**HAJNAL, Peter I. Guide to United Nations organization documentation &
publishing for students, researchers, librarians. Oceana, 1978. 450p
bibl index 78-2223. 35.00 ISBN 0-379-20257-8. C.I.P.**
A reference work by the former associate librarian at the U.N., giving an
introduction to the U.N., its structure and historical development (with
information through mid-1977), and including in a final chapter a selection
of basic documents (U.N. Charter, etc.). The emphasis is on the U.N.
publishing program—acquisition, organization, and use of documents—
with a 156-item select bibliography of publications by and about the U.N.
The appendix includes brief descriptions of various specialized international agencies that are otherwise not covered. Although not so stated, the
volume basically updates and replaces this publisher's work by Brenda
Brimmer et al., *A guide to the use of United Nations documents* (1962),
and it complements Harry N. M. Winton's *Publications of the United
Nations system: a reference guide* (CHOICE, Nov. 1973), a more
straightforward bibliography, which does include specialized agency publications as well. It is reasonably well bound but marred by the use of
needlessly large typewriter typeface (photographically reproduced), adding
greatly to the bulk. Two indexes (one to the bibliography buried in the

Continued

HAJNAL

volume, the other a fragmentary general index at the end) impede use of
the volume as a reference tool. Suitable for undergraduate academic
libraries.

GUIDE TO UNITED NATIONS
ORGANIZATION, DOCUMENTATION AND PUBLISHING

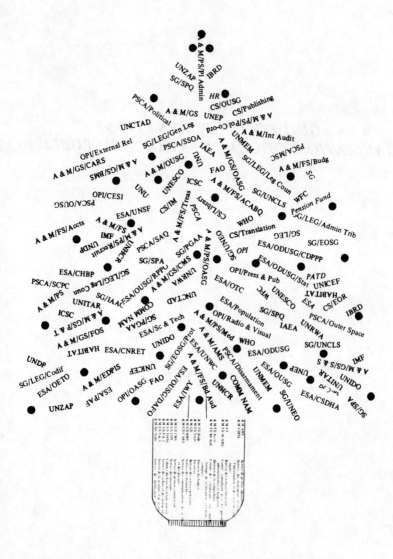

Abbreviations and Acronyms (Courtesy U.N. Secretariat News)

GUIDE
TO UNITED NATIONS ORGANIZATION, DOCUMENTATION & PUBLISHING
FOR STUDENTS, RESEARCHERS, LIBRARIANS

by
Peter I. Hajnal

Oceana Publications, Inc.
Dobbs Ferry, New York
1978

Library of Congress Cataloging in Publication Data

Hajnal, Peter I.   1936-
   Guide to United Nations Organization,
Documentation and Publishing

   Includes bibliographies and indexes.
   1. United Nations. 2. United Nations — Bibliography.
3. United Nations — Information services. 4. Libraries —
Special collections — United Nations publications. I. Title.
JX1977.H22   341.23   78-2223
ISBN 0-379-20257-8

© Copyright 1978 by Oceana Publications, Inc.

Manufactured in the United States of America

To the memory of my Father

"Nations shall beat their swords into plowshares and man shall not learn war anymore."

These words, spoken by an ancient prophet, constitute the principles which govern the activities of the United Nations.

Delegates, meeting in the session of the General Assembly, discuss not only world peace and security but also every other question which affects the lives and well-being of humanity. From thier discussions come proposals for programmes and activities in fields such as Disarmament, Atomic Energy,Environment, Peace-keeping, Apartheid, the New International Economic Order, Social Development, Population, World Food Programme and many others.

The *Guide to United Nations Organization, Documentation and Publishing* will introduce and explain to the reader the intri'cacies and structure of the Organization which carries out the multiple activities referred to above. In addition, it will inform the reader about the organization of United Nations documents and publications and will provide guidance for efficient research and information retrieval. Thus, a much needed information tool will be added and, on behalf of the Dag Hammarskjold Library, I wish to express our appreciation for the contribution to knowledge about the United Nations which the Oceana Publishing Company has made by the publication of this important book.

NATALIA I. TYULINA
Director
Dag Hammarskjold Library
United Nations, New York

TABLE OF CONTENTS

ILLUSTRATIONS, TABLES AND LISTS

Illustrations

ABBREVIATIONS AND ACRONYMS

ACDA	Asian Centre for Development Administration
ACTRSWD	Asian Centre for Training and Research in Social Welfare and Development
ASI	Asian Statistical Institute
CCOP	Committee for Co-ordination of Joint Prospecting for Mineral Resources in Asian Offshore Areas
CDC	Cairo Demographic Centre
CEDOR	Centre démographique ONU-Roumanie
CELADE	Centro Latinoamericano de Demografía
chap(s).	chapter(s)
CIENES	Centro Interamericano de Enseñanza de Estadística
CLADES	Centro Latinoamericano de Documentación Económica y Social
CMEA	Council for Mutual Economic Assistance
ECA	Economic Commission for Africa
ECAFE	Economic Commission for Asia and the Far East
ECE	Economic Commission for Europe
ECLA	Economic Commission for Latin America
ECOSOC	Economic and Social Council
ECWA	Economic Commission for Western Asia
ESAPAC	Escuela Superior de Administración Pública América Central
ESC	Economic and Social Council
ESCAP	Economic and Social Commission for Asia and the Pacific
ESCOR	Official records of the Economic and Social Council
FAO	Food and Agriculture Organization of the United Nations
FID	International Federation for Documentation
GA	General Assembly
GAOR	Official records of the General Assembly
GATT	General Agreement on Tariffs and Trade
IAEA	International Atomic Energy Agency

IBD	International Bureau for Declarations of Death
IBRD	International Bank for Reconstruction and Development
ICAO	International Civil Aviation Organization
ICAP	Instituto Centroamericano de Administración Pública
ICC	International Children's Centre
ICITO	Interim Commission for the International Trade Organization
ICJ	International Court of Justice
IDA	International Development Association
IDEP	African Institute for Economic Development and Planning
IFAD	International Fund for Agricultural Development
IFC	International Finance Corporation
IFORD	Institut de formation et de recherche démographiques
IIPS	International Institute for Population Studies
ILO	International Labour Organisation
ILPES	Instituto Latinoamericano de Planificación Económica y Social
IMCO	Inter-Governmental Maritime Consultative Organization
IMF	International Monetary Fund
INDIS	Industrial Information System (UNIDO)
INN	International Nonproprietary Name
INSEA	Institut national de la statistique et d'économique appliquée
IRO	International Refugee Organization
ISBD	International Standard Bibliographic Description
ISO	International Organization for Standardization
ITO	[Proposed] International Trade Organization
ITU	International Telecommunication Union
NGO('s)	Non-governmental organization(s)
No(s).	Number(s)
NSGT('s)	Non-self-governing territory (-ies)
OECD	Organization for Economic Co-operation and Development

ONUC	United Nations Operation in the Congo
p(p).	page(s)
PAIS	Public Affairs Information Service [Bulletin]
para(s).	paragraph(s)
Rev.	revision
RIPS	Regional Institute for Population Studies
SC	Security Council
SCOR	Official records of the Security Council
sect(s).	section(s)
SITC	Standard International Trade Classification
TC	Trusteeship Council
TCOR	Official records of the Trusteeship Council
UN	United Nations
UNAFEI	Asia and the Far East Institute for the Prevention of Crime and the Treatment of Offenders
UNBIS	[Proposed] United Nations bibliographic information system
UNCIO	United Nations Conference on International Organization, San Francisco, 1945
UNCTAD	United Nations Conference on Trade and Development
UNDI	United Nations documents index
UNDIS	United Nations documentation information system
UNDOF	United Nations Disengagement Observer Force
UNDP	United Nations Development Programme
UNEF	United Nations Emergency Force
UNEP	United Nations Environment Programme
UNESCO	United Nations Educational, Scientific and Cultural Organization
UNESOB	United Nations Economic and Social Office in Beirut
UNFICYP	United Nations Force in Cyprus
UNICEF	United Nations Children's Fund (formerly: United Nations International Children's Emergency Fund)
UNIDO	United Nations Industrial Development Organization

UNITAR   United Nations Institute for Training
          and Research
UNMOGIP   United Nations Military Observer Group
          in India and Pakistan
UNRRA   United Nations Relief and Rehabilita-
          tion Administration
UNTSO   United Nations Truce Supervision Organi-
          zation in Palestine
U.S.(A.) United States of America
USSR   Union of Soviet Socialist Republics
United
Kingdom   United Kingdom of Great Britain and
          Northern Ireland
United
States   United States of America
UPU   Universal Postal Union
vol(s).   volume(s)
WHO   World Health Organization
WIPO   World Intellectual Property Organization
WMO   World Meteorological Organization
World
Bank   International Bank for Reconstruction
          and Development

FOREWORD

I consider it very fortunate that we now have in the *Guide to United Nation's Organization, Documentation and Publishing* an accurate, up-to-date reference work on the structure, functions and evolution of the now highly complicated international organization system.

Much of the material contained in this single volume — the guide to United Nations publications, selected bibliography and the many lists and tables — will, I am sure, prove invaluable for students, teachers, researchers and others who wish to be kept informed on the expanding tasks of the United Nations family of organizations.

GENICHI AKATANI
Under Secretary-General
Department of Public Information
United Nations

ACKNOWLEDGMENTS

I should like to express my thanks to the United
Nations for providing me with study space and all possible
co-operation and assistance in the preparation of this
work. My gratitude is due also to the University of
Toronto for granting me study leave and other assistance
in the completion of my research.

The individuals who gave generously of their time
and advice are too numerous to be all listed here. I am
grateful to them for their help which contributed to
whatever merit this book may have. The responsibility
for any inaccuracies or omissions is, of course, entirely
mine.

I am especially indebted to the following
individuals: Professor Thomas Atkins of Baruch College,
City University of New York, for his excellent suggestions
and constructive criticism; Professor Dusan Djonovich of
Brooklyn College, City University of New York and Dr. Olga
Bishop of the University of Toronto, for their encourage-
ment; Mrs. Natalia I. Tyulina, Director of the Dag
Hammarskjöld Library of the United Nations and her staff,
especially Mrs. Charlotte Bedford, Miss Irene Corotneff,
Miss Kaarina Einola, Miss Graciela Gonzalez, Mr. William
Landskron, Mrs. Nina Leneman, Miss Elva Levy, Mrs. Daphne
Lincoff, Miss Luciana Marulli, Mr. Ivan Schwartz, Mr. Samuel
Sobel, Mrs. Olina Wang, and Mr. Allan Windsor; Mr. George Mc
and Mr. Harry Winton of UNITAR; Mrs. Madeleine Mitchell and
Mr. Robert N. Kenney of the UN Office of Public Information,
Mr. Charles C. Hall of the UN Department of Conference
Services; Mrs. Harry C. Priest for her untiring help in
editing the manuscript, and for her common sense and
uncommon wisdom; Miss Jillian Cook for her conscientious
typing of the manuscript; and last but by no means least,
my wife, Edna Hajnal, for her patient and valuable
assistance in preparing and improving the draft manuscript.

xxvii

INTRODUCTION

The twofold purpose of this <u>Guide</u> is to aid researchers, students, librarians and others whose work involves an awareness of United Nations activities and the use of United Nations publications and related secondary material; and to whet the appetite of those who are not familiar with the multifarious activities and resultant publications of the world organization. The United Nations is indeed a prolific publisher, now producing, in the official languages of the Organization (Arabic, Chinese, English, French, Russian, Spanish), about forty-six thousand documents annually, a good many of which are of interest to teachers, students, researchers and practitioners in the field of social sciences and other disciplines.

Sixteen years ago, Brenda Brimmer and her co-authors of <u>A Guide to the Use of United Nations Documents</u> lamented the fact that so few economists, historians and sociologists used United Nations material extensively. It is hoped that, as the activities and interests of the United Nations system of organizations have expanded to embrace most fields of human endeavour, few researchers now need to be convinced of the usefulness of keeping abreast of those activities and of the resultant documentation.

Today, it would seem an unrealistic aim to produce a complete guide of manageable size to United Nations publications. Rather than aspiring to completeness, the present work shows the range and types of publications, introduces in a systematic manner the pattern of documentation, publication, and distribution, and presents, bibliographically, a generous represent-

ative sample of primary and secondary material.
In addition, the <u>Guide</u> describes the structure, organization and functions of the
world organization, a prerequisite for a full
understanding of its complex pattern of documentation. The <u>Guide</u>, moreover, may be used as
a source of reference to factual information
such as the dates and main agenda items of special and emergency special sessions of the General Assembly; membership of the United Nations;
and names of non-governmental organizations in
consultative status with the Economic and Social
Council. The cutoff date for information included is 22 July 1977.

The <u>Guide</u> is in five parts. Part I
surveys the structure, functions and evolution
of the United Nations, and its relation to other
organizations within and outside the United Nations system. Part II describes the pattern of
United Nations publications and documentation.
Part III is a practical guide to the use, acquisition, and organization of United Nations
publications. Part IV is a select annotated
bibliography of primary and secondary material.
Part V reproduces a selection of important documents.

The appendix presents a brief survey,
with bibliographies, of intergovernmental organizations related to the United Nations.

PART I

STRUCTURE, FUNCTIONS, AND EVOLUTION
OF THE UNITED NATIONS

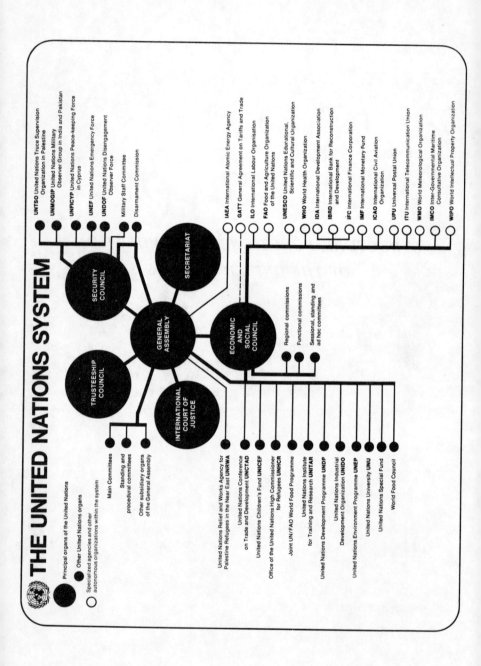

THE UNITED NATIONS SYSTEM

● Principal organs of the United Nations

● Other United Nations organs

○ Specialized agencies and other autonomous organizations within the system

Principal organs (central circles):
- SECURITY COUNCIL
- TRUSTEESHIP COUNCIL
- SECRETARIAT
- GENERAL ASSEMBLY
- INTERNATIONAL COURT OF JUSTICE
- ECONOMIC AND SOCIAL COUNCIL

General Assembly organs:
- Main Committees
- Standing and procedural committees
- Other subsidiary organs of the General Assembly

Security Council organs:
- **UNTSO** United Nations Truce Supervision Organization in Palestine
- **UNMOGIP** United Nations Military Observer Group in India and Pakistan
- **UNFICYP** United Nations Peace-keeping Force in Cyprus
- **UNEF** United Nations Emergency Force
- **UNDOF** United Nations Disengagement Observer Force
- Military Staff Committee
- Disarmament Commission

Other United Nations organs (lower):
- United Nations Relief and Works Agency for Palestine Refugees in the Near East **UNRWA**
- United Nations Conference on Trade and Development **UNCTAD**
- United Nations Children's Fund **UNICEF**
- Office of the United Nations High Commissioner for Refugees **UNHCR**
- Joint UN/FAO World Food Programme
- United Nations Institute for Training and Research **UNITAR**
- United Nations Development Programme **UNDP**
- United Nations Industrial Development Organization **UNIDO**
- United Nations Environment Programme **UNEP**
- United Nations University **UNU**
- United Nations Special Fund
- World Food Council

Economic and Social Council:
- Regional commissions
- Functional commissions
- Sessional, standing and ad hoc committees

Specialized agencies:
- **IAEA** International Atomic Energy Agency
- **GATT** General Agreement on Tariffs and Trade
- **ILO** International Labour Organisation
- **FAO** Food and Agriculture Organization of the United Nations
- **UNESCO** United Nations Educational, Scientific and Cultural Organization
- **WHO** World Health Organization
- **IDA** International Development Association
- **IBRD** International Bank for Reconstruction and Development
- **IFC** International Finance Corporation
- **IMF** International Monetary Fund
- **ICAO** International Civil Aviation Organization
- **UPU** Universal Postal Union
- **ITU** International Telecommunication Union
- **WMO** World Meteorological Organization
- **IMCO** Inter-Governmental Maritime Consultative Organization
- **WIPO** World Intellectual Property Organization

The United Nations System

CHAPTER 1

THE UNITED NATIONS CHARTER

The devastation wrought by the Second World War and the common recognition of the need to achieve peace, human rights, better international law, and social and economic progress led fifty-four nations to sign the basic document of the world Organization, the United Nations Charter. (The full text of the Charter is in Part V.)

The steps leading to the Charter are listed below:
the Inter-Allied Declaration, signed in London on 12 June 1941 by fourteen states and exiled governments;
the Atlantic Charter, signed on 14 August 1941 by Franklin D. Roosevelt and Winston Churchill;
the Declaration by United Nations, signed on 1 January 1942 at Washington, D.C. by twenty-six states and later adhered to by another twenty-one;
the declaration of a Moscow conference, signed on 30 October 1943 by representatives of the Chinese, USSR, United Kingdom and United States governments;
the 1 December 1943 Teheran declaration of Churchill, Roosevelt and Stalin;
the Dumbarton Oaks Conference of 21 August-7 October 1944;
the Yalta Conference of February 1945;

the United Nations Conference on International
Organization, also known as the San Francisco
Conference, which met from 25 April to 25 June
1945 and brought together delegates of fifty
countries.[1]

The San Francisco Conference drafted and
adopted the United Nations Charter which came
into force[2] on 24 October 1945, upon ratification by China, France, the USSR, the United Kingdom, the United States and the majority of the
other signatories. Each anniversary of that
date is observed as United Nations Day.

The Charter has so far been amended four
times, increasing the membership of the Security
Council and the Economic and Social Council and
mandating the resultant increase of the number
of required votes in those two organs. The portions affected are Articles 23, 27, 61 and 109.
In addition to formal amendment, informal amendment and interpretation are other methods of

----

[1] For more detail on the steps leading
to the Charter, see Yearbook of the
United Nations, 1946-47 (Bibliography
entry 46), pp. 1-50; and Everyman's
United Nations, 1945-1965 (Bibliography entry 44), pp. 4-9.

[2] It should be remembered that while the
Charter is the basic constitutional
document of the United Nations, it
does not, in itself, explain the functioning of the Organization any more
than the United States Constitution
explains the workings of the American
government. Inis Claude, Swords into
plowshares (Bibliography entry 23),
p.7.

Charter development.[3] Certain United Nations
organs as well as the specialized agencies may
ask the International Court of Justice for advisory opinions on the legal interpretation of
Charter provisions.

For the past several years, the General
Assembly has been considering a review of the
Charter. To this end, the Assembly, by its resolution 3349 (XXIX) of 17 December 1974, established the Ad Hoc Committee on the Charter of
the United Nations. Assembly resolution 3499
(XXX) of 15 December 1975 reconvened the Ad Hoc
Committee as the enlarged Special Committee on
the Charter of the United Nations and the Strengthening of the Role of the Organization. The
terms of reference of the Special Committee are:
> (a) To examine in detail the observa-
> tions received from Governments
> concerning:
>> (i) Suggestions and proposals
>> regarding the Charter of
>> the United Nations;
>> (ii) The strengthening of the
>> role of the United Na-
>> tions with regard to the
>> maintenance and consoli-
>> dation of international
>> peace and security, the
>> development of co-opera-
>> tion among all nations
>> and the promotion of the
>> rules of international
>> law in relations between
>> States;

------3
Leland M. Goodrich, The United Nations
in a changing world (Bibliography
entry 27), pp. 32-39. For a scholarly
commentary on Charter development, see
Goodrich, Hambro, and Simons, Charter
of the United Nations; commentary and
documents (Bibliography entry 26).

(b) To consider any additional specific proposals that Governments may make with a view to enhancing the ability of the United Nations to achieve its purposes;

(c) To list the proposals which have been made in the Committee and to identify those which have awakened special interests.[4]

In its resolution 31/28 of 3 December 1976, the General Assembly took note of the first report of the Special Committee, charged the Committee to continue its work, and invited governments to submit observations and proposals, so that the Special Committee could report to the General Assembly at its thirty-second session (fall 1977).

---

[4] Official records of the General Assembly, Thirtieth Session, Supplement No. 34.

CHAPTER 2

MEMBERSHIP OF THE UNITED NATIONS

The composition of the United Nations
has changed significantly since the founding of
the Organization. There were fifty-one original members (Poland, unable to attend the San
Francisco Conference but having signed the Charter on 15 October 1945, is numbered among the
original members.)

Under the Charter, "membership in the
United Nations is open to all . . . peace-
loving states which . . . are able and willing
to carry out [the] obligations"[5] contained in
the Charter. New members must be admitted by
a resolution or other formal decision of the
General Assembly, upon recommendation of the
Security Council. (See Fig. 3 for an example.)
Such a recommendation is considered a substantive matter in the Council and is, therefore,
subject to veto by one or more permanent members.

The General Assembly may (again, on the
recommendation of the Security Council) suspend
or expel a state from membership. There is no
Charter provision for the withdrawal of a member from the United Nations but there occurred
a case of voluntary non-participation of a member state when Indonesia decided, on 20 January

―――――――[5] United Nations, Charter (Bibliography
entry 1), Article 4.

UNITED NATIONS

SECURITY

COUNCIL

Distr.
GENERAL

S/RES/412 (1977)
7 July 1977

RESOLUTION 412 (1977)

Adopted by the Security Council at its
2021st meeting, on 7 July 1977

The Security Council,

Having examined the application of the Republic of Djibouti for admission to the United Nations (S/12357),

Recommends to the General Assembly that the Republic of Djibouti be admitted to membership in the United Nations.

Security Council Resolution Recommending the Admission of a State to U.N. Membership

77-13214

1965, to withdraw from the Organization and, on 19 September 1966, to resume co-operation with the United Nations.

Political/territorial changes may affect membership, e.g., Egypt and Syria, both original members, were a single member during their union as the United Arab Republic from 21 February 1958 to 13 October 1961. At the latter date, Syria resumed its status as an independent state and its separate membership in the United Nations. Another example: the Federation of Malaya was admitted to membership on 17 September 1957. Singapore, Sabah (formerly North Borneo) and Sarawak joined the Federation in September 1963. On 9 August 1965 Singapore became an independent state, and, on 21 September 1965, it was admitted as a separate member of the United Nations.

States not members of the United Nations may participate in some of the programmes of the Organization and may become members of specific organs or subsidiary bodies, e.g., Switzerland, not a member of the United Nations, is a member of the Economic Commission for Europe, a subsidiary body of the Economic and Social Council.

Representation of a member state can be a contentious issue in the Organization. The question of the representation of China, for instance, had been debated for many years until the General Assembly decided by its resolution No. 2758 (XXVI) of 25 October 1971 that the government of the Chinese People's Republic was the lawful representative of that state. Members of the United Nations numbered one hundred and forty-seven at the beginning of 1977. They are listed in Table I-A with the dates on which they became members. Names of original members are underlined.

A chronological (by year of admission) list of admissions to membership in the United Nations (Table I-B) reveals important landmarks in the history of the Organization, e.g., the "package deal" in which the General Assembly, by

TABLE I-A

MEMBER STATES OF THE UNITED NATIONS

<u>Member</u>	<u>Date of Admission</u>
Afghanistan	19 Nov. 1946
Albania	14 Dec. 1955
Algeria	8 Oct. 1962
Angola	1 Dec. 1976
<u>Argentina</u>	24 Oct. 1945
<u>Australia</u>	1 Nov. 1945
Austria	14 Dec. 1955
Bahamas	18 Sep. 1973
Bahrain	21 Sep. 1971
Bangladesh	17 Sep. 1974
Barbados	9 Dec. 1966
<u>Belgium</u>	27 Dec. 1945
Benin*	20 Sep. 1960
Bhutan	21 Sep. 1971
<u>Bolivia</u>	14 Nov. 1945
Botswana	17 Oct. 1966
<u>Brazil</u>	24 Oct. 1945
Bulgaria	14 Dec. 1955
Burma	19 Apr. 1948
Burundi	18 Sep. 1962
<u>Byelorussia</u>	24 Oct. 1945
<u>Canada</u>	9 Nov. 1945
Cape Verde	16 Sep. 1975

* Formerly Dahomey.

Member	Date of Admission
Central African Empire*	20 Sep. 1960
Chad	20 Sep. 1960
Chile	24 Oct. 1945
China**	24 Oct. 1945
Colombia	5 Nov. 1945
Comoros	12 Nov. 1975
Congo	20 Sep. 1960
Costa Rica	2 Nov. 1945
Cuba	24 Oct. 1945
Cyprus	20 Sep. 1960
Czechoslovakia	24 Oct. 1945
Democratic Kampuchea***	14 Dec. 1955
Democratic Yemen	14 Dec. 1967
Denmark	24 Oct. 1945
Dominican Republic	24 Oct. 1945
Ecuador	21 Dec. 1945

* Formerly Central African Republic.

** By resolution 2758 (XXVI) of 25 October 1971, the General Assembly decided "to restore all its rights to the People's Republic of China and to recognize the representatives of its Government as the only legitimate representatives of China to the United Nations, and to expel forthwith the representatives of Chiang Kai-shek from the place which they unlawfully occupy at the United Nations and in all organizations related to it".

***Formerly Cambodia.

Member	Date of Admission
Egypt*	24 Oct. 1945
El Salvador	24 Oct. 1945
Equatorial Guinea	12 Nov. 1968
Ethiopia	13 Nov. 1945
Fiji	13 Oct. 1970
Finland	14 Dec. 1955
France	24 Oct. 1945
Gabon	20 Sep. 1960
Gambia	21 Sep. 1965
German Democratic Republic	18 Sep. 1973
Germany, Federal Republic of	18 Sep. 1973
Ghana	8 Mar. 1957
Greece	25 Oct. 1945
Grenada	17 Sep. 1974
Guatemala	21 Nov. 1945
Guinea	12 Dec. 1958
Guinea-Bissau	17 Sep. 1974
Guyana	20 Sep. 1966
Haiti	24 Oct. 1945

---

* Egypt and Syria were original members of the United Nations from 24 October 1945. Following a plebiscite on 21 February 1958, the United Arab Republic was established by a union of Egypt and Syria and continued as a single member. On 13 October 1961, Syria, having resumed its status as an independent State, resumed its separate membership in the United Nations.

Member	Date of Admission
Honduras	17 Dec. 1945
Hungary	14 Dec. 1955
Iceland	19 Dec. 1946
India	30 Oct. 1945
Indonesia*	28 Sep. 1950
Iran	24 Oct. 1945
Iraq	21 Dec. 1945
Ireland	14 Dec. 1955
Israel	11 May 1949
Italy	14 Dec. 1955
Ivory Coast	20 Sep. 1960
Jamaica	18 Sep. 1962
Japan	18 Dec. 1956
Jordan	14 Dec. 1955
Kenya	16 Dec. 1963
Kuwait	14 May 1963
Lao People's Demo-cratic Republic**	14 Dec. 1955

---

* By letter of 20 January 1965, Indonesia announced its decision to withdraw from the United Nations "at this stage and under the present circumstances". By telegram of 19 September 1966, it announced its decision "to resume full co-operation with the United Nations and to resume participation in its activities". On 28 September 1966, the General Assembly took note of this decision and the President invited representatives of Indonesia to take seats in the Assembly.

** Formerly Laos.

Member	Date of Admission
Lebanon	24 Oct. 1945
Lesotho	17 Oct. 1966
Liberia	2 Nov. 1945
Libya	14 Dec. 1955
Luxembourg	24 Oct. 1945
Madagascar	20 Sep. 1960
Malawi	1 Dec. 1964
Malaysia*	17 Sep. 1957
Maldives	21 Sep. 1965
Mali	28 Sep. 1960
Malta	1 Dec. 1964
Mauritania	27 Oct. 1961
Mauritius	24 Apr. 1968
Mexico	7 Nov. 1945
Mongolia	27 Oct. 1961
Morocco	12 Nov. 1956
Mozambique	16 Sep. 1975
Nepal	14 Dec. 1955
Netherlands	10 Dec. 1945
New Zealand	24 Oct. 1945
Nicaragua	24 Oct. 1945
Niger	20 Sep. 1960
Nigeria	7 Oct. 1960

---

* The Federation of Malaya joined the United Nations on 17 September 1957. On 16 September 1963, its name was changed to Malaysia, following the admission to the new federation of Singapore, Sabah (North Borneo) and Sarawak. Singapore became an independent State on 9 August 1965 and a member of the United Nations on 21 September 1965.

Member	Date of Admission
Norway	27 Nov. 1945
Oman	7 Oct. 1971
Pakistan	30 Sep. 1947
Panama	13 Nov. 1945
Papua New Guinea	10 Oct. 1975
Paraguay	24 Oct. 1945
Peru	31 Oct. 1945
Philippines	24 Oct. 1945
Poland*	24 Oct. 1945
Portugal	14 Dec. 1955
Qatar	21 Sep. 1971
Romania	14 Dec. 1955
Rwanda	18 Sep. 1962
Samoa	15 Dec. 1976
São Tomé and Príncipe	16 Sep. 1975
Saudi Arabia	24 Oct. 1945
Senegal	28 Sep. 1960
Seychelles	21 Sep. 1976
Sierra Leone	27 Sep. 1961
Singapore	21 Sep. 1965
Somalia	20 Sep. 1960
South Africa	7 Nov. 1945
Spain	14 Dec. 1955

* Poland did not attend the San Franciso Conference. A space was left for the signature
of Poland (one of the signatories of the Declaration by United Nations). Poland signed
the Charter on 15 October 1945 and is thus
considered one of the original members.

Member	Date of Admission
Sri Lanka*	14 Dec. 1955
Sudan	12 Nov. 1956
Surinam	4 Dec. 1975
Swaziland	24 Sep. 1968
Sweden	19 Nov. 1946
Syria**	24 Oct. 1945
Thailand	16 Dec. 1946
Togo	20 Sep. 1960
Trinidad and Tobago	18 Sep. 1962
Tunisia	12 Nov. 1956
Turkey	24 Oct. 1945
Uganda	25 Oct. 1962
Ukraine	24 Oct. 1945
Union of Soviet Socialist Republics	24 Oct. 1945
United Arab Emirates	9 Dec. 1971
United Kingdom	24 Oct. 1945
United Republic of Cameroon	20 Sep. 1960

---

*   Formerly Ceylon.

** Egypt and Syria were original members of the
    United Nations from 24 October 1945. Follow-
    ing a plebiscite on 21 February 1958, the
    United Arab Republic was established by a
    union of Egypt and Syria and continued as a
    single member. On 13 October 1961, Syria,
    having resumed its status as an independent
    State, resumed its separate membership in the
    United Nations.

Member	Date of Admission
United Republic of Tanzania*	14 Dec. 1961
United States	24 Oct. 1945
Upper Volta	20 Sep. 1960
Uruguay	18 Dec. 1945
Venezuela	15 Nov. 1945
Yemen	30 Sep. 1947
Yugoslavia	24 Oct. 1945
Zaire	20 Sep. 1960
Zambia	1 Dec. 1964

---

* Tanganyika was a member of the United Nations from 14 December 1961 and Zanzibar was a member from 16 December 1963. Following the ratification on 26 April 1964 of Articles of Union between Tanganyika and Zanzibar, the United Republic of Tanganyika and Zanzibar continued as a single member, changing its name to United Republic of Tanzania on 1 November 1964.

TABLE I-B

CHRONOLOGICAL LIST OF ADMISSIONS TO MEMBERSHIP
IN THE UNITED NATIONS

Original members: Argentina, Australia, Belgium, Bolivia, Brazil, Byelorussia, Canada, Chile, China, Colombia, Costa Rica, Cuba, Czechoslovakia, Denmark, Dominican Republic, Ecuador, Egypt, El Salvador, Ethiopia, France, Greece, Guatemala, Haiti, Honduras, India, Iran, Iraq, Lebanon, Liberia, Luxembourg, Mexico, Netherlands, New Zealand, Nicaragua, Norway, Panama, Paraguay, Peru, Philippines, Poland, Saudi Arabia, South Africa, Syria, Turkey, Ukraine, Union of Soviet Socialist Republics, United Kingdom, United States, Uruguay, Vene-

zuela, Yugoslavia (51).
Admitted in 1946: Afghanistan, Iceland, Sweden, Thailand (4).
Admitted in 1947: Pakistan, Yemen (2).
Admitted in 1948: Burma (1).
Admitted in 1949: Israel (1).
Admitted in 1950: Indonesia (1).
Admitted in 1955: Albania, Austria, Bulgaria, Democratic Kampuchea, Finland, Hungary, Ireland, Italy, Jordan, Lao People's Democratic Republic, Libya, Nepal, Portugal, Romania, Spain, Sri Lanka (16).
Admitted in 1956: Japan, Morocco, Sudan, Tunisia (4).
Admitted in 1957: Ghana, Malaysia (2).
Admitted in 1958: Guinea (1).
Admitted in 1960: Benin, Central African Empire, Chad, Congo, Cyprus, Gabon, Ivory Coast, Madagascar, Mali, Niger, Nigeria, Senegal, Somalia, Togo, United Republic of Cameroon, Upper Volta, Zaire (17).
Admitted in 1961: Mauritania, Mongolia, Sierra Leone, United Republic of Tanzania (4).
Admitted in 1962: Algeria, Burundi, Jamaica, Rwanda, Trinidad and Tobago, Uganda (6).
Admitted in 1963: Kenya, Kuwait (2).
Admitted in 1964: Malawi, Malta, Zambia (3).
Admitted in 1965: Gambia, Maldives, Singapore (3).
Admitted in 1966: Barbados, Botswana, Guyana, Lesotho (4).
Admitted in 1967: Democratic Yemen (1).
Admitted in 1968: Equatorial Guinea, Mauritius, Swaziland (3).
Admitted in 1970: Fiji (1).
Admitted in 1971: Bahrain, Bhutan, Oman, Qatar, United Arab Emirates (5).
Admitted in 1973: Bahamas, German Democratic Republic, Germany (Federal Republic of) (3).
Admitted in 1974: Bangladesh, Grenada, Guinea-Bissau (3).
Admitted in 1975: Cape Verde, Comoros, Mozambique, Papua New Guinea, São Tomé and Principe, Surinam (6).
Admitted in 1976: Angola, Samoa, Seychelles (3).

(No new members were admitted in 1951, 1952, 1953, 1954, 1959, 1969, and 1972).

---

its resolution 995 (X) of 14 December 1955, admitted four socialist states and twelve western and Asian states to membership in the United Nations (see Fig. 4).

An even more significant event occurred in 1960 when, during its fifteenth session, the Assembly admitted seventeen new members, sixteen of them newly independent African states. This action marked the beginning of a shift in the composition of the Organization in favour of third-world states. The same Assembly session adopted the landmark Declaration on the Granting of Independence to Colonial Countries and Peoples (the text of the Declaration is in Part V).

995 (X). Admission of new Members to the United Nations[4]

The General Assembly,

Having received the recommendation[5] of the Security Council of 14 December 1955 that the following countries should be admitted to membership in the United Nations: Albania, Jordan, Ireland, Portugal, Hungary, Italy, Austria, Romania, Bulgaria, Finland, Ceylon, Nepal, Libya, Cambodia, Laos and Spain,

Having considered the application for membership of each of these countries,

Decides to admit the above-mentioned sixteen countries to membership in the United Nations.

555th plenary meeting,
14 December 1955.

---

[4] See also resolution 918 (X).
[5] *Official Records of the General Assembly, Tenth Session, Annexes,* agenda item 21, document A/3099.

CHAPTER 3

THE GENERAL ASSEMBLY

        The General Assembly (GA) is one of six
principal United Nations organs established by
the Charter. The others are the Security Council, the Economic and Social Council, the Trusteeship Council, the International Court of
Justice and the Secretariat.

        The General Assembly consists of repre-
sentatives of all member states of the United
Nations (Charter, Article 9). It is the main
deliberative body of the Organization. It "may
discuss any questions . . . within the scope of
the . . . Charter or relating to the powers and
functions of any [United Nations] organs" (Article 10). It may consider matters of international peace and security and may recommend measures for the peaceful settlement of situations
endangering peace, security or friendly relations among nations. It initiates studies and
makes recommendations (as per Article 13)
        for the purpose of (a) promoting inter-
        national co-operation in the political
        field and encouraging the progressive
        development of international law and
        its codification [and] (b) promoting
        international co-operation in the
        economic, social, cultural, educa-
        tional, and health fields, and assist-
        ing in the realization of human rights
        and fundamental freedoms for all with-
        out distinction as to race, sex, lan-

guage, or religion.

The Assembly receives and discusses reports of other United Nations organs, elects certain members of those organs (e.g., the non-permanent members of the Security Council), appoints the Secretary-General on the recommendation of the Security Council, and controls the finances of the Organization. Regarding the last-mentioned function, the Assembly has the power to approve the budget of the United Nations and to set the scale of assessment for the apportionment of expenses. Table II shows the programme budget for the biennium 1976-1977.

The scale of assessments for the contributions of member states to the United Nations budget for 1977, as set by Assembly resolution 31/95 B of 14 December 1976, will be found in Table III. Budgetary appropriations and scales of assessment for earlier years can be found in the Resolutions supplements of the Official records of the General Assembly. For a fully detailed budget, see Programme budget for the biennium (Bibliography entry 39).

In cases of threats to or breaches of international peace, when the Security Council cannot act for reasons of lack of unanimity among the permanent members, the Assembly is empowered by its resolution 337 (v) of 3 November 1950, called the "Uniting for peace" resolution, to take appropriate action, including the recommendation for the collective use of armed force.

The General Assembly holds its regular sessions annually, beginning, as a rule, on the third Tuesday in September and running generally until mid-December. In addition, it has been convened for special and emergency special sessions, as shown in Table IV.

Each member state of the United Nations has one vote in the General Assembly. Voting on important questions (e.g., admission of new members, budgetary matters) requires a two-

thirds majority; on other questions, a simple
majority.

The Assembly has seven main committees:
First (Political and Security) Committee
Special Political Committee
Second (Economic and Financial) Committee
Third (Social, Humanitarian and Cultural)
  Committee
Fourth (Trusteeship) Committee
Fifth (Administrative and Budgetary) Committee
Sixth (Legal) Committee

The Assembly has also established two
procedural committees: the General (Steering)
Committee, and the sessional Credentials Committee. In addition, the Assembly has created
a number of standing committees and ad hoc and
sessional subsidiary bodies.[6] The following is
a partial list of these bodies:

Standing committees and bodies
Advisory Committee on Administrative and Budget-
  ary Questions
Committee on Contributions
Board of Auditors

Subsidiary and ad hoc bodies
Conference of the Committee on Disarmament
Special Committee on the Problem of Hungary
Special Committee to Investigate Israeli Prac-
  tices affecting the Human Rights of Popula-
  tions of Occupied Territories
Special Committee against Apartheid
Scientific Committee on the Effects of Atomic
  Radiation
Committee on the Peaceful Uses of Outer Space
Committee on the Peaceful Uses of the Sea-Bed
  and Ocean Floor beyond the Limits of National
  Jurisdiction

----

[6] Blanche Finley's The structure of the
General Assembly (Bibliography entry
25) is an excellent source of information on the Assembly's subsidiary
bodies over the years.

Subsidiary and ad hoc bodies (continued)
United Nations Children's Fund (UNICEF)
Office of the United Nations High Commissioner
  for Refugees (UNHCR)
United Nations Relief and Works Agency for Pal-
  estine Refugees in the Near East (UNRWA)
United Nations University (UNU)
Committee on the Elimination of Racial Discrim-
  ination (CERD)
Panel of Experts on the Protein Problem Confront-
  ing Developing Countries
United Nations High Commissioner for Namibia
Committee on Information from Non-Self-Govern-
  ing Territories
Special Committee on the Situation with regard
  to the Implementation of the Declaration on
  the Granting of Independence to Colonial Coun-
  tries and Peoples (Special Committee of Twen-
  ty-four)
Preparatory Committee for the Twenty-fifth Anni-
  versary of the United Nations
Committee on Control and Limitation of Documen-
  tation
Working Group on Currency Instability
United Nations Capital Development Fund
International Civil Service Advisory Board
Committee on Relations with the Host Country
International Law Commission

Other bodies established or co-established by
the General Assembly
United Nations Conference on Trade and Develop-
  ment (UNCTAD)
Joint UN/FAO World Food Programme (WFP)
United Nations Institute for Training and
  Research (UNITAR)
United Nations Development Programme (UNDP)
United Nations Environment Programme (UNEP)
United Nations Industrial Development Organiza-
  tion (UNIDO)

TABLE II

UNITED NATIONS PROGRAMME BUDGET FOR THE
BIENNIUM 1976-1977

Section	Appropriation (US dollars) (originally set by resolution 3539 A (XXX) of 17 Dec. 1975, revised by resolution 31/207 A of 22 Dec. 1976
Part I. Over-all policy-making, direction and co-ordination	
1. Over-all policy-making, direction and co-ordination	21 188 900
TOTAL, part I	21 188 900
Part II. Political and peace-keeping activities	
2. Political and Security Council affairs; peace-keeping activities	47 086 400
TOTAL, part II	47 086 400
Part III. Political, trusteeship and decolonization activities	
3. Political affairs, trusteeship and decolonization activities	8 160 000
TOTAL, part III	8 160 000

Section	Appropriation (US dollars) (originally set by resolution 3539 A (XXX) of 17 Dec. 1975, revised by resolution 31/207 A of 22 Dec. 1976
Part IV. Economic, social and humanitarian activities	
4. Policy-making organs (economic and social activities)	3 464 100
5A. Department of Economic and Social Affairs	41 514 500
5B. United Nations Centre on Transnational Corporations	2 993 800
6. Economic Commission for Europe	15 202 100
7. Economic and Social Commission for Asia and the Pacific	15 238 500
8. Economic Commission for Latin America	18 336 200
9. Economic Commission for Africa	18 975 500
10. Economic Commission for Western Asia	9 826 200
11. United Nations Conference on Trade and Development	48 449 300
12. United Nations Industrial Development Organization	46 087 100
13A. United Nations Environment Programme	6 047 000
13B. Habitat: United Nations Conference on Human Settlements	957 500

Section	Appropriation (US dollars) (originally set by resolution 3539 A (XXX) of 17 Dec. 1975, revised by resolution 31/207 A of 22 Dec. 1976
Part IV. Economic, social and humanitarian activities (continued)	
14.International narcotics control	4 361 900
15.Regular programme of technical assistance	20 092 900
16.Office of the United Nations High Commissioner for Refugees	15 945 400
17.Office of the United Nations Disaster Relief Co-ordinator	1 551 000
TOTAL, part IV	269 043 000
Part V. Human rights	
18.Human rights	6 422 000
TOTAL, part V	6 422 000
Part VI. International Court of Justice	
19.International Court of Justice	5 179 700
TOTAL, part VI	5 179 700

Section	Appropriation (US dollars) (originally set by resolution 3539 A (XXX) of 17 Dec. 1975, revised by resolution 31/207 A of 22 Dec. 1976
Part VII. Legal activities	
20. Legal activities	8 031 000
TOTAL, part VII	8 031 000
Part VIII. Common services	
21. Public information	30 241 100
22. Administration, management and general services	136 229 100
23. Conference and library services	108 534 600
TOTAL, part VIII	275 004 800
Part IX. Special expenses	
24. United Nations bond issue	17 199 000
TOTAL, part IX	17 199 000
Part X. Staff assessment	
25. Staff assessment	108 570 900
TOTAL, part X	108 570 900

Section	Appropriation (US dollars) (originally set by resolution 3539 A (XXX) of 17 Dec. 1975, revised by resolution 31/207 A of 22 Dec. 1976
Part XI. Capital expenditures	
26. Construction, alteration, improvement and major maintenance of premises	18 047 200
TOTAL, part XI	18 047 200
GRAND TOTAL	783 932 900

TABLE III

SCALE OF ASSESSMENTS FOR THE CONTRIBUTIONS OF
MEMBER STATES TO THE UNITED NATIONS
BUDGET FOR THE FINANCIAL YEAR 1977

Member state	Per cent
Afghanistan	0.02
Albania	0.02
Algeria	0.10
Argentina	0.83
Australia	1.52
Austria	0.63
Bahamas	0.02
Bahrain	0.02
Bangladesh	0.04
Barbados	0.02
Belgium	1.07
Benin	0.02

Member state	Per cent
Bhutan	0.02
Bolivia	0.02
Botswana	0.02
Brazil	1.04
Bulgaria	0.13
Burma	0.02
Burundi	0.02
Byelorussian Soviet Socialist Republic	0.40
Canada	2.96
Cape Verde	0.02
Central African Empire	0.02
Chad	0.02
Chile	0.09
China	5.50
Colombia	0.11
Comoros	0.02
Congo	0.02
Costa Rica	0.02
Cuba	0.13
Cyprus	0.02
Czechoslovakia	0.87
Democratic Kampuchea	0.02
Democratic Yemen	0.02
Denmark	0.63
Dominican Republic	0.02
Ecuador	0.02
Egypt	0.08
El Salvador	0.02
Equatorial Guinea	0.02
Ethiopia	0.02
Fiji	0.02
Finland	0.41
France	5.66
Gabon	0.02
Gambia	0.02
German Democratic Republic	1.35
Germany, Federal Republic of	7.74
Ghana	0.02
Greece	0.39
Grenada	0.02
Guatemala	0.02
Guinea	0.02
Guinea-Bissau	0.02
Guyana	0.02

Member state	Per cent
Haiti	0.02
Honduras	0.02
Hungary	0.34
Iceland	0.02
India	0.70
Indonesia	0.14
Iran	0.43
Iraq	0.10
Ireland	0.15
Israel	0.24
Italy	3.30
Ivory Coast	0.02
Jamaica	0.02
Japan	8.66
Jordan	0.02
Kenya	0.02
Kuwait	0.16
Lao People's Democratic Republic	0.02
Lebanon	0.03
Lesotho	0.02
Liberia	0.02
Libyan Arab Republic	0.17
Luxembourg	0.04
Madagascar	0.02
Malawi	0.02
Malaysia	0.09
Maldives	0.02
Mali	0.02
Malta	0.02
Mauritania	0.02
Mauritius	0.02
Mexico	0.78
Mongolia	0.02
Morocco	0.05
Mozambique	0.02
Nepal	0.02
Netherlands	1.38
New Zealand	0.28
Nicaragua	0.02
Niger	0.02
Nigeria	0.13
Norway	0.43
Oman	0.02
Pakistan	0.06

Member state	Per cent
Panama	0.02
Papua New Guinea	0.02
Paraguay	0.02
Peru	0.06
Philippines	0.10
Poland	1.40
Portugal	0.20
Qatar	0.02
Romania	0.26
Rwanda	0.02
São Tomé and Príncipe	0.02
Saudi Arabia	0.24
Senegal	0.02
Sierra Leone	0.02
Singapore	0.08
Somalia	0.02
South Africa	0.40
Spain	1.53
Sri Lanka	0.02
Sudan	0.02
Surinam	0.02
Swaziland	0.02
Sweden	1.20
Syrian Arab Republic	0.02
Thailand	0.10
Togo	0.02
Trinidad and Tobago	0.02
Tunisia	0.02
Turkey	0.30
Uganda	0.02
Ukrainian Soviet Socialist Republic	1.50
Union of Soviet Socialist Republics	11.33
United Arab Emirates	0.08
United Kingdom of Great Britain and Northern Ireland	4.44
United Republic of Cameroon	0.02
United Republic of Tanzania	0.02
United States of America	25.00
Upper Volta	0.02
Uruguay	0.04
Venezuela	0.40
Yemen	0.02
Yugoslavia	0.38

Member state	Per cent
Zaire	0.02
Zambia	0.02
	100.00

States which are not members of the United Nations but which participate in certain of its activities are called upon to contribute towards the 1977 expenses of such activities on the basis of the following rates:

Non-member state	Per cent
Democratic People's Republic of Korea	0.05
Holy See	0.02
Liechtenstein	0.02
Monaco	0.02
Nauru	0.02
Republic of Korea	0.13
San Marino	0.02
Switzerland	0.96
Tonga	0.02
Western Samoa	0.02

TABLE IV

SPECIAL AND EMERGENCY SPECIAL SESSIONS OF
THE GENERAL ASSEMBLY

Session	Date	Main agenda item
1st special	28 Apr.-15 May 1947	Palestine question
2nd special	16 Apr.-14 May 1948	Palestine question
1st emergency special	1-10 Nov. 1956	Suez Canal question
2nd emergency special	4-10 Nov. 1956	Hungarian situation

TABLE IV (continued)

Session	Date	Main agenda item
3rd emergency special	8-21 Aug. 1958	Lebanon and Jordan situa tion
4th emergency special	17-20 Sept. 1960	Congo situation
3rd special	21-25 Aug. 1961	Tunisian situation
4th special	14 May-17 June 1963	Financial situation of the United Nations
5th special	21 Apr.-13 June 1967	South West Africa question
5th emergency special	17 June-18 Sept.1967	Middle East situation
6th special	9 Apr.2 May 1974	New international eco nomic order
7th special	1-16 Sept. 1975	International economic co-operation

The next special session, to be devoted to disarmament, will be convened in New York in May/June 1978.[7]

---

[7] General Assembly resolution 31/189B of 21 December 1976.

CHAPTER 4

THE SECURITY COUNCIL

The Security Council (SC) has five permanent and ten non-permanent members, the latter
elected by the General Assembly for two-year
terms. The permanent members (marked below by
asterisks) are designated as such by the Charter.
Members, as of 1977, are as follows (term of
office ends on 31 December of the year shown in
parentheses):

Benin (1977)	India (1978)	Romania (1977)
Canada (1978)	Libya (1977)	USSR*
China*	Mauritius (1978)	United Kingdom*
France*	Pakistan (1977)	United States*
Germany, Federal Republic of (1978)	Panama (1977)	Venezuela (1978)

The primary responsibility of the Security Council, as set forth in Article 24 of
the Charter, is the maintenance of international
peace and security. In accordance with that
responsibility, the Council is empowered to investigate any situation that may lead to international disputes, aggression or threats to
peace. It may make recommendations (see, for
example, Figs. 5 and 6 which illustrate two
crucial Council resolutions relating to the
Middle East: resolutions 242 (1967) and 338
(1973)) and take enforcement action ranging from
registering disapproval through economic sanctions to the use of armed force.

Resolution 242 (1967)
of 22 November 1967

The Security Council,

Expressing its continuing concern with the grave situation in the Middle East,

Emphasizing the inadmissibility of the acquisition of territory by war and the need to work for a just and lasting peace in which every State in the area can live in security,

Emphasizing further that all Member States in their acceptance of the Charter of the United Nations have undertaken a commitment to act in accordance with Article 2 of the Charter,

1. *Affirms* that the fulfilment of Charter principles requires the establishment of a just and lasting peace in the Middle East which should include the application of both the following principles:

(i) Withdrawal of Israel armed forces from territories occupied in the recent conflict;

(ii) Termination of all claims or states of belligerency and respect for and acknowledgement of the sovereignty, territorial integrity and political independence of every State in the area and their right to live in peace within secure and recognized boundaries free from threats or acts of force;

2. *Affirms further* the necessity

(a) For guaranteeing freedom of navigation through international waterways in the area;

(b) For achieving a just settlement of the refugee problem;

(c) For guaranteeing the territorial inviolability and political independence of every State in the area, through measures including the establishment of demilitarized zones;

3. *Requests* the Secretary-General to designate a Special Representative to proceed to the Middle East to establish and maintain contacts with the States concerned in order to promote agreement and assist efforts to achieve a peaceful and accepted settlement in accordance with the provisions and principles in this resolution;

Security Council Resolution 242 (1967) on the Middle East Situation

4. *Requests* the Secretary-General to report to the Security Council on the progress of the efforts of the Special Representative as soon as possible.

Adopted unanimously at the 1382nd meeting.

Resolution 338 (1973)
of 22 October 1973

The Security Council

1. *Calls upon* all parties to the present fighting to cease all firing and terminate all military activity immediately, no later than 12 hours after the moment of the adoption of this decision, in the positions they now occupy;

2. *Calls upon* the parties concerned to start immediately after the cease-fire the implementation of Security Council resolution 242 (1967) in all of its parts;

3. *Decides* that, immediately and concurrently with the cease-fire, negotiations shall start between the parties concerned under appropriate auspices aimed at establishing a just and durable peace in the Middle East.

Adopted at the 1747th meeting by 14 votes to none[27]

---

[27] One member (China) did not participate in the voting.

Security Council Resolution 338 (1973) on the Middle East Situation

The Council recommends to the General Assembly the admission of new members of the United Nations. It recommends the appointment of Secretaries-General. It exercises trusteeship functions in areas designated as "strategic". The only remaining trust territory, the Trust Territory of the Pacific Islands is, in fact, in this category.

Unlike the General Assembly and the other two Councils, which have regular and other sessions, the Security Council functions continuously and meets whenever called.

Each Council member has one vote but only permanent members have the "veto": a negative vote cast by any one permanent member will prevent the adoption of a resolution on substantive matters. Decisions on substantive matters require nine affirmative votes including as indicated above, the concurring votes (or abstentions) of all five permanent members. Decisions on procedural matters require any nine affirmative votes. At times, "the possibility of the so-called double veto arises if there is disagreement as to whether a proposal submitted to the Council is procedural or substantive."[8] A case in point is Council resolution 132 (1959) on the "Laos question" which was preceded by a decision to the effect that the vote to be taken was to be a vote on a procedural matter (see Fig. 7).

--------8

Sydney D. Bailey, Voting in the Security Council (Bloomington: Indiana University Press, 1969), p.18.

QUESTION RELATING TO LAOS

Decision

At its 848th meeting, on 7 September 1959, the Council decided that the vote that was to be taken on the draft resolution before it [3] was a vote on a procedural matter.

Adopted by 10 votes to 1 (Union of Soviet Socialist Republics).

[3] Later adopted as resolution 132 (1959).

132 (1959). Resolution of 7 September 1959

[S/4216]

The Security Council

Decides to appoint a sub-committee consisting of Argentina, Italy, Japan and Tunisia, and instructs this sub-committee to examine the statements made before the Security Council concerning Laos, to receive further statements and documents and to conduct such inquiries as it may determine necessary, and to report to the Council as soon as possible.

Adopted at the 848th meeting by 10 votes to 1 (Union of Soviet Socialist Republics).[4]

[4] See the decision preceding this resolution.

The Security Council has established[9]:

Standing committees
Committee of Experts on Rules of Procedure
Committee on the Admission of New Members

Substantive bodies
Military Staff Committee
Disarmament Commission

Ad hoc organs, e.g.,
Ad Hoc Subcommittee on Namibia
Security Council Committee Established in Pursuance of Resolution 253 (1968) concerning
   the Question of Southern Rhodesia (also known
   as Sanctions Committee)

Peacekeeping bodies, e.g.,
United Nations Truce Supervision Organization
   in Palestine (UNTSO)
United Nations Emergency Force (UNEF)
United Nations Disengagement Observer Force
   (UNDOF)
United Nations Military Observer Group in India
   and Pakistan (UNMOGIP)
United Nations Force in Cyprus (UNFICYP)

The Disarmament Commission reports both
to the Security Council and to the General Assem
bly. The International Atomic Energy Agency
(IAEA), an autonomous agency within the United
Nations system of organizations, reports annually to the General Assembly but, as appropriate,
also to the Security Council and to the Economic

---

[9]
S.D. Bailey's The procedure of the UN
Security Council (Bibliography entry
72) is a good source of information on
the structure as well as the procedure
of the Council

and Social Council. The Security Council itself submits annual and special reports to the General Assembly.

CHAPTER 5

THE ECONOMIC AND SOCIAL COUNCIL - STRUCTURE
AND FUNCTIONS

The Economic and Social Council (ESC,
ECOSOC) has 54 members, elected by the General
Assembly for three-year terms. Table V lists
members as of 1977.

TABLE V

MEMBERS OF THE ECONOMIC AND SOCIAL
COUNCIL IN 1977
(term of office expires on 31 December of the
year given in parentheses)

Afghanistan (1978)
Algeria (1978)
Argentina (1977)
Austria (1978)
Bangladesh (1978)
Bolivia (1978)
Brazil (1978)
Bulgaria (1977)
Canada (1977)
China (1977)
Colombia (1979)
Cuba (1978)
Czechoslovakia (1977)
Denmark (1977)
Ecuador (1977)
Ethiopia (1977)
France (1978)

Gabon (1977)
Germany, Federal Repub-
    lic of (1978)
Greece (1978)
Iran (1979)
Iraq (1979)
Italy (1979)
Jamaica (1979)
Japan (1977)
Kenya (1977)
Malaysia (1978)
Mauritania (1979)
Mexico (1979)
Netherlands (1979)
New Zealand (1979)
Nigeria (1978)
Norway (1977)

Pakistan (1977)
Peru (1977)
Philippines (1979)
Poland (1979)
Portugal (1978)
Rwanda (1979)
Somalia (1979)
Sudan (1979)
Syria (1979)
Togo (1978)
Tunisia (1978)

Uganda (1978)
Ukraine (1979)
USSR (1977)
United Kingdom (1977)
United States (1979)
Upper Volta (1979)
Venezuela (1978)
Yemen (1977)
Yugoslavia (1978)
Zaire (1977)

The Council, under the authority of the General Assembly, is responsible for the economic and social activities of the United Nations. In accordance with the Charter, it may initiate or conduct studies, make recommendations and submit reports "with respect to international economic, social, cultural, educational, health, and related matters and . . . may make recommendations for the purpose of promoting respect for, and observance of, human rights and fundamental freedoms for all." (Article 62.)

The Council holds two regular sessions (and, in the past few years, an organizational session) each year. Each member state has one vote, and voting requires a simple majority.

The Council has the following subsidiary bodies (see Fig. 8 for chart):

Functional commissions
Statistical Commission
Population Commission
Commission for Social Development
Commission on Human Rights
Commission on the Status of Women
Commission on Narcotic Drugs

Regional commissions
Economic Commission for Africa (ECA, Addis Ababa)
Economic and Social Commission for Asia and the Pacific (ESCAP, Bangkok; formerly called Economic Commission for Asia and the Far East)

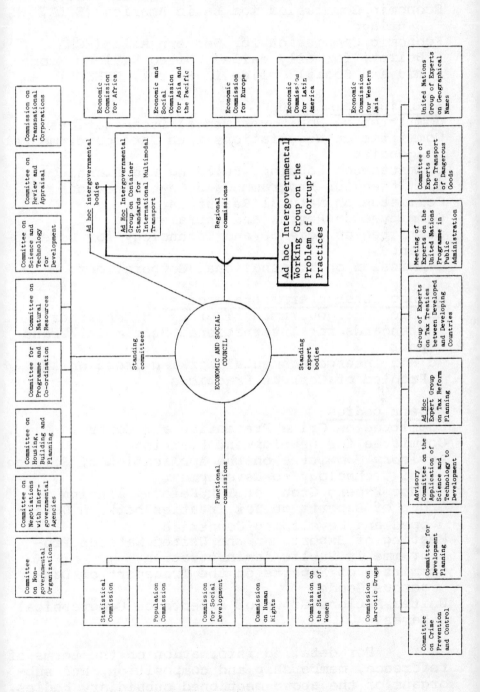

Structure of the Economic and Social Council

Regional commissions (continued)
Economic Commission for Europe (ECE, Geneva)
Economic Commission for Latin America (ECLA, Santiago)
Economic Commission for Western Asia (ECWA, Beirut; formerly called United Nations Economic and Social Office in Beirut, UNESOB)

Standing committees
Committee on Non-Governmental Organizations
Committee on Negotiations with Intergovernmental Agencies
Committee on Housing, Building and Planning
Committee for Programme and Co-ordination
Committee on Natural Resources
Committee on Review and Appraisal
Committee on Science and Technology for Development
Commission on Transnational Corporations

Ad hoc intergovernmental bodies
Ad Hoc Intergovernmental Group on Container Standards for International Multimodal Transport
Ad Hoc Intergovernmental Working Group on the Problem of Corrupt Practices

Expert bodies
Committee on Crime Prevention and Control
Committee for Development Planning
Advisory Committee on the Application of Science and Technology to Development
Ad Hoc Expert Group on Tax Reform Planning
Group of Experts on Tax Treaties between Developed and Developing Countries
Meeting of Experts on the United Nations Programme in Public Administration
Committee of Experts on the Transport of Dangerous Goods
United Nations Group of Experts on Geographical Names

For detailed information on the terms of reference, membership and composition, and sub-organs of the above-mentioned subsidiary bodies, see the following documents:

United Nations, Economic and Social Council,
Rationalization of the work of the Council:
review of the terms of reference of the sub-
sidiary bodies of the Council; note by the
Secretariat (New York, 28 January 1976; E/5453/
Rev. 1)

United Nations, Economic and Social Council,
Rationalization of the work of the Council:
review of the terms of reference of the subsidiary bodies of the Council; membership of
the Economic and Social Council and its subsidiary bodies in 1976 (New York, 15 April
1976; E/5453/Rev. 1/Add. 1)

United Nations, Economic and Social Council,
Review of the terms of reference of the subsidiary bodies of the Council; note by the
Secretariat, amendment (New York, 7 March
1977; E/5453/Rev. 1/Amend. 1)

CHAPTER 6

THE UNITED NATIONS SYSTEM OF ORGANIZATIONS; CO-ORDINATING FUNCTIONS OF THE ECONOMIC AND SOCIAL COUNCIL

The Economic and Social Council is concerned not only with the economic and social activities of the United Nations itself but also with similar activities of the intergovernmental organizations of the United Nations system. Table VI lists these organizations.

TABLE VI

THE UNITED NATIONS SYSTEM OF ORGANIZATIONS

Specialized agencies

Food and Agriculture Organization of the
    United Nations (FAO)
    Headquarters: Via delle Terme di Caracalla
                  00100 Rome, Italy
Inter-Governmental Maritime Consultative
    Organization (IMCO)
    Headquarters: 101-104 Piccadilly
                  London, WIV OAE, England
International Bank for Reconstruction and
    Development (IBRD, World Bank)
    Headquarters: 1818 H Street, N.W.
                  Washington, D.C. 20433,
                  U.S.A.

International Civil Aviation Organization
    (ICAO)
    Headquarters: Place de l'Aviation Interna-
                  tionale
                  1000 Sherbrooke Street West
                  Montreal, Quebec, Canada
                  H3A 2R2
International Development Association (IDA)
    Headquarters: 1818 H Street, N.W.
                  Washington, D.C. 20433
                  U.S.A.
International Finance Corporation (IFC)
    Headquarters: 1818 H Street, N.W.
                  Washington, D.C. 20433
                  U.S.A.
International Labour Organisation (ILO)
    Headquarters: International Labour Office
                  4, route des Morillons
                  CH-1211 Geneva 22
                  Switzerland
International Monetary Fund (IMF)
    Headquarters: 700, 19th Street, N.W.
                  Washington, D.C. 20431
                  U.S.A.
International Telecommunication Union (ITU)
    Headquarters: Place des Nations
                  1211 Geneva 20
                  Switzerland
United Nations Educational, Scientific and
    Cultural Organization (UNESCO)
    Headquarters: 7, Place de Fontenoy
                  75700 Paris, France
Universal Postal Union (UPU)
    Headquarters: Weltpoststrasse 4
                  Berne 1, Switzerland
World Health Organization (WHO)
    Headquarters: 20, avenue Appia
                  1211 Geneva, Switzerland
World Intellectual Property Organization
    (WIPO)
    Headquarters: 32, chemin des Colombettes
                  1211 Geneva 20, Switzerland
World Meteorological Organization (WMO)
    Headquarters: 41, avenue Giuseppe-Motta
                  Geneva, Switzerland

Other organizations

General Agreement on Tariffs and Trade (GATT)
Headquarters: Villa La Bocage
Palais des Nations
1211 Geneva 10, Switzerland
International Atomic Energy Agency (IAEA)
Headquarters: Kärntnerring 11
A-1010 Vienna I, Austria

These intergovernmental agencies are autonomous, each with its own basic establishing instrument, organizational structure, budget and documentation. They are related to the United Nations by individual relationship agreements. The specialized agencies submit annual reports on their activities to the Economic and Social Council while the International Atomic Energy Agency reports primarily to the General Assembly.

Another specialized agency, the International Refugee Organization (IRO), operated during the years 1946-1952. It was then terminated and some of its functions were transferred to the United Nations High Commissioner for Refugees.

Some of the specialized agencies predate the United Nations, e.g., the International Labour Organisation which was established in 1919 as an autonomous institution affiliated with the League of Nations; and the oldest specialized agency, the International Telecommunication Union which was founded in 1865 as the International Telegraph Union.

Other organizations may become specialized agencies, in response to "pressure for the creation of new agencies [and] for reviewing the relationships between the UN and the existing agencies."[10]

──────────[10] United Nations, Office of Public Information, Non-Governmental Organizations Section, Co-ordination within the UN system (New York, 5 December 1974; OPI/NGO/SB/53), p. 3.

The most current example is that of the International Fund for Agricultural Development (IFAD). The General Assembly, in its resolution 3503 (XXX) of 15 December 1975, provided that IFAD should become a specialized agency and requested the Economic and Social Council

> to arrange for the negotiation with the preparatory commission of the International Fund for Agricultural Development of an agreement with the Fund to constitute it as a specialized agency in accordance with Articles 57 and 63 of the Charter of the United Nations, to enter into such agreement, subject to the approval of the General Assembly, and to arrange with the preparatory commission for the provisional application of that agreement as appropriate.[11]

Accordingly, the Economic and Social Council's Committee on Negotiations with Intergovernmental Agencies, as charged by Council resolution 2006 (LX) of 13 May 1976, prepared a draft relationship agreement (contained in document E/5924 of 11 May 1977). The draft agreement has been transmitted to IFAD for approval.

The fourteen specialized agencies have entered into a relationship with the United Nations following a standard pattern of preparation, negotiation, elaboration and acceptance of the agreement.[12]

----

[11] United Nations, General Assembly, Res-olutions adopted during its thir-tieth session (New York, 1976; Official records of the General Assembly, Thirtieth Session, Supplement No. 34), pp. 63-64.

[12] For a detailed discussion of this process and of the machinery of co-ordination among UN organizations, see Everyman's United Nations Bibliography entry 44), pp. 487-550.

The International Atomic Energy Agency
is not a specialized agency but an autonomous
intergovernmental organization established under
the aegis of the United Nations.

The General Agreement on Tariffs and
Trade is a multilateral treaty administered by
a secretariat which was originally established
to serve as the secretariat for the Interim Commission for the International Trade Organization
(ICITO). The International Trade Organization
(ITO) itself has not been established, although
its draft charter (the "Havana Charter") was
completed in 1948.

Co-ordination is an increasingly important function of the United Nations in this age
of interdisciplinary approaches. The question
of arid zones may be cited as an example: UNESCO
has been studying it from a scientific viewpoint,
FAO and UNDP from the point of view of food production and water management. It is also an environmental problem, of concern to UNEP.

The international concern with the advancement of women also illustrates how an activity evolves into a concerted action programme
(i.e., one involving the United Nations and one
or more specialized agencies). The General Assembly initiated a study of this question in 1962.
In 1966, the Secretary-General submitted his report on the question to the Commission on the
Status of Women. The Commission approved the
report, suggesting specific goals and objectives.
On 7 November 1967, the Assembly adopted the Declaration on the Elimination of Discrimination
against Women. The Declaration embodies principles of equal rights, proposals for legislation
and regulations by member states, measures to be
taken to ensure equality of status of men and
women, of husband and wife, protection of children, prohibition of child marriages, etc. (See
Part V for the text of the Declaration.) The
1968 Teheran International Conference on Human

Rights supported these aims and measures. In
1970, the General Assembly formally adopted a
programme of concerted international action for
the advancement of women, projecting national
and international legal action, educational and
health programmes, and studies of the effects of
scientific and technological changes on women.
The programme set forth specific targets to be
achieved by the United Nations system of organizations during the second United Nations Development Decade (1970-1980).[13]

On 18 December 1972, the General Assembly adopted resolution No. 3010 (XXVII) "in
which it proclaimed 1975 as International Women's
Year and decided to devote the year to intensified action to promote equality between men and
women, to ensure the full integration of women
in the total development effort and to recognize
the importance of women's contribution[s]."[14]
The culmination of the programme of International Women's Year was the World Conference of the
International Women's Year, held in Mexico City
from 19 June to 2 July 1975. Among the proposals
of the Conference: a World Plan of Action aimed
at improving the status of women and the proclamation of the period 1975-1985 as the Decade
for Women and Development to ensure continuing
regional, national and international action.

During its thirtieth session and the
first part of its thirty-first session, the
General Assembly adopted several resolutions
aimed at enlarging the role of women and endorsing the recommendations of the Mexico City

―――――――[13] Everyman's United Nations; a summary
of activities . . . for . . . 1966-
1970. (Bibliography entry 45), pp.
161-164.

[14]
United Nations, General Assembly, Report of the Economic and Social Council on the work of its organizational
session for 1975 and of its fifty-
eight and fifty-ninth sessions. (New
York, 1975. Official records of the

Conference:

Resolution 3505 (XXX) of 15 December 1975 dealt with the integration of women in the development process

Resolution 3520 (XXX) of 15 December 1975 proclaimed the period 1976 to 1985 "United Nations Decade for Women: Equality, Development and Peace"

Resolutions 3521-3524 (XXX) of 15 December 1975 dealt with the role of women in education

Resolution 31/133 of 16 December 1976 set out criteria and proposals for the management of the Voluntary Fund for the United Nations Decade for Women (the Fund had originally been established for the International Women's Year only, by Economic and Social Council resolution 1850 (LVI) of 16 May 1974)

Resolution 31/134 of 16 December 1976 concerned itself with the improvement of the status and enlargement of role of women in education

Resolution 31/135 of 16 December 1976 endorsed Economic and Social Council resolution 1998 (LX) of 15 May 1976 in which the Council had decided to create an International Research and Training Institute for the Advancement of Women

Resolution 31/136 of 16 December 1976 approved the programme for the United Nations Decade for Women

Resolution 31/137 of 16 December 1976 requested the convening, in 1977, of a pledging conference for contributions to the Voluntary Fund for the United Nations Decade for Women

Resolution 31/175 of 21 December 1976 reaffirmed the need for effective mobilization of women in development

In addition to co-operating with the specialized agencies, GATT and the International Atomic Energy Agency, the United Nations also co-operates with institutions called United Nations affiliated bodies - a term that "refers

---

General Assembly, Thirtieth Session, Supplement No. 3), p. 17.

to institutes, centres, etc. which are related
to the United Nations by reason of special agreements or arrangements covering . . . secretariat
services . . . the services of experts and consultants, and financial support which may be
provided through the United Nations Development
Programme or by 'funds-in-trust.'"[15] Table VII
is a partial list of affiliated bodies at the
end of 1975 (as of July 1977, no new listing has
been completed by the United Nations):

TABLE VII

UNITED NATIONS AFFILIATED BODIES

African Institute for Economic Development and
   Planning, IDEP, Dakar

Asia and the Far East Institute for the Prevention of Crime and the Treatment of Offenders,
   UNAFEI, Fuchu, Japan

Asian Centre for Development Administration,
   ACDA, Kuala Lumpur, Malaysia

Asian Centre for Training and Research in Social
   Welfare and Development, ACTRSWD, Manila

Asian Coconut Community, Jakarta

Asian Development Institute, Bangkok
   Formerly: Asian Institute for Economic De-
              velopment and Planning

Asian Statistical Institute, ASI, Tokyo

Cairo Demographic Centre, CDC
   Formerly: North African Demographic Centre

————————[15]
       United Nations, Dag Hammarskjöld Li-
       brary, Office of the Director, Policy
       concerning documents and publications
       of United Nations affiliated bodies.
       [New York] 1 December 1975. (DIREC-
       TIVE/A/24/Annex I, Sub-annex 15),
       p. 1. Quoted by permission.

Centre démographique ONU-Roumanie CEDOR, Bucharest

Centre for Social and Criminological Research, Cairo

Centro Interamericano de Enseñanza de Estadística, CIENES, Santiago de Chile

Centro Latinoamericano de Demografía, CELADE, Santiago de Chile

Centro Latinoamericano de Documentación Económica y Social, CLADES, Santiago de Chile

Committee for Co-ordination of Joint Prospecting for Mineral Resources in Asian Offshore Areas, CCOP, Bangkok

East African Statistical Training Centre, Dar-es-Salaam, Tanzania

European Centre for Social Welfare Training and Research, Vienna

Institut de formation et de recherche démographiques, IFORD, Yaoundé, Cameroun

Institut national de la statistique et d'économique appliquée, INSEA, Rabat, Morocco

Institute of Statistics and Applied Economics, Kampala, Uganda

Instituto Centroamericano de Administración Pública, ICAP, San José, Costa Rica
<u>Formerly</u>: Escuela Superior de Administración Pública América Central, ESAPAC

Instituto Latinoamericano de Planificación Económica y Social, ILPES, Santiago de Chile

International Bureau for Declarations of Death, IBD, Geneva, 1952-1973

International Children's Centre, ICC, Paris

International Institute for Population Studies, IIPS, Bombay
<u>Formerly</u>: Demographic Training and Research Centre at Chembur, India

International Lead and Zinc Study Group, United Nations, New York

International Statistical Education and Research Centre, Beirut

International Statistical Education Centre, Calcutta

Latin American Institute for Social Defense, San José, Costa Rica

Regional Institute for Population Studies, RIPS, Accra, Ghana

Regional Institute for Research and Training in Statistics for the Near East, Baghdad, Iraq

CHAPTER 7

NON-GOVERNMENTAL ORGANIZATIONS IN CONSULTATIVE
STATUS WITH THE ECONOMIC AND SOCIAL COUNCIL

        The Economic and Social Council consults
regularly with a large number of non-governmental organizations (NGO's) which fall into one of
three categories:
Category I: organizations with interest and
  competence in most of the fields of activity
  of the Economic and Social Council;
Category II: organizations concerned with and
  competent in only a few fields of activity
  of the Council; and
Roster: organizations that may make specific
  contributions to the work of the Economic and
  Social Council and are consulted by the Council on an ad hoc basis.

        The non-governmental organizations may:
(a) designate authorized representatives to
serve as observers at public meetings of the
Economic and Social Council and its subsidiary
bodies; (b) submit written statements, relating
to the work of the Council and its subsidiary
bodies, for circulation as United Nations documents; and (c) consult with the United Nations
Secretariat about matters of mutual concern.

        Table VIII is a list[16] of non-governmen-
──────────[16]
        Source: United Nations, Economic and
        Social Council, Non-governmental or-
        ganizations in consultative status

tal organizations in consultative status with
the Economic and Social Council as of July 1977.
The addresses, names of officers, etc. of most
of these organizations may be obtained from the
Yearbook of international organizations, 16th
ed. (1977).

TABLE VIII

NON-GOVERNMENTAL ORGANIZATIONS IN CONSULTATIVE
STATUS WITH THE ECONOMIC AND SOCIAL COUNCIL

Category I

International Alliance of Women - Equal Rights,
Equal Responsibilities

International Association of French-Speaking
Parliamentarians

International Chamber of Commerce

International Confederation of Free Trade Unions

International Co-operative Alliance

International Council of Voluntary Agencies
(ICVA)

International Council of Women

International Council on Social Welfare

International Federation of Agricultural Producers

International Organization for Standardization
(ISO)

International Organization of Consumers Unions
(IOCU)

---

with the Economic and Social Council
in 1976 (New York, 14 July 1976;
E/INF/154); and United Nations, Economic and Social Council, Report of
the Committee on Non-Governmental
Organizations (New York, 13 April
1977; E/5934).

International Organizations of Employers
International Planned Parenthood Federation
International Union of Local Authorities
International Youth and Student Movement for
    the United Nations
Inter-Parliamentary Union
League of Red Cross Societies
Organisation of African Trade Union Unity (OATUU)
United Towns Organization
Women's International Democratic Federation
World Assembly of Youth (WAY)
World Confederation of Labour
World Federation of Democratic Youth (WFDY)
World Federation of Trade Unions (WFTU)
World Federation of United Nations Associations
    (WFUNA)
World Veterans Federation

Category II

Afro-Asian Organization for Economic Co-operation
Afro-Asian Peoples' Solidarity Organization
Agudas Israel World Organization
Airport Associations Coordinating Council (AACC)
All-African Women's Conference
All-India Women's Conference
All-Pakistan Women's Association
American Field Service, Inc.
Amnesty International
Anti-apartheid Movement, The
Anti-Slavery Society, The

Arab Lawyers Union

Associated Country Women of the World

Association for Childhood Education Internationa

Association for the Study of the World Refugee
Problem

Bahá'i International Community

Baptist World Alliance

Boy Scouts World Bureau

CARE (Cooperative for American Relief Everywhere, Inc.)

Caritas Internationalis (International Confederation of Catholic Charities)

Carnegie Endowment for International Peace

Catholic International Union for Social Service

Centre for Latin American Monetary Studies

Centro de Investigación para el Desarrollo
Económico Social

Chamber of Commerce of the United States of
America

Christian Democratic World Union

Christian Peace Conference

Church World Service, Inc.

Commission of the Churches on International
Affairs, The

Commonwealth Human Ecology Council (CHEC)

Community Development Foundation, Inc.

Consultative Council of Jewish Organizations

Co-ordinating Board of Jewish Organizations
(CBJO)

Co-ordinating Committee for International Voluntary Service

Eastern Regional Organization for Public Adminis

tration

European Association of National Productivity
Centres

European Insurance Committee

European League for Economic Co-operation

Federation for the Respect of Man and Humanity

Federation of Arab Economists, The

Foundation for the Peoples of the South Pacific,
Inc., The

Friends World Committee for Consultation

Howard League for Penal Reform

Ibero-American Institute of Aeronautic and Space
Law and Commercial Aviation

Institute for Policy Studies

Institute of Electrical and Electronic Engineers,
Inc.

Inter-American Council of Commerce and Production

Inter-American Federation of Public Relations
Association

Inter-American Federation of Touring and Automobile Clubs (FITAC)

Inter-American Planning Society

Inter-American Press Association

Inter-American Statistical Institute

International Abolitionist Federation

International Air Transport Association

International Association Against Painful Ex-
periments on Animals

International Association for Religious Freedom
(IARF)

International Association for Social Progress

International Association for the Promotion and Protection of Private Foreign Investments

International Association for the Protection of Industrial Property

International Association for Water Law (IAWL)

International Association of Democratic Lawyers

International Association of Educators for World Peace

International Association of Penal Law

International Association of Ports and Harbours (IAPH)

International Association of Schools of Social Work

International Association of Youth Magistrates

International Astronautical Federation

International Automobile Federation (FIA)

International Bar Association

International Cargo Handling Co-ordination Association

International Catholic Child Bureau

International Catholic Migration Commission

International Catholic Union of the Press

International Centre for Local Credit

International Chamber of Shipping

International Christian Union of Business Executives (UNIAPAC)

International Civil Airport Association

International College of Surgeons

International Commission of Jurists

International Commission on Irrigation and Drainage

International Committee of the Red Cross

International Co-operation for Socio-Economic Development (CIDSE)

International Council for Adult Education (ICAE)

International Council for Building Research, Studies and Documentation

International Council of Environmental Law

International Council of Jewish Women

International Council of Monuments and Sites (ICOMOS)

International Council of Scientific Unions

International Council of Social Democratic Women

International Council of Societies of Industrial Design (ICSID)

International Council on Alcoholism and Addictions

International Council on Jewish Social and Welfare Services

International Defence and Aid Fund for Southern Africa

International Federation for Housing and Planning

International Federation for Human Rights

International Federation of Beekeepers' Associations

International Federation of Business and Professional Women

International Federation of Journalists

International Federation of Landscape Architects

International Federation of Resistance Movements

International Federation of Senior Police Officers

International Federation of Settlements and Neighbourhood Centres

International Federation of Social Workers

International Federation of University Women

International Federation of Women in Legal Careers

International Federation of Women Lawyers

International Hotel Association

International Indian Treaty Council

International Institute for Vital Registration and Statistics (IIVRS)

International Institute of Administrative Sciences

International Institute of Public Finance

International Islamic Federation of Student Organizations

International Law Association

International League for Human Rights

International League of Societies for the Mentally Handicapped

International Movement for Fraternal Union Among Races and Peoples (UFER)

International Organization - Justice and Development

International Organization of Journalists (IOJ)

International Organization of Supreme Audit Institutions (INTOSAI)

International Petroleum Industry Environmental Conservation Association (IPIECA)

International Prisoners Aid Association

International Road Federation

International Road Transport Union

International Rural Housing Association

International Savings Banks Institute

International Senior Citizens Association, Inc., The

International Social Service

International Society for Criminology

International Society of Social Defence

International Statistical Institute

International Touring Alliance

International Union for Child Welfare

International Union for Conservation of Nature and Natural Resources

International Union for Inland Navigation

International Union for the Scientific Study of Population

International Union of Architects

International Union of Building Societies and Savings Associations

International Union of Family Organizations

International Union of Lawyers

International Union of Producers and Distributors of Electrical Energy

International Union of Public Transport

International Union of Railways

International University Exchange Fund

International Young Christian Workers

Jaycees International

Latin American Association of Finance Development Institutions (ALIDE)

Latin American Iron and Steel Institute

Lions International - The International Association of Lions Clubs

Lutheran World Federation

Movement for Colonial Freedom

Muslim World League (MWL)

Mutual Assistance of the Latin American Government Oil Companies (ARPEL)

Organization for International Economic Relation (IER)

OXFAM

Panafrican Institute for Development

Pan American Federation of Engineering Societies (UPADI)

Pan-Pacific and South-East Asia Women's Association

Pax Romana
International Catholic Movement for Intellectual and Cultural Affairs
International Movement of Catholic Students

Permanent International Association of Road Congresses (PIARC)

Rehabilitation International

Rotary International

Salvation Army, The

Socialist International

Society for Comparative Legislation

Society for International Development (SID)

Société internationale de prophylaxie criminelle

Soroptimist International

St. Joan's International Alliance

Studies and Expansion Society - International Scientific Association (SEC)

Union of Arab Jurists

Union of International Associations

Union of International Fairs

United Kingdom Standing Conference on the Second United Nations Development Decade

Universal Federation of Travel Agents Associations

Vienna Institute for Development

War Resisters International

Women's International League for Peace and Freedom

Women's International Zionist Organization

World Alliance of Young Men's Christian Associations

World Association of Girl Guides and Girl Scouts

World Association of World Federalists

World Confederation of Organizations of the Teaching Profession

World Conference on Religion and Peace

World Council for the Welfare of the Blind

World Council of Credit Unions, Inc. (WOCCU)

World Council of Management

World Energy Conference

World Federation for Mental Health

World Federation for the Protection of Animals

World Federation of Catholic Youth

World Federation of the Deaf

World Jewish Congress

World Leisure and Recreation Association

World Movement of Mothers

World Muslim Congress

World Peace Through Law Centre

World Population Society

World Student Christian Federation

World Trade Centers Association

World Union of Catholic Women's Organizations

World Union of Organizations for the Safeguard
of Youth

World University Service

World Women's Christian Temperance Union

World Young Women's Christian Association

Zonta International

Roster

Organizations included by virtue of action
taken by the Economic and Social Council

African Medical and Research Foundation International

American Foreign Insurance Association

Asian Development Center

Asian Youth Council

Battelle Memorial Institute

Center for Inter-American Relations

Commission to Study the Organization of Peace

Comité d'études économiques de l'industrie du
gaz

Committee for Economic Development

Committee for European Construction Equipment

Confederation of Asian Chambers of Commerce

Congress of Racial Equality (CORE)

Council of European National Youth Committees
(CENYC)

Econometric Society

Engineers Joint Council

Environmental Coalition for North America
(ENCONA)

European Alliance of Press Agencies

European Association of Refrigeration Enterprises (AEEF)

European Confederation of Woodworking Industries

European Container Manufacturers' Committee

European Mediterranean Commission Water Planning

Ex-Volunteers International

Federation of International Furniture Removers

Foundation for the Establishment of an International Criminal Court, The

Institute of International Container Lessors

International Association for Bridge and Structural Engineering

International Association for Hydrogen Energy

International Association for Research Into Income and Wealth

International Association for the Exchange of Students for Technical Experience (IASTE)

International Association of Chiefs of Police

International Association of Gerontology

International Board of Co-operation for the Developing Countries (EMCO)

International Bureau for the Supression of Traffic in Persons

International Bureau of Motor-Cycle Manufacturers

International Center for Dynamics of Development

International Committee of Outer Space Onomastics (ICOSO)

International Confederation of Associations of Experts and Consultants

International Container Bureau

International Federation for Documentation

International Federation of Chemical and General
   Workers' Unions (ICF)

International Federation of Cotton and Allied
   Textile Industries

International Federation of Forwarding Agents
   Associations

International Federation of Free Journalists

International Federation of Operational Research
   Societies

International Federation of Pedestrians

International Federation of Surveyors

International Federation of the Blind

International Federation on Ageing

International (Free) Federation of Deportees and
   Resistance Internees

International Fiscal Association

International Inner Wheel

International League of Surveillance Societies,
   The

International Movement Science and Service for a
   Just and Free World

International Olive Growers Federation

International Organization for Commerce

International Organization of Experts (ORDINEX)

International Peace Academy

International Peace Bureau

International Permanent Bureau of Automobile
   Manufacturers

International Playground Association

International Police Association

International Progress Organisation (IPO)

International Public Relations Association (IPRA)

International Real Estate Federation

International Schools Association

International Shipping Federation

International Society for Prosthetics and Orthotics

International Society for the Protection of Animals

International Solar Energy Society

International Union of Judges

International Union of Marine Insurance

International Union of Police Federations

International Union of Social Democratic Teachers

International Union of Tenants

International Voluntary Service

International Working Group for the Construction of Sports Premises (IAKS)

Latin American Confederation of Tourist Organizations (COTAL)

Latin American Official Workers' Confederation (CLATE)

Minority Rights Group

Movement Against Racism, Antisemitism and for Peace

National Indian Brotherhood

National Organization for Women (NOW)

National Parks and Conservation Association

OISCA - International (Organization for Industrial, Spiritual and Cultural Advancement - International)

Open Door International (for the Economic Emancipation of the Woman Worker)

Pan American Development Foundation

Pax Christi, International Catholic Peace Movement

Permanent International Association of Navigation Congresses

Pio Mansú International Research Centre for Environmental Structures, The

Planetary Citizens

Population Council, The

Prévention routière internationale, La (International Road Safety Association)

Quota International

SERVAS International

Society for Social Responsibility in Science

United Nations of Yoga (UNY)

United Way of America

World Alliance of Reformed Churches

World Association for Christian Communication

World Confederation for Physical Therapy

World Development Movement

World Federation of Christian Life Communities

World Union for Progressive Judaism

Young Lawyers International Association (AIJA)

Organizations placed on the Roster by
action of the Secretary-General

American Association for the Advancement of Science

Asian Environmental Society

Association for the Advancement of Agricultural Sciences in Africa

Center of Concern

Committee for International Co-ordination of National Research in Demography (CICRED)

Fauna Preservation Society, The

Foresta Institute for Ocean and Mountain Studies

Friends of the Earth (F.O.E.)

Institut de la vie

International Advisory Committee on Population and Law

International Association Against Noise

International Association on Water Pollution Research (IAWPR)

International Educational Development, Inc.

International Institute for Environment and Development

International Ocean Institute

International Society for Community Development

International Studies Association

International Union of Anthropological and Ethnological Sciences

National Audubon Society

Natural Resources Defense Council, Inc.

Organisation internationale pour le développement rural

Population Crisis Committee

Population Institute

Sierra Club

Trilateral Commission, The

World Education Inc.

World Society of Ekistics

Organizations placed on the Roster by virtue of
their consultative status with specialized
agencies or other United Nations bodies

Aerospace Medical Association	ICAO
Afro-Asian Writers' Union	UNESCO
Arab Federation of Chemical Fertilizer Producers	UNIDO
Asian Broadcasting Union	UNESCO, FAO
Association des universités partiellement ou entièrement de langue française	UNESCO
Association for the Promotion of the International Circulation of the Press	UNESCO
Association of Arab Universities	UNESCO
Association of Commonwealth Universities	UNESCO
Association of European Jute Industries	UNCTAD
Association of Official Analytical Chemists	FAO
Association of South East Asian Institutions of Higher Education	UNESCO
Baltic and International Maritime Conference, The	IMCO, UNCTAD
Biometric Society, The	WHO
B'nai B'rith International Council	UNESCO
Catholic International Education Office	UNESCO, UNICEF
Central Council for Health Education	WHO
Christian Medical Commission	WHO
Commonwealth Medical Association	WHO
Co-ordination Committee for the Textile Industries in the European Common Market	UNCTAD

Council for International Organizations of Medical Sciences (CIOMS)	WHO, UNESCO
Council of European and Japanese National Shipowners' Associations, The (CENSA)	UNCTAD
Engineering Committee on Oceanic Resources (ECOR)	IMCO
European Association for Animal Production	FAO
European Association for Personnel Management	ILO
European Association for the Trade in Jute Products	UNCTAD
European Association of Management Consultants Associations	UNIDO
European Association of Management Training Centres	UNIDO
European Association of Nitrogen Manufacturers	IMCO
European Atomic Forum	IAEA
European Broadcasting Union	UNESCO
European Center for Overseas Industrial Development	UNIDO
European Centre for the Perfection and Research for Artists taking Part in the Productions	UNESCO
European Committee of Sugar Manufacturers	UNCTAD
European Confederation of Agriculture	FAO, IAEA
European Council of Chemical Manufacturers Federations	IMCO, UNCTAD
European Federation of Associations of Engineers and Heads of Industrial Safety Services and Industrial Physicians	ILO

European Federation of National Associations of Engineers	UNESCO
European Federation of National Maintenance Societies	UNIDO
European Industrial Space Study Group - EUROSPACE	IMCO
European Mechanical Handling Confederation	ILO
European Oceanic Association	UNIDO
European Society of Culture	UNESCO
European Training and Research Centre for Theatrical Performers	UNESCO
European Tugowners Association (ETA)	IMCO
European Union of Coachbuilders	UNIDO
European Union of Public Relations	UNIDO
Eurosat S.A.	IMCO
Experiment in International Living, The	UNESCO
Fédération internationale des journalistes et écrivains du tourisme	UNESCO
Federation of Indian Chambers of Commerce and Industry	UNCTAD
Federation of Indian Export Organizations	UNCTAD
Federation of National Associations of Ship Brokers and Agents	UNCTAD
General Arab Insurance Federation	UNCTAD
Hemispheric Insurance Conference	UNCTAD
Institut du transport aerien	ICAO
Institute of International Law	ICAO
Institute on Man and Science	UNESCO
Inter-American Association of Broadcasters	UNESCO

Inter-American Association of Sanitary Engineering	WHO
Inter-American Council of Commerce and Production	UNCTAD
International Academy of Aviation and Space Medicine	ICAO
International Academy of Legal Medicine and of Social Medicine	WHO
International Aeronautical Federation	ICAO
International Agency for the Prevention of Blindness (Vision International)	UNICEF
International Aircraft Brokers Association	ICAO
International Airline Navigators Council	ICAO, WMO
International Air Safety Association	ICAO
International Association for Accidents and Traffic Medicine	WHO
International Association for Cereal Chemistry (ICC)	UNIDO
International Association for Child Psychiatry and Allied Professions	WHO
International Association for Earthquake Engineering	UNESCO
International Association for Educational and Vocational Guidance	UNESCO, ILO, UNICEF
International Association for Educational and Vocational Information	UNESCO, ILO
International Association for Mass Communication Research	UNESCO
International Association for Prevention of Blindness	WHO
International Association for the Advancement of Educational Research	UNESCO

International Association for the Evaluation of Educational Achievement	UNESCO
International Association for the Physical Sciences of the Ocean	ICAO
International Association of Agricultural Economists	FAO
International Association of Agricultural Librarians and Documentalists	FAO
International Association of Agricultural Medicine	WHO, ILO
International Association of Art - Painting, Sculpture, Graphic Art	UNESCO
International Association of Art Critics	UNESCO
International Association of Classification Societies	IMCO
International Association of Conference Interpreters	ILO
International Association of Crafts and Small and Medium-Sized Enterprises	UNIDO
International Association of Fish Meal Manufacturers	FAO
International Association of Horticultural Producers	FAO
International Association of Insurance and Reinsurance Intermediaries	UNCTAD
International Association of Legal Science	UNESCO
International Association of Lighthouse Authorities	IMCO
International Association of Literary Critics	UNESCO
International Association of Logopedics and Phoniatrics	UNESCO, WHO, UNICEF

International Association of Medical Laboratory Technologists	WHO
International Association of Microbiological Societies	WHO
International Association of Physical Oceanography (IAPO)	ICAO
International Association of Scientific Experts in Tourism	UNESCO
International Association of Students in Economics and Management	UNESCO, ILO
International Association of Theatre Critics	UNESCO
International Association of Universities	UNESCO
International Association of University Professors and Lecturers	UNESCO
International Association of Workers for Maladjusted Children	UNESCO
International Astronomical Union	WMO
International Baccalaureate Office	UNESCO
International Board on Books for Young People	UNESCO, UNICEF
International Brain Research Organization	UNESCO, WHO
International Bureau of Social Tourism	ILO, UNESCO
International Cell Research Organization	UNESCO
International Centre for Wholesale Trade	UNCTAD
International Centre of Films for Children and Young People	UNESCO, UNICEF
International Centre of Research and Information on Collective Economy	ILO
International Cocoa Trade Federation	UNCTAD

International Commission Against Concentration Camp Practices	ILO
International Commission of Agricultural Engineering	FAO, UNESCO
International Commission on Illumination	IMCO, ICAO, ILO
International Commission on Radiation Units and Measurements	WHO, IAEA
International Commission on Radiological Protection	WHO, IAEA
International Committee for Plastics in Agriculture	UNIDO
International Committee for Social Science Information and Documentation	UNESCO
International Committee of Catholic Nurses and Medico-Social Workers	WHO, ILO
International Committee on Laboratory Animals	WHO
International Community of Booksellers Associations	UNESCO
International Confederation of European Beet Growers	UNCTAD
International Confederation of Midwives	WHO, ILO, UNICEF
International Confederation of Societies of Authors and Composers	UNESCO
International Congress of University Adult Education	UNESCO
International Coordinating Committee for the Presentation of Science and the Development of Out-of-School Scientific Activities	UNESCO
International Coordinating Council of Aerospace Industries Associations	ICAO

International Copyright Society	UNESCO
International Council for Philosophy and Humanistic Studies	UNESCO
International Council for Educational Films	ILO
International Council of Aircraft Owner and Pilot Associations	ICAO
International Council of Graphic Design Associations	UNESCO
International Council of Museums	UNESCO
International Council of Nurses	WHO,ILO, UNESCO, UNICEF
International Council of Societies of Pathology	WHO
International Council of Sport and Physical Education	UNESCO
International Council on Archives	UNESCO
International Council on Correspondence Education	UNESCO
International Council on Education for Teaching	UNESCO
International Cystic Fibrosis (Mucoviscidosis) Association	WHO
International Dairy Federation	FAO, UNICEF
International Dance Council	UNESCO
International Dental Federation	WHO
International Diabetes Federation	WHO
International Economic Association	UNESCO
International Electrotechnical Commission	IMCO, WHO
International Epidemiological Association	WHO

International Ergonomics Association	ILO,WHO
International Falcon Movement	UNESCO
International Federation for Home Economics	UNICEF
International Federation for Information Processing	UNESCO
International Federation for Medical and Biological Engineering	WHO
International Federation for Parent Education	UNESCO, UNICEF
International Federation of Actors	UNESCO
International Federation of Air Line Pilots Associations	ICAO, WMO
International Federation of Automatic Control	UNIDO, UNESCO
International Federation of Catholic Universities	UNESCO
International Federation of Children's Communities	UNESCO
International Federation of Clinical Chemistry	WHO
International Federation of Fertility Societies	WHO
International Federation of Free Teachers' Unions	UNESCO
International Federation of Gynecology and Obstetrics	WHO
International Federation of Home Economics	FAO
International Federation of Independent Air Transport	ICAO
International Federation of Industrial Producers of Electricity for own Consumption	IAEA

International Federation of Library Associations	UNESCO
International Federation of Margarine Associations	FAO
International Federation of Medical Students' Associations	WHO
International Federation of Modern Language Teachers	UNESCO
International Federation of Multiple Sclerosis Societies	WHO
International Federation of Newspaper Publishers	UNESCO
International Federation of Ophthalmological Societies	WHO
International Federation of Organizations of School Correspondence and Exchanges	UNESCO
International Federation of Pharmaceutical Manufacturers Associations	WHO
International Federation of Physical Medicine and Rehabilitation	WHO
International Federation of Plantation, Agricultural and Allied Workers	FAO
International Federation of Popular Travel Organizations	UNESCO
International Federation of Purchasing and Materials Management (IFPMM)	UNCTAD
International Federation of Sports Medicine	WHO
International Federation of Surgical Colleges	WHO
International Federation of the Periodical Press	UNESCO
International Federation of the Phonographic Industry	UNESCO

International Federation of the Training Centres for the Promotion of Progressive Education	UNESCO
International Federation of Translators	UNESCO
International Federation of Workers' Educational Associations	UNESCO
International Fertility Association	WHO
International Film and Television Council	UNESCO
International Geographical Union	ICAO
International Hospital Federation	WHO
International Humanistic and Ethical Union	UNESCO
International Hydatidological Association	WHO
International Institute for Industrial Planning	UNIDO
International Institute of Music, Dance and Theatre in the Audio-Visual Media	UNESCO
International League Against Epilipsy	WHO
International League Against Rheumatism	WHO, UNICEF
International League for Child and Adult Education	UNESCO
International League of Dermatological Societies	WHO
International Leprosy Association	WHO
International Literary and Artistic Association	UNESCO
International Marine Radio Association	IMCO
International Maritime Committee	IMCO
International Maritime Pilot's Association	IMCO
International Measurement Confederation	UNIDO

International Medical Association for the Study of Living Conditions and Health	FAO
International Movement of Catholic Agricultural and Rural Youth	FAO, ILO, UNESCO
International Music Council	UNESCO
International Organization Against Trachoma	WHO
International Organization for Rural Development	UNICEF
International Paediatric Association	WHO, UNICEF
International Peace Research Association	UNESCO
International PEN	UNESCO
International Pharmaceutical Federation	WHO
International Political Science Association	UNESCO
International Publishers Association	UNESCO
International Radiation Protection Association	WHO
International Radio and Television Organization	UNESCO
International Radio-Maritime Committee	IMCO, ICAO, WMO
International Rayon and Synthetic Fibres Committee	UNCTAD
International Reading Association	UNESCO
International Round Table for the Advancement of Counselling (IRTAC)	ILO, UNICEF
International Scientific Film Association	UNESCO

International Scientific Radio Union	WMO
International Secretariat of Catholic Technologists, Agriculturists and Economists	ILO
International Ship Owners Association	UNCTAD
International Social Science Council	UNESCO, ILO
International Society for Burn Injuries	WHO
International Society for Education through Art	UNESCO
International Society for Human and Animal Mycology	WHO
International Society for Labour Law and Social Legislation	ILO
International Society for Photogrammetry	UNESCO
International Society for Research on Moors	FAO
International Society of Biometeorology	WHO,WMO
International Society of Blood Transfusion	WHO
International Society of Cardiology	WHO
International Society of Citriculture	FAO
International Society of Endocrinology	WHO
International Society of Hematology	WHO
International Society of Orthopaedic Surgery and Traumatology	WHO
International Society of Radiographers and Radiological Technicians	WHO
International Society of Radiology	WHO

International Society of Soil Science	FAO, UNESCO, WMO
International Sociological Association	UNESCO
International Solid Wastes and Public Cleansing Association	WHO
International Superphosphate and Compound Manufacturers' Association Limited	IMCO, UNCTAD, UNIDO
International Theatre Institute	UNESCO
International Transport Workers' Federation	ICAO
International Travel Journalists and Writers Federation	UNESCO
International Union Against Cancer	WHO
International Union Against the Venereal Diseases and the Treponematoses	WHO, UNICEF
International Union Against Tuberculosis	WHO, ILO, UNICEF
International Union for Health Education	WHO, UNESCO, UNICEF
International Union for the Liberty of Education	UNESCO
International Union of Aviation Insurers	ICAO
International Union of Biological Sciences	WHO
International Union of Food and Allied Workers Associations	FAO
International Union of Forestry Research Organizations	FAO
International Union of Geodesy and Geophysics	ICAO

International Union of Immunological Societies	WHO
International Union of Independent Laboratories	UNIDO
International Union of Judges	ILO
International Union of Leather Technologists and Chemists Societies	UNIDO, FAO
International Union of Nutritional Sciences	FAO, WHO, UNICEF
International Union of Pharmacology	WHO
International Union of Psychological Science	UNESCO
International Union of Pure and Applied Chemistry	WHO, FAO
International Union of School and University Health and Medicine	WHO, UNESCO
International Union of Socialist Youth	UNESCO, ILO, UNICEF
International Union of Students	UNESCO
International Water Supply Association	WHO
International Writers Guild	UNESCO
International Young Catholic Students	UNESCO
International Youth Federation for Environmental Studies and Conservation	UNESCO
International Youth Hostel Federation	UNESCO
Japan Atomic Industrial Forum, Inc.	IAEA
Joint Commission on International Aspects of Mental Retardation	WHO
Latin American and Caribbean Federation of Exporters' Associations	UNCTAD
Latin American Plastics Institute	UNIDO

Latin American Shipowners Association	UNCTAD, IMCO
Latin-American Social Science Council	UNESCO
Liaison Office of the Rubber Industries of the European Economic Community	UNCTAD
Medical Women's International Association	WHO, UNICEF
Miners' International Federation	UNCTAD
National Shippers' Councils of Europe	UNCTAD
Oil Companies' International Marine Forum	IMCO
Pacific Science Association	UNESCO, WMO
Pan-African Youth Movement	UNESCO
Pan-American Union of Associations of Engineering	UNESCO
Permanent Commission and International Association on Occupational Health	WHO, ILO
Permanent International Committee on Canned Foods	FAO
Society for Chemical Industry	UNIDO
Society for General Systems Research	UNESCO
Society of African Culture	UNESCO
Sri Aurobindo Society	UNESCO
Standing Conference of Chambers of Commerce and Industry of the European Economic Community	UNCTAD
Standing Conference of Rectors and Vice-Chancellors of the European Universities	UNESCO
Trade Unions International of Agricultural, Forestry and Plantation Workers	FAO

Trade Union International of Food, Tobacco, Hotel and Allied Industries' Workers	FAO
Transplantation Society	WHO
UNDA - Catholic International Association for Radio and Television	UNESCO
Union of Industries of the European Community	UNIDO, UNCTAD
Union of International Engineering Organizations	UNESCO, UNIDO
Union of Latin American Universities	UNESCO
Union of National Radio and Television Organizations of Africa	UNESCO, ILO
Union of Producers, Conveyors and Distributors of Electric Power in African Countries, Madagascar and Mauritius	UNIDO
United Schools International	UNESCO
United Seamen's Service	ILO
Universal Esperanto Association	UNESCO
World Association for Animal Production	FAO
World Association for Public Opinion Research	UNESCO
World Association for the School as an Instrument of Peace	UNESCO
World Association of Industrial and Technological Research Organizations	UNIDO
World Association of Societies of Pathology	WHO
World Confederation of Teachers	UNESCO
World Crafts Council	UNESCO, UNICEF
World Education Fellowship, The	UNESCO
World Federation for Medical Education	WHO
World Federation of Agricultural Workers	FAO

World Federation of Engineering Organizations	UNESCO, UNIDO
World Federation of Foreign Language Teachers Associations	UNESCO
World Federation of Hemophilia	WHO
World Federation of Medical Education	WHO
World Federation of Neurology	WHO
World Federation of Neurosurgical Societies	WHO
World Federation of Nuclear Medicine and Biology	WHO
World Federation of Occupational Therapists	WHO
World Federation of Parasitologists	WHO, FAO
World Federation of Public Health Associations	WHO
World Federation of Scientific Workers	UNESCO
World Federation of Societies of Anaesthesiologists	WHO
World Federation of Teachers' Unions	UNESCO
World Fellowship of Buddhists	UNESCO
World Medical Association	WHO, ILO
World Movement of Christian Workers	ILO
World Organization for Early Childhood Education	UNESCO, UNICEF
World ORT Union	ILO
World OSE Union (Worldwide Organisation for Child Care, Health and Hygiene Among Jews)	WHO, UNICEF
World Packaging Organization	UNIDO
World Peace Council	UNESCO, UNCTAD

World's Poultry Science Association	FAO
World Psychiatric Association	WHO
World Union of Catholic Teachers	UNESCO
World Veterinary Association	WHO, FAO
Young Christian Workers	UNESCO, ILO

CHAPTER 8

THE TRUSTEESHIP COUNCIL, AND DECOLONIZATION

The Trusteeship Council (TC) was established to supervise economic, political, social
and educational developments in territories
placed by the United Nations under the international trusteeship system. The Charter gave the
Council the power to "(a) consider reports submitted by the administering authority; (b) accept
petitions and examine them . . .; (c) provide
for periodic visits to the . . . trust territories" (Article 87).

There were altogether eleven Trust Territories, each brought into the international trusteeship system by means of trusteeship agreements:
1. Western Samoa had formerly been administered by New Zealand on behalf of the United
Kingdom under a League of Nations mandate. Under a United Nations trusteeship agreement, approved by the General Assembly on 13 December
1946 (A/RES/63(I)), the Territory was again administered by New Zealand. Western Samoa became independent on 1 January 1962 and was admitted to United Nations membership as Samoa on
15 December 1976.
2. Tanganyika had also been a League-mandated territory, administered by the United Kingdom. Under a United Nations trusteeship agreement, approved by the General Assembly on 13
December 1946 (A/RES/63(I)), the Territory was
again administered by the United Kingdom. Tan-

ganyika became independent on 9 December 1961
and joined the United Nations on 14 December 196
Following the ratification on 26 April 1964 of
the Articles of Union between Tanganyika and
Zanzibar, the United Republic of Tanganyika and
Zanzibar continued as a single United Nations
member, changing its name to United Republic of
Tanzania on 1 November 1964.

3. Ruanda-Urundi had been mandated by the
League of Nations to Belgium. Under a United
Nations trusteeship agreement, approved by the
General Assembly on 13 December 1946 (A/RES/63
(I)), the Territory was again administered by
Belgium. Ruanda-Urundi became independent on
1 July 1962 as two separate states: the Repub-
lic of Rwanda and the Kingdom of Burundi. Bu-
rundi and Rwanda were admitted to membership in
the United Nations on 18 September 1962.

4. The Cameroons under British Administration had formerly been the Cameroons under British Mandate. It was administered by the United Kingdom under a United Nations trusteeship
agreement approved by the General Assembly on
13 December 1946 (A/RES/63(I)). Following pleb-
iscites held in February 1961, the northern
part of the Territory became a province of Nigeria (Nigeria had been a United Nations member
since 7 October 1960) while the southern part
joined the former French Cameroons to form the
Federal Republic of Cameroon, later called United Republic of Cameroon. Cameroon had been a
United Nations member since 20 September 1960.

5. The Cameroons under French Administration had formerly been a League-mandated territory called French Cameroons. It was again administered by France under a United Nations trus
teeship agreement approved by the General Assem
bly on 13 December 1946 (A/RES/63(I)). The
Territory became independent as the Cameroon Republic on 1 January 1960 and was admitted to
membership in the United Nations on 20 September
1960.

6. Togoland under British Administration
had formerly been Togoland under British Mandate
It was administered by the United Kingdom under
a United Nations trusteeship agreement approved

by the General Assembly on 13 December 1946
(A/RES/63(I)). The Territory joined the Gold
Coast when the latter attained independence as
Ghana on 6 March 1957. (Ghana has been a Unit-
ed Nations member since 8 March 1957.)

7. Togoland under French Administration had
formerly been a League-mandated territory under
French administration. It was administered by
France under a United Nations trusteeship agreement approved by the General Assembly on 13 December 1946 (A/RES/63(I)). The Territory attained independence on 27 April 1960 and was admitted to United Nations membership on 20 September 1960 as Togo.

8. New Guinea had formerly been administered by Australia on behalf of the United Kingdom
under a League mandate. Under a United Nations
trusteeship agreement, approved by the General
Assembly on 13 December 1946 (A/RES/63(I)), the
Territory was again administered by Australia.
New Guinea, together with Papua, a "non-self-
governing territory", became independent on 16
September 1975 and was admitted to United Nations membership on 10 October 1975 as Papua
New Guinea.

9. Nauru had formerly been administered by
Australia under a League mandate, on the joint
behalf of Australia, New Zealand, and the United Kingdom. Under a United Nations trusteeship
agreement, approved by the General Assembly on
1 November 1947 (A/RES/140(II)), the Territory
was administered jointly by Australia, New Zealand, and the United Kingdom. Nauru became independent on 31 January 1968. It has not joined
the United Nations.

10. Somaliland under Italian Administration,
formerly Italian Somaliland, was the only Trust
Territory that had not been under a League of
Nations mandate. It was administered by Italy
under a United Nations trusteeship agreement
approved by the General Assembly on 2 December
1950 (A/RES/442(V)). Upon attaining independence on 1 July 1960, it joined the former British Somaliland to become the Republic of Somalia. Somalia was admitted to United Nations
membership on 20 September 1960.

TRUSTEESHIP AGREEMENT
FOR THE TRUST TERRITORY
OF THE PACIFIC ISLANDS

PREAMBLE

Whereas Article 75 of the Charter of the United Nations provides for th
establishment of an International Trusteeship System for the administratio
and supervision of such territories as may be placed thereunder by subse
quent agreements; and

Whereas under Article 77 of the said Charter the Trusteeship System ma
be applied to territories now held under mandate; and

Whereas on 17 December 1920 the Council of the League of Nations con
firmed a mandate for the former German islands north of the Equator t
Japan, to be administered in accordance with Article 22 of the Covenant c
the League of Nations; and

Whereas Japan, as a result of the Second World War, has ceased to exer
cise any authority in these islands;

Now, therefore, the Security Council of the United Nations, having satis
fied itself that the relevant articles of the Charter have been complied with
hereby resolves to approve the following terms of trusteeship for the Pacifi
Islands formerly under mandate to Japan:

ARTICLE 1

The Territory of the Pacific Islands, consisting of the islands formerl
held by Japan under mandate in accordance with Article 22 of the Covenar
of the League of Nations, is hereby designated as a strategic area and place
under the Trusteeship System established in the Charter of the Unitrd Na
tions. The Territory of the Pacific Islands is hereinafter referred to as th
Trust Territory.

ARTICLE 2

The United States of America is designated as the Administering Authorit
of the Trust Territory.

ARTICLE 3

The Administering Authority shall have full powers of administration
legislation, and jurisdiction over the Territory subject to the provisions c
this Agreement, and may apply to the Trust Territory, subject to any modi
fications which the Administering Authority may consider desirable, suc

A Page from the Trusteeship Agreement for the Pacific Islands

ACCORD DE TUTELLE
POUR LE TERRITOIRE SOUS TUTELLE
DES ILES DU PACIFIQUE

PREAMBULE

Considérant que l'Article 75 de la Charte des Nations Unies prévoit l'établissement d'un Régime international de tutelle pour l'administration et la surveillance des territoires qui pourront être placés sous ce Régime en vertu d'accords ultérieurs;

Considérant qu'en vertu de l'Article 77 de ladite Charte, le Régime de tutelle peut s'appliquer aux territoires actuellement sous mandat;

Considérant qu'à la date du 17 décembre 1920, le Conseil de la Société des Nations a confirmé l'octroi au Japon d'un mandat sur les îles autrefois allemandes situées au nord de l'équateur, qui serait exercé conformément à l'Article 22 du Pacte de la Société des Nations;

Considérant que le Japon, à la suite de la deuxième guerre mondiale, a cessé d'exercer une autorité quelconque sur ces îles;

En conséquence, le Conseil de sécurité des Nations Unies, s'étant assuré que les dispositions des Articles pertinents de la Charte ont été observées, décide par les présentes d'approuver les termes suivants du Régime de tutelle pour les îles du Pacifique antérieurement placées sous mandat japonais:

ARTICLE PREMIER

Le Territoire des îles du Pacifique, composé des îles placées antérieurement sous mandat japonais conformément à l'Article 22 du Pacte de la Société des Nations, est désigné par les présentes, comme zone stratégique et placé sous le Régime de tutelle établi par la Charte des Nations Unies. Le territoire des îles du Pacifique est dénommé ci-après: Territoire sous tutelle.

ARTICLE 2

Les Etats-Unis d'Amérique sont désignés comme Autorité chargée de l'administration du Territoire sous tutelle.

ARTICLE 3

L'Autorité chargée de l'administration aura pleins pouvoirs d'administration, de législation et de juridiction sur le Territoire sous réserve des dispositions du présent Accord, et pourra, sous réserve de toutes modifications qu'elle estimera désirables, appliquer dans le Territoire sous tutelle toutes

11. The Pacific Islands, formerly a League-
mandated territory administered by Japan, is the
only remaining Trust Territory. It is administered by the United States under a United Nations trusteeship agreement approved by the Security Council on 2 April 1947 (S/RES/21(1947)).
As the Territory of the Pacific Islands (also
known as Micronesia) was designated by the United Nations as a strategic area, its administration is supervised by the Security Council with
the assistance of the Trusteeship Council. (Fig
9 reproduces a page of this trusteeship agreement.)

The Trusteeship Council has not had a
fixed number of members: membership was divided equally between administering and non-admin-
istering states. As of 1977, the only members
of the Trusteeship Council are the five permanent members of the Security Council. Voting in
the Trusteeship Council requires a simple majority, each member having one vote.

Although the Trusteeship Council has
nearly completed its work, it still sends out
visiting missions and receives petitions (see
Fig. 10 for an example of the latter).

Colonial countries, referred to by the
United Nations as non-self-governing territories
(NSGT's),   as well as other less than fully
independent areas (especially Namibia and Rhodesia) have been a special concern of the United Nations. The General Assembly has passed
resolutions about non-self-governing territories
from its very first session on.   The Assembly has been especially active in this area
since the adoption, by Assembly resolution 1514
(XV) of 14 December 1960, of the Declaration on
the Granting of Independence to Colonial Countries and Peoples (see Part V for the text of
the Declaration). By its resolution 1654 (XVI)
of 27 November 1961, the Assembly established
the Special Committee on the Situation with regard to the Implementation of the Declaration on
the Granting of Independence to Colonial Coun-

TED NATIONS

JSTEESHIP

UNCIL

Distr.
GENERAL

T/PET.10/121
5 July 1977

ORIGINAL: ENGLISH

PETITION FROM THE PEOPLE OF PALAU ISLANDS CONCERNING THE
TRUST TERRITORY OF THE PACIFIC ISLANDS 1/

(Circulated in accordance with rule 85, paragraph 1, of the
rules of procedure of the Trusteeship Council)

We, the people of Palau Islands, who sign this petition have been informed
ough newspapers, radio broadcasts, and public discussions that an oil
er-port and related projects are being planned for Palau. We hereby affix
signatures to register our protest to the super-port proposal because a
ject of such magnitude will disrupt and adversely affect the land, waters,
society of Palau whereby we, the Palauan people, will not be able to control
lives and determine our destiny.

1/ Signed by 1,262 persons. The list of signatures has been placed in the
les of the Secretariat and is available to members of the Council for
nsultation. See also T/PV.1462.

-12986

Petition to the Trusteeship Council

tries and Peoples (known popularly as the Special Committee of 24).

Namibia and Rhodesia have been and continue to be of concern to the Organization as a whole. This is evidenced, for instance, by the activities of the committee established in pursuance of Security Council resolution 253(1968) on measures against Southern Rhodesia, known popularly as the Sanctions Committee.

CHAPTER 9

THE INTERNATIONAL COURT OF JUSTICE

The International Court of Justice (ICJ)
is the successor of the Permanent Court of International Justice of the League of Nations.

The Court[17], established by the Charter,
is the principal judicial organ of the United
Nations. It functions under the terms of its
Statute which is an integral part of the United
Nations Charter. All members of the United Na-
tions are automatically parties to the Court's
Statute; in addition, states not members of the
United Nations may become parties to the Statute
under conditions recommended by the Security
Council and approved by the General Assembly.
For example, Liechtenstein and San Marino have
been parties since 1950 and 1954, respectively.
A state which is not a party to the Statute may
refer cases to the Court, upon its acceptance of
the Court's jurisdiction.

──────────[17] For more information on the Court,
see Shabtai Rosenne, The World Court;
what it is and how it works, 3d, rev.
ed. (Leiden/Dobbs Ferry, N.Y.: Sijt-
hoff/Oceana, 1973) or the Court's The
International Court of Justice (The
Hague, 1976). For a good compendium
of documents and other source material, see S. Rosenne, Documents on the
International Court of Justice (Bibliography entry 64)

The court's jurisdiction extends to all cases and disputes brought before it by states. In addition, the General Assembly, the Security Council and other United Nations organs may request the Court to render advisory opinions. The Court applies (a) international conventions . . . establishing rules . . . recognized by the conte ing states; (b) international custom, as evidence of a general practice accepted as law; (c) the general principles of law . . (d) . . . judicial decisions. [The Court may] decide a case ex aequo et bono [i.e., according to fairness rather than strict application of law] if the parties agree.[18]

The Court is composed of fifteen independent judges of different nationalities, elected for nine-year terms by the Security Council and the General Assembly "from among persons of high moral character [with] qualifications required in their respective countries for appointment to the highest judicial offices, or are jurisconsults of recognized competence in international law" (Statute, Article 2). The Court elects its President and Vice-President; they are both elected for three years and take precedence over the other judges.

The following judges, listed in official order of precedence, are the present (1977) members, with nationality and end of term (each term ends on 5 February of the year indicated):

Eduardo Jiménez de Aréchaga (Uruguay) (1979),
    President
Nagendra Singh (India) (1982), Vice-President
Isaac Forster (Senegal) (1982)
André Gros (France) (1982)
Manfred Lachs (Poland) (1985)

————18
Statute of the International Court of Justice, Article 38 (see Part V for the full text of the Statute)

Hardy C. Dillard (United States) (1979)
Louis Ignacio-Pinto (Benin) (1979)
Federico de Castro (Spain) (1979)
Platon D. Morozov (USSR) (1979)
Sir Humphrey Waldock (United Kingdom) (1982)
José María Ruda (Argentina) (1982)
Hermann Mosler (Federal Republic of Germany) (1985)
Taslim O. Elias (Nigeria) (1985)
Salah El Dine Tarazi (Syria) (1985)
Shigeru Oda (Japan) (1985)

The administrative machinery of the Court is directed by its President and implemented by the Registrar with the assistance of Registry officials. The Court is considered to be permanently in session.

Between 1 April 1946 (the first time it met) and 31 July 1976, the Court had dealt with a total of 60 cases, as listed in Table IX. In those 60 cases it gave 38 judgments and 16 advisory opinions. Of the 182 orders made therein, 139 related solely to the fixing or extending of time-limits. (For more detailed information on judgments and advisory opinions of the Court see its annual Reports of judgments, advisory opinions and orders.)

TABLE IX

CASES BEFORE THE INTERNATIONAL
COURT OF JUSTICE 1946-1976

Title	Dates
(a) Contentious*	
Corfu Channel (United Kingdom v. Albania)	1947-1949
Fisheries (United Kingdom v. Norway)	1949-1951

————* In the case of proceedings instituted by means of a special agreement the names of the parties are separated by an oblique stroke.

Title	Dates
Protection of French Nationals and Protected Persons in Egypt (France v. Egypt)	1949-1950
Asylum (Colombia/Peru)	1949-1950
Rights of Nationals of the United States of America in Morocco (France v. United States)	1950-1952
Request for Interpretation of the Judgment of 20 November 1950 in the Asylum case (Colombia v. Peru)	1950
Haya de la Torre (Colombia v. Peru)	1950-1951
Ambatielos (Greece v. United Kingdom)	1951-1953
Anglo-Iranian Oil Co. (United Kingdom v. Iran)	1951-1952
Minquiers and Ecrehos (France/United Kingdom)	1951-1953
Nottebohm (Liechtenstein v. Guatemala)	1951-1955
Monetary Gold Removed from Rome in 1943 (Italy v. France, United Kingdom and United States)	1953-1954
Electricité de Beyrouth Company (France v. Lebanon)	1953-1954
Treatment in Hungary of Aircraft and Crew of United States of America (United States v. Hungary)	1954
Treatment in Hungary of Aircraft and Crew of United States of America (United States v. USSR)	1954
Aerial Incident of 10 March 1953 (United States v. Czechoslovakia)	1955-1956
Antarctica (United Kingdom v. Argentina)	1955-1956
Antarctica (United Kingdom v. Chile)	1955-1956
Aerial Incident of 7 October 1952 (United States v. USSR)	1955-1956

Title	Dates
Certain Norwegian Loans (France v. Norway)	1955-1957
Right of Passage over Indian Territory (Portugal v. India)	1955-1960
Application of the Convention of 1902 Governing the Guardianship of Infants (Netherlands v. Sweden)	1957-1958
Interhandel (Switzerland v. United States)	1957-1959
Aerial Incident of 27 July 1955 (Israel v. Bulgaria)	1957-1959
Aerial Incident of 27 July 1955 (United States v. Bulgaria)	1957-1960
Aerial Incident of 27 July 1955 (United Kingdom v. Bulgaria)	1957-1959
Sovereignty over Certain Frontier Land (Belgium/Netherlands)	1957-1959
Arbitral Award Made by the King of Spain on 23 December 1906 (Honduras v. Nicaragua)	1958-1960
Aerial Incident of 4 September 1954 (United States v. USSR)	1958
Barcelona Traction, Light and Power Company, Limited (Belgium v. Spain)	1958-1961
Compagnie du Port, des Quais et des Entrepôts de Beyrouth and Société Radio-Orient (France v. Lebanon)	1959-1960
Aerial Incident of 7 November 1954 (United States v. USSR)	1959
Temple of Preah Vihear (Cambodia v. Thailand)	1959-1962
South West Africa (Ethiopia v. South Africa; Liberia v. South Africa)	1960-1966
Northern Cameroons (Cameroon v. United Kingdom)	1961-1963

Title	Dates
Barcelona Traction, Light and Power Company, Limited (New Application: 1962) (Belgium v. Spain)	1962-1970
North Sea Continental Shelf (Federal Republic of Germany/Denmark; Federal Republic of Germany/Netherlands)	1967-1969
Appeal Relating to the Jurisdiction of the ICAO Council (India v. Pakistan)	1971-1972
Fisheries Jurisdiction (United Kingdom v. Iceland)	1972-1974
Fisheries Jurisdiction (Federal Republic of Germany v. Iceland)	1972-1974
Nuclear Tests (Australia v. France)	1973-1974
Nuclear Tests (New Zealand v. France)	1973-1974
Trial of Pakistani Prisoners of War (Pakistan v. India)	1973

(b) Advisory

Conditions of Admission of a State to Membership in the United Nations (Article 4 of Charter)	1947-1948
Reparation for Injuries Suffered in the Service of the United Nations	1948-1949
Interpretation of Peace Treaties with Bulgaria, Hungary and Romania	1949-1950
Competence of the General Assembly for the Admission of a State to the United Nations	1949-1950
International Status of South West Africa	1949-1950
Reservations to the Convention on the Prevention and Punishment of the Crime of Genocide	1950-1951
Effect of Awards of Compensation Made by the United Nations Administrative Tribunal	1953-1954

Title	Dates
Voting Procedure on Questions relating to Reports and Petitions concerning the Territory of South West Africa	1954-1955
Judgments of the Administrative Tribunal of the ILO upon Complaints Made against Unesco	1955-1956
Admissibility of Hearings of Petitioners by the Committee on South West Africa	1955-1956
Constitution of the Maritime Safety Committee of the Inter-Governmental Maritime Consultative Organization	1959-1960
Certain Expenses of the United Nations (Article 17, paragraph 2, of the Charter)	1961-1962
Legal Consequences for States of the Continued Presence of South Africa in Namibia (South West Africa) notwithstanding Security Council Resolution 276 (1970)	1970-1971
Application for Review of Judgement No. 158 of the United Nations Administrative Tribunal	1972-1973
Western Sahara	1974-1975

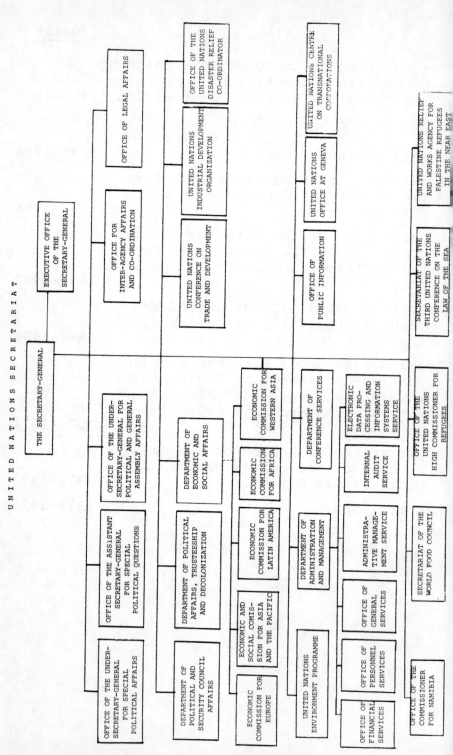

Structure of the Secretariat

CHAPTER 10

THE SECRETARIAT

The Secretariat "services the other organs of the United Nations and administers the programmes and policies laid down by them."[19] It is headed by the Secretary-General who is appointed by the General Assembly on the recommendation of the Security Council. The United Nations has had the following Secretaries-General thus far:
> Trygve Lie (Norway; 1 February 1946-10 April 1953);
> Dag Hammarskjöld (Sweden; 10 April 1953-17 September 1961);
> U Thant (Burma; 3 November 1961-31 December 1971);
> Kurt Waldheim (Austria; 1 January 1972-).

The Secretary-General is the chief administrative officer of the United Nations. He performs various functions entrusted to him by the General Assembly and the three Councils. He submits annual reports on the work of the Or-

―――――――[19] Basic facts about the United Nations, 30th anniversary ed. (Bibliography entry 43), p. 13. For an interesting recent critical appraisal, see Theodor Meron, The United Nations Secretariat; the rules and the practice (Lexington, Mass.: Heath, 1977).

ganization to the General Assembly (see Bibliography entry 41) and appoints the staff of the
Secretariat.

The staff of the Secretariat is recruite
on as wide a geographical basis as possible.
The international, impartial nature of the Secretariat is mandated by the Charter (Article
100):

In the performance of their duties the
Secretary-General and the staff shall
not seek or receive instructions from
any government or from any other authority
external to the Organization. They shall
refrain from any action which might reflect on their position as international
officials responsible only to the Organization.

Each Member of the United Nations undertakes to respect the exclusively international character of the responsibilities of the Secretary-General and
the staff and not to seek to influence
them in the discharge of their responsibilities.

The Secretariat is a continuously functioning organ, divided into the following major
units (see Fig. 11 for chart):

Officesof the Secretary-General,
comprising the Executive Office
of the Secretary-General, the Office of
the Under-Secretary-General for Special
Political Affairs, the Office of the
Assistant Secretary-General for Special
Political Questions, the Office of the
Under-Secretary-General for Political
and General Assembly Affairs, the Office
for Inter-Agency Affairs and Co-ordination, and the Office of Legal Affairs;
Department of Political and Security Council
Affairs;
Department of Political Affairs, Trusteeship
and Decolonization;
Department of Economic and Social Affairs, in-
cluding the Statistical Office and the Secre-

tariats of the five regional commissions of
the United Nations;
Secretariat of the United Nations Conference on
Trade and Development;
Secretariat of the United Nations Industrial De-
velopment Organization;
Office of the United Nations Disaster Relief Co-
ordinator;
Secretariat of the United Nations Environment
Programme;
Department of Administration and Management, in-
cluding the Office of Financial Services, the
Office of Personnel Services, the Office of
General Services, the Administrative Manage-
ment Service, the Internal Audit Service, and
the Electronic Data Processing and Information
Systems Service;
Department of Conference Services, including the
Dag Hammarskjöld Library;
Office of Public Information;
United Nations Office at Geneva;
United Nations Centre on Transnational Corpora-
tions;
Office of the Commissioner for Namibia;
Secretariat of the World Food Council;
Office of the United Nations High Commissioner
for Refugees;
Secretariat of the Third United Nations Confer-
ence on the Law of the Sea (an ad hoc unit of
the Secretariat, created to serve the third
Law of the Sea Conference);
Secretariat of the United Nations Relief and
Works Agency for Palestine Refugees in the
Near East.

In addition to the major units listed
above, the Secretariat has a number of boards
and committees; e.g.:
Advisory Board on Compensation Claims;
Appointment and Promotion Board, Committee and
Panel;
Committee on the Employment of Women in the
Secretariat;
Health and Life Insurance Committee;
Interdepartmental Committee for the Centre for
Economic and Social Information;

Inter-Departmental Training Committee;
Interdepartmental Working Group on Outer Space;
Joint Appeals Board;
Joint Disciplinary Committee;
Publications Board;
Visa Committee.

CHAPTER 11

ORGANIZATIONAL CHANGES

An organization of the size and complexity of the United Nations cannot remain, and has not remained, static in its structure and activities. It has undergone many changes and will, in response to the shifting international political and economic situation, continue to change.

A milestone on the political road of the United Nations was the Declaration on the Granting of Independence to Colonial Countries and Peoples, adopted by General Assembly resolution 1514 (XV) of 14 December 1960. (The text of the Declaration is in Part V.) Country after former colonial country gained self-determination and independence in the nineteen-fifties and sixties. The process has been almost completed by the mid-seventies. In the overwhelming majority of cases, admission to membership in the United Nations has been the logical step following independence. This has resulted in a qualitative as well as a quantitative change in the composition of the Organization. In sharp contrast to the earlier years when the United Nations was dominated by the Big Five and by the industrially developed nations, today Third World countries form the majority and act as a driving force behind United Nations decisions and activities, especially those of the General Assembly and the Economic and Social Council.

The increased preponderance of Third
World countries in the United Nations, their
desire for a more equitable distribution of the
earth's resources, and the recognition by all o:
the need for greater and more efficient development assistance were among the major factors
that impelled the world Organization to formulate proposals for structural and other changes.

In the late 1960's, two important studies were undertaken. The first was a broad
survey of the problems of international co-
operation in the area of development, conducted
by a Commission on International Development
under the chairmanship of Lester B. Pearson.[20]
The second, R.G.A. Jackson's "capacity study",
examined the role that the United Nations system of organizations has played and should play
in the process of development co-operation.[21]

In April-May 1974, the General Assembly
held its sixth special session, devoted to the
economic situation of the world. The special
session adopted a Declaration on the Establishment of a New International Economic Order and
a Programme of Action on the Establishment of
a New International Economic Order. (The texts
of these two documents are in Part V.)[22]

---

[20] Commission on International Development, Partners in development (Bibliography entry 50).

[21] United Nations, A study of the capacity of the United Nations development system (Bibliography entry 53).

[22] For a study of the new international
economic order, see Jyoti Shankar
Singh, A new international economic
order; toward a fair redistribution
of the world's resources (New York:
Praeger, c1977).

Further deliberations resulted, in May 1975, in a study prepared by the Group of Experts on the Structure of the United Nations System.[23] This study contains proposals for major restructuring of the United Nations system in order to make the Organization more capable of dealing effectively with international economic co-operation, trade, development financing and industrialization.

The twenty-ninth session of the General Assembly adopted, in its resolution 3281 (XXIX) of 12 December 1974, the Charter of economic rights and duties of states (see Part V for the text). In September 1975 the Assembly held its seventh special session devoted to international economic co-operation. The Assembly recognized the need for a new economic and social framework and, in its resolution 3362 (S-VII) of 16 September 1975, adopted unanimously, it set down basic policies, guidelines and principles of restructuring the economic and social sectors of the United Nations system of organizations, and established an Ad Hoc Committee on the Restructuring of the Economic and Social Sectors of the United Nations System. (See Part V for the text of resolution 3362 (S-VII).)

The Assembly's thirtieth and thirty-first sessions continued the active consideration of international economic issues and their effects on the United Nations system of organizations. The thirty-first session extended the mandate of the Ad Hoc Committee, requesting it to submit its final recommendations to the thirty-second session of the Assembly, through the Economic and Social Council. The thirty-first session of the Assembly was suspended on 22 December 1976, to be reconvened "solely and exclusively for the consideration of the agenda

_____ [23] United Nations, Group of Experts on the Structure of the United Nations System, A new United Nations structure for global co-operation (Bibliography entry 57).

item entitled . . . 'Development and international economic co-operation: implementation
of the decisions adopted by the General Assembly at its seventh special session'."24

In response to economic and political
aspirations, various regional and other non-
official groupings emerged during the past
several years. Regional, economic, political
or other factors provide the cohesiveness of
these groups, which often act in the United
Nations in a co-ordinated fashion.

Perhaps the best known of these groups
is the 'Group of 77' which came into being, as
a bloc of developing countries, at the first
session of the United Nations Conference on
Trade and Development in 1964. It has retained
its name, although, by 1977, it numbered the
following 114 members, including some that are
not members of the United Nations:

GROUP OF 77

Afghanistan	Brazil	Cuba
Algeria	Burma	Cyprus
Angola	Burundi	Democratic
Argentina	Cape Verde	Kampuchea
Bahamas	Central African	Democratic
Bahrain	Empire	People's
Bangladesh	Chad	Republic
Barbados	Chile	of Korea
Benin	Colombia	Democratic
Bhutan	Comoros	Yemen
Bolivia	Congo	Dominican
Botswana	Costa Rica	Republic

--------24

United Nations, Office of Public Information, Press Section, Resolutions
of the General Assembly at the first
part of its thirty-first regular session (21 September-22 December 1976;
New York, 29 December 1976; Background release GA/5571), p. 58.

Ecuador
Egypt
El Salvador
Equatorial Guinea
Ethiopia
Fiji
Gabon
Gambia
Ghana
Grenada
Guatemala
Guinea
Guinea-Bissau
Guyana
Haiti
Honduras
India
Indonesia
Iran
Iraq
Ivory Coast
Jamaica
Jordan
Kenya
Kuwait
Lao People's
  Democratic
  Republic
Lebanon
Lesotho
Liberia
Libyan Arab
  Republic
Madagascar
Malawi
Malaysia
Maldives
Mali
Malta
Mauritania
Mauritius
Mexico
Morocco
Mozambique

Nepal
Nicaragua
Niger
Nigeria
Oman
Pakistan
Palestine Lib-
  eration Or-
  ganization
Panama
Papua New
  Guinea
Paraguay
Peru
Philippines
Qatar
Republic of
  Korea
Romania
Rwanda
São Tomé and
  Príncipe
Saudi Arabia
Senegal
Seychelles
Sierra Leone
Singapore
Socialist Re-
  public of
  Viet Nam
Somalia
Sri Lanka
Sudan
Surinam
Swaziland
Syrian Arab
  Republic
Thailand
Togo
Trinidad and
  Tobago
Tunisia
Uganda
United Arab Emirates

United Repub-
  lic of
  Cameroon
United Repub-
  lic of
  Tanzania
Upper Volta
Uruguay
Venezuela
Yemen
Yugoslavia
Zaire
Zambia

Other non-official groups active in the United Nations:

Asian Group
African Group
Socialist Group
Latin American Group
Western European and Other States Group
Non-aligned Countries Group
Group of States of the Islamic Conference

CHAPTER 12

UNITED NATIONS INFORMATION CENTRES

        The establishment of United Nations in-
formation centres was first called for by General Assembly resolution 13(I) of 13 February
1946 which recommended the creation of branch
offices of the United Nations Department of Public Information (now Office of Public Information) "in order to ensure that peoples in all
parts of the world receive as full information
as possible about the United Nations."[25] Assembly resolution 595(VI) of 4 February 1952[26] approved a report of Subcommittee 8 of the Fifth
Committee, which stated that "the Department of
Public Information should establish and maintain a system of Information Centres on an adequate regional and/or linguistic basis with due
regard to actual varying needs."

        Over the years, the system of United
Nations information centres has evolved as a
major arm of the Organization's Office of Public Information. At present (1977) there are

————————[25] United Nations, General Assembly,
Official records of the General As-
sembly, First Session, First Part:
Resolutions (London, 1946), p. 17.

[26] United Nations, General Assembly,
Official records of the General Assembly, Sixth Session, Supplement No.
20 (New York, 1952), p. 82.

58 United Nations information centres and office
around the world, serving over 130 member states

        The functions of the information centres
are:
To maintain a close working relationship with
   national and local press, radio, television,
   educational authorities and governmental information services, keeping these agencies
   informed of United Nations activities in political, economic, social and humanitarian
   matters;
To operate reference libraries where documents
   of the United Nations system of organizations
   are available to educators, students, representatives of the information media and the
   general public;
To assist the regional commissions and other
   United Nations organs as well as other organizations of the United Nations system in fulfilling their needs for information;
To co-operate with field offices of the United
   Nations Development Programme;
To assist non-governmental organizations;
To assist in the translation and adaptation of
   United Nations information material into local
   languages.

        In response to General Assembly resolu-
tion 2897(XXVI) of 22 December 1971, the Secretary-General initiated a thorough review of the
system of United Nations information centres,
aimed at assessing the efficiency and resources
of the centres and improving their performance.

        Table X is a list of United Nations in-
formation centres and offices.[27]

────────27
        Source: United Nations, General As-
        sembly, Fifth Committee, Programme
        budget for the biennium 1976-1977:
        United Nations information centres
        system; report of the Secretary-
        General (New York, 7 September 1976;
        A/C.5/31/14).

TABLE X

UNITED NATIONS INFORMATION CENTRES
AND OFFICES

ACCRA (established March 1958)
Information Centre serving: Ghana, Guinea and
Sierra Leone

ADDIS ABABA (established April 1960)
Information Centre serving Ethiopia. Also
serves as Information Service for the United
Nations Economic Commission for Africa (ECA)

ALGIERS (established September 1963)
Information Centre serving Algeria

ANKARA (established March 1975)
Information Office serving Turkey

ASUNCION (established October 1962)
Information Centre serving Paraguay

ATHENS (established April 1954)
Information Centre serving: Cyprus, Greece
and Israel

BAGHDAD (established April 1963)
Information Centre serving Iraq

BANGKOK (established October 1951)
Information Centre serving: Cambodia, Lao
People's Democratic Republic, Malaysia, So-
cialist Republic of Viet Nam, Singapore and
Thailand. Also serves as Information Service
for the United Nations Economic and Social
Commission for Asia and the Pacific (ESCAP)

BEIRUT (established September 1962)
Information Centre serving: Jordan, Kuwait,
Lebanon and Syrian Arab Republic. Also serves
as Information Service for the United Nations
Economic Commission for Western Asia (ECWA)

BELGRADE (established November 1950)
Information Centre serving: Albania and
Yugoslavia

BOGOTA (established May 1954)
Information Centre serving: Colombia, Ecuador and Venezuela

BRUSSELS (established January 1975)
Information and Liaison Office serving Belgium

BUCHAREST (established June 1970)
Information Centre serving Romania

BUENOS AIRES (established November 1948)
Information Centre serving: Argentina and
Uruguay

BUJUMBURA (established June 1961)
Information Centre serving Burundi

CAIRO (established April 1949)
Information Centre serving: Egypt, Saudi
Arabia and Yemen

COLOMBO (established August 1961)
Information Centre serving Sri Lanka

COPENHAGEN (established December 1946)
Information Centre serving: Denmark, Finland,
Iceland, Norway and Sweden

DAKAR (established April 1964)
Information Centre serving: Gambia, Guinea-
Bissau, Ivory Coast, Mauritania and Senegal

DAR ES SALAAM (established June 1961)
Information Centre serving: Malawi, Uganda
and United Republic of Tanzania

GENEVA (established February 1947)
Information Centre serving: Bulgaria, Federal
Republic of Germany, Holy See, Hungary, Po-
land, Portugal, Spain and Switzerland. Also
serves as Information Service for the United
Nations Office at Geneva and the United Na-

tions Economic Commission for Europe (ECE)

ISLAMABAD (established March 1951 in Karachi)
Information Centre serving Pakistan

KABUL (established October 1959)
Information Centre serving Afghanistan

KATHMANDU (established April 1964)
Information Centre serving Nepal

KHARTOUM (established October 1963)
Information Centre serving: Sudan and Somalia

KINSHASA (established July 1964)
Information Centre serving Zaire

LAGOS (established May 1967)
Information Centre serving Nigeria

LA PAZ (established September 1963)
Information Centre serving Bolivia

LIMA (established April 1960)
Information Centre serving Peru

LOME (established May 1962)
Information Centre serving: Benin and Togo

LONDON (established January 1947)
Information Centre serving: Ireland, Netherlands and United Kingdom

LUSAKA (established October 1975)
Information Centre serving: Botswana, Namibia,
Swaziland and Zambia

MANILA (established August 1953)
Information Centre serving the Philippines

MASERU (being established)
Information Centre to serve Lesotho

MEXICO CITY (established August 1947)
Information Centre serving: Cuba, Dominican
Republic and Mexico

MONROVIA (established October 1950)
   Information Centre serving Liberia

MOSCOW (established April 1948)
   Information Centre serving: Byelorussian SSR
   Ukrainian SSR and USSR

NAIROBI (established August 1974)
   Information Centre serving Kenya

NEW DELHI (established January 1947)
   Information Centre serving: Bhutan and India

OUAGADOUGOU (being established)
   Information Centre to serve Upper Volta

PARIS (established March 1947)
   Information Centre serving: Belgium, France
   and Luxembourg

PORT MORESBY (established April 1962)
   Information Centre serving: British Solomon
   Islands and Papua New Guinea

PORT OF SPAIN (established January 1962)
   Information Centre serving: Bahamas, Barbados, Grenada, Guyana, Jamaica and Trinidad
   and Tobago

PRAGUE (established December 1947)
   Information Centre serving: Czechoslovakia
   and German Democratic Republic

RABAT (established December 1962)
   Information Centre serving Morocco

RANGOON (established June 1959)
   Information Centre serving Burma

RIO DE JANEIRO (established March 1947)
   Information Centre serving Brazil

ROME (established July 1958)
   Information Centre serving: Italy and Malta

SAN SALVADOR (established July 1960)
Information Centre serving: Belize, Costa
Rica, El Salvador, Guatemala, Honduras, Nic-
aragua and Panama

SANTIAGO (established March 1951)
Information Centre serving Chile. Also serves
as Information Service for the United Nations
Economic Commission for Latin America (ECLA)

SYDNEY (established November 1948)
Information Centre serving: Australia, Fiji
and New Zealand

TANANARIVE (established January 1963)
Information Centre serving Comoros and Madagascar

TEHERAN (established May 1950)
Information Centre serving Iran

TOKYO (established April 1958)
Information Centre serving Japan

TUNIS (established May 1960)
Information Centre serving: Libyan Arab Republic and Tunisia

VIENNA (established January 1972)
Information Centre serving Austria. Also
serves as Information Service for the United
Nations Industrial Development Organization
(UNIDO)

WASHINGTON (established October 1946)
Information Centre serving: United States of
America and Trust Territory of the Pacific
Islands

YAOUNDE (established October 1965)
Information Centre serving Cameroon, Central
African Empire and Gabon

N.B.: Countries not served by an information
centre are serviced direct from United Nations
Headquarters.

PART II

PUBLICATIONS AND DOCUMENTATION
OF THE UNITED NATIONS

CHAPTER 13

SALES PUBLICATIONS

The United Nations may consider issuing a document as a sales publication "if it is of public interest, reaches a standard of intellectual endeavour that reflects credit on the United Nations, . . . does not substantially duplicate material that has already been published . . . [and that has more than a minimal] sales potential."[28]

Major reports, studies, yearbooks, conference proceedings, many indexes and bibliographies, the Treaty series (Bibliography entry 87) and other publications of wide interest (e.g., the UN monthly chronicle; Bibliography entry 48) are issued by the United Nations as sales publications in one or more of the official languages of the Organization: Arabic, Chinese, English, French, Russian and Spanish. Since the admission to United Nations membership of the Federal Republic of Germany and the German Democratic Republic, a small number of documents have appeared in German as well.

Most sales publications bear a symbol called the sales number. The sales number indicates: (a) the language of the publication; (b) the year when issuance was planned (not necessar-

---

[28] United Nations, Secretariat, Administrative instruction (New York, 24 June 1975; ST/AI/189/ADD.17), p. 1.

ily the actual year of publication); (c) the
broad subject category; (d) a number specific
to the individual item. Example: E.71.XVII.5
is the sales number of the <u>Yearbook of international trade statistics,</u> 1969 - a publication i
English (E.) issued in 1971 (.71.) in subject
category XVII (international statistics) as the
fifth (.5.) publication in that subject categor
in 1971.

        The current subject categories are show
in Table XI.

TABLE XI

SUBJECT CATEGORIES OF UNITED NATIONS
SALES PUBLICATIONS

I	General
II.A	Economics
II.B	Economic development
II.C	World economy
II.D	Trade, finance and com- merce
II.E	European economy
II.F	Asian economy
II.G	Latin American economy
II.H	Public administration
II.K	African economy
IV	Social questions
V	International law
VII	Political and Security Council affairs
VIII	Transport and communica- tions
IX	Atomic energy
X	International administra- tion
XI	Narcotic drugs
XIII	Demography
XIV	Human rights
XV	UNITAR publications
XVI	Public finance and fisca questions
XVII	International statistics

TABLE OF CONTENTS (continued)

TABLE DES MATIERES (suite)

Page

Tableaux

Pages

JUIN 1977

Page from the Table of Contents of the *Monthly bulletin of statistics*

The following subject categories are no longer used or are now used differently:

Category III - Public health. No publications have been issued in this category since 1948. The World Health Organization issues material in this field.

Category VI - Trusteeship and non-self-governing territories. No publications have been issued in this category since 1963.

Category VI.A - Trusteeship. No publications have been issued in this category since 1957.

Category VI.B - Non-self-governing territories. No publications have been issued in this category since 1960.

Category XII - Education, science and culture. The United Nations has never issued publications in this category. UNESCO publishes material in this field.

Category XV - Relief and rehabilitation. No publication has been issued on this subject since 1947. Category XV is now used for UNITA publications.

Because of the special importance of statistics in research, it is worthwhile to list major United Nations sales publications in that field:

Statistical yearbook (Bibliography entry 95)
Yearbook of international trade statistics
Yearbook of national accounts statistics
Yearbook of construction statistics
Yearbook of industrial statistics (formerly The
  growth of world industry)
Commodity trade statistics
World energy supplies
Demographic yearbook (Bibliography entry 90)
Population and vital statistics reports
World trade annual and supplement (Bibliography
  entries 97-98)
Monthly bulletin of statistics (Bibliography
  entry 91) (see Fig. 12 for a page from the
  table of contents)
World statistics in brief; United Nations sta-
  tistical pocketbook (Bibliography entry 96)
Studies in methods and international standards:
  Standard international trade classification

(Bibliography entry 92), World weights and measures, Compendium of social statistics, Handbook of population and housing census methods, Input-output tables and analysis, Directory of international statistics (Bibliography entry 94), and many others.

The above is a partial listing of publications of the United Nations Statistical Office. Most have been issued in sales category XVII. In addition, other organs of the United Nations compile statistics on a systematic basis, e.g., the Statistical Division of the Economic Commission for Europe (issued in sales category II.E.):

Annual bulletin of electric energy statistics for Europe
Annual bulletin of general energy statistics for Europe
Annual bulletin of housing and building statistics for Europe
Annual bulletin of transport statistics for Europe
Statistics of road traffic accidents in Europe
Annual bulletin of coal statistics for Europe
Annual bulletin of gas statistics for Europe
Statistics of world trade in steel
Annual bulletin of steel statistics for Europe

the Statistics Division of the Economic and Social Commission for Asia and the Pacific (issued in sales category II.F.):
Quarterly bulletin of statistics for Asia and the Pacific
Foreign trade statistics for Asia and the Pacific
Statistical yearbook for Asia and the Pacific

the Statistics and Quantitative Analysis Division of the Economic Commission for Latin America (issued in sales category II.G.):
Statistical bulletin for Latin America

the Economic Commission for Africa (issued in sales category II.K.):
Foreign trade statistics for Africa (Series A: Direction of trade; Series B: Trade by commod-

ity)

the United Nations Conference on Trade and Development (issued in sales category II.D.):
Handbook of international trade and development
   statistics (Bibliography entry 99).

        The system of United Nations publicatio
is somewhat similar to that of the League of Nations; e.g., sales category XI, Narcotic drugs,
was also the League category for that subject.

Other examples:
Monthly list of selected articles, issued since
   1946 by the Geneva Library of the United Nations, is a direct successor to the Fortnight-
   ly (later, Monthly) list of selected articles
   that had been published since February 1929
   by the Library of the League of Nations;
Statistical yearbook (Bibliography entry 95),
   issued by the Statistical Office of the United
   Nations since 1948, succeeds the Statistical
   yearbook of the League of Nations, published
   by the League's Economic Intelligence Service
   from 1927 to 1945;
Treaty series (Bibliography entry 87), published
   by the United Nations as mandated by the Charter, succeeds the Treaty series of the League
   of Nations that had been published by the
   League in a very similar format, since 1921,
   in compliance with the terms of its Covenant.

        Many United Nations publications that
are considered documents (i.e., material published officially under the authority of a Unite
Nations organ) carry sales numbers as well as
document series symbols. Documents that are not
sales publications, naturally, have no sales
number.

        Some sales publications are issued with-
out sales numbers. Examples: the United Nations Treaty series (Bibliography entry 87) and
the UN monthly chronicle (Bibliography entry 48;
these two have no document series symbols either,
not being documents in the strict sense of the

term) and the <u>Official records</u> of the General
Assembly and the three Councils (these have
document series symbols in addition to their
<u>Official records</u> designation).

The International Court of Justice has
its own system of sales numbers: a simple
chronological sequence of Arabic numerals.

United Nations

GENERAL
ASSEMBLY
Official Records

Agenda item 12:

A N N E X E S

THIRTIETH SESSION

NEW YORK, 197

Agenda item 125:* Question of Cyprus

CONTENTS

* For the discussion of this item, see: Official Records of the General Assembly, Thirtieth Session, Special Political Committee, 975th and 976th meetings; and ibid., Plenary Meetings, 2367th, 2401st, 2404th to 2407th, 2411th and 2413th meetings.

DOCUMENT A/10242

Cyprus: request for the inclusion of an additional item in the agenda of the thirtieth session

Original: English
16 September 1975

Letter dated 16 September 1975 from the representative of Cyprus to the Secretary-General

On instructions from my Government, I have the honour to request, under rule 15 of the rules of procedure of the General Assembly, the inclusion in the agenda of the thirtieth session of the Assembly of an additional item entitled "Question of Cyprus".

In accordance with rule 20 of the rules of procedure, an explanatory memorandum relating to this request is attached hereto.

(Signed) Zenon ROSSIDES
Permanent Representative of
Cyprus to the United Nations

Explanatory memorandum

1. The question of Cyprus was an item on the agenda of the twenty-ninth session of the General Assembly and the over-all situation at the time was described in the explanatory memorandum annexed to the request for the inclusion of the item at that session.[1]

[1] See: Official Records of the General Assembly, Twenty-ninth Session, Annexes, agenda item 110, document A/9743.

2. On this item the General Assembly adopted resolution 3212 (XXIX) of 1 November 1974 unanimously, including the assenting vote of Turkey.

3. The Security Council, by its resolution 365 (1974) of 13 December 1974 endorsed the said resolution of the General Assembly, thereby giving it mandatory effect. The Council further called upon the parties concerned to implement the said resolution as soon as possible, and requested the Secretary-General to report to the Security Council on the progress of the implementation.

4. The Secretary-General, acting in compliance with the above resolution, issued, on 24 January 1975, a note verbale addressed to the parties concerned—namely, Cyprus, Greece and Turkey (see annex I below)—requiring them to supply all relevant information at an early date concerning the steps taken or contemplated to be taken by them in regard to the implementation of General Assembly resolution 3212 (XXIX).

5. The Government of Cyprus promptly responded to the Secretary-General's note verbale on 1 February 1975 (see annex II below) to the effect that it had fully carried out its responsibilities under General Assembly resolution 3212 (XXIX) and the endorsing Security Council resolution 365

Annexes (XXX) 125

A Page from an Annex of the *Official records* of the General Assembly

CHAPTER 14

OFFICIAL RECORDS

The Official records are the major final records of the General Assembly and its main committees, the Security Council, the Economic and Social Council, the Trusteeship Council, the Disarmament Commission, the International Law Commission, the Trade and Development Board of the United Nations Conference on Trade and Development, and the Industrial Development Board of the United Nations Industrial Development Organization. Other major conferences issue Official records, too.

The three components of the Official records[29] were, for many years:

I. Meeting records:
verbatim records of plenary meetings of the Assembly's First Committee, the Security Council, and the Trusteeship Council;
summary records of meetings of the Economic and Social Council, the Trade and Development Board, the Industrial Development Board, etc.;
agenda;
list of delegations;
checklists of documents issued.

---

[29] This description is based partly on: United Nations, Dag Hammarskjöld Library, United Nations documentation; a brief guide for official recipients (New York, 1974; ST/LIB/34; Bibliography entry 134).

Some meeting records are issued in printed fascicles, others, in mimeographed form. Meeting records of the International Law Commission (a subsidiary organ of the General Assembly) are in volume I of the Yearbook of the International Law Commission (Bibliography entry 66).

2. Annexes

collections of texts of documents related to and arranged by agenda items, and checklists of other documents (see Fig. 13 for a sample page. For most organs, the annexes appear in separate fascicles, for others, meeting records and annexes are in the same volume. In the case of the International Law Commission, annex-type documents appear in volume II of the Yearbook of the International Law Commission.

3. Supplements

reports of subsidiary organs and other bodies, resolutions and decisions, e.g.: the annual report of the Economic Commission for Asia and the Far East for 1969/70 comprises Supplement No. 2 of the Official records of the forty-ninth session of the Economic and Social Council;

the Report of the Secretary-General on the work of the Organization (Bibliography entry 41) is issued each year as Supplement No. 1 of the Official records of the General Assembly; the Security Council's report to the Assembly on the Council's activities (see Bibliography entry 82) appears as Supplement No. 2 of the Official records of the General Assembly.

In the past few years, changes have taken place in the component parts, form and distribution of some of the Official records. The General Assembly, in its resolution 3415(XXX) of 8 December 1975 approved several criteria to be applied to meeting records of United Nations bodies. As a result, meeting records are now issued as follows:

The verbatim records of the plenary meetings of the General Assembly and the Security Council and the summary records of the plenary meetings of the Economic and Social Council . . . continue to be

issued initially in provisional mimeographed form for limited distribution
and later in printed form, with . . .
corrections . . . incorporated, for
general distribution . . ..
    The verbatim records of the Trustee-
ship Council . . . continue to be issued
in one form only for general distribution,
subject to correction. The verbatim records of the [General Assembly's] First
Committee . . . [are now] issued in one
form only, subject to correction . . ..
    The summary records of the Main Com-
mittees of the General Assembly, the
sessional committees of the Economic and
Social Council and the Governing Council
of UNDP, the Executive Board of UNICEF,
the Trade and Development Board and the
Industrial Development Board . . . [are
now] issued in one form only . . ..
[For certain subsidiary bodies, summary
records are now issued only for discussions of substantive issues.][30]

All changes in the meeting records of
the General Assembly have been in effect from
the Assembly's 30th session (1975).

Beginning with its 56th session (1974),
the Economic and Social Council has not issued
annexes. Its Official records have consisted
of summary records of meetings, supplements,
and lists of delegations.

The Official records of the Security
Council now consist of: verbatim records of
meetings; quarterly and special supplements
containing documents; and resolutions and
decisions.

――――――[30] United Nations, General Assembly,
        Thirty-first Session, Records of
        meetings of United Nations bodies;
        note by the Secretary-General (New
        York, 10 February 1976; A/31/INF/2).

The <u>Official records</u> of the Trusteeship
Council now consist of: verbatim records of
meetings (issued in mimeographed form, with
sessional corrigenda); sessional fascicles
containing annexes; and supplements which includ
resolutions and decisions, and reports of visiting missions.

CHAPTER 15

OTHER DOCUMENTS AND PUBLICATIONS

1.   In addition to Official records and
other sales publications, the General Assembly,
the Security Council, the Economic and Social
Council, the Trusteeship Council, and many other
United Nations organs issue a vast volume of
provisional documents, working papers, draft
resolutions, information documents, etc. Much
of this material is not widely distributed outside the United Nations itself. On the other
hand, important provisional documents are usually reissued in unchanged or revised form as final
documents in the Official records or as other
sales publications.

2.   Documents of the Secretariat, too, may
be issued as provisional or internal documents
or may appear as sales publications or other
permanent documents. Many important reports,
bibliographies, guides and other compilations
are issued by Secretariat bodies, e.g., the Demographic yearbook (Bibliography entry 90) issued by the Statistical Office; The sea, legal
and political aspects; a select bibliography,
issued by the Dag Hammarskjöld Library in its
Bibliographical series; Everyman's United Nations (Bibliography entries 44-45), issued by
the Office of Public Information.

3.   Press releases, issued by the Press Section, Office of Public Information, as non-offi-
cial matter primarily for the use of information

United Nations
Press Release

Office of Public Information
Press Section
United Nations, New York

WS/822
8 JULY 1977

W E E K L Y   N E W S   S U M M A R Y

(Main developments during the week 1 - 7 July)

Secretary-General Kurt Waldheim this week elaborated on his proposal for an international institution, within the framework of the United Nations, to co-ordinate development of the world's energy resources. He was speaking in Geneva at the opening of the summer session of the Economic and Social Council.

At a Geneva press conference, the Secretary-General spoke of the latest moves towards Middle East peace negotiation. Earlier, he had addressed the opening session of the summit meeting of the Organization of African Unity (OAU) at Libreville, Gabon.

The Security Council has recommended approval of the application of the new Republic of Djibouti to join the United Nations. Approval by the General Assembly would make it the 148th Member of the Organization.

The President of the Third United Nations Conference on the Law of the Sea, H. Shirley Amerasinghe (Sri Lanka), has reported on the current state of efforts to reach an agreement to govern man's use of the oceans.

77-13162

A Page from a *U.N. Press release*   For information media – not an official recor

media, often are the first pieces of available information about new developments as they occur or about topics about which official documents would not appear until much later. Some examples to illustrate their range:

Resolutions of the General Assembly at the first part of its thirty-first regular session, 21 September - 22 December 1976. New York, 29 December 1976. xiv, 426 p. (Press release GA/5571.) Contains the text of resolutions adopted, information on voting, directory information on officers of the session, agenda, alphabetical subject index. Similar releases are issued after each session.

Security Council [meeting summaries] (Press release SC/-   ). Issued almost simultaneously with the meetings themselves.

Weekly news summary (Press release WS/-   ). Capsule review of the main developments of interest to the United Nations (see Fig. 14 for an example).

Member states of the United Nations (Press release M/-   ). A background release, listing members with dates of admission. Revised frequently to publicize each change as it occurs.

Membership of principal United Nations organs (Press release ORG/-). Annual.

Chart of agencies related to the United Nations (Press release SA/-). Shows, in tabular form, the functions, total membership, gross budget, etc., of each agency. Annual.

United Nations special observances and conferences (Reference paper). Lists and summarizes major events scheduled for the year covered and for subsequent years. Annual.

4.   The documentation of the International Court of Justice follows the pattern of the documentation of the Court's predecessor, the Per-

UNITED NATIONS DEVELOPMENT PROGRAMME

Distr.
GENERAL
UNDP/MIS/INF.55
12 December 1974
English only

UNDP: PROJECT REPORTS

Reports derestricted: March 1974 - November 1974[1]/

The following reports have been derestricted by the Governments concerned, and may now be obtained from the sources listed in the Annex to this circular:

1. ARGENTINA   - Mineral Exploration in the Northwest Region

   (ARG/70/535) Informe provisional - Exploración minera de la
                región noroeste. (Fase I). Nueva York,
                Naciones Unidas, 1973. (DP/SF/UN/101).
                Español solamente.

Executing Agency: United Nations

2. BURMA   - Mu River Irrigation Survey
   (BUR/62/505)

                Mu river irrigation survey feasibility
                study. Rome, ITALCONSULT, 1970-1973.
                3 parts plus addendum. 13 books.

                Thapanzeik dam - Final design. Rome,
                ITALCONSULT, February 1972. 3 volumes
                in 8 books including maps and drawings.

Executing Agency: United Nations

3. CHAD   - Études de preinvestissement pour l'irrigation
                de la plaine de Satégui-Deressia

   (CHD/73/002) Campagne hydrologique en 1973. Roma, Carlo Lotti
                and C., Consulting Engineers, décembre
                1973. Français seulement.

Executing Agency: International Bank for Reconstruction and Development

---

1/   Circular UNDP/MIS/INF.54 listing reports derestricted during the
      period August 1973 - February 1974, was issued on 25 March 1974.

A Page from a UNDP List of Derestricted Reports

manent Court of International Justice. The
major series (all sales publications) are:

Reports of judgments, advisory opinions and
   orders

Pleadings, oral arguments, documents

Acts and documents concerning the organization
   of the Court

Yearbook

Bibliography of the International Court of
   Justice

5.   Publications of the United Nations Development Programme differ from other United Nations publications in several respects; e.g.,
the UNDP project reports are considered to be
part of the technical assistance supplied by the
United Nations to countries requesting such assistance. The reports become the property of the
requesting country which alone can decide what
reports may be derestricted and made available
to the public.[31] Information on derestricted
country reports and their availability may be
found in:

International bibliography, information, documentation (Bibliography entry 109);

UNDP business bulletin (bimonthly publication of
   the United Nations Development Programme);

UNDP: project reports; reports derestricted
   (semi-annual listing issued by the United Nations Development Programme with the symbol
   UNDP/MIS/INF . . .; see Fig. 15 for an example);

UNDP compendium of approved projects (annual);

DP/PROJECTS (fact sheets).

----

[31] United Nations, Dag Hammarskjöld Li-
       brary, Seminar on United Nations doc-
       umentation for North American depo-
       sitory and standing order libraries
       (New York, 14-16 January 1976), pp.
       7-8.

6.   While not United Nations documents in
the strict sense of the term, two important
series must be considered in any examination of
the steps leading to the establishment of the
United Nations:

documents of the United Nations Conference on
   International Organization, San Francisco,
   1945 (the 'San Francisco Conference'; bibliography entry 17);

publications of the Preparatory Commission of
   the United Nations, London, 1945 (Bibliography
   entries 11-14).

CHAPTER 16

FORM OF UNITED NATIONS MATERIAL

          The physical form of material issued by
the United Nations varies greatly. The Organization itself issues its documents in mimeographed, offset and printed form and, increasingly but selectively, in microform.
1. Microfiche produced and sold by the United
    Nations:
Official records of the General Assembly: meet-
    ing records (plenary and committees), annexes,
    supplements
Official records of the Security Council: meet-
    ing records, supplements and special supple-
    ments, resolutions
Official records of the Economic and Social Coun-
    cil: meeting records, supplements and special
    supplements, annexes
Official records of the Trusteeship Council:
    meeting records, resolutions
United Nations Treaty series (Bibliography entry
    87) and cumulative indexes (Bibliography entry
    118)
Yearbook of the International Law Commission
    (Bibliography entry 66)
Yearbook of the United Nations (Bibliography
    entry 46)
Statistical yearbook (Bibliography entry 95)
Demographic yearbook (Bibliography entry 90)
Yearbook on human rights (Bibliography entry 61)
Yearbook of international trade statistics
Yearbook of national accounts statistics
Yearbook of the United Nations Commission on In-

ternational Trade Law
United Nations juridical yearbook
Statistical yearbook for Asia and the Pacific
Repertory of practice of United Nations organs
    (Bibliography entry 2)
Judgments of the United Nations Administrative
    Tribunal
Reports of international arbitral awards
World economic survey (Bibliography entry 54)
Foreign trade statistics for Asia and the Pacifi
Economic survey of Asia and the Pacific
Economic survey of Latin America
Mineral resources development series
Water resources series
United Nations legislative series (Bibliography
    entry 67)
International review of criminal policy
Population studies
Yearbook of industrial statistics
Documents of the United Nations Environment Pro-
    gramme
Proceedings of the international conferences on
    the peaceful uses of atomic energy
Documents of the United Nations Conference on In
    ternational Organization (Bibliography entry
    17)
Yearbook of the International Court of Justice
Reports of judgments, advisory opinions and or-
    ders of the International Court of Justice
Pleadings before the International Court of
    Justice
Documents of the United Nations Conference on
    Trade and Development
Documents of the United Nations Industrial De-
    velopment Organization
Terminology bulletins
Documents of the 1974 World Food Conference
Reports of the Sub-Commission on Prevention of
    Discrimination and Protection of Minorities
    (a subsidiary organ of the Commission on Hu-
    man Rights)
Documents of the Economic Commission for Europe

        The text of the microfiches is in nega-
tive, with the header in positive. Each fiche
is 105 mm x 148 mm (4" x 6") in size. Each

nternational Zone

ASIA: TWO THIRDS AND COUNTING

Asia now has almost two thirds of the world's people and may double its total by the year 2000. India, China and Japan have approached the problem three different ways. For more than twenty years India has sought to control her population growth with the largest birth control program in the world. Now her government is attacking poverty first, which is now seen as the root of her population difficulties. When the People's Republic of China came into being more than two decades ago she decided to attack poverty first. Now her population is leveling off. Japan's postwar economic miracle of rapid industrialization brought with it a near zero population growth, but also brought with it all of the environmental and social problems that come with industrialization. Now she, like the rest of the developed world, must deal with the two edged sword of inflation and recession. International Zone 160.

28 minutes   color   1975

ASSIGNMENT CHILDREN

Alistair Cooke gives the audience the opportunity of experiencing once again Danny Kaye's memorable journey to Asia on behalf of the United Nations Children's Fund. One of the world's great clowns contributes his own therapy of laughter in support of UNICEF's mission to the world's children. International Zone 1.

28 minutes   black and white   1961

BENEATH THE DREAM

Hong Kong has quadrupled its population during the last 20 years, by natural increase and by the influx of settlers from the Chinese mainland. A quarter of Hong Kong's more than four million people live in vast apartment blocks hemmed in by moutains and sea. Myriads more live in shanties or anchored junks in the teeming harbor. To feed the hungry, to clothe and teach needy children is a task that falls heavily upon the authorities. Into this world of struggling humanity our film travels, guided by two young Chinese girls, Fuku and Lee, each doing her part to ease misery and promote well-being. Fuku is a member of the Children's Association, which looks after 100,000 children. Lee seeks out those for whom there is no room at school, bringing them the help of the mobile library given by UNICEF. International Zone 123.

28 minutes   color   1969

BOOM TOWN

Three hundred migrants a week stream into the new Venezuelan city of Ciudad Guyana, where iron, fuel and the river highway combine to make possible a great city of the future. Its present people are mostly Venezuelan farmers and artisans, seeking to lodge in this mushrooming boom town. Many live in shanties on illegally occupied land; others secure title to building lots and put up their own dwellings. Meanwhile, the town's master plan, fashioned by the Corporación Venezolana de Guyana, struggles to keep ahead of reality while simultaneously preserving the vision of a handsome and practical future city. This film is about the role of the planner and how the United Nations contributes to the shaping of cities of the future. International Zone 87.

28 minutes   color   1967

A CALL FROM MALAYSIA

In this film, we follow a young Sarawak villager in his efforts to become a "communicator," as he learns to participate in broadcasting, telephony, radio and other modern occupations Malaysia now requires. More than eleven million people living on countless islands and one large peninsula are now united in the Federation of Malaysia and the agencies of the UN Family are at work to help them build a modern and effective country. International Zone 81.

28 minutes   color   1966

CANE ... AND ABLE

Jamaica, a nation since 1962, is struggling to build a sound economy, to find productive work and a life of dignity for all its people. United Nations cameras encounter some people that tourists rarely meet: a Scot who is helping to start a footwear industry; the editor of a daily paper, who believes Jamaicans should go abroad and bring back know-how; young people at Cobbla Camp who are getting back their faith in farming; and a dynamic Jamaican at the University of the West Indies who is also artistic director of the National Dance Company of Jamaica and who feels the Jamaican is highly motivated and, given the opportunity, can meet the challenge—he is able. International Zone 116.

28 minutes   color   1969

CATALYST

A true-life situation that helped change the lives of people in a Haitian village. A United Nations agricultural expert shows the villagers what they can do to help themselves through cooperative effort in growing and marketing. Filmed entirely in Haiti. International Zone 9.

28 minutes   black and white   1961

Iran moves to eradicate the illicit traffic in opium, morphine and heroin. This film dramatizes the actual efforts of the Iranian government with the UN's assistance. Made with the cooperation of the Iranian government and its enforcement officers. International Zone 74.

28 minutes   black and white   1966

CHIMBOTE: A BETTER PLACE TO LIVE

The earthquake of 1970 almost wiped out this Peruvian coastal city. Emergency assistance was rushed in by the international community but soon after Peru turned to the UN for help in planning a new city, one that could not be so easily wiped out by a future natural disaster. Polish town planners (who had rebuilt Warsaw after World War II) and Yugoslavs (who had restored the earthquake-shattered city of Skopje) joined Peruvian planners in constructing "A Better Place to Live." International Zone 149. Also available in Spanish.

28 minutes   color   1971

CHINA'S CHAIR

This film offers the controversial slice of history that makes up the years 1945-1971, on the China question in the United Nations, ending with the People's Republic of China being seated in the General Assembly on November 15, 1971. The comprehensive case file includes rare footage of Russia's walkout from the Security Council to protest the continued Nationalist presence, the United Nations intervention in Korea, the appearance in 1950 of General Wu of the People's Republic, and traces the international reasons why of the China votes during the twenty years that followed. International Zone 137. McGraw: $260.

28 minutes   color   1971

A Page from the *United Nations 16 mm. film catalogue*

fiche contains 60 frames at a reduction ratio
of 20:1.

2. Microfilm. For many years, the Archives Sec
tion of the United Nations microfilmed United
Nations documents and made this material available on roll microfilm. For more information,
see Index to microfilm of United Nations documents in English, 1946-1967 (Bibliography entries 119-120).

3. Sound recordings of meetings, historic event
press conferences, etc. have been produced
by the United Nations for many years. For details see Catalogue of sound recordings in the
custody of the Sound Recording Unit of the Telecommunications Section of the United Nations
(Bibliography entry 146).

4. Motion pictures and television programmes.
The United Nations has produced many individual
films and the following main series:
The UN: its Charter and organization (a basic
   series for the study of the United Nations,
   its organs and related organizations)
Man builds, man destroys (a series of half-half
   colour films, dealing with the human environment around the globe)
International zone (a series of half-hour television specials about international co-operation in various fields of human endeavour)
The new international economic order (a new seri
   of half-hour television programmes dealing
   with natural resources, capital, technology,
   and human resources)

        For a listing, with descriptions, of
United Nations films, see United Nations 16 mm
film catalogue (Bibliography entry 147; Fig. 16
shows a page from the catalogue).

5. Reprints, translations, etc. Many United
Nations documents and related publications are
issued or reissued commercially. Examples:
the Readex Microprint edition of mimeographed
   and printed documents of the United Nations,

1946 to date (<u>see</u> Bibliography entry 16)
the Xerox/University Microfilms microfiche
edition of the bibliography of the 1972
Stockholm United Nations Conference on the
Human Environment
the Kraus Reprint Corporation reissue of out-
of-print volumes of the <u>Yearbook of the United
Nations</u>, <u>Demographic yearbook</u>, <u>Statistical
Yearbook</u>, <u>United Nations legislative series</u>,
<u>Economic bulletin for Africa</u>, and many other
United Nations publications
translations (into other than official languages
of the United Nations), e.g., a Japanese
version of the <u>Statistical yearbook</u> or a
Hungarian translation of <u>The application of
computer technology for development</u>
the Unifo Publishers, Ltd. edition of International Women's Year conference documents on
microfiche, with printed index
the Oceana Publications, Inc., edition of
United Nations resolutions
<u>Who's who in the United Nations and related
agencies</u>, issued by Arno Press (<u>see</u> Bibliography entry 100).

CHAPTER 17

UNITED NATIONS DOCUMENT SERIES SYMBOLS

      Symbols of United Nations documents are complex combinations of capital or lower-case letters and, usually Arabic but sometimes Roman, numerals. The elements are separated by oblique strokes.

      The leading elements of the series symbols identify the issuing organ, e.g.,

A/-	General Assembly
CERD/-	Committee on the Elimination of Racial Discrimination
DC/-	Disarmament Commission
DP/-	United Nations Development Programme
E/-	Economic and Social Council
ID/-	United Nations Industrial Development Organization
S/-	Security Council
ST/-	Secretariat
T/-	Trusteeship Council
TD/-	United Nations Conference on Trade and Development
UNEP/-	United Nations Environment Programme
UNITAR/-	United Nations Institute for Training and Research

      Secondary elements may denote

(a) subsidiary organs, e.g.,

-/AC.../-   Ad hoc committee or other similar

                              body
-/C.../- Standing, permanent or main committe
-/CN.../- Commission
-/CONF.../- Conference
-/GC/- Governing Council
-/PC.../- Preparatory committee
-/SC.../- Sub-committee
-/Sub.../- Sub-commission
-/WG.../- Working group
-/WP.../- Working party

(b) <u>type of document</u>, e.g.,

-/INF/- Information series
-/MIN... Minutes
-/NGO/- Statements made by non-governmental
                organizations
-/PET/- Petitions
-/PV... Verbatim records of meetings (procès
                verbaux)
-/RES/- Resolutions in mimeographed form
-/SR... Summary records of meetings
-/WP... Working papers

(c) <u>modifications</u> of the original document, e.g.

-/Add... Addendum
-/Amend... Amendment
-/Corr... Corrigendum
-/Excerpt Excerpt
-/Rev... Revision
-/Summary Summary

(d) <u>distribution categories</u>:

-/L... Limited distribution
-/R... Restricted distribution

              Examples of the use of series symbols:

<u>Main committees of the General Assembly</u>

A/C.1/- First (Political and Security)
                Committee
A/SPC/- Special Political Committee
A/C.2/- Second (Economic and Financial) Com-

	mittee
A/C.3/-	Third (Social, Humanitarian and Cultural) Committee
A/C.4/-	Fourth (Trusteeship) Committee
A/C.5/-	Fifth (Administrative and Budgetary) Committee
A/C.6/-	Sixth (Legal) Committee

Other selected subsidiary bodies of the General
   Assembly

A/AC.179/-	Ad Hoc Committee on the Restructuring of the Economic and Social Sectors of the United Nations System
A/AC.182/-	Special Committee on the Charter of the United Nations and on the Strengthening of the Role of the Organization
A/CN.4/-	International Law Commission
A/CN.9/-	Commission on International Trade Law
A/CONF.62/-	Third United Nations Conference on the Law of the Sea
A/CONF.78/-	United Nations Conference on Territorial Asylum

Selected subsidiary bodies of the Economic and
   Social Council

E/C.6/-	Committee on Housing, Building and Planning
E/C.7/-	Committee on Natural Resources
E/C.8/-	Committee on Science and Technology for Development
E/CN.4/-	Commission on Human Rights
E/CN.5/-	Commission for Social Development
E/CN.11/-	Economic and Social Commission for Asia and the Pacific
E/CN.12/-	Economic Commission for Latin America
E/CN.14/-	Economic Commission for Africa
E/ECE/-	Economic Commission for Europe
E/ECWA/-	Economic Commission for Western Asia

Selected specific documents

TD/B/16/Rev.2 — Rules of procedure of the Trade and Development Board (/B/) of the United Nations Conference on Trade and Development (TD/...), second revised edition. The original Rules were issued as th 16th document in the Board's general series.

A/RES/3201 (S/VI) — General Assembly resolution 3201, adopted by the sixth special session of the Assembly. (Resolutions and most other series were numbered consecutively.

A/SPC/L.247 — A draft resolution discussed by the General Assembly's Special Political Committee. For limite distribution; issued as the 247t document in the Committee's "limited" series.

S/Agenda 1624-1683 — Provisional agenda of the 1624th through 1683rd meetings of the Security Council.

S/PV.1646 — Verbatim records (procès-verbaux of the 1646th meeting of the Security Council.

E/CN.6/549 — The 549th document issued in the general series of the Commission on the Status of Women of the Economic and Social Council

ST/LEG/SER.C/8 — United Nations juridical yearboo 1970 (Issued in 1972, it bears also the sales number E.72.V.1.) No. 8 in the juridical yearbook series of the Secretariat's Offi of Legal Affairs.

T/PET.10/68	The 68th petition received by the Trusteeship Council with respect to the Trust Territory of the Pacific Islands.

In 1975, a change took place, aimed at shortening the symbols of General Assembly documents[32] whose numerical components had, in some cases, reached five digits. At the same time, the structure of the symbol has become more complex, by the introduction of a numerical secondary element beginning with documents relating to the thirty-first session. Examples:

A/31/2	Second in the series of main documents of the General Assembly, issued for its thirty-first session
A/C.5/31/L.22	Twenty-second in the series of limited distribution documents of the Fifth Committee of the Assembly, issued during or for the thirty-first session
A/C.2/31/SR.10	Summary record of the tenth meeting of the General Assembly's Second Committee, held during the Assembly's thirty-first session
A/RES/31/2	Second resolution (in mimeographed form) adopted by the thirty-first session of the General Assembly
A/32/87/Add.1	Addendum No. 1 to the eighty-seventh in the series of main documents in the general series of

---

[32] United Nations, General Assembly, Simplification of symbol series and numbering of meetings for the General Assembly and its main committees (New York, 23 December 1975; A/INF/31/1).

UNITED NATIONS

GENERAL ASSEMBLY

SECURITY COUNCIL

Distr.
GENERAL

A/32/134
S/12357
6 July 1977
ENGLISH
ORIGINAL: FRENCH

GENERAL ASSEMBLY
Thirty-second session
Item 25 of the preliminary list*
ADMISSION OF NEW MEMBERS TO THE
  UNITED NATIONS

SECURITY COUNCIL
Thirty-second yea

Application of the Republic of Djibouti for admission to
membership in the United Nations

Note by the Secretary-General

In accordance with rule 135 of the rules of procedure of the General Assembl
and rule 59 of the provisional rules of procedure of the Security Council, the
Secretary-General has the honour to circulate herewith the application of the
Republic of Djibouti for admission to membership in the United Nations, contained
in a letter dated 30 June 1977 from the President of the Republic of Djibouti to
the Secretary-General.

---

* A/32/50/Rev.1.

77-13068

A Document Bearing Two Series Symbols

the General Assembly, issued for
its thirty-second session.

Certain documents may carry more than
one series symbol, e.g., some documents in the
general series of the General Assembly are also
considered to be documents of the Security Council and bear an A/- number as well as an S/- number (see Fig. 17 for an example).

When a document is reissued in the Official records or as a sales publication, its
series symbol remains unchanged.

The International Court of Justice does
not use document series symbols. It uses standard short titles instead, as follows:

I.C.J. Pleadings
I.C.J. Reports
I.C.J. Bibliography
I.C.J. Acts and documents
I.C.J. Yearbook

CHAPTER 18

THE COMPUTER-BASED BIBLIOGRAPHIC INFORMATION
SYSTEM OF THE UNITED NATIONS

A) UNDIS: United Nations Documentation In-
    formation System

     In 1969, the Dag Hammarskjöld Library be-
an computer-storing various files of information
xtracted from and relating to United Nations doc-
ments. The ultimate purpose of the system was
et out as
     the progressive creation, in successive
     phases, of a generalized information
     base and the establishment and operation
     of services . . . [designed] to satisfy
     the need of official and other potential
     users for specific documentary information
     on the activities of the United Nations
     and on the substantive questions dealt
     with by it over the years.[33]

     The functions of UNDIS were stated as
follows: document retrieval, selective data
storage and retrieval, compilation of indexes in
English, French, Russian and Spanish, and storage

────────33
          United Nations, Dag Hammarskjöld Li-
     brary, Computer-assisted indexing;
     background information on activities
     carried out at United Nations Head-
     quarters (New York, 1975 [?]), p. 2.

and dissemination of texts in microform.[34]

Computer-based UNDIS files include: reports, resolutions and verbatim or summary meeting records of the General Assembly, the three Councils and many of their subsidiary or related organs; sales publications; International Court of Justice publications; articles included in United Nations periodicals from 1972 on. Among the types of documents excluded from UNDIS: Treaty series, mimeographed documents of the regional commissions and of various other United Nations bodies.[35]

The information contained in the compute files is of various types: references to documents (e.g., series symbol, sales number, microfiche number), physical and substantive description of documents (e.g., author, title, distribution category; narrative summaries) and textual information extracted from documents (e.g., verbatim texts of operative paragraphs of resolutions).[36]

Products of UNDIS include: UNDEX; Unite Nations documents index (Bibliography entries 130-132; see Fig. 18 for a sample page) ad hoc information aids, etc. As of July 1977, UNDIS plans to issue:

a list of United Nations sales publications published from 1972 through 1977, arranged in sales number order and giving basic bibliographic information about each item; this will be accompanied by an author list and title list, each containing the same information as the sales number list, and a brief subject in-

---

[34] Ibid., p. 7.

[35] United Nations, Dag Hammarskjöld Library, UNDIS, the United Nations documentation information system (New York, 1974; ST/LIB/33), p.3.

[36] Ibid., pp. 3-4.

SUBJECT INDEX

LOPMENT: and international economic co-operation
ISC DOCUMENTS
  SECRETARY-GENERAL
    761202   A/31/336/Add.1

REPORTS
  COMMITTEE TO DRAW UP A CONSTITUTION FOR THE
  UNITED NATIONS INDUSTRIAL DEVELOPMENT
  ORGANIZATION AS A SPECIALIZED AGENCY
    761210   A/31/405
            A/AC.180/9

  GENERAL ASSEMBLY (31): 2nd COMMITTEE
    761217   A/31/335/Add.1

VOTING
  761119   A/31/PV.72

  761221   A/31/PV.106

LOPMENT: international strategy; implementation
MEETING RECORDS
  761221   A/31/PV.106

REPORTS
  GENERAL ASSEMBLY (31): 2nd COMMITTEE
    761217   A/31/335/Add.1

VOTING
  761221   A/31/PV.106

LOPMENT: international strategy; revision
MEETING RECORDS
  761221   A/31/PV.106

REPORTS
  GENERAL ASSEMBLY (31): 2nd COMMITTEE
    761216   A/31/436

    761218   A/31/338/Add.2

VOTING
  761221   A/31/PV.106

LOPMENT: popular participation
REPORTS
  SECRETARY-GENERAL
    760928   E/CN.5/532

ELOPMENT: UN operational activities
MEETING RECORDS
  761221   A/31/PV.106

REPORTS
  GENERAL ASSEMBLY (31): 2nd COMMITTEE
    761215   A/31/411

VOTING
  761221   A/31/PV.106

ELOPMENT ASSISTANCE
MEETING RECORDS
  761221   A/31/PV.106

REPORTS
  GENERAL ASSEMBLY (31): 2nd COMMITTEE
    761216   A/31/436

VOTING
  761221   A/31/PV.106

PLOMATIC CONFERENCE ON THE REAFFIRMATION AND
ELOPMENT OF INTERNATIONAL HUMANITARIAN LAW
PLICABLE IN ARMED CONFLICTS (Geneva 1977): results
MEETING RECORDS
  761124   A/31/PV.77

VOTING
  761124   A/31/PV.77

DIPLOMATIC RELATIONS: Vienna Convention 1961;
implementation
  MEETING RECORDS
    761213   A/31/PV.97

  REPORTS
    GENERAL ASSEMBLY (31): 6th COMMITTEE
      761210   A/31/403

  RESOLUTIONS
    761213   A/RES/31/76

  VOTING
    761213   A/31/PV.97

DIPLOMATIC VEHICLES: parking
  REPORTS
    COMMITTEE ON RELATIONS WITH THE HOST COUNTRY (5)
      761100   A/31/26
             GAOR(31)-Suppl 26

    GENERAL ASSEMBLY (31): 6th COMMITTEE
      761213   A/31/418

DIPLOMATS: protection
  REPORTS
    COMMITTEE ON RELATIONS WITH THE HOST COUNTRY (5)
      761100   A/31/26
             GAOR(31)-Suppl 26

DISABLED PERSONS
See/See also
  INTERNATIONAL YEAR FOR DISABLED PERSONS

DISABLED PERSONS: integration into community life
  REPORTS
    SECRETARY-GENERAL
      761104   E/CN.5/535

DISABLED PERSONS: rights; Declaration 1975;
implementation
  MEETING RECORDS
    761213   A/31/PV.97

  REPORTS
    GENERAL ASSEMBLY (31): 3rd COMMITTEE
      761207   A/31/389

  VOTING
    761213   A/31/PV.97

DISARMAMENT
See/See also
  MILITARY BUDGETS: reduction

DISARMAMENT: general and complete
  MEETING RECORDS
    761221   A/31/PV.106

  REPORTS
    ADVISORY COMMITTEE ON ADMINISTRATIVE AND
    BUDGETARY QUESTIONS
      761209   A/31/8/Add.14

    GENERAL ASSEMBLY (31): 1st COMMITTEE
      761210   A/31/386

  VOTING
    761221   A/31/PV.106

DISARMAMENT: role of UN; strengthening
  MEETING RECORDS
    761214   A/31/PV.98

  REPORTS
    ADVISORY COMMITTEE ON ADMINISTRATIVE AND
    BUDGETARY QUESTIONS
      761209   A/31/8/Add.14

    GENERAL ASSEMBLY (31): 1st COMMITTEE
      761208   A/31/387

A Page from the *UNDEX subject index*

dex, referring to sales numbers;
a revised list of United Nations document series
symbols (for the latest published list, <u>see</u>
Bibliography entry 129);
a thesaurus of indexing terms.

(B)   UNBIS: <u>United Nations Bibliographic Information System</u>

The aim of this new system[37] is to improve and expand bibliographic information services to internal as well as external users. The proposed system envisions:

greater bibliographic control over various types of material (UN documents as well as other library material held by the libraries of the United Nations);
on-line retrieval (for internal users);

implementation of international bibliographic standards;
input capability and access to stored information not only for the Dag Hammarskjöld Library but for substantive UN departments, libraries of the regional commissions, and so on;
production of subject bibliographies, catalogues etc., for internal users;
a union list of serials held by libraries of the United Nations system of organizations;
a comprehensive index to United Nations document and publications.

It is the last-mentioned product that is of the greatest interest to external users of United Nations documents and publications. The

―――――――[37] This information is based on the 1976 <u>Annual report</u> of the Dag Hammarskjöld Library, 1976-77 issues of the Dag Hammarskjöld Library's <u>Library newsletter</u>, and personal interviews with staff of the Dag Hammarskjöld Library during July 1977. Material used by permission of the Dag Hammarskjöld Library.

new index would be a successor to the present
JNDEX and of UNDI (Bibliography entries 135-136),
JNDEX's predecessor, and would incorporate the
best features of both.

This new product is tentatively entitled
United Nations documentation (UNDOC): current
index. Its proposed components are:

a checklist containing: list of sales
    publications; list of new series symbols;
    language versions of documents and
    publications received; list of documents
    republished; list of Official records;
    list of current periodicals; list of maps;

subject index, author index, and title index.
    It is planned that these will be as
    comprehensive as the corresponding issues
    of the checklist and that the subject index
    will give in-depth analysis of all items
    included.

In addition to the current index, present
recurrent indexes (such as the Indexes to
proceedings, Bibliography entries 122-125) and
various ad hoc bibliographies would be considered
as products of the new system.

The UNBIS pilot project began on 1
October 1976 and continues at the time of this
writing. It is hoped that the current index
will see the light of day in 1978.

PART III

USE, ACQUISITION, AND ORGANIZATION
OF UNITED NATIONS PUBLICATIONS

CHAPTER 19

RESEARCH USE OF UNITED NATIONS PUBLICATIONS

From the functional point of view, United Nations publications are considered by the Organization to fall into several categories:

(a) documents relating to the internal administration of the United Nations (budget, personnel, etc.) "are intended chiefly for the staff members of the Organization itself and for members of delegations of member states";[38]

(b) documents "concerned with the actual functioning of the Organization [and] with the implementation of its objectives and programmes - decisions, resolutions, . . . verbatim records of meetings," etc. are addressed principally to the member states;[39]

(c) yearbooks, statistics, collections of texts, etc. "are produced for a very wide range of governmental and academic specialists, research workers and technicians, industrialists and businessmen";[40]

---

[38] John Goormaghtigh, "Introductory report for Panel III: utilization of international documentation," (in Sources, organization, utilization of international documentation; Bibliography entry 110), p. 183.

[39] Ibid.

[40] Ibid., pp. 183-184.

(d)   publications "supplying information on one particular aspect or on the overall activities of" the Organization (press releases, brochures, folders or periodicals are "intended for non-specialists".[41]

Different types of users (international organizations, governments, universities, specialists and non-specialists) have widely different requirements. Lacking a common denominator, the compromise chosen here is to outline some research methods most relevant to the needs of researchers and students outside the United Nations itself.[42]

Among the factors influencing research, one might mention the research environment and the researcher's awareness of the intended audience of United Nations publications, as described in the previous paragraphs. The nature of these publications must also be properly understood. It is often discovered, for instance, that there is no single official UN monograph, single document, or publication on a given subject. Information must often be obtained from scattered documents, many of which are reportorial in style and lacking in analytical quality. On the other hand, it should be recognized that the United Nations itself, from its very beginnings, has shown considerable concern for informing the public of its aims and activities (see Chapter 12).

Basic types and methods of United Nations research

Most research problems involving United

----

[41] Ibid.

[42] The remainder of this chapter is an adaptation and updating of Chapter 2 of B. Brimmer's A guide to the use of United Nations documents (Bibliography entry 105). Used by permission of Oceana Publications, Inc.

Nations publications fall into the following
categories:

1. A study of the work of a particular organ or
   subsidiary organ;
2. A study of a particular subject, e.g., human
   rights, transnational corporations, environment;
3. A study of an administrative or organizational issue, e.g., co-ordination between
   the United Nations and the specialized
   agencies, the role of the Secretary-General,
   etc.;
4. A study of United Nations activities or documentation relating to a geographical area;
5. A study of the position of a government as
   reflected in United Nations debates.

The two main methods of research are the
historical approach and the problem-solving
approach, and combinations and variations of the
two. Depending on the particular needs of a
particular researcher, all steps in either method
will not need to be taken; in fact, in most cases,
only some of the steps will be necessary.

The following sequence is suggested for
conducting research in any of the five above-
mentioned types of problems:

(a) precise determination or "narrowing-down"
of the subject of research;
(b) determination of the United Nations organ
or subsidiary organ that deals with the subject;
(c) finding the document series symbol used by
the organ or subsidiary organ;
(d) finding the proper reference tools that
cover the series of relevant documents;
(e) locating the needed documents through the
reference tools.

The historical approach

Step 1: determining precisely the subject of
        research.

One may find that many United Nations bodies
have discussed various aspects of the same problem under a variety of headings. To take an
example: 'rice' has been discussed under the
rubrics of: the world shortage of cereals; agriculture; UNICEF; UNRRA; commodities; economic
development; the regional commissions; refugees;
statistics; technical co-operation; etc.

Step 2:   learning the structure of the United
          Nations.

The principal organs of the United Nations were
established by Article 7 of the Charter; the
functions and powers of each principal organ are
set down mainly in Articles 10-17, 24-26, 62-66,
87, 88, 92, 97-99 of the Charter and Articles
34-38 of the Statute of the International Court
of Justice. It is useful, especially for the
beginning researcher, to read these portions of
the Charter and the Statute.

Step 3:   consulting the Index to the Charter and
          the Statute of the International Court
          of Justice (New York, 1947; United Na-
          tions publication, Sales No. 47.I.15).

This would provide further subject guidance.

Step 4:   consulting the Index (volume 21) to the
          documents of the 1945 United Nations
          Conference on International Organiza-
          tion (the San Francisco Conference; see
          Bibliography entry 17).

This index gives an analytical as well as an alphabetical subject approach and a legislative
history of United Nations organs.

Some additional reference tools may be used, for
instance: the Bibliography of the Charter of the
United Nations, published by the United Nations
Library (Bibliography entry 139); the Repertory
of practice of United Nations organs (Bibliography entry 2); the Repertoire of practice of
the Security Council; the Charter of the United

ations, commentary and documents (Bibliography
ntry 26); the Public papers of the Secretaries-
eneral (Bibliography entry 10). When conducting
historical study, it is also useful to keep in
ind the United Nations' organizational and pro-
edural precedents in the League of Nations.
ome examples of works on the League that may
e consulted: Hans Aufricht's Guide to League
f Nations publications, a bibliographical sur-
ey of the work of the League, 1920-1947; F.P.
alters' History of the League of Nations; Mary
va Birchfield's Consolidated catalog of League
f Nations publications offered for sale.

Step 5: consulting the indexes to the documents
of the 1945 Preparatory Commission of
the United Nations:

(a) the Index to documents of the United Nations
Preparatory Commission, 1945-1946 (Archives
reference guide No. 1; ST/CGS/SER.A/1) and (b)
Index to documents of the United Nations Preparatory Commission, Executive Committee, 1945 (Archives reference guide No. 2; ST/CGS/SER.A/2).
See Bibliography entries 11-14 for a listing of
the publications of the Preparatory Commission.

Step 6: determining (or, at least, making an
informed guess) which organs deal with the subject of research.

This process may begin with consulting one or
more of the following sources: Yearbook of the
United Nations (Bibliography entry 46); W. Chamberlin's A chronology and fact book of the United Nations, 1941-1976 (Bibliography entry 21);
Everyman's United Nations (Bibliography entries
44-45); the annual Report of the Secretary-
General on the work of the Organization (Bibliography entry 41); reports of the major organs
to the General Assembly: the Economic and Social Council (Bibliography entry 56), the International Court of Justice (Bibliography entry
65), the Security Council (Bibliography entry
82) and the Trusteeship Council (Bibliography
entry 84). It is of value, also, to examine the

available documents of the foreign offices of
various UN member and non-member states; for instance, the series Foreign relations of the Unit
ed States.

Step 7:   ascertaining if there is a series of
          documents on the subject of research.

This step should begin with consulting the Dag
Hammarskjöld Library's List of United Nations
document series symbols (Bibliography entry 129)
which is a guide to large segments of
mimeographed and printed material on all subject
of concern to the United Nations.

Step 8:   consulting publications catalogues in
          order to ascertain whether printed pub-
          lications have appeared on the subject
          of research:

Ten years of United Nations publications, 1945
to 1955 (Bibliography entry 137); Catalogue of
United Nations publications (Bibliography entries 141-142); United Nations publications in
print (Bibliography entry 149); Publications of
the United Nations; general catalogue (Geneva:
United Nations, 1975). In the context of the
present chapter, these catalogues are listed
primarily for subject guidance in research; for
a discussion of acquisitions, see Chapter 21.
It is also useful to peruse the catalogues of
United Nations Official records (see Bibliograph
entries 143-145), H.N.M. Winton's Publications
of the United Nations system (Bibliography entry
156), T.D. Dimitrov's Documents of international
organisations (Bibliography entry 107), and
International bibliography, information, documentation (Bibliography entry 109).

Step 9: consulting the UN monthly chronicle
(Bibliography entry 48) and its predecessors,
the United Nations bulletin (issued January 1950
June 1954) and the United Nations review (issued
July 1954-December 1964).

These periodicals cover all the important activi

ties of the United Nations and include subject indexes.

Step 10:   using the Check lists of United Nations documents (Bibliography entry 140).

Each Check list was devoted to the documents of a particular organ. The Check lists cover documents issued from 1946 to 1953 and fill the gap from the beginnings of the United Nations to the first issue of UNDI (q.v., Step 13).

Step 11:   using the Index notes series to supplement the Check lists, especially for the period 1946-1949.

The Index notes were issued by the then Department of Public Information of the United Nations. To give an example: Index note 16 and its revisions listed Security Council documents.

Step 12:   using the Information papers sub-series of the principal and other organs.

These papers contain various types of useful information. Examples:
   AEC/INF/2/Rev. 2 Series symbols for documents of the Atomic Energy Commission
   A/INF/15 Disposition of agenda items of the second session of the General Assembly
   E/INF/154 Non-governmental organizations in consultative status with the Economic and Social Council in 1976
   A/INF/31/1 Simplification of symbol series and numbering of meetings for the General Assembly and its main committees.

Step 13:   consulting the United Nations documents index and the Indexes to resolutions.

The United Nations documents index (or UNDI, as it is popularly known) is a most important reference tool for the period 1950-1973, making research for that period much simpler than re-

search for the period prior to 1950. See Biblio
raphy   entries 135-136 for more information abou
UNDI.

Three indexes have been issued thus far in the
cumulative Indexes to resolutions series: Index
to resolutions of the General Assembly, 1946-
1970; Index to resolutions and other decisions
of the United Nations Conference on Trade and
Development and of the Trade and Development
Board, 1964-1972; and Index to resolutions of
the Security Council, 1946-1970. These indexes
provide subject guidance to the resolutions as
well as chronological listings. (See Bibliography   entries 108, 126-128 for more information.)

Step 14:   using UNDEX: United Nations documents
           index. UNDEX is the successor of UNDI
           beginning with 1974, although it over-
           laps with UNDI during the years 1970-
           1973. Bibliography entries 130-132
           give more information about UNDEX but
           it may be useful to outline here some
           of the ways in which it differs from
           its predecessor.

While UNDI had been a single index (although
containing various types of information), UNDEX
has been issued in three separate series: Serie
A - subject index; Series B - country index; and
Series C - list of documents issued. UNDEX Series A is somewhat comparable to the "subject
index" portion of UNDI but the former is less
complete than the latter in its coverage (it excludes, for instance, the documents of many important subsidiary organs); further, UNDEX does
not match UNDI's depth of indexing.

For its first few years of publication, UNDEX,
unlike UNDI, had not provided cross references -
a drawback that has now been remedied.

UNDEX Series B is an innovation, potentially useful to researchers who wish to trace the partic-

ipation of a country in particular United Nations activities.

A serious drawback of UNDEX Series A and B has been a lack of cumulations (UNDI had cumulated annually, followed by a commercially published multi-annual cumulation). This is now being remedied: at the time of this writing, annual cumulations of Series A and B for 1975 are in press, and cumulations for 1976 are in preparation.

UNDEX Series C is as complete in its coverage as the checklist portion of UNDI. There is, however, a difference in the publishing pattern: UNDI had been issued eleven times a year, with annual cumulations, while UNDEX Series C is issued ten times a year, with no single annual cumulation. There is, however, a de facto semi-annual cumulation, as follows:

Issues 1 and 6 list documents in the A/- (General Assembly) series

Issues 2 and 7 list documents in the E/- (Economic and Social Council) series

Issues 3 and 8 list documents in the S/- (Security Council) and T/- (Trusteeship Council) series; publications of the International Court of Justice; and sales publications

Issues 4 and 9 list documents in the ST/- (Secretariat series and in the series of the regional commissions: E/CEPAL/- (E/CN.12/-), E/ECA/- (E/CN.14/-), E/ECE/- , E/ECWA/- and E/ESCAP/- (E/CN.11/-)

Issues 5 and 10 list documents issued by other UN organs or bodies (UNCTAD, UNIDO, UNICEF, UNDP, Disarmament Commission, etc.); issue 10 also contains a consolidated list of periodicals.

Wishing to combine the best features of UNDI and UNDEX, the Dag Hammarskjöld Library is now planning to issue a new series of indexes (see Chapter 18 for more information).

Step 15: using the UN monthly chronicle (for the purely subject use of the Chroni-

UNITED NATIONS
NATIONS UNIES

No. 77 / 1

21 July 1977

DAILY LIST OF DOCUMENTS DISTRIBUTED AT HEADQUARTERS
LISTE QUOTIDIENNE DES DOCUMENTS DISTRIBUES AU SIEGE

21 July 1977

[Up to 7 a.m. – Jusqu'à 7 heures]

SYMBOL – COTE	MAIN TITLE – TITRE PRINCIPAL	Arabic Arabe	Chinese Chinois	English Anglais	French Français	Russian Russe	Spanish
	GENERAL ASSEMBLY - DOCUMENTS						
A/32/127	THIRTY-SECOND SESSION - Item 21 of the preliminary list - ELECTION OF SEVEN MEMBERS OF THE COMMITTEE FOR PROGRAMME AND CO-ORDINATION - Note by the Secretary-General	X	X	X	X	X	
A/32/151	Items 30 and 31 of the preliminary list - QUESTION OF PALESTINE - THE SITUATION IN THE MIDDLE EAST - Letter dated 18 July 1977 from the Permanent Representative of Portugal to the United Nations addressed to the Secretary-General	X	X	X	X	X	
A/C.5/32/5	FIFTH COMMITTEE - Item 100 of the preliminary list - PROGRAMME BUDGET FOR THE BIENNIUM 1978-1979 - Impact of inflation on budgets of the organizations of the United Nations system - Report of the Secretary-General		X		X		
A/AC.105/PV.170	COMMITTEE ON THE PEACEFUL USES OF OUTER SPACE - MEETING HELD ON 21 JUNE 1977, 1500			X			
A/AC.154/SR.66	COMMITTEE ON RELATIONS WITH THE HOST COUNTRY - MEETING HELD ON 15 JULY 1977, 1530			X	X		
A/AC.187/SR.1-14/ Corrigendum	PREPARATORY COMMITTEE FOR THE SPECIAL SESSION OF THE GENERAL ASSEMBLY DEVOTED TO DISARMAMENT - MEETINGS HELD FROM 28 MARCH TO 20 MAY 1977			X			
A/AC.188/L.2	AD HOC COMMITTEE ON THE DRAFTING OF AN INTERNATIONAL CONVENTION AGAINST THE TAKING OF HOSTAGES - MATERIAL ON THE TAKING OF HOSTAGES - Document prepared by the Secretariat in pursuance of paragraph 4 of General Assembly resolution 31/103					X	X
A/CN.9/WG.IV/WP.6/Add.2	UNITED NATIONS COMMISSION ON INTERNATIONAL TRADE LAW - Working Group on International Negotiable Instruments - FIFTH SESSION - DRAFT UNIFORM LAW ON INTERNATIONAL BILLS OF EXCHANGE AND INTERNATIONAL PROMISSORY NOTES - (First revision) - Working paper prepared by the Secretariat - Addendum - Articles 51 to 86			X			
A/CONF.62/C.2/L.97	THIRD CONFERENCE ON THE LAW OF THE SEA - SECOND COMMITTEE - Zambia: Revised draft articles in keeping with the Declaration of Developing Land-Locked and other Geographically Disadvantaged States adopted at Kampala in March 1974			X			
	SECURITY COUNCIL - DOCUMENTS						
S/12368	LETTER DATED 20 JULY 1977 FROM THE PERMANENT REPRESENTATIVE OF ANGOLA TO THE UNITED NATIONS ADDRESSED TO THE SECRETARY-GENERAL		X	X	X	X	X
S/RES/413 (1977)	RESOLUTION 413 - Adopted by the Security Council at its 2025th meeting, on 20 July 1977		X	X	X	X	X
	ECONOMIC AND SOCIAL COUNCIL - OFFICIAL RECORDS						
E/5945/Add.1 E/CEPAL/1030/Rev.1/Add.1	SIXTY-THIRD SESSION - ECONOMIC COMMISSION FOR LATIN AMERICA - ANNUAL REPORT - VOLUME II - Supplement No. 11A			X			X

A Page from the *Daily list of documents*

cle, see Step 9).

The Chronicle is a good source of current information: together with many other types of
material, it gives dates of meetings and thus
leads the researcher to documents of the particular organ that deals with the topic of research.

Step 16:   using sources of information for the
period after the date of the latest
issue of the UN monthly chronicle.

The following may serve as sources of information
and guides to the latest documents:
(a) UN press releases. These are produced very
speedily but are at times less accurate than
official United Nations documents (see Chapter
15 for examples of press releases);
(b) the Journal of the United Nations, which
gives: a daily account of meetings held, with
brief summaries of what action was taken; a
listing of meetings to be held; and the documents
used at meetings;
(c) the Daily list of documents distributed at
Headquarters (see Fig. 19 for a sample page).
This is issued with each day's distribution of
the documents themselves and is thus very helpful
in locating very recent documents.

Unfortunately, with a few exceptions, the above-
mentioned three sources are not generally available outside of UN Headquarters.

Step 17:   using secondary material to supplement
United Nations sources.

In searching for current information about United Nations affairs, the following are among the
recommended research tools:
newspapers of record, such as Le monde or the
    New York Times;
current events services and indexes, such as
    Keesing's contemporary archives (see Bibliog-
    raphy entry 33), Facts on file, Deadline data
    on world affairs or PAIS bulletin (see Bibliog-

raphy entry 113);
somewhat less current but more scholarly publications, e.g., <u>International organization</u> (see
  Bibliography entry 32).

An example of the historical approach:
a study of the evolution of the role of the Secretary-General.

(Step 2)   Research may begin with reading the
           relevant portions of the Charter, es-
           pecially Articles 97-101, for general
           guidance.

(Step 4)   Detailed information on the history
           of these Charter provisions will be
           found in the documents of the San
           Francisco Conference.

For the interpretation of Charter provisions,
<u>Charter of the United Nations; commentary and
documents</u> is an excellent source. For a comprehensive summary of United Nations action in
accordance with Charter provisions, the <u>Reper-
tory of practice of United Nations organs</u> is
invaluable. Another useful set is the <u>Public
papers of the Secretaries-General</u>. For a survey
of League of Nations antecedents, documents of
the League and works about the League (such as
F.P. Walters' <u>History of the League of Nations</u>)
should be consulted.

(Step 5)   The documents of the UN Preparatory
           Commission should also be examined.

(Step 6)   For a chronological narrative of
           United Nations activities, including
           activities of the Secretaries-General,
           <u>see</u> the <u>Yearbook of the United Nations</u>
           and the annual <u>Report of the Secretary-
           General</u>. This should be supplemented
           by the annual <u>Introduction to the re-
           port of the Secretary-General</u> (see
           Bibliography entry 42), which contains
           personal observations of the incum-
           bent Secretary-General.

(Step 9)   Consulting the UN monthly chronicle
           will be helpful for current informa-
           tion.

(Step 13) UNDI and the Indexes to resolutions
           will lead the researcher to documents
           of interest, and so will

(Step 14) Series A of UNDEX.

(Step 16) UN press releases, if available, bring
           the researcher up to date.

(Step 17) Secondary material about the UN in
           general and the Secretary-General in
           particular, should be consulted.

The problem-solving approach

        Certain types of research problems,
especially those involving the study of a geographical area or the study of the position of
a member state in United Nations debates, lend
themselves to a step-by-step approach that is
not necessarily historical.

Problem 1:   In searching for documents about a
particular member state or geographical area,
it is necessary to consult various reference
tools, applicable to the time period of interest:
the UN monthly chronicle, publications
catalogues, the Check lists of United Nations
documents, UNDI, UNDEX, the Indexes to resolutions, the Indexes to proceedings (see Bibliography entries 122-125), and other Indexes
described above. (See also 'historical approach'
steps 7-10 and 13-16.)

Problem 2:   In addition to indexes, another good
source of information on national aspects of
particular problems is found in the replies of
governments to questionnaires sent out by the
United Nations. References to these replies
will be found in the Check lists of United Nations documents, UNDI, and UNDEX. (See also
'historical approach' steps 10, 13 and 14.)

Problem 3: Resolutions of various organs often deal with information required from some or all member states in connection with particular subjects; e.g., forced labour, fiscal administration, administration of non-self-governing territories. Resolutions, therefore, should be consulted, with the aid of the Indexes to resolutions where applicable. (See also 'historical approach' step 13.)

Problem 4: The Secretary-General's reports on the implementation of resolutions often note compliance or non-compliance with United Nations requests. These reports may be located by using the Disposition of agenda items prior to 1952 and the Indexes to proceedings thereafter (see Bibliography entries 122-125 for a description of the latter).

Problem 5: General policy statements by a particular government on major world issues may be found in the Official records of the General Assembly. At the beginning of each session of the Assembly, the chief delegate (or, quite often, the foreign minister) of each member state usually makes a statement on his government's views on major issues before the United Nations. These statements appear in the 'meeting records' portion of the Official records under the agenda item "General debate".

Problem 6: To trace implementation of general policy statements by member states in terms of United Nations activities, it is useful to consult the Official records of the principal organs and their sub-organs, with the aid of the catalogues of Official records (see Bibliography entries 143-145) where applicable. The annexes of the Official records (or other annex-type documents) are particularly valuable in the problem-solving approach, as they give a sessional or annual documentary history of items appearing on the agenda of the principal organs. (See Chapter 14 for a detailed description of Official records.)

Problem 7: The Disposition of agenda items and
its successor, Indexes to proceedings, contain
listings of delegations of the member states and
of subjects on which the delegations made statements, with references to specific meetings at
which the statements were made.

Problem 8: To verify how a particular state
voted in United Nations organs, various sources
may be used. One may begin by consulting the
Yearbook of the United Nations and continue with
the meeting records portion of the Official records of the organ in question. For recent
meetings, information about voting on important
issues may be found in the UN monthly chronicle.
Lynn Schopen's Nations on record (Bibliography
entry 116) is a chronological listing of roll-
call votes at plenary meetings of the General
Assembly, 1946 through 1973. Beginning with the
Assembly's thirtieth session (1975), the Index
to proceedings of the General Assembly includes
an annex containing a voting chart of resolutions
adopted by recorded or roll-call vote. Beginning with 1976, the Index to proceedings of the
Security Council includes an annex containing a
voting chart of resolutions adopted by the Council during the year covered.

Problem 9: To trace a specific subject, e.g.,
transnational ("multinational") corporations,
one may begin with UNDEX Series A (Subject index)
and its predecessor, the UNDI Subject index.
These two indexes will refer to many, though
not all, relevant documents which can then be
consulted: reports and working documents of the
Commission on Transnational Corporations, Official records of the Economic and Social Council
and of the General Assembly (use the Indexes to
proceedings of these two organs). Consult the
annual reports (and, if available, the working
documents) of the regional commissions and of
other organs interested in transnationals:
UNCTAD, UNIDO, etc.

Problem 10: To ascertain whether the General
Assembly or the Security Council adopted a res-

olution on a particular question and to find
the text of the resolution, consult the cumulative Indexes to resolutions of the General Assem
bly and the Security Council for the period
1946-1970. For 1971 and subsequent years, consult the Indexes to proceedings or the UNDI Subject index and its successor, the UNDEX Subject
index. Find the text of the resolution in the
collected sessional edition of the resolutions
in the Official records of the General Assembly
and the collected annual edition of the resolutions of the Security Council. For very recent
resolutions, consult the mimeographed document
containing the individual resolution of the
General Assembly (under the symbol A/[session
number]/RES/-) and the Security Council (S/
RES/-   ). Detailed information on action
leading to the resolution and on related documents issued can be found with the help of the
Index to proceedings of the General Assembly
and of the Security Council.

Problem 11: To find a full bibliographic descri
tion of a particular document, consult UNDEX
Series C (List of documents issued) and its
predecessor, the UNDI cumulative checklist. For
1946-1949 documents, consult Check lists of
United Nations documents.

Conclusions on the step-process (historical and
problem-solving)

As mentioned above, only some of the
steps described in this chapter will be needed
for most types of research. Only the individual
researcher can determine which processes are
appropriate to a particular research problem.

As a general rule, it is important to
avoid unnecessary duplication. For instance, in
'historical approach' step 6, the researcher
would not need to consult both the Yearbook of
the United Nations and the Report of the Secretary-General for the same year. The latter is
a relatively brief narrative while the former
is very detailed but appears after a considerabl

time-lag. It follows that the Secretary-General's report should be used only as an alternative for recent years for which the Yearbook is not yet available.

It is often possible to find short-cuts in one's research. The following two sequences are suggested as typical short-cuts:

1. For a historical survey:
(A) Step 7: List of United Nations document series symbols
(B) Step 8: Publications catalogues
(C) Step 10: Check lists of United Nations documents
(D) Step 13: UNDI
(E) Step 14: UNDEX

2. For a 'problem-solving' or mixed approach:
(A) Everyman's United Nations, to find the particular UN organ or activity and the time period relevant to the research problem;
(B) Yearbook of the United Nations, for greater detail;
(C) Report of the Secretary-General, or reports of the other principal organs, to the General Assembly, for more recent information;
(D) UN monthly chronicle, for the most recent material.

Specialized research tools to supplement the general sources introduced above:

(a) Statistical sources. The United Nations Statistical Office and other United Nations bodies issue numerous statistical yearbooks, periodicals, monographs on statistical methodology, and other statistical series and studies, all of which are valuable to researchers. (See Chapter 13 and Bibliography entries 90-99 for more detail about many of these publications.)

Example of the use of statistical sources: to find statistics on international trade between two specific countries and/or in a specific commodity, consult the Yearbook of inter-

national trade statistics, the Commodity trade
statistics, the World trade annual, and the
Handbook of international trade and development
statistics. For very recent data, information
may be found (although in less detail) in the
Monthly bulletin of statistics.

(b) Legal sources. The most important series
are:
United Nations Treaty series and its cumulative
  indexes (see Bibliography entries 87 and 118,
  respectively, for more detail);
Statement of treaties and international agreements registered or filed and recorded with
  the Secretariat (see Bibliography entry 89)
  This is a guide to legal instruments whose
  texts have not yet been published in the
  Treaty series;
International tax agreements. This is a comprehensive compilation of tax agreements concluded since 1843. Volume 8, World guide to international tax agreements, is a tabular index to this looseleaf service;
Multilateral treaties in respect of which the
  Secretary-General performs depositary functions (see Bibliography entry 88);
United Nations legislative series (see Bibliography entry 67);
Publications of the International Court of Justice: Reports of judgments, advisory opinions
  and orders; Pleadings, oral arguments, documents; Acts and documents concerning the organization of the Court; Yearbook; Bibliography of the International Court of Justice.

    Example of the use of legal sources:
to ascertain whether a particular state signed
or ratified a treaty or an agreement, consult
Multilateral treaties in respect of which the
Secretary-General performs depositary functions.
This will also indicate the volume and page
number of the Treaty series where the text of
the treaty or agreement can be found. For information about more recent (or recently modi-
fied) treaties, consult the Statement of treaties
and international agreements registered or filed
and recorded with the Secretariat.

CHAPTER 20

HOW TO CITE UNITED NATIONS PUBLICATIONS

There are no uniform standards of style
to be followed when citing United Nations publications in bibliographies, footnotes and other
references. The United Nations itself uses a
style manual[43] supplemented by editorial direc-
tives issued from time to time by the Secretariat.
An especially important editorial directive on
the subject of footnotes and other references
was issued in 1973.[44] Another useful citation
guide was prepared by M.H. Rothman.[45]

Turabian's manual[46] and the Anglo-

---

[43] United Nations, Dag Hammarskjöld
Library, Bibliographical style manual
(Bibliography entry 121).

[44] United Nations, Secretariat, Editorial
directive [on footnotes and other
references] (New York, 8 June 1973;
ST/CS/SER.A/14).

[45] Marie H. Rothman, Citation rules and
forms for United Nations documents
and publications (Bibliography entry
114).

[46] Kate L. Turabian, A manual for writers
of term papers, theses, and dissertations (3d, rev. ed. Chicago: University of Chicago Press, 1967.)

American cataloguing rules[47] now incorporating, in a revised chapter 6,[48] the International Standard Bibliographic Descriptions (monographs) [ISBD (M)] are highly recommended.

The following rules and examples are condensed from editorial directive ST/CS/SER.A/1 (<u>supra</u>, footnote 44):

<u>Footnote references to mimeographed documents</u>

(a) A direct reference to a mimeographed document is normally made by inserting the document series symbol in parentheses in the text, following the words to be referenced. The following abbreviations should be used, as appropriate:

chapter, chapters	chap., chaps.
number, numbers	No., Nos.
page, pages	p., pp.
paragraph, paragraphs	para., paras.
section, sections	sect., sects.
volume, volumes	vol., vols.

Examples:
<u>Official records of the General Assembly</u>
<u>Twenty-fifth Session, Supplement No. 3,</u>
chap. X, paras. 447-451.

. . . in the report of the Special Committee (A/8081, para.6)

The following terms should not be abbreviated:

resolution
part
document

---

[47] <u>Anglo-American cataloging rules</u> (Chicago: American Library Association, 1967).

[48] <u>_____, Chapter 6: Separately published monographs</u> (Chicago: American Library Association, 1974).

preamble
annex
Article(s) (of the Charter of the United
    Nations)
Supplement

(b) An indirect reference or one that
would cause an awkward interruption in the con-
tinuity of the text should be given in a footnote. Example:

"Research had provided some evidence to support
that study."*

*See also E/CN ..../0000; and E/CN....
    /0001, chap. II.

Footnote references to United Nations publications

In references to United Nations publications, the full title, underlined or italic,
should be given either in the text,* if convenient, or in the footnote.** In the latter case,
the indication of the sales number should appear
in parentheses. Examples:

". . . in the 1967 Report on the world social
situation."*

* United Nations publication, Sales
    No. E.68.IV.9.

** 1967 Report on the world social
    situation (United Nations publica-
    tion, Sales No. E.68.IV.9).

Footnote references to a specific chapter in a publication

The title of a chapter to which specific
reference is made should be given in a footnote
only if necessary; it should not be given if it
appears, quoted exactly or not, in the text.
Examples:

". . . a study of the determinants of labour
supply in Europe in the period 1950-1980,"*

  *   Economic survey of Europe in 1968:
      the European economy in 1968 (United
      Nations publication, Sales No.
      E.69.II.E.1), chap. III.

". . . in a study published in 1969."**

  ** Economic survey of Europe in 1968:
      the European economy in 1968 (United
      Nations publication, Sales No.
      E.69.II.E.1), chap. III, "Determi-
      nants of labour supply in Europe,
      1950-1980".

Footnote references to signed articles in United
   Nations periodicals

      Signed articles in United Nations peri-
odicals are treated in the same way as articles
in any other periodical. Example:
      La C. Verman, "Standardization in a
      developing economy," Industrialization
      and productivity, Bulletin 7 (United
      Nations publication, Sales No. 64.II.B.1
      p. 39.

Footnote references to Official records

      References to documents or meeting
records that appear in the various Official
records series of United Nations organs should
be given in footnotes. Footnotes referring to
Official records comprise the following four
elements:
      (1) Series (e.g., Official records of
           the General Assembly)
      (2) Session
      (3) Volume (e.g., Plenary meetings,
           Annexes, Supplements)
      (4) Special reference within the volume
           (meeting, paragraph, document
           symbol)

Example:

> Official records of the Economic and
> Social Council, Fifty-second Session,
> Supplement No. 3, chap. III.

The document symbol or meeting number
may appear either in the text, preceding the
footnote indicator, or in the footnote itself.
Example:

". . . that his delegation would have preferred
 the original draft"*

> * Official records of the General
>   Assembly, Twenty-fifth Session,
>   Annexes, agenda items 27, 28, 29,
>   30, 31, 93 and 94, document A/8191.

When a meeting number is referred to, a
footnote giving the Official records reference,
if any, should be given if the session is not
made clear in the text. Example:

"The Committee had considered the question at
 its 1470th meeting."*

> * Official records of the General
>   Assembly, Twenty-first Session,
>   First Committee.

If there are repeated references to a meeting
record that has been reproduced in the Official
records, a footnote giving the full reference
should be inserted the first time the number
appears in the text but not thereafter.

The existence of addenda or corrigenda
should be indicated. Examples:

> Official records of the General Assembly,
> Twenty-fifth Session, Supplement No. 8A,
> document A/8008/Add. 13.

> Official records of the General Assembly,
> Twenty-fifth Session, Supplement No. 8
> and corrigenda.

Further examples of correct footnote references to <u>Official records</u> are given below:

GENERAL ASSEMBLY

1. Meeting records (plenary):
    <u>Official records of the General Assembly</u>
    <u>First part of First Session, Plenary</u>
    <u>meetings</u>, 17th meeting.

2. Meeting records (committee):
    <u>Official records of the General Assembly</u>
    <u>Third Session, Part II, Fifth Committee,</u>
    182d meeting.

3. Supplements:
    <u>Official records of the General Assembly</u>
    <u>Second part of First Session, Supplement</u>
    No. 2, chap. III, para. 79.

4. Annexes:
    <u>Official records of the General Assembly</u>
    <u>Fourth Session, Sixth Committee, Annex,</u>
    document A/997, para. 26.

5. <u>Official records of the General Assembly</u>
    <u>Fifth Session, Annexes</u>, agenda item 3,
    document A/C.3/172.

6. <u>Official records of the General Assembly</u>
    <u>Nineteenth Session, Annexes</u>, annex No.
    21, document A/5721.

SECURITY COUNCIL

1. Meeting records:
    <u>Official records of the Security Council,</u>
    <u>Third Year, No. 97</u>, 337th meeting.

2. <u>Official records of the Security Council,</u>
    <u>Eleventh Year</u>, 749th meeting, para.3.

3. Supplements:
    <u>Official records of the Security Council,</u>
    <u>Ninth Year, Supplement for January,</u>

February and March 1954, document S/3185.

ECONOMIC AND SOCIAL COUNCIL

1. Annexes:
Official records of the Economic and
Social Council, Ninth Session, Annex,
p. 292, document E/1400.

2. Official records of the Economic and
Social Council, Eleventh Session,
Annexes, agenda item 24, document E/1660.

3. Meeting records:
Official records of the Economic and
Social Council, Resumed Eighteenth
Session, 834th meeting.

4. Official records of the Economic and
Social Council, Twenty-eighth Session,
1071st meeting.

5. Supplements:
Official records of the Economic and
Social Council, Twenty-fourth Session,
Supplement No. 3, chap. II.

TRUSTEESHIP COUNCIL

1. Supplements:
Official records of the Trusteeship
Council, Fifth Special Session,
Supplement No. 2.

2. Meeting records:
Official records of the Trusteeship
Council, Twenty-second Session, 909th
meeting.

DISARMAMENT COMMISSION

Supplements:
Official records of the Disarmament

Commission, Supplement for January to
December 1965, document DC/227, para. 3.

Footnote references to resolutions

References to resolutions of the General
Assembly, the Security Council, the Economic and
Social Council, and the Trusteeship Council
should be made as in the following examples:

"The Economic and Social Council, by its resolution 1535 (XLIX), had established a Standing
Committee on Natural Resources composed of 27
members."   [No footnote reference.]

"No agreement has yet been reached on liability
for damage caused by the launching of objects
into outer space, though the General Assembly
has on several occasions indicated the importance it attaches to this question."*

*   For instance, in resolutions 2260
(XXII) of 3 November 1967 and 2600
(XXIV) of 16 December 1969.

In references to resolutions of subsidiary or ad hoc bodies, it may be useful to infor
the reader where the text appears. Examples:

"By its resolution 2 (XXIV), the Sub-Commission
had decided that the working group . . ."*

*   E/CN.4/1070, chap. XII.

"The Commission on the Status of Women, by its
resolution 3 (XXIII), had made recommendations
concerning the appointment of qualified women
to the highest ranks of the international civil
service."**

** Official records of the Economic and
Social Council, Forty-eighth Session,
Supplement No. 6, chap. XII.

Footnote references to records of the International Law Commission

The printed records of the International Law Commission appear in yearbooks, volume I of each Yearbook containing records of the Commission's sessions and volume II containing documents. In the years before 1962, volumes I and II bore the same sales number, followed by the indication "Vol. I" or "Vol. II". Since 1962 a different sales number has been assigned to each volume, and the volume number is no longer part of the sales number. Examples:

Yearbook of the International Law Commission, 1959, vol. II (United Nations publication, Sales No. 59.V.1, Vol. II).

Yearbook of the International Law Commission, 1969, vol. II (United Nations publication, Sales No. E.70.V.8).

Footnote references to the United Nations Treaty series

References to instruments printed in the United Nations Treaty series may be made by volume and page number. It is not necessary to give the year of the volume, which often is many years later than the year of the instrument referred to; nor is it necessary to give the number of the instrument. If the reference is to the instrument as a whole, the page reference should be to the page on which it starts; if the reference is to a specific part of the instrument, the corresponding page number(s) should be given. Examples:

". . . the Egyptian-Israeli General Armistice Agreement, signed at Rhodes on 24 February 1949."*

* United Nations, Treaty series, vol. 42, p. 251.

". . . in article 8 of the Trade Agreement between the Kingdom of Greece and the Republic of Cyprus."**

>   ** United Nations, <u>Treaty series</u>, vol. 609, p. 24.

If the title of the instrument referred to is not given in the text, it should be given in the footnote. Example:

> Convention on the Settlement of Investment Disputes between States and Nationals of Other States (United Nations, <u>Treaty series</u>, vol. 575, p. 159

<u>Footnote references to reports of a United Nations seminar</u>

Examples:

1. <u>Technico-economic, organizational and administrative aspects of inland water-borne transport: Report of the United Nations Interregional Symposium, Leningrad, 9-29 September 1968</u> (ST/TAO/SER.C/114).

2. <u>Seminar on the Effects of Scientific and Technological Developments on the Status of Women, Iasi, Romania, 5-18 August 196</u> (ST/TAO/HR/37).

3. <u>Report of the Interregional Seminar on the Training of Professional and Voluntary Youth Leaders, Holte, Denmark, 6-22 October 1969</u> (United Nations publication, Sales No. E.70.II.H.4).

<u>Footnote references to proceedings of a United Nations conference</u>

References to volumes of the proceedings of a United Nations conference should include the title as it appears on the title page, the volume number and title, if there is more than one volume, the United Nations publication sales

umber, and, if necessary, the precise reference
n the volume. Example:

> Proceedings of the World Population
> Conference, Belgrade, 30 August-10
> September 1965, vol. I. Summary report
> (United Nations publication, Sales No.
> 66.XIII.5), meeting B.5, "Projections
> of urban and rural population, economi-
> cally active population, households
> and families," Statement by the
> Moderator, pp. 272-279.

References to papers contributed to the
conference should include the name of the author,
the title of the paper within quotation marks,
the title of the proceedings, the volume number
and title, the sales number, and the page number
s) in the volume.

Footnote references to the 'Statistical papers' series

Examples:
1. Population and vital statistics report:
   data available as of 1 January 1971,
   Statistical papers, series A, vol.
   XXIII, No. 1 (ST/STAT/SER.A/95).

2. Methodology of demographic sample
   surveys, Statistical papers, series
   M, No. 51 (United Nations publication,
   Sales No. E.71.XVII.11).

Footnote references to the Monthly bulletin of statistics

Example:
> Monthly bulletin of statistics, vol.
> XXXI, No. 6 (June 1977).

Footnote references to the Report of the Preparatory Commission of the United Nations

Example:
> Report of the Preparatory Commission

<u>of the United Nations</u> (PC/20), chap.
VIII, sect. 2, paras. 59-60.

Footnote references to documents of the San Francisco Conference, 1945

References to official documents (mimeographed or printed) of the United Nations Conference on International Organization, held in San Francisco in 1945, should be by symbol only. Example:

United Nations Conference on International Organization, II/1/34.

References to unofficial (typewritten) verbatim minutes should give the name of the organ, the date of the meeting, the number of the bound volume and the page number. Example:

United Nations Conference on International Organization, Steering Committee, 5 May 1945, vol. 68, p.13.

Footnote references to advisory opinions of the International Court of Justice

In references to advisory opinions of the International Court of Justice, the title should be cited as shown on the verso of the front cover of the volume referred to. Example:

<u>Certain expenses of the United Nations
(Article 17, paragraph 2, of the
Charter), Advisory opinion of 20 July
1962: I.C.J. Reports 1962</u>, p. 151.

Listing of United Nations documents in bibliographies

In "mixed" bibliographies, listing United Nations documents and other material (books published by commercial publishers, government publications, etc.) the words "United Nations" should appear in the author position, that is,

t the beginning of each entry. The following
nformation should also be given, as appropriate,
n the order shown: the name of the organ or
ffice responsible for issuing the document; the
itle (initial capital letters being used only
or the first word and for proper nouns); the
ate of publication; the pagination; the document
eries symbol in parentheses; a reference to the
fficial records in which the document appears.
he following information should also appear, as
ppropriate: the distribution classification
if "Limited"); the United Nations publication
ales number; the title and symbol of the Year-
ook of the International Law Commission.
xamples:

.   United Nations. Department of Economic
    and Social Affairs. World economic
    survey, 1960. 1961. 237 p. (United
    Nations publication, Sales No. 61.II.C.1)

.   United Nations. Economic Commission for
    Asia and the Far East. Contribution of
    rural community development programmes
    to national economic development; note
    by the Executive Secretary. 24 January
    1961. 5 p. (E/CN.11/L.96) Limited
    distribution.

3. United Nations. General Assembly. Report
    of the Secretary-General on the work of
    the Organization, 16 June 1960-15 June
    1961. 1961. 181 p. (Official records
    of the General Assembly, Sixteenth Session,
    Supplement No. 1)

    In a bibliography that lists United
Nations publications and/or documents only, they
could be arranged by symbol, in alphanumerical
order. The same information should be given as
indicated above, except that the document series
symbol, taking the place of the author, should
be indicated by a subheading in the listing.
Examples:

United Nations General Assembly

A/4427. Comprehensive review of the
United Nations Joint Staff Pension
Fund; Report of the Pension Review
Group. 5 August 1960. 54 p. (Official
records of the General Assembly, Fifteent
Session, Annexes, agenda item 63)

United Nations Economic and Social Council

E/3525-E/ICEF/431. United Nations
Children's Fund. Report of the Executive
Board, 8-19 June 1961. [1961.] 54 p.
(Official records of the Economic and
Social Council, Thirty-second Session,
Supplement No. 13B)

CHAPTER 21

HOW TO OBTAIN UNITED NATIONS PUBLICATIONS

Distribution categories

For purposes of distribution, United Nations documents are classified in several categories:

(a) General distribution: basic documents, final meeting records, resolutions and other decisions of main organs, studies and reports, etc. These documents receive the widest distribution.

(b) Limited distribution: documents of temporary or ephemeral nature, e.g., draft resolutions, draft reports, papers relating to agenda. These documents are produced in smaller quantities than those for general distribution and are distributed only to official recipients and others "likely to be immediately interested in the work of the body concerned".[49] The contents of many "limited distribution" documents eventually find their way into "general distribution" documents such as the final report of the body to which they were first submitted. The Readex Microprint edition of United Nations documents (see Bibliography entry 16) includes many "limited distribution" items. (See Fig. 20 for an example of a "limited distribution" document.)

————————[49] United Nations, Dag Hammarskjöld Library, United Nations documentation; a brief guide for official recipients (New York, 1974; ST/LIB/34), p. 10.

UNITED NATIONS

ECONOMIC
AND
SOCIAL COUNCIL

Distr.
LIMITED

E/CONF.69/L.14
23 June 1977

ENGLISH ONLY

THIRD UNITED NATIONS CONFERENCE ON THE
  STANDARDIZATION OF GEOGRAPHICAL NAMES
Athens, 17 August-7 September 1977
Item 15 (b) of the provisional agenda.
  Writing Systems: (b) Writing of names
  from unwritten languages.

THE TREATMENT OF TOPONYMS IN MANITOBA FROM
LANGUAGES WITHOUT AN ALPHABET*

Paper presented by Canada

* Paper prepared by Michael Munro, head of field research for the Toponymy
Division, Surveys and Mapping Branch, Department of Energy, Mines and Resources,
Ottawa.

(c) Restricted distribution: "documents and
meeting records whose contents require at the
time of issuance that they not be made public.
The distribution of these documents and records
is determined by the originating office".[50]
Having met certain conditions, such as the
passage of time, many "restricted distribution"
documents are subsequently derestricted. At
present, the United Nations does not make these
derestricted documents widely available, although
such documents may be consulted in libraries of
United Nations organizations. The United Nations
Development Programme is one of the exceptions:
it regularly lists its derestricted project
reports (see supra, Chapter 15).

(d) Other distribution categories include "For
participants only":
provisional documents (unrevised, uncorrected
    texts issued to participants of meetings and
    some others, and later reissued as formal
    documents);
working papers;
conference room papers;
other informal documents.

Types of distribution

(a) Official distribution. The United Nations
distributes its documents and other publications
to permanent missions of the member states,
permanent observers, ministries and other
governmental addresses of member and non-member
states; the press and other information media;
the United Nations Secretariat, including the
libraries; other organs of the United Nations;
international governmental and non-governmental
organizations; specialized agencies and other
related organizations; United Nations information centres; depository libraries (more information on depository libraries is given
below).

──────────[50] Ibid.

(b) <u>Depository libraries</u>. "In order to make its
documents and publications available throughout
the world, the United Nations maintains a system
of depository libraries."[51] Depository libraries
are designated by the United Nations Publication
Board on the advice of the director of the Dag
Hammarskjöld Library and according to specific
criteria. Depository libraries receive "general
distribution" material in the official language
of their choice. Deposit may be partial
(<u>Official records</u> of the major organs, sales
publications, subscription periodicals, the
<u>Treaty series</u>, and certain mimeographed documents)
or full (in addition to the above types of publications, full depositories are entitled to all
generally distributed UN documents and publications, whether printed, mimeographed, or reproduced by offset). The annual growth of holdings
is 10-14 linear feet of shelf-space for a partial
depository collection and 18-20 linear feet for
a full depository.

     Depository libraries are expected "to
place the material received in the care of
qualified library staff, to keep it in good
order and to make it accessible to the public,
free of charge, at reasonable hours"[52] and to
fulfil other conditions of deposit. Since 1
January 1975 most depositories have been required to pay an annual contribution: full
depositories in developing countries, U.S. $300
per year; partial depositories, $200 per year;
full depositories in developed countries, $800
per year; partial depositories, $500 per year.
Table XII lists depository libraries as of
January 1977.

―――――――――[51]
     United Nations, Secretariat, <u>Instruc-</u>
     <u>tions for depository libraries</u>
     <u>receiving United Nations material</u>
     (New York, 31 March 1977; ST/LIB/13/
     Rev.3), Annex I, p. 1.

[52] <u>Ibid</u>., Annex I, pp. 2-3.

c) <u>Standing order service</u>. This service was
established by the United Nations in order to
enable purchasers to receive a continuous supply
of recurrent titles, series or other types of
United Nations publications. There are five
types of standing orders:

over-all: includes publications in all subject
   categories, UNICEF publications and <u>Official</u>
   <u>records</u>. Excludes mimeographed documents,
   subscription periodicals and International
   Court of Justice publications. The annual
   cost varies: in 1976, the cost of an over-all
   standing order was around U.S. $3,000;

subject-category: standing orders may be placed
   for one or more subject categories (for a
   description of subject categories and of
   sales numbers in general, <u>see supra</u>, Chapter
   13) or for the <u>Official records</u> of one or more
   United Nations organs;

title and series: one or more recurrent titles
   (e.g., <u>Yearbook of the United Nations, Indexes</u>
   <u>to proceedings, World economic survey, Statis-</u>
   <u>tical yearbook for Asia and the Pacific,</u>
   <u>Resolutions of the General Assembly, United</u>
   <u>Nations legislative series</u>) may be obtained
   on standing order;

mimeographed documents: certain classes of
   mimeographed documents (e.g., those of the
   Security Council and the Disarmament Commission) may be purchased, in English, on annual
   subscription;

International Court of Justice publications:
   one or more series (Reports, Pleadings,
   Bibliography, Yearbook) are available on
   standing order.

(d) <u>Subscription periodicals</u>. The following
United Nations periodicals are available on
subscription as of 1977:

Monthly bulletin of statistics
Commodity trade statistics
Statistical indicators of short term economic
    changes in ECE countries
Industrial research and development news
Population and vital statistics report
Bulletin on narcotics
Current bibliographical information (Dag
    Hammarskjöld Library)
UN monthly chronicle
Objective: justice
Monthly bibliography; a subject compilation of
    newly acquired books, official documents and
    periodicals (formerly: Monthly list of books,
    catalogued in the [Geneva] Library of the
    United Nations)
Monthly list of selected articles (Geneva
    Library of the United Nations)
UNDEX; United Nations documents index

Availability of sales publications and other
United Nations material

        All sales publications in print may be
obtained from:

United Nations   or   United Nations
    Publications   Publications
Room A-3315   Palais des Nations
New York,   1211 Geneva 10
N.Y.   10017   Switzerland
U.S.A.

or from booksellers and sales agents for United
Nations publications throughout the world.
Detailed information about all sales items, with
current prices, is available from United Nations
Publications.

        The average in-print time for sales pub-
lications is five to seven years. Mimeographed
documents remain available for two years, as a
rule. Official records are usually available
for five years, except for resolutions which
are kept in stock on a continuing basis.

Some out-of-print United Nations publications may be obtained in reprint from:

Kraus Reprint Corporation
Route 100
Millwood
New York   10546
U.S.A.

Catalogues are available on request from Kraus.

Newsletters, information bulletins and other publications of various United Nations organs that are not available through regular sales channels may sometimes be obtained by writing to the issuing organ, e.g.:

Documents and Publishing Section
Economic Commission for Africa
P.O. Box 3001
Addis Ababa, Ethiopia

Documents and Sales Publications
Economic Commission for Latin America
Edificio Naciones Unidas
Avenida Dag Hammarskjöld, Casilla 179-D
Santiago, Chile

Documents Reproduction Unit
Economic and Social Commission for Asia
   and the Pacific
Sala Santitham, Rajadamnern Avenue
Bangkok, Thailand

Documents Officer
Economic Commission for Western Asia
P.O. Box 35099
Amman, Jordan

Distribution and Sales Section
United Nations Office at Geneva
Palais des Nations
1211 Geneva 10, Switzerland
(for Economic Commission for Europe and
   UNCTAD material)

The Registrar
International Court of Justice
Peace Palace
The Hague, 2012, Netherlands

Documents Distribution Service
United Nations Industrial Development
   Organization
Felderhaus, Room F-724
Rathausplatz 2
A-1010 Vienna, Austria

United Nations publications in microform (see also Chapter 16). Official records of the General Assembly and of the three Councils, the Treaty series, the Repertory of practice of United Nations organs and many of the yearbooks and other publications are obtainable from United Nations Publications on 105 mm x 148 mm negative microfiche at a reduction of 20:1, each fiche containing 60 frames. Microfiche is also available from Unifo, Publishers, Inc., P.O. Box 89, White Plains, New York 10605, U.S.A. Unifo will supply catalogues on request.

The Archives Section of the United Nations microfilmed large sets of United Nations documents from 1947 to 1968. Films of unrestric ed documents are available from United Nations Publications on roll microfilm (each reel a 100 feet of 16 mm unperforated safety film).

The Readex Microprint Corporation has produced microprints of United Nations documents (see Bibliography entry 16). They are available from: Readex Microprint Publications, 5 Union Square, New York, New York 10003, U.S.A.

Other commercial firms have microfilmed certain types of United Nations documents. For instance, derestricted UNDP country project reports can be purchased, on microfiche, from University Microfilms, Inc., 300 North Zeeb Road, Ann Arbor, Michigan 48106, U.S.A.

Sound recordings have been taken of meetings of

United Nations organs, press conferences and events relating to United Nations functions and activities (see also Chapter 16). Some of these disks and tapes may be available from United Nations, Archives Section, New York, New York 10017, U.S.A.

16 mm motion pictures and television programmes have been produced by the United Nations from the beginning of the existence of the Organization (see also Chapter 16). Films are available world-wide, for purchase or rental, from the following sources:

in Canada: Cinemedia, Ltd.
P.O. Box 332
Agincourt, Ontario

in the U.S.A.: FMS Films, Inc.
P.O. Box 7316
Alexandria, Virginia 22307
(rental)

Great Plains National Instructional Television Library
P.O. Box 80669
Lincoln, Nebraska 68501
(purchase and rental: Man builds, man destroys series only)

Journal Films, Inc.
930 Pitner Avenue
Evanston, Illinois 60202
(purchase)

McGraw-Hill Films
1221 Avenue of the Americas
New York, New York 10020
(purchase and rental)

New York University Film Library
26 Washington Place
New York, New York 10003
(rental)

Sterling Educational Films
241 East 34th Street
New York, New York 10016
(purchase)

Films may also be purchased direct from the
Radio and Visual Services Division, United
Nations, New York, New York, 10017.

In other countries, selected United
Nations films are available on loan from United
Nations information centres. (See Chapter 12
for a description and list of information
centres.)

Acquisition tools. The following catalogues
and other sources are useful:
Ten years of United Nations publications, 1945
  to 1955 (Bibliography entry 137)
Catalogue [of] United Nations publications, 1967
  (Bibliography entry 141)
Catalogue [of] United Nations publications,
  1968-69 (Bibliography entry 142)
United Nations publications in print; a check-
  list (Bibliography entry 149)
United Nations Official records, 1948-62
  (Bibliography entry 143)
United Nations Official records, 1962-70 and
  Supplement, 1970-72 (Bibliography entries
  144-145)
Publications of the International Court of
  Justice (Bibliography entry 138)
UNDEX; United Nations documents index. Series
  C: list of documents issued (Bibliography
  entry 132)
Microfiche (price-list) (Bibliography entry 148)

Most of the above-mentioned catalogues
and lists are available from United Nations
Publications, sales agents and other booksellers
(some may no longer be in print but may be consulted at depository and other libraries).

Index to microfilm of United Nations documents
  in English (Bibliography entries 119-120).
  The two issues of this index cover 1946-1967.

Catalogue of sound recordings (Bibliography
   entry 146)
United Nations 16 mm film catalogue, 1975-76
   (Bibliography entry 147)
International bibliography, information, doc-
   umentation (Bibliography entry 109)
UNDP business bulletin
UNDP project reports: reports derestricted.

The last two publications are available from:

>   United Nations Development Programme
>   Information Division
>   1 United Nations Plaza
>   New York, New York 10017
>   U.S.A.

When consulting any of the above, it is
essential to remember that prices are subject
to change. United Nations Publications (see
supra for New York and Geneva addresses) will
supply current prices on request.

What to acquire

B. Brimmer defines large, medium and
small collections of United Nations documents
and publications as follows:

>   Large collection: from one receiving and
>   processing all printed and mimeographed
>   material in one or more languages to one
>   receiving and processing all printed items
>   in one language.

>   Medium collection: from one receiving the
>   printed Official records of all the main
>   organs, plus selected sales . . . items
>   to one receiving a selection of about 100
>   items a year.

>   Small collection: from one receiving about
>   a dozen book-sized items and two periodicals
>   to one limited to a selection of less than
>   half a dozen items a year.[53]

──────────[53] B. Brimmer, op, cit., p. 91.

While large collections (generally depository libraries) are fairly comprehensive and medium collections are developed according to the specific needs of the institution (such as curricula in the case of universities), small collections consist of a selection of basic material. Individuals would acquire United Nations publications even more selectively: they may, for example, want to own Everyman's United Nations or Basic facts about the United Nations and subscribe to the UN monthly chronicle.

The following is a suggested list of basic material for a small collection in a library or other institution:

Primary material

Yearbook of the United Nations (Bibliography entry 46)

Everyman's United Nations (Bibliography entries 44-45)

Statistical yearbook (Bibliography entry 95) or World statistics in brief (Bibliography entry 96)

World economic survey (Bibliography entry 54)

UN monthly chronicle (Bibliography entry 48)

Basic facts about the United Nations (Bibliography entry 43)

Report of the Secretary-General on the work of the Organization (Bibliography entry 41)

and one or more of the following:

Report of the Economic and Social Council (Bibliography entry 56)

Report of the Security Council (Bibliography entry 82)

Report of the Trusteeship Council (Bibliography entry 84)

Proposed programme budget for the biennium (Bibliography entry 40)

Medium-term plan . . . (Bibliography entry 38)

Demographic yearbook (Bibliography entry 90)

Yearbook on human rights (Bibliography entry 61)

Yearbook of the International Court of Justice

Handbook of international trade and development statistics (Bibliography entry 99)
Economic survey of Europe
Economic bulletin for Europe
Economic and social survey of Asia and the Pacific
Economic bulletin for Asia and the Pacific
Economic survey of Latin America
CEPAL review (formerly: Economic bulletin for Latin America)
Economic survey of Africa
Economic bulletin for Africa

Secondary material
Annual review of United Nations affairs (Bibliography entry 19)
International organization (Bibliography entry 32)
Chamberlin, A chronology and fact book of the United Nations (Bibliography entry 21)
Claude, Swords into plowshares (Bibliography entry 23)
Goodrich, Charter of the United Nations; commentary and documents (Bibliography entry 26)
Goodrich, The United Nations in a changing world (Bibliography entry 27)
Sachs, The United Nations; a handbook (Bibliography entry 36)

TABLE XII

UNITED NATIONS DEPOSITORY LIBRARIES

Afghanistan
Kabul University
Library
Kabul

Algeria
Bibliothèque Nationale
d'Algerie
Alger

Argentina
Biblioteca del Congreso
de la Nación
Buenos Aires

Centro de Documentación
Internacional
Buenos Aires

Universidad Nacional de
Córdoba
Biblioteca Mayor
Córdoba

Universidad Nacional de
Cuyo
Mendoza

Biblioteca Argentina
"Dr. Juan Alvarez"
Rosario

Australia
The State Library of
South Australia
Adelaide 5001

State Library of
Queensland
Brisbane 4000

Australian Parliamen-
tary Library
Parliament House
Canberra 2600

National Library of
Australia
Canberra 2600

State Library of
Victoria
Melbourne 3000

State Reference Library
The Library Board of
Western Australia
Perth 6000

The Library of New
South Wales
Sydney 2000

Austria
Österreichische
Nationalbibliothek
A-1014 Wien

ahrain

ahrain Public Libraries
anama

angladesh

acca University Library
acca-2

arbados

niversity of the West
   Indies
ave Hill Campus
ridgetown

elgium

ibliothèque du Parle-
   ment
alais de la Nation
ruxelles

ibliothèque Royale
   Albert ler
000 Bruxelles

Jniversité Catholique
   de Louvain
Bibliothèque Centrale
3000 Louvain

Bolivia

Biblioteca Nacional de
   Bolivia
Sucre

Botswana

National Library of
   Botswana
Gaborone

Brazil

Biblioteca da Câmara
   dos Deputados
Palácio do Congresso
   Nacional
Brasília, D.F.

Biblioteca-Depositária
   das Nações Unidas
Faculdade de Dereito
   da Universidade
   Federal do Rio Grande
   do Sul
90000 Pôrto Alegre

Biblioteca Nacional do
   Río de Janeiro
Río de Janeiro

Fundação de Pesquisas-
   CPE
40000 Salvador, Bahia

Biblioteca Mario de
   Andrade
São Paulo

Bulgaria

Sofiiski Universitet
   "Kliment Ohridsky"
Biblioteka
Sofia

Burma

National Library
Rangoon

Byelorussian Soviet
Socialist Republic

Gosudarstvennaya Bib-
   lioteka BSSR imeni
   V.I. Lenina, Minsk 30

Canada

University of Alberta
The Library
Edmonton

University of New
Brunswick
Harriet Irving Library
Fredericton E3B 5H5

Dalhousie University
Library
Halifax

Queen's University
Douglas Library
Kingston K7L 5C4

McGill University
Libraries
McLennan Library
Montréal 101

Université de Montréal
Bibliothèque des Scien-
ces Humaines et Socia-
les
Montréal H3C 3T2

University of Ottawa
Institute for Inter-
national Co-operation
Ottawa K1N 6N5

Université Laval
Bibliothèque
Québec G1K 7P4

University of Saskatche-
wan
Murray Memorial Library
Saskatoon S7N OWO

Canadian Institute of
International Affair
Toronto M5S 2V9

University of Toronto
Library
Toronto M5S 1A5

University of British
Columbia
The Library
Vancouver 8

Provincial Library of
Manitoba
Winnipeg R3C OV8

Chile

Biblioteca del Congre-
so Nacional
Santiago

Biblioteca Nacional
Santiago

China

Chungking Library
Chungking

National Library of
Peking
Peking 7

Colombia

Biblioteca Nacional
Bogotá

Universidad del Valle
Departamento de Bib-
liotecas
Cali

osta Rica

iblioteca Nacional
"Manuel Obregón"
an José

uba

iblioteca Nacional
"José Martí"
a Habana

yprus

inistry of Education
ibrary
icosia

zechoslovakia

Univerzitná Knižnica
85 17 Bratislava

Universitní Knihovna
01 87 Brno

Knihovna Federálního
Shromáždení CSSR
10 02 Praha 1

Státní Knihovna CSR
10 01 Praha 1

Democratic Kampuchea

Bibliothèque Nationale
Phnom Penh

Denmark

Statsbiblioteket
Universitetsparken
DK-8000 Århus C

Det Kongelige Bibliotek
DK-1219 København K

Dominican Republic

Universidad Autónoma
de Santo Domingo
Biblioteca Central
Santo Domingo

Ecuador

Biblioteca Nacional
Quito

Egypt

Dar el-Kutub
Cairo

El Salvador

Biblioteca Nacional de
El Salvador
San Salvador

Ethiopia

Haile Selassie I
University Library
Addis Ababa

Fiji

The University of the
South Pacific
Laucala Bay
Suva

Finland

Åbo Akademi
Förenta Nationernas
Deposatory
20500 Åbo 50

Eduskunnan Kirjasto
SF-00102 Helsinki 10

Finland (continued)

Tampereen Yliopiston
  Kirjasto
SF-33100 Tampere 10

France

Bibliothèque Interuni-
  versitaire d'Aix-
  Marseille
13626 Aix-en-Provence

Bibliothèque Interuni-
  versitaire de Lyon
69363 Lyon Cedex 2

Bibliothèque Interuni-
  versitaire de Nancy
54042 Nancy

Bibliothèque Cujas de
  Droit et Sciences
  Économiques
Service des Publications
  Internationales
75005 Paris Ve

Bibliothèque de l'Assem-
  blée Nationale
Service de la Documen-
  tation Étrangère
Paris VIIe

Bibliothèque Nationale
Service des Publications
  officielles
75084 Paris

Fondation Nationale des
  Sciences Politiques
75341 Paris

Bibliothèque Nationale
  et Universitaire
67070 Strasbourg

Bibliothèque Interuni-
  versitaire de Bordeau
Droit et Sciences
  économiques
33405 Talence

**German Democratic
Republic**

Deutsche Staatsbiblio-
  thek
1080 Berlin

Friedrich-Schiller-
  Universität
Institut für Völkerrech
69 Jena

Deutsche Bücherei
701 Leipzig

**Germany, Federal
Republic of**

Freie Universität Berli
Universitätsbibliothek
1000 Berlin 33

Staatsbibliothek Preus-
  sischer Kulturbesitz
1000 Berlin 30

Deutscher Bundestag
Bundeshaus-Bibliothek
53000 Bonn

Hamburgisches Welt-
  Wirtschafts-Archiv
2000 Hamburg 36

Max Planck-Institut für
  Ausländisches Öffent-
  liches Recht und
  Völkerrecht
D-6900 Heidelberg

Germany, Federal
Republic of (continued)
Institut für Interna-
tionales Recht an der
Universität Kiel
2300 Kiel

Bayerische Staats-
bibliothek
8000 München 34

Ghana

Ghana Library Board
Accra

University of Ghana
Balme Library
Legon

Greece

Bibliothèque de la
Chambre des Députés
Hellénique
Ancien Palais Royal
Athènes

Bibliothèque Nationale
Athènes

Institute of Interna-
tional Public Law and
International Rela-
tions
Thessaloniki

Guatemala

Biblioteca Nacional
Ciudad de Guatemala

Guyana

University of Guyana
Library
Georgetown

Haiti

Bibliothèque Nationale
de Port-au-Prince
Port-au-Prince

Honduras

Universidad Nacional
Autónoma
Tegucigalpa, D.C.

Hungary

Országgyűlési Könyvtár
Budapest V

Iceland

Landsbókasafn Islands
Reykjavik

India

University of Bombay
University Library
Bombay-1

National Library
Belvedere
Calcutta-700 027

Panjab University
Library of the Depart-
ment of Laws
Chandigarh

University of Delhi
Delhi School of Econom-
ics
Ratan Tata Library
Delhi 110007

Karnatak University
Library
Dharwar-580003

India (continued)

Osmania University
   Library
Hyderabad 500007

Uttar Pradesh Civil
   Secretariat Library
Lucknow

Connemara Public Library
Madras-60000

Indian Council of World
   Affairs Library
New Delhi 110001

Parliament Library
Lok Sabha Secretariat
Parliament House
New Delhi 110001

Servants of India
   Society's Library
Poona-411004

Kerala University
   Library
Trivandrum 1

Banaras Hindu University
   Library
Varanasi-221005

Indonesia

Dewan Perwakilan Rakjat
   Republik Indonesia
Jakarta

Perpustakaan Museum
   Pusat
Jakarta 1/22

Gadjah Mada Universitas
Jogjakarta

Iran

The Pahlavi University
College of Arts and
   Science Library
Shiraz

Library of the Majlis
Teheran

University of Teheran
Centre for Graduate
   International Studies
Library, Faculty of Law
   and Political Science
Teheran

Iraq

University of Baghdad
Central Library
Baghdad

University of Mosul
Central Library
Mosul

Ireland

National Library of
   Ireland
Dublin 2

Israel

The Jewish National and
   University Library
Jerusalem 91-000

The Knesset Library
Jerusalem

Italy

Biblioteca Nazionale
   Centrale
50122 Firenze

Italy (continued)

Università Cattolica del
Sacro Cuore
Biblioteca
20123 Milano

Università degli Studi
di Padova
Istituto di Diritto
Pubblico
Padova

Institut international
pour l'unification du
droit privé
Bibliothèque
00184 Roma

Società Italiana per la
Organizzazione Inter-
nazionale
00186 Roma

Università degli Studi
di Trieste
Instituto di Diritto In-
ternazionale e Legis-
lazione Comparata
Trieste

Centro d'Informazione
delle Nazioni Unite
Palazzetto Venezia
Piazza San Marco 50
Venezia

Ivory Coast

Bibliothèque Nationale
Abidjan

Jamaica

The Institute of Jamaica
Library
Kingston

University of the West
Indies
Library
Mona

Japan

Seinan Gakuin Univer-
sity
Library
Fukuoka 814

Kyushu United Nations
Depository Library
Fukuoka City 810

Hiroshima University
Library
Hiroshima

Tohoku University
Library
Kawauchi, Sendai

Kobe University
Research Institute for
Economics and Business
Administration
Rokko, Kobe

Kyoto United Nations
Depository Library
Kyoto

Aichi Prefectural
Labour Centre
Library
Nagoya City

Hokkaido University
Faculty of Economics
and Business Adminis-
tration
Library
Sapporo 060

Japan (continued)

National Diet Library
Tokyo 100

University of Tokyo
General Library
Tokyo 113

Jordan

University of Jordan
Library
Amman

Kenya

University of Nairobi
Library
Nairobi

Korea (Republic)

Korea University
Library
Seoul

Kuwait

Kuwait University
   Libraries
Kuwait

Ministry of Foreign
   Affairs
The Library
Kuwait

Lao People's Democratic
Republic

Bibliothèque
Institut Royal de Droit
   et d'Administration
Vientiane

Lebanon

Bibliothèque Nationale
Beyrouth

Lesotho

University of Botswana,
   Lesotho and Swaziland
Library
Roma

Liberia

University of Liberia
Libraries
Monrovia

Libya

University of Libya
The Main Library
Benghazi

Central Bank of Libya
Economic Research
   Library
Tripoli

Luxembourg

Bibliothèque Nationale
Luxembourg

Madagascar

Bibliothèque Universi-
   taire
Tananarive

Malaysia

National Library of
   Malaysia
Kuala Lumpur

alta

byal Malta Library
alletta

auritius

he University of Mauri-
    tius
ibrary
educt

exico

iblioteca Nacional
éxico 1, D.F.

niversidad Autónoma de
    Nuevo León
acultad de Economía
iblioteca Consuelo
    Meyer L.
onterrey

niversidad Veracruzana
nstituto de Investiga-
    ciones y Estudios
    Superiores Económicos
    y Sociales
alapa

ongolia

osudarstvennaia Publi-
    chnaia Biblioteka MNR
lan-Bator

orocco

niversité Mohamed V
aculté des Sciences
    Juridiques,
    Économiques et
    Sociales
abat Agdal

Nepal

Tribhuvan University
Library
Kirtipur, Kathmandu

Netherlands

Universiteits-Biblio-
    theek
Amsterdam

Koninklijke Bibliotheek
's-Gravenhage

Rijksuniversiteit te
    Groningen
Bibliotheek
Groningen

Rijksuniversiteit te
    Leiden
Bibliotheek
Leiden

Katholieke Universiteit
Bibliotheek
Nijmegen

New Zealand

Auckland Public Library
Auckland 1

General Assembly Library
Parliament House
Wellington 1

Victoria University of
    Wellington
The Library, Wellington

Nicaragua

Biblioteca Nacional
Managua, D.N.

Niger
École Nationale d'Ad-
  ministration de Niamey
Niamey

Nigeria
University of Ife
  Library
Ile - Ife

National Library of
  Nigeria
P.M.B. 12626 Lagos

University of Nigeria
Nnamdi Azikiwe Library
Nsukka

Ahmadu Bello University
Kashim Ibrahim Library
Zaria

Norway
Universitetsbiblioteket
  i Bergen
Bergen

Det Norske Nobelin-
  stitutt
Biblioteket
Oslo 2

Universitets biblioteket
N-7000 Trondheim

Pakistan
National Assembly
Library
Islamabad

University of Sind
Central Library
Jamshoro

Karachi University
Library
Karachi 32

Punjab University
Library
Lahore 2/12

University of Peshawar
Library
Peshawar 1

Panama
Biblioteca Nacional
Panamá

Papua New Guinea
University of Papua
  New Guinea
The Library
Boroko

Paraguay
Biblioteca Nacional
Asunción

Peru
Cámara de Diputados
Biblioteca
Lima

Biblioteca Nacional
Lima

Philippines
University of Mindanao
  Library
Davao City

National Library
Ermita, Manila

Philippines (continued)

University of the
   Philippines Library
Diliman
Quezon City D-505

Poland

Biblioteka Sejmowa
0-902 Warszawa

Polski Instytut Spraw
   Miedzynarodowych
0-950 Warszawa

Biblioteka Narodowa
0-973 Warszawa

Portugal

Biblioteca Geral da
   Universidade
Coimbra

Biblioteca Nacional de
   Lisboa
Lisboa-5

Puerto Rico

Universidad de Puerto
   Rico
Biblioteca General
Río Piedras 00931

Romania

Academiei Republicii
   Socialiste România
Biblioteca
Bucuresti

Rwanda

Université Nationale
   du Rwanda
Bibliothèque
Butare

Samoa

The Nelson Memorial
   Public Library
Apia

Saudi Arabia

King Abdulaziz Univer-
   sity Library
Jeddah

State Public Library
Riyadh

Senegal

Assemblée Nationale
Secrétariat Général
Section de la Biblio-
   thèque
Dakar

Université de Dakar
Bibliothèque
Dakar

Sierra Leone

University of Sierra
   Leone
Fourah Bay College
Library
Freetown

Singapore

National Library
Singapore 6

Somalia

University Institute of
   Somalia
Mogadishu

South Africa

Library of Parliament
Cape Town

South African Library
Cape Town 8001

State Library
Pretoria

Spain

Universidad de Barcelona
Facultad de Derecho
Biblioteca
Barcelona 17

Biblioteca Nacional
Madrid

Escuela diplomatica
Ministerio de Asuntos
   Exteriores
Madrid

Universidad de Valencia
Facultad de Derecho
Biblioteca
Valencia

Sri Lanka

The Law Society of Sri
   Lanka, Colombo 12

Sudan

University of Khartoum
Library
Khartoum

Surinam

Universiteit van
   Suriname
Instituut voor Inter-
   nationaal Recht en
   Internationale
   Betrekkinger
Paramaribo

Swaziland

Swaziland National
   Library
Manzini

Sweden

Kungliga Biblioteket
S-102 41 Stockholm 5

Riksdagsbiblioteket
S-100 12 Stockholm

Lunds Universitets-
   biblioteket
S-221 03 Lund

Dag Hammarskjöld
   Biblioteket
S-751 27 Uppsala 1

Switzerland

Eidgenössische Parla-
   ments- und Zentral-
   bibliothek
CH-3003 Bern

witzerland (continued)

nstitut universitaire
  de hautes études in-
  ternationales
ibliothèque
H-1211 Geneva 21

ibliothèque Publique et
  Universitaire de
  Genève
H-1211 Geneva 4

yria

amascus University
nited Arab Library
amascus

hailand

ational Library
angkok 3

ogo

ibliothèque Nationale
  du Togo
omé

rinidad and Tobago

niversity of the West
  Indies
ibrary
t. Augustine

unisia

niversité de Tunis
aculté de droit et des
  sciences politiques
  et économiques
ampus universitaire
unis

Turkey

Millî Kütüphane
Ankara

Istanbul Universitesi
  Kütüphanesi
Istanbul-Beyazit

Uganda

Makerere University
Library
Kampala

Ukrainian Soviet
Socialist Republic

Akademiia Nauk Ukrain-
  skoi SSR
Tsentral'naia Nauchnaia
Biblioteka
Kiev 17

Union of Soviet Socia-
list Republics

Tsentral'naia Nauchnaia
  Biblioteka Lenin-
  Gradskogo Gosudarstven-
  nogo Universiteta
  imeni A.A. Zhdanova
Leningrad

Akademiia Nauk SSSR
Moskva 19

Gosudarstvennaia Bib-
  lioteka SSSR imeni
  V.I. Lenina
Moskva

Union of Soviet Socia-
list Republics (con-
tinued)

Vilniaus Valstybinis V.
Kapsuko vardo Univer-
sitetas
Moksliné Biblioteka
232633 Vilnius

United Kingdom

The National Library of
Wales
Aberystwyth SY23 3BU

Belfast Public Libraries
Central Library
Belfast BT1 2EA

Birmingham Public Li-
braries
Reference Library
Birmingham B3 3HQ

Cambridge University
University Library
Cambridge CB3 9DR

University College
The Library
Cardiff CF1 1XL

National Library of
Scotland
Edinburgh EH1 1EW

The University of Sussex
The Institute of Devel-
opment Studies
The Library
Falmer, Brighton BN1 9RE

The Mitchell Library
Glasgow G3 7DN

Liverpool City Librar-
ies
Liverpool L3 8EW

The British Library
Reference Division
Department of Printed
Books
London WC1B 3DG

London School of Eco-
nomics and Political
Science
British Library of
Political and Eco-
nomic Science
London WC2A 2AE

The Royal Institute of
International Affair
London 4W1Y 4LE

Manchester Public
Libraries
Central Library
Manchester M2 5PD

Oxford University
Bodleian Library
Department of Printed
Books
Oxford OX1 3BG

United Republic of
Tanzania

University of Dar es
Salaam
The Library
Dar es Salaam

United States of America

California

University of California, Berkeley
General Library
Berkeley 94720

Los Angeles Public Library
Los Angeles 90017

University of California Library
University Research Library
Los Angeles 90024

The Stanford University Libraries
Stanford 94305

Colorado

Denver Public Library
Denver 80203

Connecticut

Yale University Library
New Haven 06520

District of Columbia

Library of Congress
Washington, D.C. 20504

Florida

The Florida State University
Robert Manning Strozier Library
Tallahassee 32306

Hawaii

University of Hawaii Library
Honolulu 96822

Illinois

Library of International Relations
Chicago 60611

University of Chicago
The Joseph Regenstein Library
Chicago 60637

Northwestern University Library
Evanston 60201

University of Illinois Library
Education and Social Sciences Library
100 Library
Urbana 61801

Indiana

Indiana University
The University Libraries
Bloomington 47401

Iowa

The University of Iowa
The University Libraries
Iowa City 52240

Kansas

University of Kansas Libraries
Lawrence 66045

Kentucky

University of Kentucky
Libraries
Margaret I. King Library
Lexington 40506

Louisiana

Louisiana State University
Library
Baton Rouge 70803

Maryland

The Johns Hopkins University
The Milton S. Eisenhower
Library
Baltimore 21218

Massachusetts

Boston Public Library
Boston 02117

Harvard College Library
Cambridge 02138

Michigan

The University of
Michigan
The Harlan Hatcher
Graduate Library
Ann Arbor 48109

Minnesota

University of Minnesota
Wilson Library
Minneapolis 55455

Nevada

The University of Nevada
The University Library
Reno 89507

New Jersey

Princeton University
Pliny Fisk Library
Princeton 08540

New York

Cornell University
Libraries
Olin Library
Ithaca 14853

Columbia University
Law Library
New York 10027

Council on Foreign
Relations, Inc.
New York 10021

New York Public Library
New York 10017

New York University
Elmer Holmes Bobst
Library
New York 10003

North Carolina

The University of North
Carolina
Wilson Library
Chapel Hill 27514

Ohio

Cleveland Public Library
Cleveland 44114

Pennsylvania

University of Pennsylvania
The Charles Patterson
Van Pelt Library
Philadelphia 19104

hode Island

rown University
he John D. Rockfeller,
 Jr. Library
rovidence 02912

ennessee

oint Universities
 Libraries
ashville 37203

exas

niversity of Texas
 Library at Austin
he Library
ustin 78712

Jtah

Jniversity of Utah
Jniversity Libraries
;alt Lake City 84112

/irginia

Jniversity of Virginia
\lderman Library
:harlottesville, Va.
 22901

Vashington

Jniversity of Washington
Libraries
Government Documents
 Center
Seattle 98195

Uruguay

Biblioteca Nacional
Hemeroteca
Montevideo

Venezuela

Biblioteca Nacional
Caracas

Yugoslavia

Institut za Medju-
 narodnu Politiku
 i Privredu
Biblioteka
Beograd '

Savezna Skupstina
Beograd

Univerzitet u Beogradu
Pravni Fakultet
Biblioteka
11000 Beograd

Univerziteta Ljubljana
Pravni Fakultet
Ljubljana

Univerzitet Kiril I
 Metódij Skofoje
Praven Fakultet
Biblioteka
Skopje

Sveučilište u Zagrebu
Pravni Fakultet
Biblioteka
41001 Zagreb

Zambia

University of Zambia
The University Library
Lusaka

CHAPTER 22

HOW TO ORGANIZE A COLLECTION OF UNITED NATIONS
PUBLICATIONS

There are various methods of filing or
shelving United Nations publications. A few
approaches are indicated here.

(a) Alphanumerical arrangement by document series
symbol. An especially useful approach for full
depository libraries. The best guide for this
arrangement is the Dag Hammarskjöld Library's
List of United Nations document series symbols
(ST/LIB/SER.B/5/Rev.2: see Bibliography entry
129) plus its updating in part 2 of the cumulative index of United Nations documents index
(Bibliography entry 135), which carries the
listing of series symbols through 1973. A new
revision of the List of United Nations document
series symbols is in preparation.

Documents carrying multiple symbols
must, of course, be filed or shelved under the
symbol of the parent body or under the first
listed symbol, with cross references placed
under the other symbol(s). Institutions that
receive more than one copy of each document may
file or shelve copies of multiple-symbol documents under each symbol.

(b) Arrangement of Official records. The United

Nations recommends[54] filing or shelving these
separately by organ and session (for the Securi-
Council, by year), with cross references under
the series symbols. Arrangement of the Officia:
records of different organs may vary but the
general pattern of shelving can be: plenary
meeting records; committee meeting records;
annexes; supplements; special supplements. (See
Chapter 14 for a detailed description of Officia
records.)

(c) Arrangement by sales category (and within
each category by year) may be suitable for
partial depositories or institutions that have
standing orders. Because of the nature of the
sales number system, (see Chapter 13 for more
detail), this arrangement would result in a
broad subject classification. The United Nation
publications in print; checklist (Bibliography
entry 149) may serve as a guide to this arrangement.

(d) For publications carrying neither series
symbol nor sales number, libraries could adopt,
if desired, the simple classification scheme
used by the Dag Hammarskjöld Library. The call
number contains the elements of authorship, form
designation and title cutter. For example, the
United Nations review (predecessor of the UN

---

[54] United Nations documentation; a brief
guide for official recipients (Biblio
raphy entry 134), pp. 14-18. Also:
Graciela Faridi, Some problems in the
maintenance of United Nations depository collections and their possible
solutions (New York, 1972); and
United Nations, Secretariat, Instructions for depository libraries receiv
ing United Nations material (New York
31 March 1977; ST/LIB/13/Rev. 3),
pp. 13-14.

monthly chronicle) would carry the call number
UNST DPI (05) UN7:

UNST	United Nations Secretariat
DPI	Department of Public Information
(05)	form designation for serials
UN7	title cutter

(e) Alphabetical arrangement by title may be
convenient for recurrent publications that carry
no sales number or series symbol (e.g., the
Treaty series, Bibliography entry 87) or for
serials with non-consecutive series symbols.

(f) A classified arrangement is another possibility, although full cataloguing and classification require the use of considerable staff
time and other resources. The main consequence
of a purely subject classification would be the
dispersal of the documents of a given organ
throughout the collection. One suggestion of
remedying this problem involves an expansion of
the "J" class of the Library of Congress classification.[55] An institution with a very small
United Nations collection would likely catalogue
and classify its UN publications, integrating
them into its general collection.

(g) Separate files arranged by title or names of
issuing organs may be set up for heavily used
material such as yearbooks, compilations of
resolutions, annual reports of the Secretary-
General and of major bodies to the General
Assembly, Indexes to proceedings.

---

[55] Mina Pease, "J.01000 through J.09999 -
the plain J and international organization," (In Sources, organization, utilization of international documentation,
Bibliography entry 110), pp. 383-391.

PART IV

SOURCES OF INFORMATION:
A SELECT ANNOTATED BIBLIOGRAPHY
OF WORKS BY AND ABOUT THE UNITED NATIONS

(A) BASIC INSTRUMENTS, PROCEDURES, ETC.

1. United Nations. Charter of the United
    Nations and Statute of the International
    Court of Justice. New York: United
    Nations, Office of Public Information,
    1974. iv, 57 p.

    The Charter is the basic instrument of the
    UN. It sets out: the purposes and princi-
    ples of the Organization; basic rules
    affecting membership in the UN; composition,
    functions, powers and procedures of the
    principal organs; principles and organiza-
    tional aspects of such major international
    concern as the pacific settlement of dis-
    putes, international economic co-operation,
    non-self-governing territories and the in-
    ternational trusteeship system; amendment
    procedure; signature and ratification pro-
    cedure.

    The Statute of ICJ forms an integral part
    of the Charter. It sets out principles
    and rules governing the organization, com-
    petence, and procedures of the Court.

    In addition to separate editions, the text
    of the Charter and of the ICJ Statute can
    be found in Everyman's United Nations
    (q.v., entry No. 44) and in the Yearbook of
    the United Nations (q.v., entry No. 46).
    It is also included in part V of the present
    volume.

2. United Nations. Repertory of practice of
    United Nations organs. New York, 1955.
    5 v. + index.

    A comprehensive summary of decisions of UN
    organs, with other related material,arranged
    in the order of Charter Articles on
    which each decision was based. The index
    volume contains a consolidated table of con-
    tents of the five main volumes and an al-

phabetical subject index. Kept up to date
by supplements. Issued with United Nations
publication sales numbers.

3. United Nations. Economic and Social Council. Rules of procedure of the Economic
and Social Council. New York, 1975. vi,
32 p. (E/5715; United Nations publication,
Sales No. E.75.I.15)

The basic instrument of the Council, setting
forth rules for holding sessions, drawing
up and disposition of agenda, representation, election and powers of officers, conduct of business, voting, etc.

4. United Nations. General Assembly. Rules
of procedure of the General Assembly.
New York, 1974. xix, 84 p. (A/520/Rev.12;
United Nations publication, Sales No.
E.74.I.6)

The basic instrument of the Assembly. Sets
forth rules for convening and conducting
sessions; composition of delegations;
election and terms of reference of officers
and committees; conduct of business, etc.
Includes index.

Supplemented by:

5. United Nations. General Assembly. Amend-
ment to the Rules of procedure of the
General Assembly. New York, 1977. 1 p.
(A/520/Rev.12/Amend.1)

Amends Rule 158.

6. United Nations. International Court of
Justice. Rules of Court, adopted on 6 May
1946, as amended on 10 May 1972. [The
Hague] 1972. 31 p. (Acts and documents
concerning the organization of the Court,
No. 2)

The Rules of Court are set down under the following headings: constitution and working of the Court; contentious proceedings (procedure before the full Court; procedure before the Chambers; judgments; etc.); advisory opinions.

Supplemented by:

7. United Nations. International Court of Justice. Resolution concerning the internal judicial practice of the Court (Rules of Court, Article 33). [The Hague] 1976. 4 p.

A revision of the Court's 1968 resolution concerning internal judicial practice.

8. United Nations. Security Council. Provisional rules of procedure of the Security Council (January 1974). New York, 1974. 12 p. (S/96/Rev.6; United Nations publication, Sales No. E.74.I.5)

First adopted by the Council at its first meeting and amended a number of times, the rules of procedure of the Security Council exist in provisional form only. They contain rules for calling and conducting meetings, adoption and disposition of agenda items, representation and credentials, matters pertaining to the presidency of the Council, voting procedure, rules for issuing records, etc.

9. United Nations. Trusteeship Council. Rules of procedure of the Trusteeship Council (as amended up to and including its twenty-ninth session). New York, 1962. iii, 19 p. (T/1/Rev.6; United Nations publication, Sales No. E.62.I.23.)

The basic instrument of the Trusteeship Council. Contains rules for conducting sessions and other business, for issuing records, for the organization of subsidiary

bodies, visits to trust territories, annua
reports of administering authorities and
other aspects of the work of the Council.

(B)   COLLECTIONS OF PRIMARY SOURCES

10.   Cordier, Andrew and Foote, Wilder, eds.
      Public papers of the Secretaries-General
      of the United Nations. New York: Columbia
      University Press, 1969-

      A substantial selection, with commentaries
      from the public papers of the Secretaries-
      General. Includes official documents (e.g
      periodic and special reports to United
      Nations organs, statements made at meet-
      ings of United Nations bodies, communica-
      tions to governments) as well as non-offi-
      cial material such as addresses given out-
      side the United Nations, radio and tele-
      vision broadcasts, press conference tran-
      scripts. Most material in the non-officia
      category is available only in press
      releases that are not widely distributed
      by the United Nations.

      Volumes issued thus far in the series:
      v.1: Trygve Lie, 1946-1953;
      v.2: Dag Hammarskjöld, 1953-1956;
      v.3: Dag Hammarskjöld, 1956-1957;
      v.4: Dag Hammarskjöld, 1958-1960;
      v.5: Dag Hammarskjöld, 1960-1961;
      v.6: U Thant, 1961-1964;
      v.7: U Thant, 1965-1967.

      Each volume has an informative introductior
      and an index.

11-
14.   Preparatory Commission of the United Na-
      tions. Publications. London, 1945.

      The Preparatory Commission held its first
      session in San Francisco on 27 June 1945
      and its second in London from 24 November
      to 24 December 1945. The following docu-

ments were issued:

11. Report of the Preparatory Commission of
the United Nations. 182 p. (Doc. PC/20)
12. Report of the Executive Committee of the
Preparatory Commission of the United
Nations. 144 p. (Doc. PC/EX/113/Rev.1)
13. Preparatory Commission of the United Nations. Handbook; a Delegation and Secretariat directory. Rev. ed. 48 p.
14. Journal of the Preparatory Commission, with
eight supplements containing the summary
records of the meetings of the eight committees of the Commission.

15. Spröte, Wolfgang, ed. Die Vereinten Nationen und Ihre Spezialorganisationen.
Berlin: Staatsverlag der Deutschen Demo-
kratischen Republik, 1976 [?]-

A compendium of documents of the United
Nations system of organizations. In addition to authentic texts in English, French
and/or Russian, German translation is provided. Each volume has an informative introduction and a brief index. In all, the
following twenty volumes are planned:

1: Die Entstehung der UNO
2: Die Hauptorgane der UNO
3: UNO-Resolutionen zu politischen und
rechtlichen Grundfragen
4: Mandate und Verfahrensregeln ökono-
mischer UNO-Organe
5: UNO-Resolutionen zu Grundfragen der
internationalen Wirtschaftsbeziehungen
6: UNO-Resolutionen zu Grundfragen des
internationalen Handels, der internationalen Währungs- und Finanzbeziehun-
gen und der regionalen ökonomischen
Zusammenarbeit
7: Die Weltgesundheitsorganisation
8: Die Organisation der Vereinten Nationen für Erziehung, Wissenschaft und
Kultur
9: Die Weltorganisation für Meteorologie

10: Der Weltpostverein
11: Der Internationale Fernmeldeverein
12: Die Internationale Arbeitsorganisation
13: Die Internationale Organisation für Zivilluftfahrt
14: Die Zwischenstaatliche Beratende Seeschiffahrtsorganisation
15: Die Organisation für Ernährung und Landwirtschaft
16: Die Internationale Atomenergieorganisation
17: Die Weltbankgruppe
18: Weltorganisation für geistiges Eigentum
19: Organisation der Vereinten Nationen für industrielle Entwicklung
20: Registerband

16. United Nations. Mimeographed and printed documents, 1946- . New York: Readex Microprint Corp.

A fairly comprehensive collection, in micro print. Contains the official records of the General Assembly, Economic and Social Council, Security Council, Trusteeship Council, United Nations Conference on Trade and Development, etc.; other documents, including "limited distribution" documents, of most United Nations bodies and subsidiary bodies, and the Journal of the United Nations. Excludes most documents issued by the Secretariat and some conference proceedings.

17. United Nations Conference on International Organization, San Francisco, 1945. Documents. New York: United Nations, 1945-55. 22 v.

The first fifteen volumes contain the English and French texts of the major documents of the Conference and were published, together with volume 16 (Index), jointly by the United Nations Information Organization and the U.S. Library of Congress. Volumes 17-20 (documents of the Co-ordination

Committee and the Advisory Committee of
Jurists) were issued by the UN in 1954.
Volumes 21 and 22, General index, with (a)
legislative history and analytical subject
index and (b) alphabetical subject index,
in English and French, complete the set.

(C) ACTIVITIES OF THE UNITED NATIONS: GENERAL

18. Akademiia nauk SSSR. Institut mirovoĭ
ėkonomiki i mezhdunarodnykh otnosheniĭ.
OON; itogi, tendentsii, perspektivy. Moscow: Izdatel'stvo "Mezhdunarodnye otnoshe-
niia," 1970. 544 p.

This book, issued on the occasion of the
twenty-fifth anniversary of the United
Nations, is the product of the collaboration of several historians, economists and
jurists of the Soviet Union, the German
Democratic Republic, Poland and Czechoslovakia. The work reviews the activities of
the Organization, and examines trends and
perspectives. It discusses the following
topics: the role and place of the UN in
international relations; the principle of
universality; the maintenance of international peace and security; problems of
regional security; the problem of disarmament; UN activities in the peaceful use
of outer space; the struggle for the liqui-
dation of colonial and racist régimes;
newly independent states; economic problems
of developing countries; social problems;
the development and codification of international law; the competence of the principal organs of the UN; the future of the
UN and its Charter.

Includes bibliographical references and a
separate short bibliography of Soviet
works.

19. Annual review of United Nations affairs,
     1949-   . Dobbs Ferry, N.Y.: Oceana.

     A detailed review of the major activities
     of the UN during the year covered. In-
     cludes numerous references to documents
     and full texts of selected important docu-
     ments. Volumes for 1949-1955/56 issued
     under the auspices of the New York Univer-
     sity Graduate Program of Studies in the
     United Nations.

20. Barros, James, ed. The United Nations:
     past, present, and future. New York:
     Free Press, 1972. 279 p.

     A collection of six essays on the princi-
     pal activities and/or organs of the UN:
     the Security Council, the General Assembly,
     the Secretary-General, decolonization, the
     development of international law, and the
     economic, social and technical activities
     of the UN. The editor's introduction
     traces the history and evolution of the
     world organization. There is a brief sub-
     ject index.

21. Chamberlin, Waldo; Hovet, Thomas; and Hovet
     Erica. A chronology and fact book of the
     United Nations, 1941-1976. Dobbs Ferry,
     N.Y.: Oceana, 1976. 302 p.

     Chronological listing, sub-arranged by sub-
     ject, of important events leading to the
     establishment of the United Nations, and
     of the important issues dealt with in the
     various organs of the world body. In-
     cludes tables showing membership of the
     United Nations and of its principal organs;
     officers of the major organs; United Na-
     tions budgets and scales of assessment;
     brief information about the United Nations
     system. A documentary annex contains the
     texts of the Charter and the Rules of pro-
     cedure of the General Assembly. There is

a subject index.

22. Claude, Inis L. The changing United Nations. New York: Random House, 1968. xix, 140 p.

A collection of five essays, focusing on the changing nature of the United Nations during its first two decades. The three major factors of change, as the author sees them, were: the thermonuclear revolution and the consequent revival of the disarmament issue; the polarization brought about by the cold war, with the changing attitudes of the great powers toward the United Nations; and the process of decolonization which both affected and was affected by the United Nations. There is an essay on collective legitimization as perhaps the most important political function of the United Nations. The final essay analyzes the nature of trends discernible in the late nineteen-sixties: the trend toward universality, the increasing numerical preponderance of newly emergent states, the persistence of superpowers, the UN's growing involvement with economic development, and the Organization's peace-keeping functions.

23. Claude, Inis L. Swords into plowshares; the problems and progress of international organization. 4th ed. New York: Random House, c1971. xii, 514 p.

The focus of this book is international organization as a process, with primary attention to organizations of the United Nations system as representative aspects of that process.

The first part is devoted to historical background material: the development of international organization in the nineteenth century, the League of Nations, and the origins of the United Nations system.

The focus then shifts to constitutional problems: problems of membership, of regionalism, of voting and veto, of constitutional interpretation and development, of the international secretariat. Next, the author delineates various approaches to peace through international organization: peaceful settlement of disputes, collective security, disarmament, preventive diplomacy, the Grand Debate approach, trusteeship, and the functional approach. The final part is entitled The future of world order: it deals with the movement for world government, and the progress and prospects of international organization.

Useful lists of suggested readings accompany each chapter.

Appendices present texts of the League's Covenant, the UN Charter, the North Atlantic Treaty, the list of members of the UN and summary costs of the UN system.

24.   Falk, Richard and Mendlovitz, Saul H., eds.   The strategy of world order.   v. 3: The United Nations.   New York: World Law Fund, 1966.   xv, 848 p.

Part of a four-volume work whose aim is "to study the subject of world order from the interrelated perspectives of international law, international organization, disarmament, and economic development" [Prefatory note.] The whole work is built on the model of World peace through world law by Grenville Clark and Louis B. Sohn.

The objective of volume 3 is to examine the contribution of the United Nations to world order. Essays and primary material included are grouped as follows: the League of Nations and the United Nations; the relevance of law to the operations of

the United Nations; membership of the
United Nations; the Security Council, the
General Assembly; the Secretariat and the
Secretary-General; the limitations on the
authority of the United Nations, and apartheid in South Africa; procedures for pacific settlement; procedures for coercive
settlement; financing; evaluation of the
United Nations.

In addition to bibliographic footnotes,
most chapters indicate "coordinate reading"
in World peace through world law.

25. Finley, Blanche. The structure of the UN
General Assembly: its committees, commis-
sions and other organisms, 1946-73. Dobbs
Ferry, N.Y.: Oceana, 1977. 3 v.

A historical survey of most ad hoc committees, standing committees and other subsidiary organs set up by the General Assembly. Excludes sessional bodies such as the
main committees, and some semi-autonomous
bodies, such as the United Nations Conference on Trade and Development and the United
Nations Development Programme.

Information about each organ includes: number and date of establishing resolution,
terms of reference, membership, action
taken by the organ, with references to reports issued. Annexes include: membership
of the United Nations, list of General
Assembly resolutions, selected reference
sources concerning the General Assembly.
There is a subject index.

26. Goodrich, Leland M.; Hambro, Edvard; and
Simons, Anne Patricia. Charter of the
United Nations; commentary and documents.
3d, rev. ed. New York: Columbia University
Press, c1969. xvii, 732 p.

The purpose of the authors is to show how,
through interpretation of the Charter, fun-

damental changes in the United Nations
have taken place during the first twenty
years of the existence of the Organization
The work is a detailed, scholarly commentary on the Charter, article by article.
The authors analyze the interpretation of
Charter provisions by various United Nations bodies.

There are bibliographical footnotes, an
index, and an appendix containing the
texts of the Covenant of the League of
Nations, the Dumbarton Oaks Proposals,
the UN Charter and the ICJ Statute.

27.   Goodrich, Leland M. The United Nations in
      a changing world. New York: Columbia Uni-
      versity Press, 1974. xi, 280 p.

The book focuses on the evolution of the
United Nations in its structure, functions
and procedures. The author begins with a
comparison of the League of Nations and
the United Nations, continues with a discussion of the development of the organization and functions of the United Nations,
and ends with a prediction of the future
role of the Organization. There are numerous bibliographic footnotes (but no consolidated bibliography), references to documents, and an index.

28.   Goodspeed, Stephen S. The nature and func-
      tion of international organization. 2d ed
      New York: Oxford University Press, 1967.
      xii, 733 p.

An explanation and evaluation of the objectives, procedures, competence, and environment of international governmental organizations. The author begins by examining
the League of Nations antecedents of the
United Nations system, then continues by
scrutinizing the organizational framework,
constitutional problems, political, legal,

administrative, welfare, and trusteeship
functions of the United Nations system of
organizations. The work closes with a discussion of regionalism and reflections on
the future of the United Nations system.
There is a select bibliography, appendices,
and an index.

29. Gordenker, Leon, ed. The United Nations
in international politics. Princeton
University Press, 1971. 241 p.

A collection of six essays: on the place
of the United Nations in the international
system; the United Nations and the League
of Nations; the successes and failures of
the General Assembly; responses of the
United Nations to conflicts; the United
Nations and economic and social change;
various systems of operation in the United
Nations.

30. Gregg, Robert W., and Barkun, Michael, eds.
The United Nations system and its functions;
selected readings. Princeton: Van Nostrand,
c1968. iv, 460 p.

A collection of twenty-five essays grouped
around six generic functions of the United
Nations system: articulation and aggre-
gation of interests; communications; social-
ization and recruitment; conflict management; redistribution; integration. These
functions are considered by the editors to
subsume all activities of the UN system:
political, legal, economic, social, judicial, etc. There is no index or consolidated bibliography, although there are numerous bibliographical footnotes.

31. International conciliation. no. 1-587.
New York: Carnegie Endowment for International Peace, 1907-Mar. 1972.

Each number was devoted to a specific topic
of international interest. From 1946 to

1971, each year's fall issue gave a survey
of matters to be discussed during that
fall's session of the General Assembly.

32. International organization. v. 1- ;
Feb. 1947-   Madison, Wis.: University of Wisconsin Press.

Co-sponsored by the World Peace Foundation
Has many scholarly articles of interest to
researchers working in fields involving
the UN.

33. Keesing's contemporary archives; weekly
record of important world events. v.1-
1 July 1931-   London: Keesing's.

A loose-leaf digest of current affairs,
abstracted from press, broadcasting, official and other sources. Good coverage of
the organizations of the United Nations
system. Includes excerpts from texts of
selected important documents and speeches.
Illustrated with maps and tables. Accompanied by cumulative name and subject
index.

34. Luard, David Evan Trant. International
agencies; the emerging framework of interdependence. Dobbs Ferry, N.Y.: Oceana,
c1977. xii, 338 p.

An examination of the framework of international organizations and the issues they
deal with. Most organizations of the UN
system and some outside it are treated.
The work is arranged in chapters on various
areas of international concern: postal services , telecommunications, sea transport,
air transport, space, the sea-bed, the Ant-
arctic, meteorology, energy, labour,
health, social policy, trade, money, development. The standard-setting, rule-
making, monetary, technical, informational
and other functions of international organizations are analyzed.

35. Nicholas, H.G. <u>The United Nations as a political institution</u>. 5th ed. London: Oxford University Press, 1975. 263 p.

The author's purpose is to describe the United Nations as an established political institution, in terms of its processes and products. Introductory chapters on the Organization's origin, evolution, and the comparison of its Charter with the Covenant of the League of Nations are followed by an examination of the Security Council, the General Assembly, the Economic and Social Council, the Trusteeship Council, the specialized agencies, the International Court of Justice, the Secretariat, and the membership of the Organization. There is a select bibliography (with some brief annotations) and an index. An appendix contains the text of the Charter.

36. Sachs, Moshe, ed. <u>The United Nations; a handbook on the United Nations, its structure, history, purposes, activities and agencies</u>. New York: Worldmark Press, c1977. x, 246 p.

This paperback version of the United Nations volume of the <u>Worldmark encyclopedia of the nations</u> gives a brief historical background of the Organization, followed by informative chapters on the principal organs and activities of the United Nations and its related organizations.

Includes bibliographies.

37. Tavares de Sá, Hernane. <u>The play within the play; the inside story of the UN</u>. 1st ed. New York: Knopf, 1966. xi, 309, vii p.

A perceptive account of the nature and activities of the UN, including behind-the-scenes activities, based on the

author's personal experience and observations while he was UN Undersecretary for
Public Information from 1960 to 1965.

38. United Nations. General Assembly. Medium-term plan for the period 1974-1977--
New York. (Official records of
the General Assembly, Supplement No. 6A)

Prepared every two years for the following four years. Part I presents perspec-
tive analyses and programme highlights;
Part II gives detailed programmes by activ
ity (agriculture, international justice
and law, international trade, human rights
etc.); Part III contains special analyses
and evaluations.

39. United Nations. General Assembly. Programme budget for the biennium, 1974-
1975-- New York. (Official records of the General Assembly, Supplement
No. 6B)

Contains detailed schedules of budget
appropriations and income estimates for
the biennium, as approved by the General
Assembly.

Prior to the establishment of the biennial
budget cycle, the United Nations had issued Budget for the financial year. (Official records of the General Assembly,
Supplement No. 6A)

The nature and purposes of the budget are
set out in the Proposed programme budget
for the biennium (q.v., entry 40) and in
a related report of the Advisory Committee on Administrative and Budgetary Questions which appears as Supplement No. 8
of the Official records of the General
Assembly.

40. United Nations. General Assembly. <u>Pro-
     posed programme budget for the biennium,</u>
     <u>1974-1975--</u>   New York. (<u>Official</u>
     <u>records</u> of the General Assembly, 28th-
     Session, Supplement No. 6)

     Contains a description of the activities
     and functions of all United Nations organs
     and subsidiary organs and a detailed state-
     ment of the financial resources needed to
     support all programmes and activities.

     The expenditure estimates are grouped by
     activity: overall policy-making, direction
     and co-ordination; political, Security
     Council and peace-keeping activities; eco-
     nomic, social and humanitarian activities;
     trusteeship and decolonization; common serv-
     ices; special expenses; etc. Income esti-
     mates are divided into general income, in-
     come from staff assessment and revenue-
     producing activities.

     Prior to the establishment of the biennial
     budget cycle, the United Nations had issued
     annual <u>Budget estimates</u> (<u>Official records</u>
     of the <u>General Assembly,</u> Supplement No. 6)

     The <u>Proposed programme budget</u> should be
     consulted in conjunction with the <u>Medium-</u>
     <u>term plan</u> (q.v., entry 38) and the <u>Pro-</u>
     <u>gramme budget</u> for the biennium (q.v., entry
     39)

41. United Nations. General Assembly. <u>Report</u>
     <u>of the Secretary-General on the work of</u>
     <u>the Organization, 1946-</u>   . New York.
     (<u>Official records</u> of the General Assembly,
     Supplement No. 1)

     A very useful, detailed guide to the year's
     activities. Chapters are arranged by type
     of activity (peace-keeping operations,
     disarmament and related matters, human
     rights questions, economic and social activ-
     ities, etc.). Includes references to

relevant documents.

42.   United Nations. General Assembly. Introduction to the report of the Secretary-
General on the work of the Organization,
1956-   . New York. (Official records
of the General Assembly, Supplement No. 1A

Contains personal observations of the incumbent Secretary-General on various items
before the UN and his remarks on related
topics.

Formerly included in the Report of the
Secretary-General on the work of the Organization (q.v., entry 41)

43.   United Nations. Office of Public Information. Basic facts about the United Nations; a summary of its purposes, structure, activities. Thirtieth anniversary
ed. New York, 1975. iv, 114 p. (United
Nations publication , Sales No. E.75.I.13)

An outline of the history, structure and
the main activities of the UN, with information on the related inter-governmental organizations.

Basic facts is issued at irregular intervals. A new edition is in preparation as
of July 1977.

44.   United Nations. Office of Public Information. Everyman's United Nations; a complete handbook of the activities and evolution of the United Nations during its
first twenty years, 1945-1965. 8th ed.
New York, 1968. 634 p. (United Nations
publication, Sales No. E.67.I.2)

A guide to the structure and activities of
the UN and the related inter-governmental
organizations. It is more concise and
popular in style than the Yearbook of the
United Nations (q.v., entry 46). Arranged

by broad subject areas, each chapter is a
chronological narrative. Appendices include the texts of the Charter, the ICJ
Statute and the Universal Declaration of
Human Rights. There is a detailed alphabetical index.

45. United Nations. Office of Public Information. Everyman's United Nations; a summary of the activities of the United Nations during the five-year period 1966-
1970. New York, 1971. 248 p. (United
Nations publication, Sales No. E.71.I.10)

Together with the 8th edition of Everyman's,
provides an account of the first twenty-
five years of activities of the organizations of the United Nations system.

Everyman's United Nations is issued at
irregular intervals.

46. United Nations. Office of Public Information. Yearbook of the United Nations.
1946/47-   . New York.

A comprehensive annual record of the activities, proceedings and decisions of the
UN, with briefer summaries of the activities of the affiliated inter-governmental
organizations. Arranged by broad subject
areas such as political and security questions, economic and social questions. Includes many documentary references and complete texts of resolutions. Appendices
include texts of the Charter and of the
ICJ Statute, roster of the UN, list of UN
information centres and offices around the
world and an alphabetical subject and name
index. The first edition of the Yearbook
not only covers UN activities during 1946/
47 but includes also a history of the conferences preceding the signing of the
Charter and an account of the origin and
evolution of the UN.

Issued with United Nations publication
sales number.

47.   United Nations Institute for Training and
Development. UNITAR Conference on the
Future, Moscow, 1974. The United Nations
and the future; proceedings. Moscow, 1976
463 p. (United Nations publication, Sales
No. E.76.XV.CR/6)

Text of papers presented, and summary of
discussions at the conference, organized
by UNITAR in co-operation with the Institute of World Economy and International
Relations of the Academy of Sciences of
the USSR and the USSR State Committee for
Science and Technology.

The papers and discussions deal with three
interrelated subjects:
- the future of the United Nations,
  with particular reference to future
  resources and technological issues
  (including such papers as "Technological change and its implications
  for the United Nations", "The future
  of the United Nations; a political
  overview");
- the future in the United Nations,
  with particular reference to future
  resources and technological issues
  ("New aspects of the United Nations
  activities in the light of the energ
  and raw materials crisis", "Fore-
  casting in international organizations; needs and possibilities",
  etc.);
- national experience in undertaking
  future studies and long-range planning (papers on African, Soviet,
  and Swedish studies, and a comparative analysis).

48.   United Nations monthly chronicle.
      1965-   . New York.

      Issued by the UN Office of Public Informa-
      tion. Contains a summary of the month's
      activities, as did its predecessors, the
      United Nations bulletin (issued January
      1950-June 1954) and the United Nations
      review (July 1954-December 1964).

      Regular features are: Record of the month
      (political and security, economic and
      social, human rights, legal, and adminis-
      trative and budgetary activities); Notes
      of the month (brief news items, calendar
      of meetings, list of important documents
      issued).

49.   Wood, Robert S., ed. The process of in-
      ternational organization. New York: Ran-
      dom House, c1971. ix, 525 p.

      An anthology of writings on international
      organization in general and the United
      Nations in particular. The contents are
      assembled under the following headings:
      nature and development of international
      organization (including essays on inter-
      national politics, and historical and in-
      tellectual background); forms and processes
      of international organization (including
      essays on constitutional interpreta-
      tion and development, parliamentary di-
      plomacy, and the Secretariat); uses and
      purposes of international organization
      (collective security and preventive diplo-
      macy, disarmament, trusteeship and decolo-
      nization, etc.); problems and prospects of
      international organization.

      There are bibliographic and explanatory
      notes but no consolidated bibliography or
      index.

(D)   ACTIVITIES OF THE UNITED NATIONS: ECONOMIC
      AND SOCIAL DEVELOPMENT

50.   Commission on International Development.
      Partners in development; report of the
      Commission. New York: Praeger, 1969.
      xvi, 400 p.

      The Commission on International Develop-
      ment was set up on the initiative of the
      International Bank for Reconstruction and
      Development. Under the chairmanship of
      Lester B. Pearson, this international
      commission of development experts examined
      all relevant questions. The report survey:
      two decades (the nineteen-fifties and six-
      ties) of development, especially as applie(
      to developing nations; examines the private
      and official (bilateral and multilateral)
      development aid in the areas of financing,
      trade, population, education and others;
      analyzes the role of international organi-
      zations (the United Nations, the World
      Bank group, the OECD, regional banks such
      as the Inter-American Development Bank,
      etc.); and sets forth recommendations.

51.   Moss, Alfred George and Winton, Harry N.M.,
      comps. A new international economic order;
      selected documents, 1945-1975. New York:
      UNITAR, 1976. 2 v.   (UNITAR document servic€
      No. 1)

      A selection of resolutions, declarations,
      joint programmes of action of United Na-
      tions and other bodies. Among the docu-
      ments reproduced: Cairo Declaration of the
      Developing Countries (1962); Joint Declara-
      tion of the Group of 77 at UNCTAD I (1964);
      resolutions of the first three sessions
      (1964, 1968 and 1972) of the United Nation$
      Conference on Trade and Development; Joint
      Statement by the Socialist Countries on
      the Second Development Decade and Social
      Progress (1970); World Population Plan of

Action (1974); excerpts from the Lomé Convention (1975); OECD Declaration on Relations with Developing Countries (1975); important General Assembly resolutions relating to economic development; many others. There is a subject index.

52. Sharp, Walter R. The United Nations Economic and Social Council. New York: Columbia University Press, 1969. xii, 322 p. (Columbia University studies in international organization, 5)

A systematic examination of the Economic and Social Council from its inception through the first half of 1968. The author traces the Charter functions of the Council, the operational context, the role of human actors in the Council, decision-making, the Council's role as a world policy forum, interagency coordination, programme planning and appraisal, the changing patterns of the Council, and the future of the Council. Includes some controversial recommendations of the author.

53. United Nations. A study of the capacity of the United Nations development system. Geneva, 1969. 2 v. (DP/5, United Nations publication, Sales No. E.70.I.10)

Also known popularly as the Jackson report, after its principal author, R.G.A. Jackson. A detailed, frank examination of the role that the UN system of organizations plays in the process of the development of the Third World. The study (a) examines the character, content, organization, administration, financing and procedures of the complex development system which consists of various parts of the UN itself (UNCTAD, UNDP, UNICEF, UNIDO and other bodies) as well as about a dozen specialized agencies; (b) recommends organizational and other changes in order to make the system more efficient.

54. United Nations. Dept. of Economic and
     Social Affairs. <u>World economic survey</u>.
     No. 1-   ; 1945/47-   . New York
     (ST/ESA/-   ).

     Comprehensive annual review and analysis
     of world economic conditions. Volumes for
     1955- issued in two parts, part I dealing
     with a special topic (e.g., part I of the
     1963 volume deals with population and de-
     velopment) and part II reporting on cur-
     rent economic developments.

     Accompanied by irregular supplements. Is-
     sued with United Nations publication sales
     numbers.

55. United Nations. Economic and Social Coun-
     cil. <u>Resolutions and decisions</u>. New York
     (<u>Official records</u> of the Economic and So-
     cial Council, Supplement No. 1)

     Each issue contains sessional agenda, text
     of resolutions and decisions, and check-
     list of resolutions and decisions.

56. United Nations. General Assembly. <u>Report
     of the Economic and Social Council on the
     work of its ... sessions</u>. New York.
     (<u>Official records</u> of the General Assembly,
     Supplement No. 3)

     Summary of the work of the Council's ses-
     sions held during the report year, grouped
     by type of questions as considered by the
     various organs of the Council. Includes
     texts of important documents (e.g., draft
     resolutions) and references to other docu-
     ments. An annex includes agenda, calendar
     of conferences, directory information, etc

57. United Nations. Group of Experts on the
     Structure of the United Nations System.
     <u>A new United Nations structure for global
     economic co-operation</u>. New York, 1975.
     xvii, 112 p. (E/AC.62/9, United Nations

publication, Sales No. E.75.II.A.7)

Contains proposals for major restructuring
of the United Nations system in order to
make it more effective in dealing with international co-operation in economic development, industrialization, trade, development financing.

58. United Nations Development Programme. The
United Nations Development Programme; ques-
tions and answers. Rev. ed. New York,
Sept. 1975. iv, 40 p.

Describes the origins, aims, policies, pro-
gramming, implementation methods, financing, accomplishments, and organizational
structure of the United Nations Development Programme. Each subject section is
arranged as a short text followed by a
question-and-answer presentation.

59. United Nations Fund for Population Activities. Inventory of population projects in
developing countries around the world,
1973/74. New York, 1975. 397 p.

An inventory of sources of funding for
various categories of population projects.
Part I is an overview of donor agencies in
the field of population: United Nations
organizations; bilateral governmental organizations; non-governmental organizations. Part II is a description of individual country programmes. For each country included, the following information is
given: basic demographic statistics, governmental population policies, external
assistance. Part III discusses regional,
interregional and global programmes. Part
IV contains a brief bibliography and a
directory of sources of information. Part
V contains a country index and a subject
index.

Excludes population activities within developed countries.

60. United Nations Industrial Development Or-
     ganization. <u>Industrial development ab-</u>
     <u>stracts</u>. No. 1-   New York, 1971-
        (ID/-   ; UNIDO/LIB/SER.B/-   )

     A guide to published and unpublished doc-
     uments on industrialization: major stud-
     ies and reports, articles from <u>Industria</u>
     <u>research and development news</u> and <u>Indus-</u>
     <u>trialization and productivity</u> bulletin,
     technical assistance reports, Industrial
     Development Board documents, etc.

     Consists of three parts: subject index,
     author index, and abstracts. The abstract
     are arranged numerically, by computer
     access number. The descriptors used are
     taken from UNIDO's <u>Thesaurus of industri-</u>
     <u>al development terms</u>. The indexing and
     abstracting are done in Vienna by INDIS
     (UNIDO's Industrial Information System).
     There is a cumulative index.

(E) ACTIVITIES OF THE UNITED NATIONS: HUMAN
     RIGHTS

61. United Nations. <u>Yearbook on human rights</u>.
     1946-   . New York.

     Annual compendium of constitutional and
     legislative provisions, governmental de-
     crees, administrative orders and court
     decisions, of UN member states, bearing
     on human rights. Also contains similar
     information about trust and non-self-gov-
     erning territories as well as interna-
     tional agreements relating to human rights
     Human rights covered include civil and
     political rights as well as economic,
     social and cultural rights. There is an
     alphabetical index arranged in accordance
     with rights enumerated in the Universal
     Declaration of Human Rights.

Issued with United Nations publication
sales numbers.

62. United Nations. Secretariat. <u>United Na-
tions action in the field of human rights</u>.
New York, 1974. xiv, 212 p. (ST/HR/2;
United Nations publication, Sales No.
E.74.XIV.2)

A review of UN activities in the field of
human rights from the establishment of
the Organization through 1972. Part I
deals with measures taken within the United Nations in the field of human rights:
Charter provisions; the Universal Declaration of Human Rights; the International
Covenant on Economic, Social and Cultural
Rights; the International Covenant on Civil
and Political Rights and the Optional Protocol; right of self-determination; elimination of racial and religious discrimination; apartheid, equality of men and
women; human rights in armed conflicts;
human rights and scientific and technological developments; war crimes; etc. Part
II deals with methods used by the UN in
the field of human rights: institutional
and organizational arrangements; international instruments; implementation machinery and procedures; studies and documentation.

(F) ACTIVITIES OF THE UNITED NATIONS: JUDICIAL
AND LEGAL

63. Castañeda, Jorge. <u>Valor jurídico de las
resoluciones de las Naciones Unidas</u>.
Mexico City: Colegio de México, 1967.
xi, 203 p. (Centro de Estudios Interna-
cionales, Publicaciones, 3)

Examines the legal characteristics of United Nations resolutions of the following
types: resolutions concerning the structure and functions of the Organization;

resolutions relating to international
peace and security; resolutions that determine the existence of particular facts
or legal situations; resolutions whose
force originates in the Charter; resolutions registering an agreement between
members of organs of the UN as well as
members of the League of Nations, the
specialized agencies and inter-American
organizations; resolutions containing
declarations.

Lacks index or consolidated bibliography
but includes bibliographical footnotes.

64.   Rosenne, Shabtai, ed. Documents on the
International Court of Justice. Leiden/
Dobbs Ferry, N.Y.:   Sijthoff/Oceana, 1974.
xi, 391 p.

Contains basic source texts such as the
UN Charter, the ICJ Statute, rules of the
Court, material on privileges and immunities, General Assembly resolutions dealing
with the Court, national declarations of
acceptance of compulsory jurisdiction,
judicial statistics, Court finances.

65.   United Nations. General Assembly. Report
of the International Court of Justice.
New York.   (Official records of the General Assembly, Supplement No. 5)

Brief guide to the composition, jurisdiction and judicial work of the Court during the report year, with lists of publications and documents of the Court.

66.   United Nations. International Law Commission. Yearbook of the International Law
Commission.   1949-   (A/CN.4/SER.A/-   ).

Constitutes the official records of the
Commission. As of 1950, there have been
two volumes per year: Volume I contains
the summary records of the annual session,

with a listing of members, officers and
agenda items; Volume II contains documents
of the session, arranged by agenda items.
Vol. II also includes the report of the
Commission to the General Assembly and
checklists of sessional documents. Issued
with United Nations publication sales numbers.

67. United Nations. Office of Legal Affairs.
United Nations legislative series.
v. 1-   , New York, 1951-   (ST/LEG/SER.
B/-   )

Collection of legislative texts and texts
of international treaties and agreements
in matters of international concern. Volumes embrace topics such as the law of
the sea, laws concerning nationality,
legal provisions concerning international
organizations, laws and regulations regarding diplomatic and consular privileges
and immunities, material on the succession
of states. Issued with United Nations
publication sales numbers.

68. United Nations Conference on the Law of
the Sea, 1st, Geneva 1958. Official records. Geneva. 7 v. (A/CONF.13/-   ;
United Nations publication, Sales No.
58.V.4)

Contains documents, summary records of
meetings, list of delegations and of officers of the Conference, other documents:
v.1: Preparatory documents
v.2: Plenary meetings
v.3: First Committee (Territorial Sea
     and Contiguous Zone)
v.4: Second Committee (High Seas:
     General Régime)
v.5: Third Committee (High Seas: Fish-
     ing, Conservation of Living
     Resources
v.6: Fourth Committee (Continental Shelf)
v.7: Fifth Committee (Question of Free

Access to the Sea of Land-locked
Countries)

69.   United Nations Conference on the Law of
the Sea, 2d, Geneva 1960. <u>Official record</u>
Geneva. 2 v.

Vol. [1] (A/CONF.19/-   ; United Nations
publication, Sales No. 60.V.6) contains
the summary records of plenary meetings
and of meetings of the Committee of the
Whole, and annexes (documents relating to
the Conference, including the Final Act).

Vol. [2] (United Nations publication, Sales
No. 62.V.3) contains the verbatim records
of the general debate of the Committee of
the Whole.

70.   United Nations Conference on the Law of
the Sea, 3d, 1973-   . <u>Official records.</u>
New York.

Contains summary records of meetings and
documents of the Conference. The following volumes have been published as of July
1977:

v.1:   First Session, New York, 3-15 December 1973; Second Session, Caracas,
20 June-29 August 1974. Summary records of plenary and General Committee meetings (United Nations publication, Sales No. E.75.V.3)
v.2:   Second Session, Caracas, 20 June-29
August 1974. Summary records of
meetings of the First, Second, and
Third committees (United Nations publication, Sales No. E.75.V.4)
v.3:   First Session, New York, 3-15 December 1973; Second Session, Caracas,
20 June-29 August 1974. Documents
of the Conference (United Nations
publication, Sales No. E.75.V.5)
v.4:   Third Session, Geneva, 17 March-9 May
1975. Summary records of plenary and

committee meetings; documents of the
Conference (United Nations publication, Sales No. E.75.V.10)

v.5: Fourth Session, New York, 15 March-
7 May 1976. Summary records of plenary and committee meetings; documents (United Nations publication,
Sales No. E.76.V.8)

v.6: Fifth Session, New York, 2 August-
17 September 1976. Summary records
of plenary and committee meetings;
documents (United Nations publication, Sales No. E.77.V.2)

The Sixth Session of the Conference met in
New York, 23 May-15 July 1977. Pending
publication of the official records, the
documents of the Sixth Session are available in mimeographed form, under document
series symbol A/CONF.62/-   .

The Seventh Session of the Conference is
scheduled to be held in Geneva, from 28
March to 12 or 19 May 1978.

71. United Nations law reports; unofficial
reports concerning legal matters in the
United Nations. 1-   ; Sept. 1966-
New York: Walker.

Monthly digest of matters of legal concern
dealt with in various UN organs.

(G) ACTIVITIES OF THE UNITED NATIONS: PEACE
AND SECURITY

72. Bailey, Sydney Dawson. The procedure of
the UN Security Council. Oxford: Claren-
don Press, 1975. xii, 424 p.

A sequel to the author's Voting in the Security Council.

The following are the principal matters
discussed: institutional framework of the
Council; procedures concerning meetings;

participants in the activities of the Coun
cil; decision-making process; relations
with other organs; subsidiary organs of th
Council; the need for change. Includes a
select bibliography, copious references,
and index.

73. James, Alan. The politics of peace-keepin
New York: Praeger, c1969. 452 p. (Studi
in international security, 12)

A study of the United Nations' peace-keeping operations up to mid-1968. The author
discusses three categories of peace-keeping and related action, under the headings
"Patching-up" (investigation, mediation,
supervision, administration), "Prophylaxis
(accusation, sedation, obstruction, refrigeration), and "Proselytism" (invalida-
tion, coercion).

There is a select bibliography and an index.

74. Journal of peace research. v. 1-   ;
1964-   . Oslo: Universitetsforlaget.

Published under the auspices of the International Peace Research Association and
edited at the International Peace Research
Institute, Oslo, this scholarly quarterly
includes occasional articles on the UN
system as it relates to international peace
and security.

75. Larus, Joel, ed. From collective security
to preventive diplomacy; readings in international organization and the maintenance of peace. New York: Wiley, c1965.
xi, 556 p.

An anthology of essays and primary sources
on the League of Nations and the United
Nations. Included are eight case histo-
ries: four political crises of the League

era (the Greek-Bulgarian incident of 1925,
the Sino-Japanese dispute of 1931-1933,
the Italo-Ethiopian dispute of 1935-1936,
the Finnish-Russian conflict of 1939) and
four within the United Nations experience:
Korea, Suez, Hungary and the Congo.
Appendices contain the League's Covenant
and the United Nations Charter.

76. Manin, Philippe. L'Organisation des Nations Unies et le maintien de la paix; le
respect du consentement de l'état. Paris:
Librairie générale de droit et de juris-
prudence R. Pichon et R. Durand-Auzias,
1971. iv, 343 p. (Bibliothèque de droit
international, t. 60)

The main thrust of this work is the dual
role of the consent of states in UN peace-
keeping operations: consent as a limitation of the maintenance of peace, and consent as the foundation of United Nations
actions. The author examines the problem
of the need for state consent; the nature
of peace and security activities of the Security Council and the General Assembly;
the ways in which state consent may limit
Council and Assembly action; the scope and
extent of consent; the nature of United
Nations action as a contractual operation,
including legal and financial aspects.
Includes index and bibliography.

77. O'Brien, Conor Cruise. To Katanga and back;
a UN case history. New York: Simon and
Schuster, c1962. ix, 370 p.

A candid, personal narrative of ONUC, the
UN Operation in the Congo in 1960-61 in
which the author's mission as UN representative was to see to the implementation of
the Security Council resolution calling for
the withdrawal from the Congo of Belgian
and other foreign military personnel,
advisers, and mercenaries. The author, an
Irish diplomat and noted literary figure,

came under sharp criticism for his actions and statements from inside as well as outside the UN.

78. Peace research abstracts journal.
     v. 1-   ; June 1964-   Oakville,
     Ont.: Canadian Peace Research Institute.

Contains abstracts of journal articles, papers and monographs published in various countries and languages on all aspects of world affairs, war and peace. Many of the abstracts deal with the UN and other international organizations. Volumes for 1972- have been published with the assistance of UNESCO as an official publication of the International Peace Research Association. Arranged by coded subjects. Monthly, with annual author and subject indexes.

79. Peace research abstracts journal. Coding manual. Clarkson, Ont.: Canadian Peace Research Institute, c1967. 36 p.

Description of the classification system used in Peace research abstract journal (q.v., entry 78), detailed coding index, and alphabetical subject index.

80. Rikhye, Indar Jit; Harbottle, Michael; and Egge, Bjørn. The thin blue line; international peacekeeping and its future. New Haven: Yale University Press, 1974. xvi, 353 p. maps.

The authors, three senior military officials active in United Nations peacekeeping operations, examine activities relating to international conflict and peacekeeping conducted by the United Nations (the Middle East, the Congo and Cyprus are used as main case studies) and outside of the Organizatio (e.g., Indochina). This is followed by a consideration of future international conflict control. Maps, a bibliography and an index enhance the usefulness of the work.

81. United Nations. Conference of the Committee on Disarmament. <u>Comprehensive study of the question of nuclear-weapon-free zones in all its aspects; special report</u>. New York, 1976. iii, 98 p. (A/10027/Add. 1; United Nations publication, Sales No. E.76.I.7)

The study, carried out by the Ad Hoc Group of Qualified Governmental Experts for the Study of the Question of Nuclear-Weapon-Free Zones, traces the historical background of "military denuclearization" of various areas; discusses the concept of nuclear-weapon-free zones; sets out the responsibilities of states within and without the zones; and deals with the issues of verification and control, nuclear-weapon-free zones and international law, and the peaceful uses of nuclear energy. Also contains (verbatim) comments of members of the Conference of the Committee on Disarmament, and a Mexican working paper offering relevant draft definitions.

82. United Nations. General Assembly. <u>Report of the Security Council</u>. (Official records of the General Assembly, Supplement No. 2)

A summary of and guide to the year's activities. Part I outlines questions considered by the Council under its responsibility for the maintenance of international peace and security; part II, other matters considered by the Council; part III, note on the work of the Military Staff Committee; part IV, matters brought to the Council's attention but not discussed during the report year. Includes texts of important documents, references to other documents and summary records of meetings. Appendices give directory information, list of meetings, checklist of resolutions adopted.

(H)   ACTIVITIES OF THE UNITED NATIONS: TRUSTEE-
      SHIP AND DECOLONIZATION

83.   United Nations. General Assembly. Report
      of the Special Committee on the Situation
      with Regard to the Implementation of the
      Declaration on the Granting of Independ-
      ence to Colonial Countries and Peoples.
      New York, 1962-   (Official records
      of the General Assembly, 17th-   Session)

      Information on: establishment, organiza-
      tion and activities of the Special Commit-
      tee; dissemination of information on de-
      colonization; visiting missions to non-
      self-governing territories; foreign econom-
      ic, military and other interests affect-
      ing the territories; implementation of the
      declaration on decolonization; Southern
      Rhodesia; Namibia; other territories
      (e.g., Gibraltar, American Samoa and Guam,
      Falkland Islands). Includes documentary
      annexes.

      The first report of the Special Committee
      appeared as an addendum to agenda item 25
      in the annexes of the Official records of
      the General Assembly, seventeenth session.
      In recent years, the reports have been
      issued as supplements of the Official re-
      cords of the General Assembly.

84.   United Nations. General Assembly. Re-
      port of the Trusteeship Council. Offi-
      cial records of the General Assembly,
      Supplement No. 4)

      Summary of the year's activities: exam-
      ination of reports and petitions, visits
      to trust territories, conditions prevail-
      ing in trust territories. Includes direc-
      tory information, information on meetings
      held during the year and references to
      documents.

85. United Nations. Trusteeship Council.
    Resolutions. New York. (Official re-
    cords of the Trusteeship Council, Supple-
    ment No. 1)

    Contains agenda, resolutions adopted and
    other decisions taken by the Council.
    Issued sessionally.

(I) TREATIES AND AGREEMENTS

86. Grenville, John A.S. The major interna-
    tional treaties, 1914-1973; a history and
    guide with texts. London: Methuen & Co.,
    1974. xxix, 575 p.

    A brief history and analysis of major
    treaties and agreements, with texts of
    the most important ones. Comprises chap-
    ters such as Introduction to international
    treaties; Secret agreements and treaties
    of the first world war; Peace settlements
    and the League of Nations, 1919-23; The
    collapse of the territorial settlements
    of Versailles, 1931-38; The Allied con-
    ferences and the political settlement of
    Europe, 1943-45 (including text of the
    1942 United Nations Declaration); the
    United Nations (including texts of the
    UN Charter, of the IMF Articles of Agree-
    ment and of the IBRD Articles of Agree-
    ment); The peace treaties, 1945-72; The
    major international conflicts, treaties
    and agreements of 1973.

    Includes maps, bibliography and index.

87. United Nations. Treaty series; treaties
    and international agreements registered
    or filed and recorded with the Secretar-
    iat of the United Nations. v. 1-   ;
    1946/47-   New York.

    Collection of authentic texts of treaties
    and international agreements, published
    to satisfy a Charter (Article 102) obliga-

tion. The instruments are reproduced in
the original languages, with English and
French translation where applicable. Eac
volume has five parts: Part I contains
international agreements concluded by
states (at least one of which is a member
of the United Nations) and registered wit
the Secretariat; Part II includes genera:
international agreements, i.e., those cor
cluded before the entry into force of the
Charter or those concluded between or
among non-member states or international
organizations; Annex A records subsequent
action (accessions, ratifications, etc.)
relating to treaties previously registere
Annex B, subsequent action relating to
treaties filed and recorded; Annex C, sut
sequent actions relating to treaties and
agreements concluded during the existence
of the League of Nations.

There is a cumulative index (q.v., entry
118), each volume of which covers 50 or
100 volumes of the Treaty series.

88.   United Nations. Office of Legal Affairs.
Multilateral treaties in respect of which
the Secretary-General performs depositary
functions. List of signatures, ratifications, accessions, etc., as at 31 Dec.
1967-   New York.   (ST/LEG/SER.D/-

Comprehensive annual list of signatures,
ratifications, accessions, etc. relating
to multilateral treaties deposited with
the Secretary-General. Each successive
issue cumulates information about the
status of each treaty. The information
is presented in two parts: Part I, United Nations multilateral treaties; Part
II, League of Nations multilateral treaties. Part I is subdivided by subjects
(e.g., Human rights, Obscene publications
International trade and development, Economic statistics, Law of the sea, etc.)
Part II lists treaties in the order in

which the League of Nations originally
listed them. Information given about each
treaty includes name; entry into force;
registration date and number; reference to
the volume of the Treaty series where the
full text is to be found; information on
the method of adoption; listing of states,
with dates of signature, ratification, etc.,
texts of declarations and reservations by
states; other information. Issued with
United Nations publication sales numbers.

Supersedes an earlier publication entitled
Signatures, ratifications, accessions,
acceptances, etc., concerning the multilateral conventions and agreements in respect of which the Secretary-General acts
as depositary (United Nations publication,
Sales No. 1949.V.9) and its supplements
1-24.

89. United Nations. Office of Legal Affairs.
Statement of treaties and international
agreements registered or filed and recorded
with the Secretariat.   Feb. 1947-
New York. (ST/LEG/SER.A/-   )

Issued monthly, in English and French.
Each issue is in two parts: Part I, Treaties and agreements registered in accordance with Article 102 (1) of the Charter;
Part II, Treaties and agreements filed and
recorded in accordance with General Assembly regulations. Entries for each agreement give the registration and recording
number, title, date of conclusion, date
and method of entry into force, authentic
languages of the text, names of states or
other authorities involved.

Annexes contain information on accessions,
ratifications, supplementary agreements
and other subsequent actions affecting
agreements. There is a subject/country
index. For authentic texts of agreements,
see Treaty series, entry 87.

Issued with United Nations publication
sales numbers.

(J)   STATISTICS

90.   United Nations. Statistical Office.   Demographic yearbook. 1st-   issue; 1948-
New York.   (ST/ESA/STAT/SER.R/-   )

Compendium of demographic statistics from
about 250 geographical entities of the
world.   Tables give population, mortality,
natality, nuptiality, divorce and migration
statistics.   Each issue includes a lengthy
article on a special topic.   Issues for
1963-   include cumulative subject indexes   in English and French.   Issued with
United Nations publication sales numbers.

91.   United Nations.   Statistical Office. Monthly   bulletin of statistics.   No. 1-   ;
Jan. 1947-   . New York. (ST/STAT/SER.Q/
)

Keeps the Statistical yearbook (q.v., entr
95) up to date.   Contains international
tables (often with annual, quarterly and
monthly figures) of industrial, trade,
transport, population, production, national accounts and miscellaneous other statistics.   Each issue includes selected
special features.   An English and French
cumulative country index is featured in
the March, June, September and December
issues.

92-
94.   United Nations.   Statistical Office.   Statistical papers.   Series M.   No. 1-
Jan. 1949-   . New York. (ST/ESA/STAT/SER
M/1-   )

One of several series of collections of
statistical monographs.   Some important
publications issued in Series M:
92.   - Standard international trade classifi-

cation, revision 2. (Statistical papers, Series M, No. 34/Rev.2, United Nations publication, Sales No. E.75. XVII.6.) A numerical classification of commodities. Indispensable when using internationally comparable trade-by-commodity data as published in United Nations statistical sources, e.g., Yearbook of international trade statistics, World trade annual, q.v., entries 97-98; as well as other, e.g., OECD, statistics.

93. - United Nations standard country or area code for statistical use (Statistical papers, Series M, No. 49/Rev. 1, United Nations publication, Sales No. E.75. XVII.8) Alphabetical list of countries or areas giving 3-digit numerical codes, official names of countries or areas, standard abbreviations, and ISO (International Organization for Standardization) 2-letter and 3-letter alphabetical codes.

94. - Directory of international statistics (Statistical papers, Series M, No. 56, United Nations publication, Sales No. E.75.XVII.11.) A guide to international statistical services (performed by the UN, the specialized agencies, OECD, CMEA, the Statistical Office of the European Communities, etc.), series, standards, and computerized statistics.

95. United Nations. Statistical Office. Statistical yearbook. 1st-   issue; 1948-   . New York (ST/ESA/STAT/SER.S/-)

Annual summary of population, manpower, agricultural, social, financial, industrial, manufacturing, energy, trade, etc., statistics of the countries of the world. Data are presented in a series of tables grouped in chapters by subject. Sources

of data (national statistical offices and
intergovernmental bodies) are cited and
the tables are accompanied by copious
notes, glossaries and explanatory remarks
Tables usually give time series of several
years. Issued with United Nations publication sales numbers.

The Statistical yearbook is part of a co-
ordinated set of periodic statistical publications. Other publications in this interrelated set include the Demographic
yearbook (q.v., entry 90), Yearbook of
national accounts statistics, World energy
supplies, Yearbook of industrial statistics (formerly The growth of world industry), Yearbook of international trade statistics, Yearbook of construction statistics, Commodity trade statistics, Monthly
bulletin of statistics (q.v., entry 91),
Population and vital statistics report.
In addition to these UN publications, the
following major publications of specialized
agencies are considered as components
of the set of statistical serials: Yearbook of labour statistics (ILO); Production yearbook, Trade yearbook, Yearbook
of fishery statistics, Yearbook of forest
products (FAO); Statistical yearbook
(UNESCO); World health statistics annual
(WHO); International financial statistics
(IMF); Digest of statistics - airline traf
fic (ICAO).

96.   United Nations. Statistical Office. United Nations statistical pocketbook. 1st-
ed. New York, 1976-   (Statistical papers, series V; ST/ESA/STAT/SER.V/-
)

Annual compilation of basic international
statistics. In two parts: Part I contains demographic, economic and social
statistics for the world as a whole, for
selected regions, and for major countries.
Part II presents important statistical in-

dicators (population, national accounts, production, consumption, transport and communications, finance, external trade, international travel, prices, health, education) for individual countries. Includes sketch maps of continents.

Added title: World statistics in brief.

Issued with United Nations publication sales numbers.

97. United Nations. Statistical Office. World trade annual. 1963-   . New York, Walker.

A compendium of both summary and detailed statistics of exports and imports of the principal developed countries of the world, excluding eastern Europe. Arranged, in several volumes each year, by commodity. Tables show names of commodities with SITC number, total value in U.S. dollars of imports and exports of individual countries and a further breakdown by principal trading partner.

98. United Nations. Statistical Office. World trade annual. Supplement: trade of the industrialized nations with eastern Europe and the developing nations. 1964-   . New York, Walker.

Covers material in a similar manner as the main work. Arranged by geographical area or country.

99. United Nations Conference on Trade and Development. Handbook of international trade and development statistics. Manuel de statistiques du commerce international et du développement. 1967-   . New York. (TD/STAT./-   )

Comprehensive collection of statistical data on world trade and development. Ma-

jor groups of statistics included are:
value of world trade by regions and countries; volume, unit value, and terms of
trade index numbers by regions; commodity
prices; structure of imports and exports
by selected commodity groups; summary of
exports and imports by selected regions o:
origin and destination; imports and exports for individual countries by commodi
structure; major exports of developing
countries by leading exporters; financial
flows, aid, and balance of payments for de
veloping countries; some basic indicators
of development. Many time series are give
from 1950.

Full editions are normally issued at each
quadrennial session of the Conference,
with annual supplements during intervening
years.

Continues a publication with the same titl
first issued in 1964 under document symbol
E/CONF.46/12/Add.1.

Issued with United Nations publications
sales numbers.

(K)   BIOGRAPHIES

100. Who's who in the United Nations and relate
      agencies. 1st-   ed.; 1975-   .
      New York: Arno Press.

Contains biographies of more than 3,700
senior staff members of the secretariats
of the organizations of the UN system and
senior personnel of missions. Includes a
structural breakdown of the secretariats,
directory information about UN offices
around the world and other reference material.

(L) GLOSSARIES

101. United Nations. Division of Narcotic
Drugs. Multilingual list of narcotic
drugs under international control. 3d
ed. New York, 1968. xvii, 273 p. (E/CN.
7/513; United Nations publication Sales
No. E/F/R/S.69.XI.1)

Alphabetical (Roman alphabet) listing of
names of narcotic drugs subject to international control by virtue of various conventions. Cross references are given from
chemical names and synonyms to the main
term used in the list. Entries give, for
each drug: the International Non-proprie-
tary Name (INN); common synonyms in English, French, Spanish and Russian; nature and (structural and empirical) formula of the substance; trade names; code
designations; regime of control applicable to the substance in accordance with
treaties.

There are supplementary lists of drugs in
Arabic, Chinese, Greek, Hebrew, Japanese,
Korean, Russian and Thai.

102. United Nations. Documentation and Terminology Service. Law of the sea terminology. New York, 1975. 276 p. (Terminology bulletin No. 297/Rev.1; ST/CS/SER.
F/297/Rev.1)

A list of about 900 titles, terms and ex-
pressions (both legal and technical) relating to the law of the sea and oceanography, arranged alphabetically in English. Each entry gives French, Russian,
and Spanish equivalents. French, Russian,
and Spanish indexes refer to entry numbers in the main list.

Complements the terminology bulletin
titled Oceanography (q.v., entries 103-
104), which contains non-legal terms.

103.   United Nations. Office of Conference
       Services. Oceanography; list of terms
       relating to oceanography and marine re-
       sources. New York, 1971.   445 p.   (Termi
       nology bulletin No. 265.   ST/CS/SER.F/26

       A list of equivalent terms in English,
       French, Spanish, Russian, and Chinese.
       Contains 3,000 entries plus 1,000 syno-
       nyms. Includes such topics as geology,
       meteorology, ocean chemistry, ecology,
       etc. Arranged alphabetically (in Eng-
       lish). Includes also common acronyms
       and abbreviations of various organiza-
       tions and programmes concerned with
       oceanography. Issued by the Documenta-
       tion and Terminology Service of the
       Office of Conference Services.

       Complements the terminology bulletin
       titled Law of the sea terminology (q.v.,
       entry 102), which contains legal terms.

104.   United Nations. Office of Conference
       Services. Oceanography; list of terms
       relating to oceanography and marine re-
       sources. Addendum. New York, 1974.
       193 p.   (ST/CS/SER.F/265/Add.1)

       Contains French, Spanish and Russian in-
       dexes, referring to entry numbers in the
       main work (entry 103).

(M)   BIBLIOGRAPHIES, INDEXES, GUIDES

105.   Brimmer, Brenda. A guide to the use of
       United Nations documents, including ref-
       erence to the specialized agencies and
       special UN bodies. Dobbs Ferry, N.Y.:
       Oceana, 1962.   xv, 272 p.

       A selective guide, based on the holdings
       of the UN collection of the New York Uni-
       versity Library. Although some sections
       are now out of date, this is still an
       excellent handbook for researchers, li-

brarians and others working with UN documents. Part I, Methods and problems
of research (including a description of
the UN documentation system and guidelines for organizing UN document collections) is especially useful.

106. Deardorff, John. United Nations Security
Council index, 1946-1964. Columbus:
United Nations Collection, Ohio State
University Library, 1969. vi, 100 leaves.

An index of Security Council documents in
the United Nations collection of the Ohio
State University Library. References are
made to the part of the Official records
or to other sources where each document
may be located. Preliminary material includes a list of abbreviations.

107. Dimitrov, Theodore Delchev. Documents of
international organisations; a bibliographic handbook. London: International
University Publications, 1973. xv, 301
p.

A bibliography (some items with brief
annotations) covering documents of UN
organizations and other inter-governmental bodies. Lists material published by
and about the organizations. Arranged by
sections such as Purposes and functions,
How to use international documentation,
Bibliographic control, Modern trends:
Operational information systems. Includes a directory of international governmental organizations, a list of abbreviations, an author index and a corporate
body index.

108. Hajnal, Peter I. "Indexes to resolutions;
a reference series issued by the United
Nations Library." Government publications review, v. 2 (1975), pp. 31-40.

This article examines the scope, arrange-

ment, method of compilation and terminol
ogy of the Index to resolutions of the
General Assembly, 1946-1970, Index to
resolutions and other decisions of the
United Nations Conference on Trade and
Development and of the Trade and Develop
ment Board, 1964-1972 and Index to resol
tions of the Security Council, 1946-1970
and indicates the relationship of these
indexes to other indexing products of th
United Nations Library.

109.   International bibliography, information,
documentation. v. 1-   ; Mar. 1973-
New York, Bowker/Unipub.

A quarterly, current-awareness bibliography of organizations in the UN system
and other international governmental organizations. List books, periodicals,
maps, microforms, audiovisual material,
etc. Excludes working documents. Gives
directory information and news of activities and programmes as well as informatic
on how to obtain publications. Arranged
in three sections: information and news;
bibliographic record (by subject); perioc
icals record (alphabetical). Has a cumu
lative annual subject index and a cumulative annual list of periodicals.

110.   International Symposium on the Documentation of the United Nations and Other
Intergovernmental Organizations, Geneva,
1972. Sources, organization, utilization
of international documentation; proceedings of the ... Symposium ....The Hague:
International Federation for Documentation, 1974. 586 p. (FID publication,
506)

A useful collection of conference papers,
covering most aspects of the production,
distribution, acquisition, organization,
bibliographic control and use of the documents of UN organizations and other in-

tergovernmental agencies.

111. McConaughy, John Bothwell. A student's guide to United Nations documents and their use. New York: Council on International Relations and United Nations Affairs, c1969. 17 p.

A concise guide to primary UN documents, with a selected bibliography of sources of information about the UN. Includes a brief but useful guide to suggested research methods.

112. New Zealand. Ministry of Foreign Affairs. United Nations handbook. 1961- . Wellington. (Its Publication)

A useful, concise annual. Gives a brief survey of Charter provisions relating to the principal organs of the United Nations, information on the structure and composition of those organs and their subsidiary bodies. Membership lists are included for a number of subsidiary organs as well as the principal organs. Concise information, including directory information and membership, is presented about special bodies of the United Nations (UNICEF, UNDP, etc.) as well as about specialized agencies and other related organizations.

Title varies: United Nations and specialized agencies handbook, 1961-67; United Nations and related agencies handbook, 1968-72 (not published in 1970).

Includes index.

113. Public Affairs Information Service. Bulletin. v.1- 1915- . New York.

PAIS is a subject index to English-language monographs, pamphlets, reports and over 1,000 periodicals in the social sci-

ences. Provides good coverage of important publications of international organ
zations, including the organizations of
the United Nations system. Weekly, with
five cumulations a year, the last one
being an annual cumulation. A cumulativ
subject index for 1915-1974 has been issued by Carrollton Press.

114.   Rothman, Marie H. Citation rules and
forms for United Nations documents and
publications. Brooklyn, N.Y.: Long Island University Press, 1971. 64 p.

A fairly detailed guide, with many illus
trative examples, for citation of UN do
uments, sales publications, periodical
articles, etc. in bibliographies, footnotes and other references.

115.   Royal Institute of International Affairs
Library. Index to United Nations documents to December 1947, and Supplements,
No. 1-3, Jan. 1948-Dec. 1949. London,
1948-50. 4 pts. in 1 v.

An alphabetical listing (mostly by subject but there are some author entries
as well) of UN documents and periodicals
and some publications of the affiliated
inter-governmental organizations. References are made to document series symbols and to periodical articles. To some
extent, this index fills the gap for the
period 1946-49, not covered by UNDI (q.v.
entry 135).

116.   Schopen, Lynn [and others]. Nations on
record; United Nations General Assembly
roll-call votes (1946-1973). Oakville,
Ont.: Canadian Peace Research Institute,
1975. 515 p. + index.

A chronologically arranged listing of the
record of member states' votes in plenary
sessions of the General Assembly. Refer-

ences are given to the location of the
votes in the <u>Official records</u> of the
Assembly, to document symbols, numbers
of resolutions adopted, etc. Excludes
decisions taken by other than roll-call
vote: consensus, show-of-hands, etc.,
and votes in the committees of the Assembly. Includes an alphabetical subject
index.

117. Stevens, Robert D. and Stevens, Helen C.,
eds. <u>Reader in documents of international organizations</u>. Washington: Micro-
card Editions Books, 1973. xii, 410 p.

Designed primarily for generalist librarians, this collection of essays ranges
from well-documented scholarly contributions to schematic pieces and from selected primary documents to descriptions
of particular types of documents, organization structures and activities.

The book is divided into the following
parts: Characteristics of international
documents; the League of Nations; specialized agencies of the League of Nations;
the transition from League to United Nations; the United Nations; the specialized agencies of the United Nations; non-
governmental and regional organizations.

Lacks index.

118. United Nations. <u>Cumulative index to the
United Nations Treaty series</u>. No. 1-
New York, 1957- .

These indexes, issued by the Office of
Legal Affairs but prepared by the Dag
Hammarskjöld Library, appear in separate
English and French editions. They bear
no sales codes or series symbols. Eleven
numbers have been published to date, covering volumes 1-750 of the <u>Treaty series</u>
(q.v., entry 87).

Each index contains the following three
sections:
a)   a listing of treaties and internatic
      al agreements arranged in the order
      of date of signature, date of openir
      for signature or accession, or date
      of extension, modification, etc.
b)   a similar chronological listing of
      general international agreements
c)   an alphabetical index of broad sub-
      jects and names of parties to the
      treaties and international agreement

119. United Nations. Archives Section. Inde
      to microfilm of United Nations documents
      in English, 1946-1961. New York, 1963.
      v, 279 p. (Archives special guide, No.
      14)

      Cumulative guide to English-language
      United Nations documents microfilmed up
      to 1962. Arranged by document series
      symbol.

      Brought up to date by:

120. United Nations. Archives Section. Inde
      to microfilm of United Nations documents
      in English. Supplement, 1962-1967. New
      York, 1970. v, 82 p. (Archives special
      guide, No. 14, Supplement No. 1)

121. United Nations. Dag Hammarskjöld Librar
      Bibliographical style manual. New York,
      1963. vi, 62 p. (ST/LIB/SER.B/8; Unite
      Nations publication, Sales No. 63.I.5)

      Although designed primarily for the use
      of the UN Secretariat, this is a useful,
      detailed guide for any researcher who
      wishes to cite government publications,
      United Nations and League of Nations doc
      uments and other books, periodicals,
      pamphlets and newspapers in a bibliograp
      ically correct form.

A new edition is in preparation as of
July 1977.

122-
125.   United Nations. Dag Hammarskjöld Library.
Index to proceedings ....New York. (ST/
LIB/SER.B/-   )

These indexes are bibliographical guides
to the proceedings and documentation of
the General Assembly, the Security Council, the Economic and Social Council and
the Trusteeship Council.

The indexes are issued in four series:

122.   .   . Index to proceedings of
the General Assembly, 1950/51-   .
(ST/LIB/SER.B/A-)   1 issue per session.

123.   .   . Index to proceedings of
the Security Council, 1964-   . (ST/LIB/
SER.B/S-)   1 issue per year.

124.   .   . Index to proceedings of
the Economic and Social Council, 1952-
. (ST/LIB/SER.B/E-)   2 issues per
year.

125.   .   . Index to proceedings of
the Trusteeship Council, 1952-   . (ST/
LIB/SER.B/T-)   1 issue per year.

Each index has: an introduction including
lists of officers, checklists of meetings
of the main organ and its committees, lists
of member states and their terms of office;
agenda, with reference to subject headings
used in the subject index; subject index,
arranged alphabetically and including information on documentation, discussion in
committee and in plenary and disposition
of each agenda item; index to speeches,
arranged alphabetically by country and
subdivided by subject discussed; numerical list of documents, arranged by series

symbol, with information on republicatio

Beginning with the General Assembly's
30th session, the Index to proceedings o
the General Assembly includes an annex
containing a voting chart of resolutions
adopted by recorded or roll-call vote.
Beginning with 1976, the Index to proceedings of the Security Council include
an annex containing a voting chart of
resolutions adopted by the Council durin
the year covered.

All four Indexes to proceedings are
issued with United Nations publication
sales numbers.

126-
128.   United Nations. Dag Hammarskjöld Librar
Index to resolutions .... New York. (ST
LIB/SER.H/-   )

These indexes are cumulative guides to
information contained in or referred to
in resolutions and other decisions
adopted by major organs of the UN.

Indexes issued to date are:

126.   .   . Index to resolutions of
the General Assembly, 1946-1970. 2 v.
(ST/LIB/SER.H/1; United Nations publication, Sales No. E.72.I.3 and E.72.I.14)

127.   .   . Index to resolutions and
other decisions of the United Nations
Conference on Trade and Development and
of the Trade and Development Board, 1964
1972. (ST/LIB/SER.H/2; United Nations
publication, Sales No. E.73.I.5); and

128.   .   . Index to resolutions of
the Security Council, 1946-1970. (ST/LI
SER.H/3; United Nations publication, Sal
No. E.73.I.16)

Each index consists of two parts: a) numerical list (containing resolution number, title or subject, date of adoption and reference to the document in which the text is to be found); b) subject index, arranged alphabetically and comprising references to the substantive contents of resolutions and other decisions.

A similar index to resolutions of the Economic and Social Council, 1946-70 is in preparation.

129. United Nations. Dag Hammarskjöld Library. List of United Nations document series symbols. New York, 1970. 171 p. (ST/ LIB/SER.B/5/Rev.2; United Nations publication, Sales No. E.70.I.21)

An alphanumeric list of series symbols, with information on the names of issuing organs and on beginning and ending dates of each series. Includes also an alphabetical index of series titles and broad subjects. Was kept up to date by annual additions in UNDI (q.v., entry 135), cumulative index, part 2. A new revised edition is in preparation as of July 1977.

130-
132. United Nations. Dag Hammarskjöld Library. UNDEX; United Nations documents index. v. 1-   ; Jan. 1970-   . New York. (ST/LIB/SER.I/-   )

A product of UNDIS, the partially computer-based information system developed by the Dag Hammarskjöld Library. Supersedes the Library's United Nations documents index (q.v., entry 135). Covers UN documents and publications other than restricted material and internal papers. Excludes certain types of documents that had been indexed in UNDI, e.g., documents of main committees of the General

Assembly. Issued irregularly in 1970-73, ten times a year as of January 1974

UNDEX is issued in three series:

130. . . . Series A. Sub-ject index. (ST/LIB/SER.I/A)

Arranged alphabetically. Each entry consists of the following: (1) subject statement; (2) type of document (e.g., meeting records, voting, bibliographies reports, resolutions); (3) author (personal or corporate); (4) date; (5) document series symbol(s). Now includes see/see also references from subjects to organizational names, from broad subjects to specific subjects, etc.

131. . . . Series B. Country index. (ST/LIB/SER.I/B)

Alphabetical. Each entry consists of the following elements: (1) name of country (2) type of action (e.g., membership, statements in debates, voting - yes, voting - no, documents submitted); (3) the subject to which the action relates; (4) document series symbol.

132. . . . Series C. List of documents issued. (ST/LIB/SER.I/C)

Arranged by series symbol, with full bibliographic description. Each year, issues 1 and 6 list General Assembly documents; issues 2 and 7, Economic and Social Council documents; issues 3 and 8 Security Council and Trusteeship Council documents, International Court of Justice publications, sales publications; issues 4 and 9, Secretariat and regional commission publications; issues 5 and 10, documents in all other series. Issue 10 includes a list of periodicals.

Series A and B are issued in English,
French, Russian and Spanish; Series C,
in English and French. Annual cumulation
of Series A and B for 1975 are in press;
1976 cumulations of Series A and B are
in preparation, as of July 1977.

133. United Nations. Dag Hammarskjöld Library.
UNDIS, the United Nations documentation
information system; a handbook of products and services. New York, 1974.
iii, 37 p. illus. (ST/LIB/33)

Basic information about UNDIS, a computer-
based information storage and retrieval system developed and implemented
by the Dag Hammarskjöld Library. Describes present and planned products and
services, computer-based UNDIS files,
types of information stored; gives suggestions for the use of products and
services.

134. United Nations. Dag Hammarskjöld Library.
United Nations documentation; a brief
guide for official recipients. New York,
1974. 25 p. (ST/LIB/34)

A practical guide to United Nations documents, their distribution and availability; arrangement and maintenance of
collections of United Nations documents;
and indexes published by the United Nations.

135. United Nations. Dag Hammarskjöld Library.
United Nations documents index. v. 1-
24; Jan. 1950-Dec. 1973. New York. (ST/
LIB/SER.E/-   )

UNDI, as the index is commonly known, is
a list of and index to UN documents other
than restricted material and internal
papers. Printed publications of the International Court of Justice are covered.
1950-62 issues of UNDI included a selec-

tive index to documents of intergovernmental organizations affiliated with the
UN.

Issued monthly (combined issues for July
and August), with annual cumulations.
Prior to 1963, only the subject index
cumulated.

Monthly issues contain: checklist of do-
uments and publications, by symbol,
with full bibliographic description;
listing, by series symbol, of documents
received by the Dag Hammarskjöld Library;
list of mimeographed documents reissued
in the Official records and elsewhere;
list of sales publications; alphabetical
subject-author-title index, often called
subject index, with cross references.
Longer entries are subarranged by form
subheadings: reports, resolutions, other
documents, draft resolutions, financial
implications, meeting records. References are to series symbols and/or sales
numbers.

Annual cumulations contain: cumulative
index, part 1 - author-title-subject;
cumulative index, part 2 - listing by
series symbol, list of documents reissued, list of sales publications, list
of new series symbols; cumulative checklist - a consolidation of the monthly
checklists.

Superseded by the Library's UNDEX; United Nations documents index (q.v., entries 130-132).

136.   United Nations. Dag Hammarskjöld Library
United Nations documents index; cumulate
index. Millwood, N.Y.: Kraus-Thomson,
1974-

Cumulates the first thirteen volumes
(1950-1962) of the subject[/author/title

indexes of UNDI (q.v., entry 135). Issued
commercially, in four volumes. Another
cumulation (v. 14-24, 1963-74) is planned.

137. United Nations. Dept. of Public Information. Ten years of United Nations publications, 1945 to 1955; a complete catalogue. New York, 1955. 271 p. (ST/DPI/
SER.F/7; United Nations publication, Sales
No. 1955.I.8)

A "comprehensive guide to the Official
records and publications and periodicals"
of the UN from the 1945 San Francisco
Conference to the end of 1954. Includes
a selection of League of Nations documents. The first section (sales publications) is arranged by sales number; the
second section lists Official records.
There is an alphabetical index.

138. United Nations. International Court of
Justice. Publications of the Internation-
al Court of Justice; catalogue. The
Hague, 1975. 23 p.

A numerical listing of all sales publications of the Court from its establishment in 1946 until 16 June 1975. Includes an alphabetical index of all cases
before the Court and information on the
various ICJ series.

139. United Nations. Library. A bibliography of the Charter of the United Nations.
New York, 1955. 128 p.

List almost three thousand books, periodicals and documents about the Charter.

140. United Nations. Library. Check list of
United Nations documents. 1946-53. New
York. 20 v. (ST/LIB/SER.F/-   )

Lists United Nations documents issued

between 1946-53. The check list fills
the gap from 1946 to the beginning of
publication of the United Nations documents index (q.v., entry 135).

Arranged in separate parts, each one devoted to the documents of a particular
organ and each one containing: information on the organization and membership
of the organ concerned, a list of documents arranged by entry number and series
symbol, a subject index, a personal name
index, etc.

The following parts have been issued:
- Part 2, no. 1: Security Council, 1946-
  1949. Jan. 1953. 188 p. (ST/LIB/SER.
  F/2; United Nations publication, Sales
  No. 1953.I.3)
- Part 3: Atomic Energy Commission, 1946-
  1952. Jul. 1953. 46 p. (ST/LIB/SER.F/
  3; United Nations publication, Sales No.
  1953.I.16)
- Part 4, no. 1: Trusteeship Council,
  1947-1948. Feb. 1949. 59 p. (ST/LIB/
  SER.F/4:1; United Nations publication,
  Sales No. 1949.I.2)
- Part 4, no. 2: Trusteeship Council,
  1948. Mar. 1949. 39 p. (ST/LIB/SER.F/
  4:2; United Nations publication, Sales
  No. 1949.I.5)
- Part 4, no. 3: Trusteeship Council,
  1949. Jul. 1951. 115 p. (ST/LIB/SER.
  F/4:3; United Nations publication, Sales
  No. 1951.I.17)
- Part 5, no. 1: Economic and Social
  Council, 1946-1947. Feb. 1949. 230 p.
  (ST/LIB/SER.F/5:1; United Nations pub-
  lication, Sales No. 1949.I.4)
- Part 5, no. 2: Economic and Social
  Council, 1948. Oct. 1951.   (ST/
  LIB/SER.F/5:2; United Nations publica-
  tion, Sales No. 1951.I.27)
- Part 5, no. 3: Economic and Social
  Council, 1949. Sep. 1952. 233 p. (ST/
  LIB/SER.F/5:3; United Nations publica-

tion, Sales No. 1952.I.4)
- Part 6A, no. 1: Economic and Employment Commission, 1947-1949. Sep. 1952. 63 p. (ST/LIB/SER.F/6A:1; United Nations publication, Sales No. 1952.I.10)
- Part 6B, no. 1: Transport and Communications Commission, 1946-1949. Dec. 1951. 43 p. (ST/LIB/SER.F/6B:1; United Nations publication, Sales No. 1951. I.18)
- Part 6C, no. 1: Statistical Commission, 1947-1949. Jan. 1952. 51 p. (ST/LIB/ SER.F/6C:1; United Nations publication, Sales No. 1951.I.19)
- Part 6D, no. 1: Commission on Human Rights, 1947-1949. Sept. 1952. 111 p. (ST/LIB/SER.F/6D:1; United Nations publication, Sales No. 1952.I.6)
- Part 6E, no. 1: Social Commission, 1946-1949. Mar. 1952. 84 p. (ST/LIB/ SER.F/6E:1; United Nations publication, Sales No. 1951.I.20)
- Part 6F, no. 1: Commission on the Status of Women, 1947-1949. Aug. 1951. 42 p. (ST/LIB/SER.F/6F:1; United Nations publication, Sales No. 1951.I.21)
- Part 6H, no. 1: Fiscal Commission, 1947-1948. Feb. 1949. 11 p. (ST/LIB/ SER.F/6H:1; United Nations publication, Sales No. 1949.I.6)
- Part 6H, no. 2: Fiscal Commission, 1949. Jan. 1952. 32 p. (ST/LIB/SER.F/6H:2; United Nations publication, Sales No. 1951.I.22)
- Part 6J, no. 1: Population Commission, 1947-1949. Dec. 1951. 32 p. (ST/LIB/ SER.F/6J:1; United Nations publication, Sales No. 1951.I.23)
- Part 7B, no. 1: Economic Commission for Asia and the Far East, 1947-1949. Oct. 1951. 91 p. (ST/LIB/SER.F/7B:1; United Nations publication, Sales No. 1951.I.26)
- Part 7C, no. 1: Economic Commission for Latin America, 1948-1949. Jan. 1952. 41 p. (ST/LIB/SER.F/7C:1;

United Nations publication, Sales No.
1951.I.28)
- Part 8, no. 1: United Nations Emergenc
Fund and United Nations Appeal for Chil
dren, 1946-1949. Jan. 1953. 58 p.
(ST/LIB/SER.F/8:1; United Nations publication, Sales No. 1953.I.5)
N.B. Part 1 (General Assembly and its
subsidiary organs), 6G (Commission on
Narcotic Drugs), 7A (Economic Commission
for Europe), and 9 (Secretariat publications) never issued.

141. United Nations. Office of Conference
Services. Catalogue of United Nations
publications. New York, 1967. vi, 276
p. (ST/CS/SER.J/9).

A listing of all sales publications issued from 1945 to 1966, arranged by broac
subjects. The entries give bibliographic
identification, brief annotations,
sales numbers, prices, etc. There is an
alphabetical subject/title index and an
index arranged by sales number.

142. United Nations. Office of Conference
Services. Catalogue of United Nations
publications, 1968-1969.

Updated by annual publications-in-print
lists (q.v., entry 149).

143. United Nations. Office of Conference
Services. United Nations Official re-
cords, 1948-1962; a reference catalogue.
New York, 1963. 107 p. (ST/CS/SER.J/2;
United Nations publication, Sales No.
64.I.3).

A catalogue of the Official records of
the General Assembly, the three Councils,
the Atomic Energy Commission, the Disarmament Commission, and the Yearbook of
the International Law Commission; of the
documents of the United Nations Confer-

ence on International Organization, 1945,
and of publications of the Preparatory
Commission of the United Nations. Updated by:

144. United Nations. Office of Conference
Services. United Nations Official records, 1962-1970.

145. United Nations. Office of Conference
Services. United Nations Official records, 1962-1970. Supplement, 1970-1972.

146. United Nations. Office of General Services. Catalogue of sound recordings in
the custody of the Sound Recording Unit
of the Telecommunications Section of the
United Nations as of 31 December 1972.
New York, 19 January 1973. 75 p. (ST/
OGS/SER.F/1/Rev.1)

In three parts: (A) a list, by subject
or name of organ, of United Nations proceedings which have been recorded for preservation. References are made to year of
meeting, disc number, place of meeting;
(B) a similar list, by name of organ, of
recordings of the proceedings of specialized agencies and other non-UN organs;
(C) a subject and name list of other
sound recordings (ceremonies, press conferences, etc.).

147. United Nations. Radio and Visual Services
Division. United Nations 16 mm film
catalogue, 1975-76. New York [1976].
43 p. illus.

An annotated list of films in the "International zone" series, "Man builds, man
destroys" series, "The UN; its Charter
and organization" series and other United
Nations films. Entries give description
of contents, indication of length, colour
and year of release, and language versions
available. Includes information on how to

obtain United Nations films, subject index and title index.

148.   United Nations. Sales Section. <u>Micro-</u>
<u>fiche</u>. New York, 1977.   12 p.

Lists, with prices, United Nations publications available for sale on 105 mm x
148 mm negative microfiche, each fiche
containing 60 frames at a 20:1 reduction.
Documents on microfiche include <u>Official</u>
<u>records</u> of the General Assembly <u>and of</u>
the three Councils; <u>Treaty series</u> and
cumulative indexes; <u>Documents of</u> the Unit
ed Nations Conference on International
Organization, San Francisco, 1945; recurrent publications such as the <u>Yearbook</u>
<u>of the United Nations</u>, the <u>Demographic</u>
<u>yearbook</u>, etc.

Similar price-lists are issued annually.

149.   United Nations. Sales Section. <u>United</u>
<u>Nations publications in print, 1977;</u>
<u>checklist</u>. New York, 1977.   ii, 45 p.

Together with previous annual books-in-
print lists, updates the <u>Catalogue of</u>
<u>United Nations publications</u> (q.v., entrie
141-142) and is itself updated by quarterly checklists.

150.   United Nations. Sound Recording Unit.
<u>List of speeches and visits made by heads</u>
<u>of state and dignitaries, 1945-1972</u>. New
York, 1973.   iii, 81, 6 p.   (ST/OGS/SER.
F/4)

A chronological index of visits and
speeches, giving names, countries and
titles of visitors/speakers, duration of
visits, identification of meetings at
which speeches were made. Updated
periodically.

151. United Nations Children's Fund. Geograph-
     ical index to UNICEF documents, 1946
     to 1972. New York, 1974. 324 p. (E/ICEF/
     INDEX/2).

     A listing, by document symbol, of UNICEF
     documents relevant to specific countries
     or geographical regions. Arranged in six
     sequences, each further subdivided by
     country or area: Africa, Asia, Eastern
     Mediterranean, Europe, the Americas, In-
     terregional. Lacks subject index and
     consolidated country/area index.

152. United Nations Conference on Trade and
     Development. Information Service. Guide
     to UNCTAD publications, covering the peri-
     od from the first Conference to the end
     of 1969. Geneva. 73 p.

     Lists reports, studies and basic refer-
     ence documents issued by UNCTAD and by
     its Trade and Development Board and other
     subsidiary bodies. Arranged by the fol-
     lowing categories: basic documents,
     trade and development policies and trends,
     development aid, commodities, manufactures,
     preferences, shipping, regional eco-
     nomic groupings, trade with socialist coun-
     tries, second development decade, miscel-
     laneous items, statistical documents.
     Many entries are annotated.

     Kept up to date by annual or biennial
     supplements.

153. United Nations Industrial Development Or-
     ganization. Documents list. 1967-   .
     New York. (ID/SER.G/-   ).

     Alphanumeric lists of major printed pub-
     lications, Industrial Development Board
     documents, publications of meetings and
     conferences, information series, and
     sales publications. Contains subject in-
     dex to major studies and reports and sub-

ject index of conferences, expert working
groups, workshops and seminars. Each
year's issue cumulates previous issues.
Successor to its Index to documents issued
by the Committee for Industrial Development . . . (q.v., entry 154).

154. United Nations Industrial Development Organization. Index to documents issued by
the Committee for Industrial Development,
Centre for Industrial Development and Division for Industrial Development from inception to end of 1966. v, 114 p. New
York. (ID/SER.G/1).

Alphanumeric listing, by series symbol
and sales number, of documents issued by
the three bodies from 1961 through 1966,
including a listing of restricted documents. Alphabetical index. Continued by
its Documents list (q.v., entry 153).

155. University Microfilms International. United Nations; a keyword dissertation biblio-
ography. Ann Arbor, Mich. [1975?] [ii,]
41 p.

A listing of 345 doctoral dissertations
about the United Nations and related international organizations. Each entry
shows author, title, degree earned, name
of degree-granting institution, year degree was granted, pagination, reference
to location of abstract in Dissertation
abstracts international, and order number
for acquiring a full text reproduction of
the dissertation.

Arranged in two parts: keyword title
index and author index.

156. Winton, Harry N.M. Publications of the
United Nations system; a reference guide.
New York: Bowker, 1972. xi, 202 p.

A survey of the structure, main activities

and publications of the UN and of the
affiliated intergovernmental organizations.
Part I, Organizations of the UN system
and their publications; part II, Selected
reference publications of the UN system,
with annotated entries, arranged by broad
subject; part III, Periodicals of the UN
system. Includes a subject index.

INDEX TO THE BIBLIOGRAPHY

(Numbers refer to bibliography entries)

United Nations.

Dag Hammarskjöld Library.

United Nations.

Dept. of Economic and Social Affairs.
World economic survey (54)

Dept. of Public Information. *Ten years of United Nations publications, 1945-1955* (137)

Division of Narcotic Drugs. *Multilingual list of narcotic drugs under international control* (101)

Documentation and Terminology Service.
Law of the sea terminology (102)

Economic and Social Council.

Report [to the General Assembly] (56)

Resolutions and decisions (55)

Rules of procedure (3)

General Assembly.

Budget estimates (40)

Budget for the financial year (39)

Introduction to the report of the Secretary-General on the work of the Organization (42)

Medium-term plan (38)

Programme budget for the biennium (39)

Proposed programme budget for the biennium (40)

Report of the Economic and Social Council (56)

Report of the International Court of Justice (65)

Report of the Secretary-General on the work of the Organization (41)

  General Assembly.
    Report of the Security Council (82)

    *Report of the Special Committee on the
    Situation with Regard to the Implementation
    of the Declaration on the Granting of Inde-
    pendence to Colonial Countries and Peoples* (83)

    Report of the Trusteeship Council (84)

    Rules of procedure (4-5)

  Group of Experts on the Structure of the
  United Nations System. *A new United Nations
  structure for global economic co-operation* (57)

  International Court of Justice.
    *Publications of the International Court
    of Justice; catalogue* (138)

    Report [to the General Assembly] (65)

    Rules of Court (6-7)

    Statute (1)

  International Law Commission. *Yearbook
  of the International Law Commission* (66)

  Library.
    *A bibliography of the Charter of the
    United Nations* (139)

    Check list of United Nations documents (140)

  Office of Conference Services.
    *Catalogue of United Nations publications
    (1967-69)* (141-142)

    *Oceanography; list of terms relating to
    oceanography and marine resources* (103-104)

PART V
DOCUMENTS

CHARTER
of the
UNITED NATIONS
and
STATUTE
of the
INTERNATIONAL
COURT OF JUSTICE

CHARTER OF THE UNITED NATIONS

WE THE PEOPLES OF THE UNITED NATIONS
determined

to save succeeding generations from the scourge of war, which
twice in our lifetime has brought untold sorrow to mankind, and
to reaffirm faith in fundamental human rights, in the dignity
and worth of the human person, in the equal rights of men
and women and of nations large and small, and
to establish conditions under which justice and respect for the
obligations arising from treaties and other sources of international law can be maintained, and
to promote social progress and better standards of life in larger
freedom,

and for these ends

to practice tolerance and live together in peace with one another
as good neighbours, and
to unite our strength to maintain international peace and security, and
to ensure, by the acceptance of principles and the institution of
methods, that armed force shall not be used, save in the common interest, and
to employ international machinery for the promotion of the
economic and social advancement of all peoples,

have resolved to combine our efforts

to accomplish these aims

Accordingly, our respective Governments, through representatives assembled in the city of San Francisco, who have exhibited
their full powers found to be in good and due form, have
agreed to the present Charter of the United Nations and do
hereby establish an international organization to be known as
the United Nations.

CHAPTER I
PURPOSES AND PRINCIPLES

ARTICLE 1

The Purposes of the United Nations are:
1. To maintain international peace and security, and to
that end: to take effective collective measures for the prevention and removal of threats to the peace, and for the suppression
of acts of aggression or other breaches of the peace, and to
bring about by peaceful means, and in conformity with the
principles of justice and international law, adjustment or settlement of international disputes or situations which might lead
to a breach of the peace;
2. To develop friendly relations among nations based on
respect for the principle of equal rights and self-determination
of peoples, and to take other appropriate measures to strengthen
universal peace;
3. To achieve international co-operation in solving international problems of an economic, social, cultural, or humanitarian character, and in promoting and encouraging respect for
human rights and for fundamental freedoms for all without
distinction as to race, sex, language, or religion; and
4. To be a centre for harmonizing the actions of nations
in the attainment of these common ends.

ARTICLE 2

The Organization and its Members, in pursuit of the Purposes stated in Article 1, shall act in accordance with the following Principles.

1. The Organization is based on the principle of the sovereign equality of all its Members.

2. All Members, in order to ensure to all of them the rights and benefits resulting from membership, shall fulfil in good faith the obligations assumed by them in accordance with the present Charter.

3. All Members shall settle their international disputes by peaceful means in such a manner that international peace and security, and justice, are not endangered.

4. All Members shall refrain in their international relations from the threat or use of force against the territorial integrity or political independence of any state, or in any other manner inconsistent with the Purposes of the United Nations.

5. All Members shall give the United Nations every assistance in any action it takes in accordance with the present Charter, and shall refrain from giving assistance to any state against which the United Nations is taking preventive or enforcement action.

6. The Organization shall ensure that states which are not Members of the United Nations act in accordance with these Principles so far as may be necessary for the maintenance of international peace and security.

7. Nothing contained in the present Charter shall authorize the United Nations to intervene in matters which are essentially within the domestic jurisdiction of any state or shall require the Members to submit such matters to settlement under the present Charter; but this principle shall not prejudice the application of enforcement measures under Chapter VII.

CHAPTER II
MEMBERSHIP

ARTICLE 3

The original Members of the United Nations shall be the states which, having participated in the United Nations Conference on International Organization at San Francisco, or having previously signed the Declaration by United Nations of 1 January 1942, sign the present Charter and ratify it in accordance with Article 110.

ARTICLE 4

1. Membership in the United Nations is open to all other peace-loving states which accept the obligations contained in the present Charter and, in the judgment of the Organization, are able and willing to carry out these obligations.

2. The admission of any such state to membership in the United Nations will be effected by a decision of the General Assembly upon the recommendation of the Security Council.

ARTICLE 5

A Member of the United Nations against which preventive or enforcement action has been taken by the Security Council may be suspended from the exercise of the rights and privileges of membership by the General Assembly upon the recommendation of the Security Council. The exercise of these rights and privileges may be restored by the Security Council.

ARTICLE 6

A Member of the United Nations which has persistently violated the Principles contained in the present Charter may be

expelled from the Organization by the General Assembly upon
the recommendation of the Security Council.

CHAPTER III
ORGANS

ARTICLE 7

1. There are established as the principal organs of the
United Nations: a General Assembly, a Security Council, an
Economic and Social Council, a Trusteeship Council, an Inter-
national Court of Justice, and a Secretariat.

2. Such subsidiary organs as may be found necessary may
be established in accordance with the present Charter.

ARTICLE 8

The United Nations shall place no restrictions on the
eligibility of men and women to participate in any capacity
and under conditions of equality in its principal and subsidiary
organs.

CHAPTER IV
THE GENERAL ASSEMBLY

Composition
ARTICLE 9

1. The General Assembly shall consist of all the Members
of the United Nations.

2. Each Member shall have not more than five representatives in the General Assembly.

Functions and Powers
ARTICLE 10

The General Assembly may discuss any questions or any
matters within the scope of the present Charter or relating to
the powers and functions of any organs provided for in the
present Charter, and, except as provided in Article 12, may
make recommendations to the Members of the United Nations
or to the Security Council or to both on any such questions or
matters.

ARTICLE 11

1. The General Assembly may consider the general principles of co-operation in the maintenance of international peace
and security, including the principles governing disarmament
and the regulation of armaments, and may make recommendations with regard to such principles to the Members or to the
Security Council or to both.

2. The General Assembly may discuss any questions relating to the maintenance of international peace and security
brought before it by any Member of the United Nations, or by
the Security Council, or by a state which is not a Member of
the United Nations in accordance with Article 35, paragraph 2,
and, except as provided in Article 12, may make recommendations with regard to any such questions to the state or states
concerned or to the Security Council or to both. Any such
question on which action is necessary shall be referred to the
Security Council by the General Assembly either before or after
discussion.

3. The General Assembly may call the attention of the
Security Council to situations which are likely to endanger
international peace and security.

4. The powers of the General Assembly set forth in this
Article shall not limit the general scope of Article 10.

ARTICLE 12

1. While the Security Council is exercising in respect of

any dispute or situation the functions assigned to it in the present Charter, the General Assembly shall not make any recommendation with regard to that dispute or situation unless the Security Council so requests.

2. The Secretary-General, with the consent of the Security Council, shall notify the General Assembly at each session of any matters relative to the maintenance of international peace and security which are being dealt with by the Security Council and shall similarly notify the General Assembly, or the Members of the United Nations if the General Assembly is not in session, immediately the Security Council ceases to deal with such matters.

ARTICLE 13

1. The General Assembly shall initiate studies and make recommendations for the purpose of:

   a. promoting international co-operation in the political field and encouraging the progressive development of international law and its codification;

   b. promoting international co-operation in the economic, social, cultural, educational, and health fields, and assisting in the realization of human rights and fundamental freedoms for all without distinction as to race, sex, language, or religion.

2. The further responsibilities, functions and powers of the General Assembly with respect to matters mentioned in paragraph 1(b) above are set forth in Chapters IX and X.

ARTICLE 14

Subject to the provisions of Article 12, the General Assembly may recommend measures for the peaceful adjustment of any situation, regardless of origin, which it deems likely to impair the general welfare or friendly relations among nations, including situations resulting from a violation of the provisions of the present Charter setting forth the Purposes and Principles of the United Nations.

ARTICLE 15

1. The General Assembly shall receive and consider annual and special reports from the Security Council; these reports shall include an account of the measures that the Security Council has decided upon or taken to maintain international peace and security.

2. The General Assembly shall receive and consider reports from the other organs of the United Nations.

ARTICLE 16

The General Assembly shall perform such functions with respect to the international trusteeship system as are assigned to it under Chapters XII and XIII, including the approval of the trusteeship agreements for areas not designated as strategic.

ARTICLE 17

1. The General Assembly shall consider and approve the budget of the Organization.

2. The expenses of the Organization shall be borne by the Members as apportioned by the General Assembly.

3. The General Assembly shall consider and approve any financial and budgetary arrangements with specialized agencies referred to in Article 57 and shall examine the administrative budgets of such specialized agencies with a view to making recommendations to the agencies concerned.

Voting

ARTICLE 18

1. Each member of the General Assembly shall have one vote.

2. Decisions of the General Assembly on important questions shall be made by a two-thirds majority of the members present and voting. These questions shall include: recommendations with respect to the maintenance of international peace and security, the election of the non-permanent members of the Security Council, the election of the members of the Economic and Social Council, the election of members of the Trusteeship Council in accordance with paragraph 1(c) of Article 86, the admission of new Members to the United Nations, the suspension of the rights and privileges of membership, the expulsion of Members, questions relating to the operation of the trusteeship system, and budgetary questions.

3. Decisions on other questions, including the determination of additional categories of questions to be decided by a two-thirds majority, shall be made by a majority of the members present and voting.

ARTICLE 19

A Member of the United Nations which is in arrears in the payment of its financial contributions to the Organization shall have no vote in the General Assembly if the amount of its arrears equals or exceeds the amount of the contributions due from it for the preceding two full years. The General Assembly may, nevertheless, permit such a Member to vote if it is satisfied that the failure to pay is due to conditions beyond the control of the Member.

Procedure

ARTICLE 20

The General Assembly shall meet in regular annual sessions and in such special sessions as occasion may require. Special sessions shall be convoked by the Secretary-General at the request of the Security Council or of a majority of the Members of the United Nations.

ARTICLE 21

The General Assembly shall adopt its own rules of procedure. It shall elect its President for each session.

ARTICLE 22

The General Assembly may establish such subsidiary organs as it deems necessary for the performance of its functions.

CHAPTER V
THE SECURITY COUNCIL

Composition

ARTICLE 23

1. The Security Council shall consist of fifteen Members of the United Nations. The Republic of China, France, the Union of Soviet Socialist Republics, the United Kingdom of Great Britain and Northern Ireland, and the United States of America shall be permanent members of the Security Council. The General Assembly shall elect ten other Members of the United Nations to be non-permanent members of the Security Council, due regard being specially paid, in the first instance to the contribution of Members of the United Nations to the maintenance of international peace and security and to the other purposes of the Organization, and also to equitable geographical distribution.

2. The non-permanent members of the Security Council shall be elected for a term of two years. In the first election of the non-permanent members after the increase of the membership of the Security Council from eleven to fifteen, two of the

four additional members shall be chosen for a term of one year. A retiring member shall not be eligible for immediate re-election.

3. Each member of the Security Council shall have one representative.

Functions and Powers

ARTICLE 24

1. In order to ensure prompt and effective action by the United Nations, its Members confer on the Security Council primary responsibility for the maintenance of international peace and security, and agree that in carrying out its duties under this responsibility the Security Council acts on their behalf.

2. In discharging these duties the Security Council shall act in accordance with the Purposes and Principles of the United Nations. The specific powers granted to the Security Council for the discharge of these duties are laid down in Chapters VI, VII, VIII, and XII.

3. The Security Council shall submit annual and, when necessary, special reports to the General Assembly for its consideration.

ARTICLE 25

The Members of the United Nations agree to accept and carry out the decisions of the Security Council in accordance with the present Charter.

ARTICLE 26

In order to promote the establishment and maintenance of international peace and security with the least diversion for armaments of the world's human and economic resources, the Security Council shall be responsible for formulating, with the assistance of the Military Staff Committee referred to in Article 47, plans to be submitted to the Members of the United Nations for the establishment of a system for the regulation of armaments.

Voting

ARTICLE 27

1. Each member of the Security Council shall have one vote.

2. Decisions of the Security Council on procedural matters shall be made by an affirmative vote of nine members.

3. Decisions of the Security Council on all other matters shall be made by an affirmative vote of nine members including the concurring votes of the permanent members; provided that, in decisions under Chapter VI, and under paragraph 3 of Article 52, a party to a dispute shall abstain from voting.

Procedure

ARTICLE 28

1. The Security Council shall be so organized as to be able to function continuously. Each member of the Security Council shall for this purpose be represented at all times at the seat of the Organization.

2. The Security Council shall hold periodic meetings at which each of its members may, if it so desires, be represented by a member of the government or by some other specially designated representative.

3. The Security Council may hold meetings at such places other than the seat of the Organization as in its judgment will best facilitate its work.

ARTICLE 29

The Security Council may establish such subsidiary organs as it deems necessary for the performance of its functions.

The Security Council shall adopt its own rules of procedure, including the method of selecting its President.

Any Member of the United Nations which is not a member of the Security Council may participate, without vote, in the discussion of any question brought before the Security Council whenever the latter considers that the interests of that Member are specially affected.

Any Member of the United Nations which is not a member of the Security Council or any state which is not a Member of the United Nations, if it is a party to a dispute under consideration by the Security Council, shall be invited to participate, without vote, in the discussion relating to the dispute. The Security Council shall lay down such conditions as it deems just for the participation of a state which is not a Member of the United Nations.

CHAPTER VI
PACIFIC SETTLEMENT OF DISPUTES

1. The parties to any dispute, the continuance of which is likely to endanger the maintenance of international peace and security, shall, first of all, seek a solution by negotiation, enquiry, mediation, conciliation, arbitration, judicial settlement, resort to regional agencies or arrangements, or other peaceful means of their own choice.

2. The Security Council shall, when it deems necessary, call upon the parties to settle their dispute by such means.

The Security Council may investigate any dispute, or any situation which might lead to international friction or give rise to a dispute, in order to determine whether the continuance of the dispute or situation is likely to endanger the maintenance of international peace and security.

1. Any Member of the United Nations may bring any dispute, or any situation of the nature referred to in Article 34, to the attention of the Security Council or of the General Assembly.

2. A state which is not a Member of the United Nations may bring to the attention of the Security Council or of the General Assembly any dispute to which it is a party if it accepts in advance, for the purposes of the dispute, the obligations of pacific settlement provided in the present Charter.

3. The proceedings of the General Assembly in respect of matters brought to its attention under this Article will be subject to the provisions of Articles 11 and 12.

1. The Security Council may, at any stage of a dispute of the nature referred to in Article 33 or of a situation of like nature, recommend appropriate procedures or methods of adjustment.

2. The Security Council should take into consideration any procedures for the settlement of the dispute which have already been adopted by the parties.

3. In making recommendations under this Article the Security Council should also take into consideration that legal disputes should as a general rule be referred by the parties to

the International Court of Justice in accordance with the provisions of the Statute of the Court.

ARTICLE 37

1. Should the parties to a dispute of the nature referred to in Article 33 fail to settle it by the means indicated in that Article, they shall refer it to the Security Council.

2. If the Security Council deems that the continuance of the dispute is in fact likely to endanger the maintenance of international peace and security, it shall decide whether to take action under Article 36 or to recommend such terms of settlement as it may consider appropriate.

ARTICLE 38

Without prejudice to the provisions of Articles 33 to 37, the Security Council may, if all the parties to any dispute so request, make recommendations to the parties with a view to a pacific settlement of the dispute.

CHAPTER VII
ACTION WITH RESPECT TO THREATS TO THE PEACE, BREACHES OF THE PEACE, AND ACTS OF AGGRESSION

ARTICLE 39

The Security Council shall determine the existence of any threat to the peace, breach of the peace, or act of aggression and shall make recommendations, or decide what measures shall be taken in accordance with Articles 41 and 42, to maintain or restore international peace and security.

ARTICLE 40

In order to prevent an aggravation of the situation, the Security Council may, before making the recommendations or deciding upon the measures provided for in Article 39, call upon the parties concerned to comply with such provisional measures as it deems necessary or desirable. Such provisional measures shall be without prejudice to the rights, claims, or position of the parties concerned. The Security Council shall duly take account of failure to comply with such provisional measures.

ARTICLE 41

The Security Council may decide what measures not involving the use of armed force are to be employed to give effect to its decisions, and it may call upon the Members of the United Nations to apply such measures. These may include complete or partial interruption of economic relations and of rail, sea, air, postal, telegraphic, radio, and other means of communication, and the severance of diplomatic relations.

ARTICLE 42

Should the Security Council consider that measures provided for in Article 41 would be inadequate or have proved to be inadequate, it may take such action by air, sea, or land forces as may be necessary to maintain or restore international peace and security. Such action may include demonstrations, blockade, and other operations by air, sea, or land forces of Members of the United Nations.

ARTICLE 43

1. All Members of the United Nations, in order to contribute to the maintenance of international peace and security, undertake to make available to the Security Council, on its call and in accordance with a special agreement or agreements, armed forces, assistance, and facilities, including rights of passage, necessary for the purpose of maintaining international peace and security.

2. Such agreement or agreements shall govern the numbers and types of forces, their degree of readiness and general location, and the nature of the facilities and assistance to be provided.

3. The agreement or agreements shall be negotiated as soon as possible on the initiative of the Security Council. They shall be concluded between the Security Council and Members or between the Security Council and groups of Members and shall be subject to ratification by the signatory states in accordance with their respective constitutional processes.

ARTICLE 44

When the Security Council has decided to use force it shall, before calling upon a Member not represented on it to provide armed forces in fulfilment of the obligations assumed under Article 43, invite that Member, if the Member so desires, to participate in the decisions of the Security Council concerning the employment of contingents of that Member's armed forces.

ARTICLE 45

In order to enable the United Nations to take urgent military measures, Members shall hold immediately available national air-force contingents for combined international enforcement action. The strength and degree of readiness of these contingents and plans for their combined action shall be determined, within the limits laid down in the special agreement or agreements referred to in Article 43, by the Security Council with the assistance of the Military Staff Committee.

ARTICLE 46

Plans for the application of armed force shall be made by the Security Council with the assistance of the Military Staff Committee.

ARTICLE 47

1. There shall be established a Military Staff Committee to advise and assist the Security Council on all questions relating to the Security Council's military requirements for the maintenance of international peace and security, the employment and command of forces placed at its disposal, the regulation of armaments, and possible disarmament.

2. The Military Staff Committee shall consist of the Chiefs of Staff of the permanent members of the Security Council or their representatives. Any Member of the United Nations not permanently represented on the Committee shall be invited by the Committee to be associated with it when the efficient discharge of the Committee's responsibilities requires the participation of that Member in its work.

3. The Military Staff Committee shall be responsible under the Security Council for the strategic direction of any armed forces placed at the disposal of the Security Council. Questions relating to the command of such forces shall be worked out subsequently.

4. The Military Staff Committee, with the authorization of the Security Council and after consultation with appropriate regional agencies, may establish regional sub-committees.

ARTICLE 48

1. The action required to carry out the decisions of the Security Council for the maintenance of international peace and security shall be taken by all the Members of the United Nations or by some of them, as the Security Council may determine.

2. Such decisions shall be carried out by the Members of the United Nations directly and through their action in the

appropriate international agencies of which they are members.

ARTICLE 49

The Members of the United Nations shall join in affording mutual assistance in carrying out the measures decided upon by the Security Council.

ARTICLE 50

If preventive or enforcement measures against any state are taken by the Security Council, any other state, whether a Member of the United Nations or not, which finds itself confronted with special economic problems arising from the carrying out of those measures shall have the right to consult the Security Council with regard to a solution of those problems.

ARTICLE 51

Nothing in the present Charter shall impair the inherent right of individual or collective self-defence if an armed attack occurs against a Member of the United Nations, until the Security Council has taken measures necessary to maintain international peace and security. Measures taken by Members in the exercise of this right of self-defence shall be immediately reported to the Security Council and shall not in any way affect the authority and responsibility of the Security Council under the present Charter to take at any time such action as it deems necessary in order to maintain or restore international peace and security.

CHAPTER VIII
REGIONAL ARRANGEMENTS

ARTICLE 52

1. Nothing in the present Charter precludes the existence of regional arrangements or agencies for dealing with such matters relating to the maintenance of international peace and security as are appropriate for regional action, provided that such arrangements or agencies and their activities are consistent with the Purposes and Principles of the United Nations.

2. The Members of the United Nations entering into such arrangements or constituting such agencies shall make every effort to achieve pacific settlement of local disputes through such regional arrangements or by such regional agencies before referring them to the Security Council.

3. The Security Council shall encourage the development of pacific settlement of local disputes through such regional arrangements or by such regional agencies either on the initiative of the states concerned or by reference from the Security Council.

4. This Article in no way impairs the application of Articles 34 and 35.

ARTICLE 53

1. The Security Council shall, where appropriate, utilize such regional arrangements or agencies for enforcement action under its authority. But no enforcement action shall be taken under regional arrangements or by regional agencies without the authorization of the Security Council, with the exception of measures against any enemy state, as defined in paragraph 2 of this Article, provided for pursuant to Article 107 or in regional arrangements directed against renewal of aggressive policy on the part of any such state, until such time as the Organization may, on request of the Governments concerned, be charged with the responsibility for preventing further aggression by such a state.

2. The term enemy state as used in paragraph 1 of this Article applies to any state which during the Second World

War has been an enemy of any signatory of the present Charter.

ARTICLE 54

The Security Council shall at all times be kept fully informed of activities undertaken or in contemplation under regional arrangements or by regional agencies for the maintenance of international peace and security.

CHAPTER IX
INTERNATIONAL ECONOMIC AND SOCIAL CO-OPERATION

ARTICLE 55

With a view to the creation of conditions of stability and well-being which are necessary for peaceful and friendly relations among nations based on respect for the principle of equal rights and self-determination of peoples, the United Nations shall promote:

    a. higher standards of living, full employment, and conditions of economic and social progress and development;

    b. solutions of international economic, social, health, and related problems; and international cultural and educational co-operation; and

    c. universal respect for, and observance of, human rights and fundamental freedoms for all without distinction as to race, sex, language, or religion.

ARTICLE 56

All Members pledge themselves to take joint and separate action in co-operation with the Organization for the achievement of the purposes set forth in Article 55.

ARTICLE 57

1. The various specialized agencies, established by intergovernmental agreement and having wide international responsibilities, as defined in their basic instruments, in economic, social, cultural, educational, health, and related fields, shall be brought into relationship with the United Nations in accordance with the provisions of Article 63.

2. Such agencies thus brought into relationship with the United Nations are hereinafter referred to as specialized agencies.

ARTICLE 58

The Organization shall make recommendations for the co-ordination of the policies and activities of the specialized agencies.

ARTICLE 59

The Organization shall, where appropriate, initiate negotiations among the states concerned for the creation of any new specialized agencies required for the accomplishment of the purposes set forth in Article 55.

ARTICLE 60

Responsibility for the discharge of the functions of the Organization set forth in this Chapter shall be vested in the General Assembly and, under the authority of the General Assembly, in the Economic and Social Council, which shall have for this purpose the powers set forth in Chapter X.

CHAPTER X
THE ECONOMIC AND SOCIAL COUNCIL

Composition
ARTICLE 61

1. The Economic and Social Council shall consist of fifty-

four Members of the United Nations elected by the General Assembly.

2. Subject to the provisions of paragraph 3, eighteen members of the Economic and Social Council shall be elected each year for a term of three years. A retiring member shall be eligible for immediate re-election.

3. At the first election after the increase in the membership of the Economic and Social Council from twenty-seven to fifty-four members, in addition to the members elected in place of the nine members whose term of office expires at the end of that year, twenty-seven additional members shall be elected. Of these twenty-seven additional members, the term of office of nine members so elected shall expire at the end of one year, and of nine other members at the end of two years, in accordance with arrangements made by the General Assembly.

4. Each member of the Economic and Social Council shall have one representative.

Functions and Powers
ARTICLE 62

1. The Economic and Social Council may make or initiate studies and reports with respect to international economic, social, cultural, educational, health, and related matters and may make recommendations with respect to any such matters to the General Assembly, to the Members of the United Nations, and to the specialized agencies concerned.

2. It may make recommendations for the purpose of promoting respect for, and observance of, human rights and fundamental freedoms for all.

3. It may prepare draft conventions for submission to the General Assembly, with respect to matters falling within its competence.

4. It may call, in accordance with the rules prescribed by the United Nations, international conferences on matters falling within its competence.

ARTICLE 63

1. The Economic and Social Council may enter into agreements with any of the agencies referred to in Article 57, defining the terms on which the agency concerned shall be brought into relationship with the United Nations. Such agreements shall be subject to approval by the General Assembly.

2. It may co-ordinate the activities of the specialized agencies through consultation with and recommendations to such agencies and through recommendations to the General Assembly and to the Members of the United Nations.

ARTICLE 64

1. The Economic and Social Council may take appropriate steps to obtain regular reports from the specialized agencies. It may make arrangements with the Members of the United Nations and with the specialized agencies to obtain reports on the steps taken to give effect to its own recommendations and to recommendations on matters falling within its competence made by the General Assembly.

2. It may communicate its observations on these reports to the General Assembly.

ARTICLE 65

The Economic and Social Council may furnish information to the Security Council and shall assist the Security Council upon its request.

ARTICLE 66

1. The Economic and Social Council shall perform such functions as fall within its competence in connexion with the carrying out of the recommendations of the General Assembly.

2. It may, with the approval of the General Assembly, perform services at the request of Members of the United Nations and at the request of specialized agencies.

3. It shall perform such other functions as are specified elsewhere in the present Charter or as may be assigned to it by the General Assembly.

Voting

ARTICLE 67

1. Each member of the Economic and Social Council shall have one vote.

2. Decisions of the Economic and Social Council shall be made by a majority of the members present and voting.

Procedure

ARTICLE 68

The Economic and Social Council shall set up commissions in economic and social fields and for the promotion of human rights, and such other commissions as may be required for the performance of its functions.

ARTICLE 69

The Economic and Social Council shall invite any Member of the United Nations to participate, without vote, in its deliberations on any matter of particular concern to that Member.

ARTICLE 70

The Economic and Social Council may make arrangements for representatives of the specialized agencies to participate, without vote, in its deliberations and in those of the commissions established by it, and for its representatives to participate in the deliberations of the specialized agencies.

ARTICLE 71

The Economic and Social Council may make suitable arrangements for consultation with non-governmental organizations which are concerned with matters within its competence. Such arrangements may be made with international organizations and, where appropriate, with national organizations after consultation with the Member of the United Nations concerned.

ARTICLE 72

1. The Economic and Social Council shall adopt its own rules of procedure, including the method of selecting its President.

2. The Economic and Social Council shall meet as required in accordance with its rules, which shall include provision for the convening of meetings on the request of a majority of its members.

CHAPTER XI
DECLARATION REGARDING NON-SELF-GOVERNING TERRITORIES

ARTICLE 73

Members of the United Nations which have or assume responsibilities for the administration of territories whose peoples have not yet attained a full measure of self-government recognize the principle that the interests of the inhabitants of these territories are paramount, and accept as a sacred trust the obligation to promote to the utmost, within the system of international peace and security established by the present Charter, the well-being of the inhabitants of these territories, and, to this end:

> a. to ensure, with due respect for the culture of the peoples concerned, their political, economic, social, and educational advancement, their just treatment, and their protection against abuses;
>
> b. to develop self-government, to take due account of the political aspirations of the peoples, and to assist them in the progressive development of their free political institutions, according to the particular circumstances of each territory and its peoples and their varying stages of advancement;
>
> c. to further international peace and security;
>
> d. to promote constructive measures of development, to encourage research, and to co-operate with one another and, when and where appropriate, with specialized international bodies with a view to the practical achievement of the social, economic, and scientific purposes set forth in this Article; and
>
> e. to transmit regularly to the Secretary-General for information purposes, subject to such limitation as security and constitutional considerations may require, statistical and other information of a technical nature relating to economic, social, and educational conditions in the territories for which they are respectively responsible other than those territories to which Chapters XII and XIII apply.

ARTICLE 74

Members of the United Nations also agree that their policy in respect of the territories to which this Chapter applies, no less than in respect of their metropolitan areas, must be based on the general principle of good-neighbourliness, due account being taken of the interests and well-being of the rest of the world, in social, economic, and commercial matters.

CHAPTER XII

INTERNATIONAL TRUSTEESHIP SYSTEM

ARTICLE 75

The United Nations shall establish under its authority an international trusteeship system for the administration and supervision of such territories as may be placed thereunder by subsequent individual agreements. These territories are hereinafter referred to as trust territories.

ARTICLE 76

The basic objectives of the trusteeship system, in accordance with the Purposes of the United Nations laid down in Article 1 of the present Charter, shall be:

> a. to further international peace and security;
>
> b. to promote the political, economic, social, and educational advancement of the inhabitants of the trust territories, and their progressive development towards self-government or independence as may be appropriate to the particular circumstances of each territory and its peoples and the freely expressed wishes of the peoples concerned, and as may be provided by the terms of each trusteeship agreement;
>
> c. to encourage respect for human rights and for fundamental freedoms for all without distinction as to race, sex, language, or religion, and to encourage recognition of the

interdependence of the peoples of the world; and

d. to ensure equal treatment in social, economic, and commercial matters for all Members of the United Nations and their nationals, and also equal treatment for the latter in the administration of justice, without prejudice to the attainment of the foregoing objectives and subject to the provisions of Article 80.

ARTICLE 77

1. The trusteeship system shall apply to such territories in the following categories as may be placed thereunder by means of trusteeship agreements:

a. territories now held under mandate;

b. territories which may be detached from enemy states as a result of the Second World War; and

c. territories voluntarily placed under the system by states responsible for their administration.

2. It will be a matter for subsequent agreement as to which territories in the foregoing categories will be brought under the trusteeship system and upon what terms.

ARTICLE 78

The trusteeship system shall not apply to territories which have become Members of the United Nations, relationship among which shall be based on respect for the principle of sovereign equality.

ARTICLE 79

The terms of trusteeship for each territory to be placed under the trusteeship system, including any alteration or amendment, shall be agreed upon by the states directly concerned, including the mandatory power in the case of territories held under mandate by a Member of the United Nations, and shall be approved as provided for in Articles 83 and 85.

ARTICLE 80

1. Except as may be agreed upon in individual trusteeship agreements, made under Articles 77, 79, and 81, placing each territory under the trusteeship system, and until such agreements have been concluded, nothing in this Chapter shall be construed in or of itself to alter in any manner the rights whatsoever of any states or any peoples or the terms of existing international instruments to which Members of the United Nations may respectively be parties.

2. Paragraph 1 of this Article shall not be interpreted as giving grounds for delay or postponement of the negotiation and conclusion of agreements for placing mandated and other territories under the trusteeship system as provided for in Article 77.

ARTICLE 81

The trusteeship agreement shall in each case include the terms under which the trust territory will be administered and designate the authority which will exercise the administration of the trust territory. Such authority, hereinafter called the administering authority, may be one or more states or the Organization itself.

ARTICLE 82

There may be designated, in any trusteeship agreement, a strategic area or areas which may include part or all of the trust territory to which the agreement applies, without prejudice to any special agreement or agreements made under Article 43.

ARTICLE 83

1. All functions of the United Nations relating to strategic areas, including the approval of the terms of the trusteeship agreements and of their alteration or amendment, shall be

exercised by the Security Council.

2. The basic objectives set forth in Article 76 shall be applicable to the people of each strategic area.

3. The Security Council shall, subject to the provisions of the trusteeship agreements and without prejudice to security considerations, avail itself of the assistance of the Trusteeship Council to perform those functions of the United Nations under the trusteeship system relating to political, economic, social, and educational matters in the strategic areas.

ARTICLE 84

It shall be the duty of the administering authority to ensure that the trust territory shall play its part in the maintenance of international peace and security. To this end the administering authority may make use of volunteer forces, facilities, and assistance from the trust territory in carrying out the obligations towards the Security Council undertaken in this regard by the administering authority, as well as for local defence and the maintenance of law and order within the trust territory.

ARTICLE 85

1. The functions of the United Nations with regard to trusteeship agreements for all areas not designated as strategic, including the approval of the terms of the trusteeship agreements and of their alteration or amendment, shall be exercised by the General Assembly.

2. The Trusteeship Council, operating under the authority of the General Assembly, shall assist the General Assembly in carrying out these functions.

CHAPTER XIII
THE TRUSTEESHIP COUNCIL

Composition
ARTICLE 86

1. The Trusteeship Council shall consist of the following Members of the United Nations:

    a. those Members administering trust territories;

    b. such of those Members mentioned by name in Article 23 as are not administering trust territories; and

    c. as many other Members elected for three-year terms by the General Assembly as may be necessary to ensure that the total number of members of the Trusteeship Council is equally divided between those Members of the United Nations which administer trust territories and those which do not.

2. Each member of the Trusteeship Council shall designate one specially qualified person to represent it therein.

Functions and Powers
ARTICLE 87

The General Assembly and, under its authority, the Trusteeship Council, in carrying out their functions, may:

    a. consider reports submitted by the administering authority;

    b. accept petitions and examine them in consultation with the administering authority;

    c. provide for periodic visits to the respective trust territories at times agreed upon with the administering authority; and

    d. take these and other actions in conformity with the terms of the trusteeship agreements.

ARTICLE 88

The Trusteeship Council shall formulate a questionnaire on the political, economic, social, and educational advancement of the inhabitants of each trust territory, and the administering authority for each trust territory within the competence of the General Assembly shall make an annual report to the General Assembly upon the basis of such questionnaire.

Voting

ARTICLE 89

1. Each member of the Trusteeship Council shall have one vote.

2. Decisions of the Trusteeship Council shall be made by a majority of the members present and voting.

Procedure

ARTICLE 90

1. The Trusteeship Council shall adopt its own rules of procedure, including the method of selecting its President.

2. The Trusteeship Council shall meet as required in accordance with its rules, which shall include provision for the convening of meetings on the request of a majority of its members.

ARTICLE 91

The Trusteeship Council shall, when appropriate, avail itself of the assistance of the Economic and Social Council and of the specialized agencies in regard to matters with which they are respectively concerned.

CHAPTER XIV

THE INTERNATIONAL COURT OF JUSTICE

ARTICLE 92

The International Court of Justice shall be the principal judicial organ of the United Nations. It shall function in accordance with the annexed Statute, which is based upon the Statute of the Permanent Court of International Justice and forms an integral part of the present Charter.

ARTICLE 93

1. All Members of the United Nations are *ipso facto* parties to the Statute of the International Court of Justice.

2. A state which is not a Member of the United Nations may become a party to the Statute of the International Court of Justice on conditions to be determined in each case by the General Assembly upon the recommendation of the Security Council.

ARTICLE 94

1. Each Member of the United Nations undertakes to comply with the decision of the International Court of Justice in any case to which it is a party.

2. If any party to a case fails to perform the obligations incumbent upon it under a judgment rendered by the Court, the other party may have recourse to the Security Council, which may, if it deems necessary, make recommendations or decide upon measures to be taken to give effect to the judgment.

ARTICLE 95

Nothing in the present Charter shall prevent Members of the United Nations from entrusting the solution of their differences to other tribunals by virtue of agreements already in existence or which may be concluded in the future.

ARTICLE 96

1. The General Assembly or the Security Council may request the International Court of Justice to give an advisory

opinion on any legal question.

2. Other organs of the United Nations and specialized agencies, which may at any time be so authorized by the General Assembly, may also request advisory opinions of the Court on legal questions arising within the scope of their activities.

CHAPTER XV
THE SECRETARIAT

ARTICLE 97

The Secretariat shall comprise a Secretary-General and such staff as the Organization may require. The Secretary-General shall be appointed by the General Assembly upon the recommendation of the Security Council. He shall be the chief administrative officer of the Organization.

ARTICLE 98

The Secretary-General shall act in that capacity in all meetings of the General Assembly, of the Security Council, of the Economic and Social Council, and of the Trusteeship Council, and shall perform such other functions as are entrusted to him by these organs. The Secretary-General shall make an annual report to the General Assembly on the work of the Organization.

ARTICLE 99

The Secretary-General may bring to the attention of the Security Council any matter which in his opinion may threaten the maintenance of international peace and security.

ARTICLE 100

1. In the performance of their duties the Secretary-General and the staff shall not seek or receive instructions from any government or from any other authority external to the Organization. They shall refrain from any action which might reflect on their position as international officials responsible only to the Organization.

2. Each Member of the United Nations undertakes to respect the exclusively international character of the responsibilities of the Secretary-General and the staff and not to seek to influence them in the discharge of their responsibilities.

ARTICLE 101

1. The staff shall be appointed by the Secretary-General under regulations established by the General Assembly.

2. Appropriate staffs shall be permanently assigned to the Economic and Social Council, the Trusteeship Council, and, as required, to other organs of the United Nations. These staffs shall form a part of the Secretariat.

3. The paramount consideration in the employment of the staff and in the determination of the conditions of service shall be the necessity of securing the highest standards of efficiency, competence, and integrity. Due regard shall be paid to the importance of recruiting the staff on as wide a geographical basis as possible.

CHAPTER XVI
MISCELLANEOUS PROVISIONS

ARTICLE 102

1. Every treaty and every international agreement entered into by any Member of the United Nations after the present Charter comes into force shall as soon as possible be registered with the Secretariat and published by it.

2. No party to any such treaty or international agreement which has not been registered in accordance with the provisions of paragraph 1 of this Article may invoke that treaty or agreement before any organ of the United Nations.

ARTICLE 103

In the event of a conflict between the obligations of the Members of the United Nations under the present Charter and their obligations under any other international agreement, their obligations under the present Charter shall prevail.

ARTICLE 104

The Organization shall enjoy in the territory of each of its Members such legal capacity as may be necessary for the exercise of its functions and the fulfilment of its purposes.

ARTICLE 105

1. The Organization shall enjoy in the territory of each of its Members such privileges and immunities as are necessary for the fulfilment of its purposes.

2. Representatives of the Members of the United Nations and officials of the Organization shall similarly enjoy such privileges and immunities as are necessary for the independent exercise of their functions in connexion with the Organization.

3. The General Assembly may make recommendations with a view to determining the details of the application of paragraphs 1 and 2 of this Article or may propose conventions to the Members of the United Nations for this purpose.

CHAPTER XVII

TRANSITIONAL SECURITY ARRANGEMENTS

ARTICLE 106

Pending the coming into force of such special agreements referred to in Article 43 as in the opinion of the Security Council enable it to begin the exercise of its responsibilities under Article 42, the parties to the Four-Nation Declaration, signed at Moscow, 30 October 1943, and France, shall, in accordance with the provisions of paragraph 5 of that Declaration, consult with one another and as occasion requires with other Members of the United Nations with a view to such joint action on behalf of the Organization as may be necessary for the purpose of maintaining international peace and security.

ARTICLE 107

Nothing in the present Charter shall invalidate or preclude action, in relation to any state which during the Second World War has been an enemy of any signatory to the present Charter, taken or authorized as a result of that war by the Governments having responsibility for such action.

CHAPTER XVIII

AMENDMENTS

ARTICLE 108

Amendments to the present Charter shall come into force for all Members of the United Nations when they have been adopted by a vote of two thirds of the members of the General Assembly and ratified in accordance with their respective constitutional processes by two thirds of the Members of the United Nations, including all the permanent members of the Security Council.

ARTICLE 109

1. A General Conference of the Members of the United Nations for the purpose of reviewing the present Charter may be held at a date and place to be fixed by a two-thirds vote of the members of the General Assembly and by a vote of any nine members of the Security Council. Each Member of the United Nations shall have one vote in the conference.

2. Any alteration of the present Charter recommended by

a two-thirds vote of the conference shall take effect when ratified in accordance with their respective constitutional processes by two thirds of the Members of the United Nations including all the permanent members of the Security Council.

3. If such a conference has not been held before the tenth annual session of the General Assembly following the coming into force of the present Charter, the proposal to call such a conference shall be placed on the agenda of that session of the General Assembly, and the conference shall be held if so decided by a majority vote of the members of the General Assembly and by a vote of any seven members of the Security Council.

CHAPTER XIX

RATIFICATION AND SIGNATURE

ARTICLE 110

1. The present Charter shall be ratified by the signatory states in accordance with their respective constitutional processes.

2. The ratifications shall be deposited with the Government of the United States of America, which shall notify all the signatory states of each deposit as well as the Secretary-General of the Organization when he has been appointed.

3. The present Charter shall come into force upon the deposit of ratifications by the Republic of China, France, the Union of Soviet Socialist Republics, the United Kingdom of Great Britain and Northern Ireland, and the United States of America, and by a majority of the other signatory states. A protocol of the ratifications deposited shall thereupon be drawn up by the Government of the United States of America which shall communicate copies thereof to all the signatory states.

4. The states signatory to the present Charter which ratify it after it has come into force will become original Members of the United Nations on the date of the deposit of their respective ratifications.

ARTICLE 111

The present Charter, of which the Chinese, French, Russian, English, and Spanish texts are equally authentic, shall remain deposited in the archives of the Government of the United States of America. Duly certified copies thereof shall be transmitted by that Government to the Governments of the other signatory states.

IN FAITH WHEREOF the representatives of the Governments of the United Nations have signed the present Charter.

DONE at the city of San Francisco the twenty-sixth day of June, one thousand nine hundred and forty-five.

STATUTE OF THE INTERNATIONAL COURT OF JUSTICE

ARTICLE 1

The International Court of Justice established by the Charter of the United Nations as the principal judicial organ of the United Nations shall be constituted and shall function in accordance with the provisions of the present Statute.

CHAPTER I

ORGANIZATION OF THE COURT

ARTICLE 2

The Court shall be composed of a body of independent judges, elected regardless of their nationality from among persons of high moral character, who possess the qualifications required in their respective countries for appointment to the highest judicial offices, or are jurisconsults of recognized competence in international law.

ARTICLE 3

1. The Court shall consist of fifteen members, no two of whom may be nationals of the same state.

2. A person who for the purposes of membership in the Court could be regarded as a national of more than one state shall be deemed to be a national of the one in which he ordinarily exercises civil and political rights.

ARTICLE 4

1. The members of the Court shall be elected by the General Assembly and by the Security Council from a list of persons nominated by the national groups in the Permanent Court of Arbitration, in accordance with the following provisions.

2. In the case of Members of the United Nations not represented in the Permanent Court of Arbitration, candidates shall be nominated by national groups appointed for this purpose by their governments under the same conditions as those prescribed for members of the Permanent Court of Arbitration by Article 44 of the Convention of The Hague of 1907 for the pacific settlement of international disputes.

3. The conditions under which a state which is a party to the present Statute but is not a Member of the United Nations may participate in electing the members of the Court shall, in the absence of a special agreement, be laid down by the General Assembly upon recommendation of the Security Council.

ARTICLE 5

1. At least three months before the date of the election, the Secretary-General of the United Nations shall address a written request to the members of the Permanent Court of Arbitration belonging to the states which are parties to the present Statute, and to the members of the national groups appointed under Article 4, paragraph 2, inviting them to undertake, within a given time, by national groups, the nomination of persons in a position to accept the duties of a member of the Court.

2. No group may nominate more than four persons, not more than two of whom shall be of their own nationality. In no case may the number of candidates nominated by a group be more than double the number of seats to be filled.

ARTICLE 6

Before making these nominations, each national group is recommended to consult its highest court of justice, its legal faculties and schools of law, and its national academies and national sections of international academies devoted to the study of law.

ARTICLE 7

1. The Secretary-General shall prepare a list in alphabetical order of all the persons thus nominated. Save as provided in Article 12, paragraph 2, these shall be the only persons eligible.

2. The Secretary-General shall submit this list to the General Assembly and to the Security Council.

ARTICLE 8

The General Assembly and the Security Council shall proceed independently of one another to elect the members of the Court.

ARTICLE 9

At every election, the electors shall bear in mind not only that the persons to be elected should individually possess the qualifications required, but also that in the body as a whole the representation of the main forms of civilization and of the principal legal systems of the world should be assured.

ARTICLE 10

1. Those candidates who obtain an absolute majority of votes in the General Assembly and in the Security Council shall be considered as elected.

2. Any vote of the Security Council, whether for the election of judges or for the appointment of members of the conference envisaged in Article 12, shall be taken without any distinction between permanent and non-permanent members of the Security Council.

3. In the event of more than one national of the same state obtaining an absolute majority of the votes both of the General Assembly and of the Security Council, the eldest of these only shall be considered as elected.

ARTICLE 11

If, after the first meeting held for the purpose of the election, one or more seats remain to be filled, a second and, if necessary, a third meeting shall take place.

ARTICLE 12

1. If, after the third meeting, one or more seats still remain unfilled, a joint conference consisting of six members, three appointed by the General Assembly and three by the Security Council, may be formed at any time at the request of either the General Assembly or the Security Council, for the purpose of choosing by the vote of an absolute majority one name for each seat still vacant, to submit to the General Assembly and the Security Council for their respective acceptance.

2. If the joint conference is unanimously agreed upon any person who fulfils the required conditions, he may be included in its list, even though he was not included in the list of nominations referred to in Article 7.

3. If the joint conference is satisfied that it will not be successful in procuring an election, those members of the Court who have already been elected shall, within a period to be fixed by the Security Council, proceed to fill the vacant seats by selection from among those candidates who have obtained votes either in the General Assembly or in the Security Council.

4. In the event of an equality of votes among the judges, the eldest judge shall have a casting vote.

ARTICLE 13

1. The members of the Court shall be elected for nine years and may be re-elected; provided, however, that of the judges elected at the first election, the terms of five judges shall expire at the end of three years and the terms of five more judges shall expire at the end of six years.

2. The judges whose terms are to expire at the end of the above-mentioned initial periods of three and six years shall be chosen by lot to be drawn by the Secretary-General immediately after the first election has been completed.

3. The members of the Court shall continue to discharge their duties until their places have been filled. Though replaced, they shall finish any cases which they may have begun.

4. In the case of the resignation of a member of the Court, the resignation shall be addressed to the President of the Court for transmission to the Secretary-General. This last notification makes the place vacant.

ARTICLE 14

Vacancies shall be filled by the same method as that laid

down for the first election, subject to the following provision: the Secretary-General shall, within one month of the occurrence of the vacancy, proceed to issue the invitations provided for in Article 5, and the date of the election shall be fixed by the Security Council.

ARTICLE 15

A member of the Court elected to replace a member whose term of office has not expired shall hold office for the remainder of his predecessor's term.

ARTICLE 16

1. No member of the Court may exercise any political or administrative function, or engage in any other occupation of a professional nature.

2. Any doubt on this point shall be settled by the decision of the Court.

ARTICLE 17

1. No member of the Court may act as agent, counsel, or advocate in any case.

2. No member may participate in the decision of any case in which he has previously taken part as agent, counsel, or advocate for one of the parties, or as a member of a national or international court, or of a commission of enquiry, or in any other capacity.

3. Any doubt on this point shall be settled by the decision of the Court.

ARTICLE 18

1. No member of the Court can be dismissed unless, in the unanimous opinion of the other members, he has ceased to fulfil the required conditions.

2. Formal notification thereof shall be made to the Secretary-General by the Registrar.

3. This notification makes the place vacant.

ARTICLE 19

The members of the Court, when engaged on the business of the Court, shall enjoy diplomatic privileges and immunities.

ARTICLE 20

Every member of the Court shall, before taking up his duties, make a solemn declaration in open court that he will exercise his powers impartially and conscientiously.

ARTICLE 21

1. The Court shall elect its President and Vice-President for three years; they may be re-elected.

2. The Court shall appoint its Registrar and may provide for the appointment of such other officers as may be necessary.

ARTICLE 22

1. The seat of the Court shall be established at The Hague. This, however, shall not prevent the Court from sitting and exercising its functions elsewhere whenever the Court considers it desirable.

2. The President and the Registrar shall reside at the seat of the Court.

ARTICLE 23

1. The Court shall remain permanently in session, except during the judicial vacations, the dates and duration of which shall be fixed by the Court.

2. Members of the Court are entitled to periodic leave, the dates and duration of which shall be fixed by the Court, having in mind the distance between The Hague and the home of each judge.

3. Members of the Court shall be bound, unless they are

on leave or prevented from attending by illness or other serious reasons duly explained to the President, to hold themselves permanently at the disposal of the Court.

ARTICLE 24

1. If, for some special reason, a member of the Court considers that he should not take part in the decision of a particular case, he shall so inform the President.

2. If the President considers that for some special reason one of the members of the Court should not sit in a particular case, he shall give him notice accordingly.

3. If in any such case the member of the Court and the President disagree, the matter shall be settled by the decision of the Court.

ARTICLE 25

1. The full Court shall sit except when it is expressly provided otherwise in the present Statute.

2. Subject to the condition that the number of judges available to constitute the Court is not thereby reduced below eleven, the Rules of the Court may provide for allowing one or more judges, according to circumstances and in rotation, to be dispensed from sitting.

3. A quorum of nine judges shall suffice to constitute the Court.

ARTICLE 26

1. The Court may from time to time form one or more chambers, composed of three or more judges as the Court may determine, for dealing with particular categories of cases; for example, labour cases and cases relating to transit and communications.

2. The Court may at any time form a chamber for dealing with a particular case. The number of judges to constitute such a chamber shall be determined by the Court with the approval of the parties.

3. Cases shall be heard and determined by the chambers provided for in this Article if the parties so request.

ARTICLE 27

A judgment given by any of the chambers provided for in Articles 26 and 29 shall be considered as rendered by the Court.

ARTICLE 28

The chambers provided for in Articles 26 and 29 may, with the consent of the parties, sit and exercise their functions elsewhere than at The Hague.

ARTICLE 29

With a view to the speedy dispatch of business, the Court shall form annually a chamber composed of five judges which, at the request of the parties, may hear and determine cases by summary procedure. In addition, two judges shall be selected for the purpose of replacing judges who find it impossible to sit.

ARTICLE 30

1. The Court shall frame rules for carrying out its functions. In particular, it shall lay down rules of procedure.

2. The Rules of the Court may provide for assessors to sit with the Court or with any of its chambers, without the right to vote.

ARTICLE 31

1. Judges of the nationality of each of the parties shall retain their right to sit in the case before the Court.

2. If the Court includes upon the Bench a judge of the nationality of one of the parties, any other party may choose a

person to sit as judge. Such person shall be chosen preferably from among those persons who have been nominated as candidates as provided in Articles 4 and 5.

3. If the Court includes upon the Bench no judge of the nationality of the parties, each of these parties may proceed to choose a judge as provided in paragraph 2 of this Article.

4. The provisions of this Article shall apply to the case of Articles 26 and 29. In such cases, the President shall request one or, if necessary, two of the members of the Court forming the chamber to give place to the members of the Court of the nationality of the parties concerned, and, failing such, or if they are unable to be present, to the judges specially chosen by the parties.

5. Should there be several parties in the same interest, they shall, for the purpose of the preceding provisions, be reckoned as one party only. Any doubt upon this point shall be settled by the decision of the Court.

6. Judges chosen as laid down in paragraphs 2, 3, and 4 of this Article shall fulfil the conditions required by Articles 2, 17 (paragraph 2), 20, and 24 of the present Statute. They shall take part in the decision on terms of complete equality with their colleagues.

ARTICLE 32

1. Each member of the Court shall receive an annual salary.

2. The President shall receive a special annual allowance.

3. The Vice-President shall receive a special allowance for every day on which he acts as President.

4. The judges chosen under Article 31, other than members of the Court, shall receive compensation for each day on which they exercise their functions.

5. These salaries, allowances, and compensation shall be fixed by the General Assembly. They may not be decreased during the term of office.

6. The salary of the Registrar shall be fixed by the General Assembly on the proposal of the Court.

7. Regulations made by the General Assembly shall fix the conditions under which retirement pensions may be given to members of the Court and to the Registrar, and the conditions under which members of the Court and the Registrar shall have their travelling expenses refunded.

8. The above salaries, allowances, and compensation shall be free of all taxation.

ARTICLE 33

The expenses of the Court shall be borne by the United Nations in such a manner as shall be decided by the General Assembly.

CHAPTER II
COMPETENCE OF THE COURT
ARTICLE 34

1. Only states may be parties in cases before the Court.

2. The Court, subject to and in conformity with its Rules, may request of public international organizations information relevant to cases before it, and shall receive such information presented by such organizations on their own initiative.

3. Whenever the construction of the constituent instrument of a public international organization or of an international convention adopted thereunder is in question in a case before the Court, the Registrar shall so notify the public international organization concerned and shall communicate to it

copies of all the written proceedings.

1. The Court shall be open to the states parties to the present Statute.

2. The conditions under which the Court shall be open to other states shall, subject to the special provisions contained in treaties in force, be laid down by the Security Council, but in no case shall such conditions place the parties in a position of inequality before the Court.

3. When a state which is not a Member of the United Nations is a party to a case, the Court shall fix the amount which that party is to contribute towards the expenses of the Court. This provision shall not apply if such state is bearing a share of the expenses of the Court.

1. The jurisdiction of the Court comprises all cases which the parties refer to it and all matters specially provided for in the Charter of the United Nations or in treaties and conventions in force.

2. The states parties to the present Statute may at any time declare that they recognize as compulsory *ipso facto* and without special agreement, in relation to any other state accepting the same obligation, the jurisdiction of the Court in all legal disputes concerning:

  a. the interpretation of a treaty;

  b. any question of international law;

  c. the existence of any fact which, if established, would constitute a breach of an international obligation;

  d. the nature or extent of the reparation to be made for the breach of an international obligation.

3. The declarations referred to above may be made unconditionally or on condition of reciprocity on the part of several or certain states, or for a certain time.

4. Such declarations shall be deposited with the Secretary-General of the United Nations, who shall transmit copies thereof to the parties to the Statute and to the Registrar of the Court.

5. Declarations made under Article 36 of the Statute of the Permanent Court of International Justice and which are still in force shall be deemed, as between the parties to the present Statute, to be acceptances of the compulsory jurisdiction of the International Court of Justice for the period which they still have to run and in accordance with their terms.

6. In the event of a dispute as to whether the Court has jurisdiction, the matter shall be settled by the decision of the Court.

Whenever a treaty or convention in force provides for reference of a matter to a tribunal to have been instituted by the League of Nations, or to the Permanent Court of International Justice, the matter shall, as between the parties to the present Statute, be referred to the International Court of Justice.

1. The Court, whose function is to decide in accordance with international law such disputes as are submitted to it, shall apply:

  a. international conventions, whether general or particular, establishing rules expressly recognized by the contesting states;

  b. international custom, as evidence of a general practice accepted as law;

c. the general principles of law recognized by civilized nations;

d. subject to the provisions of Article 59, judicial decisions and the teachings of the most highly qualified publicists of the various nations, as subsidiary means for the determination of rules of law.

2. This provision shall not prejudice the power of the Court to decide a case *ex aequo et bono*, if the parties agree thereto.

CHAPTER III
PROCEDURE

ARTICLE 39

1. The official languages of the Court shall be French and English. If the parties agree that the case shall be conducted in French, the judgment shall be delivered in French. If the parties agree that the case shall be conducted in English, the judgment shall be delivered in English.

2. In the absence of an agreement as to which language shall be employed, each party may, in the pleadings, use the language which it prefers; the decision of the Court shall be given in French and English. In this case the Court shall at the same time determine which of the two texts shall be considered as authoritative.

3. The Court shall, at the request of any party, authorize a language other than French or English to be used by that party.

ARTICLE 40

1. Cases are brought before the Court, as the case may be, either by the notification of the special agreement or by a written application addressed to the Registrar. In either case the subject of the dispute and the parties shall be indicated.

2. The Registrar shall forthwith communicate the application to all concerned.

3. He shall also notify the Members of the United Nations through the Secretary-General, and also any other states entitled to appear before the Court.

ARTICLE 41

1. The Court shall have the power to indicate, if it considers that circumstances so require, any provisional measures which ought to be taken to preserve the respective rights of either party.

2. Pending the final decision, notice of the measures suggested shall forthwith be given to the parties and to the Security Council.

ARTICLE 42

1. The parties shall be represented by agents.

2. They may have the assistance of counsel or advocates before the Court.

3. The agents, counsel, and advocates of parties before the Court shall enjoy the privileges and immunities necessary to the independent exercise of their duties.

ARTICLE 43

1. The procedure shall consist of two parts: written and oral.

2. The written proceedings shall consist of the communication to the Court and to the parties of memorials, countermemorials and, if necessary, replies; also all papers and documents in support.

3. These communications shall be made through the Registrar, in the order and within the time fixed by the Court.

4. A certified copy of every document produced by one

party shall be communicated to the other party.

5. The oral proceedings shall consist of the hearing by the Court of witnesses, experts, agents, counsel, and advocates.

ARTICLE 44

1. For the service of all notices upon persons other than the agents, counsel, and advocates, the Court shall apply direct to the government of the state upon whose territory the notice has to be served.

2. The same provision shall apply whenever steps are to be taken to procure evidence on the spot.

ARTICLE 45

The hearing shall be under the control of the President or, if he is unable to preside, of the Vice-President; if neither is able to preside, the senior judge present shall preside.

ARTICLE 46

The hearing in Court shall be public, unless the Court shall decide otherwise, or unless the parties demand that the public be not admitted.

ARTICLE 47

1. Minutes shall be made at each hearing and signed by the Registrar and the President.

2. These minutes alone shall be authentic.

ARTICLE 48

The Court shall make orders for the conduct of the case, shall decide the form and time in which each party must conclude its arguments, and make all arrangements connected with the taking of evidence.

ARTICLE 49

The Court may, even before the hearing begins, call upon the agents to produce any document or to supply any explanations. Formal note shall be taken of any refusal.

ARTICLE 50

The Court may, at any time, entrust any individual, body, bureau, commission, or other organization that it may select, with the task of carrying out an enquiry or giving an expert opinion.

ARTICLE 51

During the hearing any relevant questions are to be put to the witnesses and experts under the conditions laid down by the Court in the rules of procedure referred to in Article 30.

ARTICLE 52

After the Court has received the proofs and evidence within the time specified for the purpose, it may refuse to accept any further oral or written evidence that one party may desire to present unless the other side consents.

ARTICLE 53

1. Whenever one of the parties does not appear before the Court, or fails to defend its case, the other party may call upon the Court to decide in favour of its claim.

2. The Court must, before doing so, satisfy itself, not only that it has jurisdiction in accordance with Articles 36 and 37, but also that the claim is well founded in fact and law.

ARTICLE 54

1. When, subject to the control of the Court, the agents, counsel, and advocates have completed their presentation of the case, the President shall declare the hearing closed.

2. The Court shall withdraw to consider the judgment.

3. The deliberations of the Court shall take place in private and remain secret.

ARTICLE 55

1. All questions shall be decided by a majority of the

judges present.

2. In the event of an equality of votes, the President or the judge who acts in his place shall have a casting vote.

ARTICLE 56

1. The judgment shall state the reasons on which it is based.

2. It shall contain the names of the judges who have taken part in the decision.

ARTICLE 57

If the judgment does not represent in whole or in part the unanimous opinion of the judges, any judge shall be entitled to deliver a separate opinion.

ARTICLE 58

The judgment shall be signed by the President and by the Registrar. It shall be read in open court, due notice having been given to the agents.

ARTICLE 59

The decision of the Court has no binding force except between the parties and in respect of that particular case.

ARTICLE 60

The judgment is final and without appeal. In the event of dispute as to the meaning or scope of the judgment, the Court shall construe it upon the request of any party.

ARTICLE 61

1. An application for revision of a judgment may be made only when it is based upon the discovery of some fact of such a nature as to be a decisive factor, which fact was, when the judgment was given, unknown to the Court and also to the party claiming revision, always provided that such ignorance was not due to negligence.

2. The proceedings for revision shall be opened by a judgment of the Court expressly recording the existence of the new fact, recognizing that it has such a character as to lay the case open to revision, and declaring the application admissible on this ground.

3. The Court may require previous compliance with the terms of the judgment before it admits proceedings in revision.

4. The application for revision must be made at latest within six months of the discovery of the new fact.

5. No application for revision may be made after the lapse of ten years from the date of the judgment.

ARTICLE 62

1. Should a state consider that it has an interest of a legal nature which may be affected by the decision in the case, it may submit a request to the Court to be permitted to intervene.

2. It shall be for the Court to decide upon this request.

ARTICLE 63

1. Whenever the construction of a convention to which states other than those concerned in the case are parties is in question, the Registrar shall notify all such states forthwith.

2. Every state so notified has the right to intervene in the proceedings; but if it uses this right, the construction given by the judgment will be equally binding upon it.

ARTICLE 64

Unless otherwise decided by the Court, each party shall bear its own costs.

CHAPTER IV
ADVISORY OPINIONS

ARTICLE 65

1. The Court may give an advisory opinion on any legal question at the request of whatever body may be authorized by or in accordance with the Charter of the United Nations to make such a request.

2. Questions upon which the advisory opinion of the Court is asked shall be laid before the Court by means of a written request containing an exact statement of the question upon which an opinion is required, and accompanied by all documents likely to throw light upon the question.

ARTICLE 66

1. The Registrar shall forthwith give notice of the request for an advisory opinion to all states entitled to appear before the Court.

2. The Registrar shall also, by means of a special and direct communication, notify any state entitled to appear before the Court or international organization considered by the Court, or, should it not be sitting, by the President, as likely to be able to furnish information on the question, that the Court will be prepared to receive, within a time limit to be fixed by the President, written statements, or to hear, at a public sitting to be held for the purpose, oral statements relating to the question.

3. Should any such state entitled to appear before the Court have failed to receive the special communication referred to in paragraph 2 of this Article, such state may express a desire to submit a written statement or to be heard; and the Court will decide.

4. States and organizations having presented written or oral statements or both shall be permitted to comment on the statements made by other states or organizations in the form, to the extent, and within the time limits which the Court, or, should it not be sitting, the President, shall decide in each particular case. Accordingly, the Registrar shall in due time communicate any such written statements to states and organizations having submitted similar statements.

ARTICLE 67

The Court shall deliver its advisory opinions in open court, notice having been given to the Secretary-General and to the representatives of Members of the United Nations, of other states and of international organizations immediately concerned.

ARTICLE 68

In the exercise of its advisory functions the Court shall further be guided by the provisions of the present Statute which apply in contentious cases to the extent to which it recognizes them to be applicable.

CHAPTER V
AMENDMENT

ARTICLE 69

Amendments to the present Statute shall be effected by the same procedure as is provided by the Charter of the United Nations for amendments to that Charter, subject however to any provisions which the General Assembly upon recommendation of the Security Council may adopt concerning the participation of states which are parties to the present Statute but are not Members of the United Nations.

ARTICLE 70

The Court shall have power to propose such amendments

to the present Statute as it may deem necessary, through written communications to the Secretary-General, for consideration in conformity with the provisions of Article 69.

UNIVERSAL DECLARATION OF HUMAN RIGHTS

PREAMBLE

Whereas recognition of the inherent dignity and of the equal and inalienable rights of all members of the human family is the foundation of freedom, justice and peace in the world,

Whereas disregard and contempt for human rights have resulted in barbarous acts which have outraged the conscience of mankind, and the advent of a world in which human beings shall enjoy freedom of speech and belief and freedom from fear and want has been proclaimed as the highest aspiration of the common people,

Whereas it is essential, if man is not to be compelled to have recourse, as a last resort, to rebellion against tyranny and oppression, that human rights should be protected by the rule of law,

Whereas it is essential to promote the development of friendly relations between nations,

DÉCLARATION UNIVERSELLE DES DROITS DE L'HOMME

PRÉAMBULE

Considérant que la reconnaissance de la dignité inhérente à tous les membres de la famille humaine et de leurs droits égaux et inaliénables constitue le fondement de la liberté, de la justice et de la paix dans le monde,

Considérant que la méconnaissance et le mépris des droits de l'homme ont conduit à des actes de barbarie qui révoltent la conscience de l'humanité et que l'avènement d'un monde où les êtres humains seront libres de parler et de croire, libérés de la terreur et de la misère, a été proclamé comme la plus haute aspiration de l'homme,

Considérant qu'il est essentiel que les droits de l'homme soient protégés par un régime de droit pour que l'homme ne soit pas contraint, en suprême recours, à la révolte contre la tyrannie et l'oppression,

Considérant qu'il est essentiel d'encourager le développement de relations amicales entre nations,

Whereas the peoples of the United Nations have in the Charter reaffirmed their faith in fundamental human rights, in the dignity and worth of the human person and in the equal rights of men and women and have determined to promote social progress and better standards of life in larger freedom,

Whereas Member States have pledged themselves to achieve, in co-operation with the United Nations, the promotion of universal respect for and observance of human rights and fundamental freedoms,

Whereas a common understanding of these rights and freedoms is of the greatest importance for the full realization of this pledge,

Now, therefore,

The General Assembly

Proclaims this Universal Declaration of Human Rights as a common standard of achievement for all peoples and all nations, to the end that every individual and every organ of society, keeping this Declaration constantly in mind, shall strive by teaching and education to promote respect for these rights and freedoms and by progressive measures, national and international, to secure their universal and effective recognition and observance, both among the peoples of Member States themselves and among the peoples of territories under their jurisdiction.

ARTICLE 1

All human beings are born free and equal in dignity and rights. They are endowed with reason and conscience and should act towards one another in a spirit of brotherhood.

ARTICLE 2

Everyone is entitled to all the rights and freedoms set forth in this Declaration, without distinction of any kind, such as race, colour, sex, language, religion, political or other opinion, national or social origin, property, birth or other status.

Furthermore, no distinction shall be made on the basis of the political, jurisdictional or international status of the country or territory to which a person belongs, whether it be independent, trust, non-self-governing or under any other limitation of sovereignty.

ARTICLE 3

Everyone has the right to life, liberty and the security of person.

Considérant que dans la Charte les peuples des Nations Unies ont proclamé à nouveau leur foi dans les droits fondamentaux de l'homme, dans la dignité et la valeur de la personne humaine, dans l'égalité des droits des hommes et des femmes, et qu'ils se sont déclarés résolus à favoriser le progrès social et à instaurer de meilleures conditions de vie dans une liberté plus grande,

Considérant que les États Membres se sont engagés à assurer, en coopération avec l'Organisation des Nations Unies, le respect universel et effectif des droits de l'homme et des libertés fondamentales,

Considérant qu'une conception commune de ces droits et libertés est de la plus haute importance pour remplir pleinement cet engagement,

L'Assemblée générale

Proclame la présente Déclaration universelle des droits de l'homme comme l'idéal commun à atteindre par tous les peuples et toutes les nations afin que tous les individus et tous les organes de la société, ayant cette Déclaration constamment à l'esprit, s'efforcent, par l'enseignement et l'éducation, de développer le respect de ces droits et libertés et d'en assurer, par des mesures progressives d'ordre national et international, la reconnaissance et l'application universelles et effectives, tant parmi les populations des États Membres eux-mêmes que parmi celles des territoires placés sous leur juridiction.

ARTICLE PREMIER

Tous les êtres humains naissent libres et égaux en dignité et en droits. Ils sont doués de raison et de conscience et doivent agir les uns envers les autres dans un esprit de fraternité.

ARTICLE 2

Chacun peut se prévaloir de tous les droits et de toutes les libertés proclamés dans la présente Déclaration, sans distinction aucune, notamment de race, de couleur, de sexe, de langue, de religion, d'opinion politique ou de toute autre opinion, d'origine nationale ou sociale, de fortune, de naissance ou de toute autre situation.

De plus, il ne sera fait aucune distinction fondée sur le statut politique, juridique ou international du pays ou du territoire dont une personne est ressortissante, que ce pays ou territoire soit indépendant, sous tutelle, non autonome ou soumis à une limitation quelconque de souveraineté.

ARTICLE 3

Tout individu a droit à la vie, à la liberté et à la sûreté de sa personne.

ARTICLE 4

No one shall be held in slavery or servitude; slavery and the slave trade shall be prohibited in all their forms.

ARTICLE 5

No one shall be subjected to torture or to cruel, inhuman or degrading treatment or punishment.

ARTICLE 6

Everyone has the right to recognition everywhere as a person before the law.

ARTICLE 7

All are equal before the law and are entitled without any discrimination to equal protection of the law. All are entitled to equal protection against any discrimination in violation of this Declaration and against any incitement to such discrimination.

ARTICLE 8

Everyone has the right to an effective remedy by the competent national tribunals for acts violating the fundamental rights granted him by the constitution or by law.

ARTICLE 9

No one shall be subjected to arbitrary arrest, detention or exile.

ARTICLE 10

Everyone is entitled in full equality to a fair and public hearing by an independent and impartial tribunal, in the determination of his rights and obligations and of any criminal charge against him.

ARTICLE 11

1. Everyone charged with a penal offence has the right to be presumed innocent until proved guilty according to law in a public trial at which he has had all the guarantees necessary for his defence.

2. No one shall be held guilty of any penal offence on account of any act or omission which did not constitute a penal offence, under national or international law, at the time when it was committed. Nor shall a heavier penalty be imposed than the one that was applicable at the time the penal offence was committed.

ARTICLE 12

No one shall be subjected to arbitrary interference with his privacy, family, home or correspondence, nor to attacks upon his honour and reputation. Everyone has the right to the pro-

ARTICLE 4

Nul ne sera tenu en esclavage ni en servitude; l'esclavage et la traite des esclaves sont interdits sous toutes leurs formes.

ARTICLE 5

Nul ne sera soumis à la torture, ni à des peines ou traitements cruels, inhumains ou dégradants.

ARTICLE 6

Chacun a le droit à la reconnaissance en tous lieux de sa personnalité juridique.

ARTICLE 7

Tous sont égaux devant la loi et ont droit sans distinction à une égale protection de la loi. Tous ont droit à une protection égale contre toute discrimination qui violerait la présente Déclaration et contre toute provocation à une telle discrimination.

ARTICLE 8

Toute personne a droit à un recours effectif devant les juridictions nationales compétentes contre les actes violant les droits fondamentaux qui lui sont reconnus par la constitution ou par la loi.

ARTICLE 9

Nul ne peut être arbitrairement arrêté, détenu ni exilé.

ARTICLE 10

Toute personne a droit, en pleine égalité, à ce que sa cause soit entendue équitablement et publiquement par un tribunal indépendant et impartial, qui décidera. soit de ses droits et obligations, soit du bien fondé de toute accusation en matière pénale dirigée contre elle.

ARTICLE 11

1. Toute personne accusée d'un acte délictueux est présumée innocente jusqu'à ce que sa culpabilité ait été légalement établie au cours d'un procès public où toutes les garanties nécessaires à sa défense lui auront été assurées.

2. Nul ne sera ondamné pour des actions ou omissions qui, au moment où elles ont été commises, ne constituaient pas un acte délictueux d'après le droit national ou international. De même, il ne sera infligé aucune peine plus forte que celle qui était applicable au moment où l'acte délictueux a été commis.

ARTICLE 12

Nul ne sera l'objet d'immixtions arbitraires dans sa vie privée, sa famille, son domicile ou sa correspondance, ni d'atteintes à son honneur et à sa réputation. Toute personne a droit à la

tection of the law against such interference or attacks. '

ARTICLE 13

1. Everyone has the right to freedom of movement and residence within the borders of each State.

2. Everyone has the right to leave any country, including his own, and to return to his country.

ARTICLE 14

1. Everyone has the right to seek and to enjoy in other countries asylum from persecution.

2. This right may not be invoked in the case of prosecutions genuinely arising from non-political crimes or from acts contrary to the purposes and principles of the United Nations.

ARTICLE 15

1. Everyone has the right to a nationality.
2. No one shall be arbitrarily deprived of his nationality nor denied the right to change his nationality.

ARTICLE 16

1. Men and women of full age, without any limitation due to race, nationality or religion, have the right to marry and to found a family. They are entitled to equal rights as to marriage, during marriage and at its dissolution.

2. Marriage shall be entered into only with the free and full consent of the intending spouses.

3. The family is the natural and fundamental group unit of society and is entitled to protection by society and the State.

ARTICLE 17

1. Everyone has the right to own property alone as well as in association with others.

2. No one shall be arbitrarily deprived of his property.

ARTICLE 18

Everyone has the right to freedom of thought, conscience and religion; this right includes freedom to change his religion or belief, and freedom, either alone or in community with others and in public or private, to manifest his religion or belief in teaching, practice, worship and observance.

ARTICLE 19

Everyone has the right to freedom of opinion and expression; this right includes freedom to

---

protection de la loi contre de telles immixtions ou de telles atteintes.

ARTICLE 13

1. Toute personne a le droit de circuler librement et de choisir sa résidence à l'intérieur d'un État.

2. Toute personne a le droit de quitter tout pays, y compris le sien, et de revenir dans son pays.

ARTICLE 14

1. Devant la persécution, toute personne a le droit de chercher asile et de bénéficier de l'asile en d'autres pays.

2. Ce droit ne peut être invoqué dans le cas de poursuites réellement fondées sur un crime de droit commun ou sur des agissements contraires aux buts et aux principes des Nations Unies.

ARTICLE 15

1. Tout individu a droit à une nationalité.
2. Nul ne peut être arbitrairement privé de sa nationalité, ni du droit de changer de nationalité.

ARTICLE 16

1. A partir de l'âge nubile, l'homme et la femme, sans aucune restriction quant à la race, la nationalité ou la religion, ont le droit de se marier et de fonder une famille. Ils ont des droits égaux au regard du mariage, durant le mariage et lors de sa dissolution.

2. Le mariage ne peut être conclu qu'avec le libre et plein consentement des futurs époux.

3. La famille est l'elément naturel et fondamental de la société et a droit à la protection de la société et de l'État.

ARTICLE 17

1. Toute personne, aussi bien seule qu'en collectivité, a droit à la propriété.

2. Nul ne peut être arbitrairement privé de sa propriété.

ARTICLE 18

Toute personne a droit à la liberté de pensée, de conscience et de religion; ce droit implique la liberté de changer de religion ou de conviction ainsi que la liberté de manifester sa religion ou sa conviction, seule ou en commun, tant en public qu'en privé, par l'enseignement, les pratiques, le culte et l'accomplissement des rites.

ARTICLE 19

Tout individu a droit à la liberté d'opinion et d'expression, ce qui implique le droit de ne

hold opinions without interference and to seek, receive and impart information and ideas through any media and regardless of frontiers.

ARTICLE 20

1. Everyone has the right to freedom of peaceful assembly and association.

2. No one may be compelled to belong to an association.

ARTICLE 21

1. Everyone has the right to take part in the government of his country, directly or through freely chosen representatives.

2. Everyone has the right of equal access to public service in his country.

3. The will of the people shall be the basis of the authority of government; this will shall be expressed in periodic and genuine elections which shall be by universal and equal suffrage and shall be held by secret vote or by equivalent free voting procedures.

ARTICLE 22

Everyone, as a member of society, has the right to social security and is entitled to realization, through national effort and international co-operation and in accordance with the organization and resources of each State, of the economic, social and cultural rights indispensable for his dignity and the free development of his personality.

ARTICLE 23

1. Everyone has the right to work, to free choice of employment, to just and favourable conditions of work and to protection against unemployment.

2. Everyone, without any discrimination, has the right to equal pay for equal work.

3. Everyone who works has the right to just and favourable remuneration ensuring for himself and his family an existence worthy of human dignity, and supplemented, if necessary, by other means of social protection.

4. Everyone has the right to form and to join trade unions for the protection of his interests.

ARTICLE 24

Everyone has the right to rest and leisure, including reasonable limitation of working hours and periodic holidays with pay.

---

pas être inquiété pour ses opinions et celui de chercher, de recevoir et de répandre, sans considérations de frontières, les informations et les idées par quelque moyen d'expression que ce soit.

ARTICLE 20

1. Toute personne a droit à la liberté de réunion et d'association pacifiques.

2. Nul ne peut être obligé de faire partie d'une association.

ARTICLE 21

1. Toute personne a le droit de prendre part à la direction des affaires publiques de son pays, soit directement, soit par l'intermédiaire de représentants librement choisis.

2. Toute personne a droit à accéder, dans des conditions d'égalité, aux fonctions publiques de son pays.

3. La volonté du peuple est le fondement de l'autorité des pouvoirs publics; cette volonté doit s'exprimer par des élections honnêtes qui doivent avoir lieu périodiquement, au suffrage universel égal et au vote secret ou suivant une procédure équivalente assurant la liberté du vote.

ARTICLE 22

Toute personne, en tant que membre de la société, a droit à la sécurité sociale; elle est fondée à obtenir la satisfaction des droits économiques, sociaux et culturels indispensables à sa dignité et au libre développement de sa personnalité, grâce à l'effort national et à la coopération internationale, compte tenu de l'organisation et des ressources de chaque pays.

ARTICLE 23

1. Toute personne a droit au travail, au libre choix de son travail, à des conditions équitables et satisfaisantes de travail et à la protection contre le chômage.

2. Tous ont droit, sans aucune discrimination, à un salaire égal pour un travail égal.

3. Quiconque travaille a droit à une rémunération équitable et satisfaisante lui assurant ainsi qu'à sa famille une existence conforme à la dignité humaine et complétée, s'il y a lieu, par tous autres moyens de protection sociale.

4. Toute personne a le droit de fonder avec d'autres des syndicats et de s'affilier à des syndicats pour la défense de ses intérêts.

ARTICLE 24

Toute personne a droit au repos et aux loisirs et notamment à une limitation raisonnable de la durée du travail et à des congés payés périodiques.

Article 25

1. Everyone has the right to a standard of living adequate for the health and well-being of himself and of his family, including food, clothing, housing and medical care and necessary social services, and the right to security in the event of unemployment, sickness, disability, widowhood, old age or other lack of livelihood in circumstances beyond his control.

2. Motherhood and childhood are entitled to special care and assistance. All children, whether born in or out of wedlock, shall enjoy the same social protection.

Article 26

1. Everyone has the right to education. Education shall be free, at least in the elementary and fundamental stages. Elementary education shall be compulsory. Technical and professional education shall be made generally available and higher education shall be equally accessible to all on the basis of merit.

2. Education shall be directed to the full development of the human personality and to the strengthening of respect for human rights and fundamental freedoms. It shall promote understanding, tolerance and friendship among all nations, racial or religious groups, and shall further the activities of the United Nations for the maintenance of peace.

3. Parents have a prior right to choose the kind of education that shall be given to their children.

Article 27

1. Everyone has the right freely to participate in the cultural life of the community, to enjoy the arts and to share in scientific advancement and its benefits.

2. Everyone has the right to the protection of the moral and material interests resulting from any scientific, literary or artistic production of which he is the author.

Article 28

Everyone is entitled to a social and international order in which the rights and freedoms set forth in this Declaration can be fully realized.

Article 29

1. Everyone has duties to the community in which alone the free and full development of his personality is possible.

Article 25

1. Toute personne a droit à un niveau de vie suffisant pour assurer sa santé, son bien-être et ceux de sa famille, notamment pour l'alimentation, l'habillement, le logement, les soins médicaux ainsi que pour les services sociaux nécessaires; elle a droit à la sécurité en cas de chômage, de maladie, d'invalidité, de veuvage, de vieillesse ou dans les autres cas de perte de ses moyens de subsistance par suite de circonstances indépendantes de sa volonté.

2. La maternité et l'enfance ont droit à une aide et à une assistance spéciales. Tous les enfants, qu'ils soient nés dans le mariage ou hors mariage, jouissent de la même protection sociale.

Article 26

1. Toute personne a droit à l'éducation. L'éducation doit être gratuite, au moins en ce qui concerne l'enseignement élémentaire et fondamental. L'enseignement élémentaire est obligatoire. L'enseignement technique et professionnel doit être généralisé; l'accès aux études supérieures doit être ouvert en pleine égalité à tous en fonction de leur mérite.

2. L'éducation doit viser au plein épanouissement de la personnalité humaine et au renforcement du respect des droits de l'homme et des libertés fondamentales. Elle doit favoriser la compréhension, la tolérance et l'amitié entre toutes les nations et tous les groupes raciaux ou religieux, ainsi que le développement des activités des Nations Unies pour le maintien de la paix.

3. Les parents ont, par priorité, le droit de choisir le genre d'éducation à donner à leurs enfants.

Article 27

1. Toute personne a le droit de prendre part librement à la vie culturelle de la communauté, de jouir des arts et de participer au progrès scientifique et aux bienfaits qui en résultent.

2. Chacun a droit à la protection des intérêts moraux et matériels découlant de toute production scientifique, littéraire ou artistique dont il est l'auteur.

Article 28

Toute personne a droit à ce que règne, sur le plan social et sur le plan international, un ordre tel que les droits et libertés énoncés dans la présente Déclaration puissent y trouver plein effet.

Article 29

1. L'individu a des devoirs envers la communauté dans laquelle seule le libre et plein développement de sa personnalité est possible.

2. In the exercise of his rights and freedoms, everyone shall be subject only to such limitations as are determined by law solely for the purpose of securing due recognition and respect for the rights and freedoms of others and of meeting the just requirements of morality, public order and the general welfare in a democratic society.

3. These rights and freedoms may in no case be exercised contrary to the purposes and principles of the United Nations.

ARTICLE 30

Nothing in this Declaration may be interpreted as implying for any State, group or person any right to engage in any activity or to perform any act aimed at the destruction of any of the rights and freedoms set forth herein.

Hundred and eighty-third plenary meeting.
10 December 1948.

B

RIGHT OF PETITION

The General Assembly,

Considering that the right of petition is an essential human right, as is recognized in the Constitutions of a great number of countries,

Having considered the draft article on petitions in document A/C.3/306 and the amendments offered thereto by Cuba and France,

Decides not to take any action on this matter at the present session;

Requests the Economic and Social Council to ask the Commission on Human Rights to give further examination to the problem of petitions when studying the draft covenant on human rights and measures of implementation, in order to enable the General Assembly to consider what further action, if any, should be taken at its next regular session regarding the problem of petitions.

Hundred and eighty-third plenary meeting,
10 December 1948.

C

FATE OF MINORITIES

The General Assembly,

Considering that the United Nations cannot remain indifferent to the fate of minorities,

Considering that it is difficult to adopt a uniform solution of this complex and delicate question, which has special aspects in each State in which it arises,

2. Dans l'exercice de ses droits et dans la jouissance de ses libertés, chacun n'est soumis qu'aux limitations établies par la loi exclusivement en vue d'assurer la reconnaissance et le respect des droits et libertés d'autrui et afin de satisfaire aux justes exigences de la morale, de l'ordre public et du bien-être général dans une société démocratique.

3. Ces droits et libertés ne pourront, en aucun cas, s'exercer contrairement aux buts et aux principes des Nations Unies.

ARTICLE 30

Aucune disposition de la présente Déclaration ne peut être interprétée comme impliquant pour un État, un groupement ou un individu un droit quelconque de se livrer à une activité ou d'accomplir un acte visant à la destruction des droits et libertés qui y sont énoncés.

Cent-quatre-vingt-troisième séance plénière.
le 10 décembre 1948.

B

DROIT DE PÉTITION

L'Assemblée générale,

Considérant que le droit de pétition est un des droits essentiels de l'homme, comme le reconnaissent les constitutions de nombreux pays,

Ayant examiné le projet d'article relatif aux pétitions qui figure dans le document A/C.3/306 et les amendements à cet article déposés par Cuba et la France,

Décide de ne prendre aucune mesure à ce sujet au cours de la présente session;

Prie le Conseil économique et social d'inviter la Commission des droits de l'homme à procéder à un nouvel examen du problème des pétitions lorsqu'elle examinera le projet de pacte relatif aux droits de l'homme et aux mesures de mise en œuvre, afin que l'Assemblée générale puisse, au cours de sa prochaine session ordinaire, examiner quelles mesures doivent être prises, s'il y a lieu d'en prendre, en ce qui concerne le problème des pétitions.

Cent-quatre-vingt-troisième séance plénière,
le 10 décembre 1948

C

SORT DES MINORITÉS

L'Assemblée générale,

Considérant que les Nations Unies ne peuvent pas demeurer indifférentes au sort des minorités,

Considérant qu'il est difficile d'adopter une solution uniforme de cette question complexe et délicate qui revêt des aspects particuliers dans chaque État où elle se pose,

Considering the universal character of the Declaration of Human Rights,

Decides not to deal in a specific provision with the question of minorities in the text of this Declaration;

Refers to the Economic and Social Council the texts submitted by the delegations of the Union of Soviet Socialist Republics, Yugoslavia and Denmark on this subject contained in document A/C.3/307/Rev. 2, and requests the Council to ask the Commission on Human Rights and the Sub-Commission on the Prevention of Discrimination and the Protection of Minorities to make a thorough study of the problem of minorities, in order that the United Nations may be able to take effective measures for the protection of racial, national, religious or linguistic minorities.

Hundred and eighty-third plenary meeting.
10 December 1948.

Considérant le caractère universel de la Déclaration des droits de l'homme,

Décide de ne pas traiter par une disposition spécifique dans le corps de cette Déclaration la question des minorités;

Renvoie au Conseil économique et social les textes soumis par les délégations de l'Union des Républiques socialistes soviétiques, de la Yougoslavie et du Danemark sur cette question dans le document A/C.3/307/Rev. 2, et prie le Conseil d'inviter la Commission des droits de l'homme et la Sous-Commission de la lutte contre les mesures discriminatoires et de la protection des minorités à procéder à un examen approfondi du problème des minorités, afin que l'Organisation des Nations Unies puisse adopter des mesures efficaces de protection des minorités raciales, nationales, religieuses et linguistiques.

Cent-quatre-vingt-troisième séance plénière,
le 10 décembre 1948.

(c) The Optional Protocol to the International Covenant on Civil and Political Rights;

2. *Expresses the hope* that the Covenants and the Optional Protocol will be signed and ratified or acceded to without delay and come into force at an early date;

3. *Requests* the Secretary-General to submit to the General Assembly at its future sessions reports concerning the state of ratifications of the Covenants and of the Optional Protocol which the Assembly will consider as a separate agenda item.

1496th plenary meeting,
16 December 1966.

ANNEX

International Covenant on Economic, Social and Cultural Rights

PREAMBLE

The States Parties to the present Covenant,

Considering that, in accordance with the principles proclaimed in the Charter of the United Nations, recognition of the inherent dignity and of the equal and inalienable rights of all members of the human family is the foundation of freedom, justice and peace in the world,

Recognising that these rights derive from the inherent dignity of the human person,

Recognising that, in accordance with the Universal Declaration of Human Rights, the ideal of free human beings enjoying freedom from fear and want can only be achieved if conditions are created whereby everyone may enjoy his economic, social and cultural rights, as well as his civil and political rights,

Considering the obligation of States under the Charter of the United Nations to promote universal respect for, and observance of, human rights and freedoms,

Realizing that the individual, having duties to other individuals and to the community to which he belongs, is under a responsibility to strive for the promotion and observance of the rights recognized in the present Covenant,

Agree upon the following articles:

PART I

Article 1

1. All peoples have the right of self-determination. By virtue of that right they freely determine their political status and freely pursue their economic, social and cultural development.

2. All peoples may, for their own ends, freely dispose of their natural wealth and resources without prejudice to any obligations arising out of international economic co-operation, based upon the principle of mutual benefit, and international law. In no case may a people be deprived of its own means of subsistence.

3. The States Parties to the present Covenant, including those having responsibility for the administration of Non-Self-Governing and Trust Territories, shall promote the realization of the right of self-determination, and shall respect that right, in conformity with the provisions of the Charter of the United Nations.

PART II

Article 2

1. Each State Party to the present Covenant undertakes to take steps, individually and through international assistance and co-operation, especially economic and technical, to the maximum of its available resources, with a view to achieving progressively the full realization of the rights recognized in the present Covenant by all appropriate means, including particularly the adoption of legislative measures.

2. The States Parties to the present Covenant undertake to guarantee that the rights enunciated in the present Covenant

2200 (XXI). International Covenant on Economic, Social and Cultural Rights, International Covenant on Civil and Political Rights and Optional Protocol to the International Covenant on Civil and Political Rights

A

The General Assembly,

Considering that one of the purposes of the United Nations, as stated in Articles 1 and 55 of the Charter, is to promote universal respect for, and observance of, human rights and fundamental freedoms for all without distinction as to race, sex, language or religion,

Considering that in Article 56 of the Charter all Members of the United Nations have pledged themselves to take joint and separate action in co-operation with the Organization for the achievement of that purpose,

Recalling the proclamation by the General Assembly on 10 December 1948 of the Universal Declaration of Human Rights as a common standard of achievement for all peoples and all nations,

Having considered since its ninth session the draft International Covenants on Human Rights prepared by the Commission on Human Rights and transmitted to it by Economic and Social Council resolution 545 B (XVIII) of 29 July 1954, and having completed the elaboration of the Covenants at its twenty-first session,

1. *Adopts* and opens for signature, ratification and accession the following international instruments, the texts of which are annexed to the present resolution:

(a) The International Covenant on Economic, Social and Cultural Rights;

(b) The International Covenant on Civil and Political Rights;

⁹ A/6349, annex II, A/C.3/L.1341/Rev.1, A/C.3L.1383/Rev.1, A/C.3/L.1384-1386, A/C.3/L.1400 and Corr.1, A/C.3/L.1401, A/C.3/L.1403, and A/C.3/L.1406.

will be exercised without discrimination of any kind as to race, colour, sex, language, religion, political or other opinion, national or social origin, property, birth or other status.

3. Developing countries, with due regard to human rights and their national economy, may determine to what extent they would guarantee the economic rights recognized in the present Covenant to non-nationals.

Article 3

The States Parties to the present Covenant undertake to ensure the equal right of men and women to the enjoyment of all economic, social and cultural rights set forth in the present Covenant.

Article 4

The States Parties to the present Covenant recognize that, in the enjoyment of those rights provided by the State in conformity with the present Covenant, the State may subject such rights only to such limitations as are determined by law only in so far as this may be compatible with the nature of these rights and solely for the purpose of promoting the general welfare in a democratic society.

Article 5

1. Nothing in the present Covenant may be interpreted as implying for any State, group or person any right to engage in any activity or to perform any act aimed at the destruction of any of the rights or freedoms recognized herein, or at their limitation to a greater extent than is provided for in the present Covenant.

2. No restriction upon or derogation from any of the fundamental human rights recognized or existing in any country in virtue of law, conventions, regulations or custom shall be admitted on the pretext that the present Covenant does not recognize such rights or that it recognizes them to a lesser extent.

PART III

Article 6

1. The States Parties to the present Covenant recognize the right to work, which includes the right of everyone to the opportunity to gain his living by work which he freely chooses or accepts, and will take appropriate steps to safeguard this right.

2. The steps to be taken by a State Party to the present Covenant to achieve the full realization of this right shall include technical and vocational guidance and training programmes, policies and techniques to achieve steady economic, social and cultural development and full and productive employment under conditions safeguarding fundamental political and economic freedoms to the individual.

Article 7

The States Parties to the present Covenant recognize the right of everyone to the enjoyment of just and favourable conditions of work which ensure, in particular:

(a) Remuneration which provides all workers, as a minimum, with:

(i) Fair wages and equal renumeration for work of equal value without distinction of any kind, in particular women being guaranteed conditions of work not inferior to those enjoyed by men, with equal pay for equal work;

(ii) A decent living for themselves and their families in accordance with the provisions of the present Covenant;

(b) Safe and healthy working conditions;

(c) Equal opportunity for everyone to be promoted in his employment to an appropriate higher level, subject to no considerations other than those of seniority and competence;

(d) Rest, leisure and reasonable limitation of working hours and periodic holidays with pay, as well as remuneration for public holidays.

Article 8

1. The States Parties to the present Covenant undertake to ensure:

(a) The right of everyone to form trade unions and join the trade union of his choice, subject only to the rules of the organization concerned, for the promotion and protection of his economic and social interests. No restrictions may be placed on the exercise of this right other than those prescribed by law and which are necessary in a democratic society in the interests of national security or public order or for the protection of the rights and freedoms of others;

(b) The right of trade unions to establish national federations or confederations and the right of the latter to form or join international trade-union organizations;

(c) The right of trade unions to function freely subject to no limitations other than those prescribed by law and which are necessary in a democratic society in the interests of national security or public order or for the protection of the rights and freedoms of others;

(d) The right to strike, provided that it is exercised in conformity with the laws of the particular country.

2. This article shall not prevent the imposition of lawful restrictions on the exercise of these rights by members of the armed forces or of the police or of the administration of the State.

3. Nothing in this article shall authorize States Parties to the International Labour Organisation Convention of 1948 concerning Freedom of Association and Protection of the Right to Organize to take legislative measures which would prejudice, or apply the law in such a manner as would prejudice, the guarantees provided for in that Convention.

Article 9

The States Parties to the present Covenant recognize the right of everyone to social security, including social insurance.

Article 10

The States Parties to the present Covenant recognize that:

1. The widest possible protection and assistance should be accorded to the family, which is the natural and fundamental group unit of society, particularly for its establishment and while it is responsible for the care and education of dependent children. Marriage must be entered into with the free consent of the intending spouses.

2. Special protection should be accorded to mothers during a reasonable period before and after childbirth. During such period working mothers should be accorded paid leave or leave with adequate social security benefits.

3. Special measures of protection and assistance should be taken on behalf of all children and young persons without any discrimination for reasons of parentage or other conditions. Children and young persons should be protected from economic and social exploitation. Their employment in work harmful to their morals or health or dangerous to life or likely to hamper their normal development should be punishable by law. States should also set age limits below which the paid employment of child labour should be prohibited and punishable by law.

Article 11

1. The States Parties to the present Covenant recognize the right of everyone to an adequate standard of living for himself and his family, including adequate food, clothing and housing, and to the continuous improvement of living conditions. The States Parties will take appropriate steps to ensure the realization of this right, recognizing to this effect the essential importance of international co-operation based on free consent.

2. The States Parties to the present Covenant, recognizing the fundamental right of everyone to be free from hunger, shall take, individually and through international co-operation, the measures, including specific programmes, which are needed:

(a) To improve methods of production, conservation and distribution of food by making full use of technical and scientific knowledge, by disseminating knowledge of the principles of nutrition and by developing or reforming agrarian systems in such a way as to achieve the most efficient development and utilization of natural resources;

(b) Taking into account the problems of both food-importing and food-exporting countries, to ensure an equitable distribution of world food supplies in relation to need.

Article 12

1. The States Parties to the present Covenant recognize the right of everyone to the enjoyment of the highest attainable standard of physical and mental health.

2. The steps to be taken by the States Parties to the present Covenant to achieve the full realization of this right shall include those necessary for:

(a) The provision for the reduction of the stillbirth-rate and of infant mortality and for the healthy development of the child;

(b) The improvement of all aspects of environmental and industrial hygiene;

(c) The prevention, treatment and control of epidemic, endemic, occupational and other diseases;

(d) The creation of conditions which would assure to all medical service and medical attention in the event of sickness.

Article 13

1. The States Parties to the present Covenant recognize the right of everyone to education. They agree that education shall be directed to the full development of the human personality and the sense of its dignity, and shall strengthen the respect for human rights and fundamental freedoms. They further agree that education shall enable all persons to participate effectively in a free society, promote understanding, tolerance and friendship among all nations and all racial, ethnic or religious groups, and further the activities of the United Nations for the maintenance of peace.

2. The States Parties to the present Covenant recognize that, with a view to achieving the full realization of this right:

(a) Primary education shall be compulsory and available free to all;

(b) Secondary education in its different forms, including technical and vocational secondary education, shall be made generally available and accessible to all by every appropriate means, and in particular by the progressive introduction of free education;

(c) Higher education shall be made equally accessible to all, on the basis of capacity, by every appropriate means, and in particular by the progressive introduction of free education;

(d) Fundamental education shall be encouraged or intensified as far as possible for those persons who have not received or completed the whole period of their primary education;

(e) The development of a system of schools at all levels shall be actively pursued, an adequate fellowship system shall be established, and the material conditions of teaching staff shall be continuously improved.

3. The States Parties to the present Covenant undertake to have respect for the liberty of parents and, when applicable, legal guardians to choose for their children schools, other than those established by the public authorities, which conform to such minimum educational standards as may be laid down or approved by the State and to ensure the religious and moral education of their children in conformity with their own convictions.

4. No part of this article shall be construed so as to interfere with the liberty of individuals and bodies to establish and direct educational institutions, subject always to the observance of the principles set forth in paragraph 1 of this article and to the requirement that the education given in such institutions shall conform to such minimum standards as may be laid down by the State.

Article 14

Each State Party to the present Covenant which, at the time of becoming a Party, has not been able to secure in its metropolitan territory or other territories under its jurisdiction compulsory primary education, free of charge, undertakes, within two years, to work out and adopt a detailed plan of action for the progressive implementation, within a reasonable number of years, to be fixed in the plan, of the principle of compulsory education free of charge for all.

Article 15

1. The States Parties to the present Covenant recognize the right of everyone:

(a) To take part in cultural life;

(b) To enjoy the benefits of scientific progress and its applications;

(c) To benefit from the protection of the moral and material interests resulting from any scientific, literary or artistic production of which he is the author.

2. The steps to be taken by the States Parties to the present Covenant to achieve the full realization of this right shall include those necessary for the conservation, the development and the diffusion of science and culture.

3. The States Parties to the present Covenant undertake to respect the freedom indispensable for scientific research and creative activity.

4. The States Parties to the present Covenant recognize the benefits to be derived from the encouragement and development of international contacts and co-operation in the scientific and cultural fields.

PART IV

Article 16

1. The States Parties to the present Covenant undertake to submit in conformity with this part of the Covenant reports on the measures which they have adopted and the progress made in achieving the observance of the rights recognized herein.

2. (a) All reports shall be submitted to the Secretary-General of the United Nations, who shall transmit copies to the Economic and Social Council for consideration in accordance with the provisions of the present Covenant;

(b) The Secretary-General of the United Nations shall also transmit to the specialized agencies copies of the reports, or any relevant parts therefrom, from States Parties to the present Covenant which are also members of these specialized agencies in so far as these reports, or parts therefrom, relate to any matters which fall within the responsibilities of the said agencies in accordance with their constitutional instruments.

Article 17

1. The States Parties to the present Covenant shall furnish their reports in stages, in accordance with a programme to be established by the Economic and Social Council within one year of the entry into force of the present Covenant after consultation with the States Parties and the specialized agencies concerned.

2. Reports may indicate factors and difficulties affecting the degree of fulfilment of obligations under the present Covenant.

3. Where relevant information has previously been furnished to the United Nations or to any specialized agency by any State Party to the present Covenant, it will not be necessary to reproduce that information, but a precise reference to the information so furnished will suffice.

Article 18

Pursuant to its responsibilities under the Charter of the United Nations in the field of human rights and fundamental freedoms, the Economic and Social Council may make arrangements with the specialized agencies in respect of their reporting to it on the progress made in achieving the observance of the provisions of the present Covenant falling within the scope of their activities. These reports may include particulars of decisions and recommendations on such implementation adopted by their competent organs.

Article 19

The Economic and Social Council may transmit to the Commission on Human Rights for study and general recommendation or, as appropriate, for information the reports concerning human rights submitted by States in accordance with articles 16 and 17, and those concerning human rights submitted by the specialized agencies in accordance with article 18.

Article 20

The States Parties to the present Covenant and the specialized agencies concerned may submit comments to the Economic and Social Council on any general recommendation under article 19 or reference to such general recommendation in any report of the Commission on Human Rights or any documentation referred to therein.

Article 21

The Economic and Social Council may submit from time to time to the General Assembly reports with recommendations of a general nature and a summary of the information received from the States Parties to the present Covenant and the specialized agencies on the measures taken and the progress made in achieving general observance of the rights recognized in the present Covenant.

Article 22

The Economic and Social Council may bring to the attention of other organs of the United Nations, their subsidiary organs and specialized agencies concerned with furnishing technical assistance any matters arising out of the reports referred to in this part of the present Covenant which may assist such bodies in deciding, each within its field of competence, on the advisability of international measures likely to contribute to the effective progressive implementation of the present Covenant.

Article 23

The States Parties to the present Covenant agree that international action for the achievement of the rights recognized in the present Covenant includes such methods as the conclusion of conventions, the adoption of recommendations, the furnishing of technical assistance and the holding of regional meetings and technical meetings for the purpose of consultation and study organized in conjunction with the Governments concerned.

Article 24

Nothing in the present Covenant shall be interpreted as impairing the provisions of the Charter of the United Nations and of the constitutions of the specialized agencies which define the respective responsibilities of the various organs of the United Nations and of the specialized agencies in regard to the matters dealt with in the present Covenant.

Article 25

Nothing in the present Covenant shall be interpreted as impairing the inherent right of all peoples to enjoy and utilize fully and freely their natural wealth and resources.

Part V

Article 26

1. The present Covenant is open for signature by any State Member of the United Nations or member of any of its specialized agencies, by any State Party to the Statute of the International Court of Justice, and by any other State which has been invited by the General Assembly of the United Nations to become a party to the present Covenant.

2. The present Covenant is subject to ratification. Instruments of ratification shall be deposited with the Secretary-General of the United Nations.

3. The present Covenant shall be open to accession by any State referred to in paragraph 1 of this article.

4. Accession shall be effected by the deposit of an instrument of accession with the Secretary-General of the United Nations.

5. The Secretary-General of the United Nations shall inform all States which have signed the present Covenant or acceded to it of the deposit of each instrument of ratification or accession.

Article 27

1. The present Covenant shall enter into force three months after the date of the deposit with the Secretary-General of the United Nations of the thirty-fifth instrument of ratification or instrument of accession.

2. For each State ratifying the present Covenant or acceding to it after the deposit of the thirty-fifth instrument of ratification or instrument of accession, the present Covenant shall enter into force three months after the date of the deposit of its own instrument of ratification or instrument of accession.

Article 28

The provisions of the present Covenant shall extend to all parts of federal States without any limitations or exceptions.

Article 29

1. Any State Party to the present Covenant may propose an amendment and file it with the Secretary-General of the United Nations. The Secretary-General shall thereupon communicate any proposed amendments to the States Parties to the present Covenant with a request that they notify him whether they favour a conference of States Parties for the purpose of considering and voting upon the proposals. In the event that at least one third of the States Parties favour such a conference, the Secretary-General shall convene the conference under the auspices of the United Nations. Any amendment adopted by a majority of the States Parties present and voting at the conference shall be submitted to the General Assembly of the United Nations for approval.

2. Amendments shall come into force when they have been approved by the General Assembly of the United Nations and accepted by a two-thirds majority of the States Parties to the present Covenant in accordance with their respective constitutional processes.

3. When amendments come into force they shall be binding on those States Parties which have accepted them, other States Parties still being bound by the provisions of the present Covenant and any earlier amendment which they have accepted.

Article 30

Irrespective of the notifications made under article 26, paragraph 5, the Secretary-General of the United Nations shall inform all States referred to in paragraph 1 of the same article of the following particulars:

(a) Signatures, ratifications and accessions under article 26;

(b) The date of the entry into force of the present Covenant under article 27 and the date of the entry into force of any amendments under article 29.

Article 31

1. The present Covenant, of which the Chinese, English, French, Russian and Spanish texts are equally authentic, shall be deposited in the archives of the United Nations.

2. The Secretary-General of the United Nations shall transmit certified copies of the present Covenant to all States referred to in article 26.

International Covenant on Civil and Political Rights

Preamble

The States Parties to the present Covenant,

Considering that, in accordance with the principles proclaimed in the Charter of the United Nations, recognition of the inherent dignity and of the equal and inalienable rights of all members of the human family is the foundation of freedom, justice and peace in the world,

Recognizing that these rights derive from the inherent dignity of the human person,

Recognizing that, in accordance with the Universal Declaration of Human Rights, the ideal of free human beings enjoying civil and political freedom and freedom from fear and want can only be achieved if conditions are created whereby everyone may enjoy his civil and political rights, as well as his economic, social and cultural rights,

Considering the obligation of States under the Charter of the United Nations to promote universal respect for, and observance of, human rights and freedoms,

Realizing that the individual, having duties to other individuals and to the community to which he belongs, is under a responsibility to strive for the promotion and observance of the rights recognized in the present Covenant,

Agree upon the following articles :

PART I

Article 1

1. All peoples have the right of self-determination. By virtue of that right they freely determine their political status and freely pursue their economic, social and cultural development.

2. All peoples may, for their own ends, freely dispose of their natural wealth and resources without prejudice to any obligations arising out of international economic co-operation, based upon the principle of mutual benefit, and international law. In no case may a people be deprived of its own means of subsistence.

3. The States Parties to the present Covenant, including those having responsibility for the administration of Non-Self-Governing and Trust Territories, shall promote the realization of the right of self-determination, and shall respect that right, in conformity with the provisions of the Charter of the United Nations.

PART II

Article 2

1. Each State Party to the present Covenant undertakes to respect and to ensure to all individuals within its territory and subject to its jurisdiction the rights recognized in the present Covenant, without distinction of any kind, such as race, colour, sex, language, religion, political or other opinion, national or social origin, property, birth or other status.

2. Where not already provided for by existing legislative or other measures, each State Party to the present Covenant undertakes to take the necessary steps, in accordance with its constitutional processes and with the provisions of the present Covenant, to adopt such legislative or other measures as may be necessary to give effect to the rights recognized in the present Covenant.

3. Each State Party to the present Covenant undertakes:

(a) To ensure that any person whose rights or freedoms as herein recognized are violated shall have an effective remedy, notwithstanding that the violation has been committed by persons acting in an official capacity ;

(b) To ensure that any person claiming such a remedy shall have his right thereto determined by competent judicial, administrative or legislative authorities, or by any other competent authority provided for by the legal system of the State, and to develop the possibilities of judicial remedy ;

(c) To ensure that the competent authorities shall enforce such remedies when granted.

Article 3

The States Parties to the present Covenant undertake to ensure the equal right of men and women to the enjoyment of all civil and political rights set forth in the present Covenant.

Article 4

1. In time of public emergency which threatens the life of the nation and the existence of which is officially proclaimed, the States Parties to the present Covenant may take measures derogating from their obligations under the present Covenant to the extent strictly required by the exigencies of the situation, provided that such measures are not inconsistent with their other obligations under international law and do not involve discrimination solely on the ground of race, colour, sex, language, religion or social origin.

2. No derogation from articles 6, 7, 8 (paragraphs 1 and 2), 11, 15, 16 and 18 may be made under this provision.

3. Any State Party to the present Covenant availing itself of the right of derogation shall immediately inform the other States Parties to the present Covenant, through the intermediary of the Secretary-General of the United Nations, of the provisions from which it has derogated and of the reasons by which it was actuated. A further communication shall be made, through the same intermediary, on the date on which it terminates such derogation.

Article 5

1. Nothing in the present Covenant may be interpreted as implying for any State, group or person any right to engage in any activity or perform any act aimed at the destruction of any of the rights and freedoms recognized herein or at their limitation to a greater extent than is provided for in the present Covenant.

2. There shall be no restriction upon or derogation from any of the fundamental human rights recognized or existing in any State Party to the present Covenant pursuant to law, conventions, regulations or custom on the pretext that the present Covenant does not recognize such rights or that it recognizes them to a lesser extent.

PART III

Article 6

1. Every human being has the inherent right to life. This right shall be protected by law. No one shall be arbitrarily deprived of his life.

2. In countries which have not abolished the death penalty, sentence of death may be imposed only for the most serious crimes in accordance with the law in force at the time of the commission of the crime and not contrary to the provisions of the present Covenant and to the Convention on the Prevention and Punishment of the Crime of Genocide. This penalty can only be carried out pursuant to a final judgement rendered by a competent court.

3. When deprivation of life constitutes the crime of genocide, it is understood that nothing in this article shall authorize any State Party to the present Covenant to derogate in any way from any obligation assumed under the provisions of the Convention on the Prevention and Punishment of the Crime of Genocide.

4. Anyone sentenced to death shall have the right to seek pardon or commutation of the sentence. Amnesty, pardon or commutation of the sentence of death may be granted in all cases.

5. Sentence of death shall not be imposed for crimes committed by persons below eighteen years of age and shall not be carried out on pregnant women.

6. Nothing in this article shall be invoked to delay or to prevent the abolition of capital punishment by any State Party to the present Covenant.

Article 7

No one shall be subjected to torture or to cruel, inhuman or degrading treatment or punishment. In particular, no one shall be subjected without his free consent to medical or scientific experimentation.

Article 8

1. No one shall be held in slavery; slavery and the slave-trade in all their forms shall be prohibited.

2. No one shall be held in servitude.

3. (a) No one shall be required to perform forced or compulsory labour;

(b) Paragraph 3 (a) shall not be held to preclude, in countries where imprisonment with hard labour may be imposed as a punishment for a crime, the performance of hard labour in pursuance of a sentence to such punishment by a competent court;

(c) For the purpose of this paragraph the term "forced or compulsory labour" shall not include:

(i) Any work or service, not referred to in sub-paragraph (b), normally required of a person who is under detention in consequence of a lawful order of a court, or of a person during conditional release from such detention;

(ii) Any service of a military character and, in countries where conscientious objection is recognized, any national service required by law of conscientious objectors;

(iii) Any service exacted in cases of emergency or calamity threatening the life or well-being of the community;

(iv) Any work or service which forms part of normal civil obligations.

Article 9

1. Everyone has the right to liberty and security of person. No one shall be subjected to arbitrary arrest or detention. No one shall be deprived of his liberty except on such grounds and in accordance with such procedure as are established by law.

2. Anyone who is arrested shall be informed, at the time of arrest, of the reasons for his arrest and shall be promptly informed of any charges against him.

3. Anyone arrested or detained on a criminal charge shall be brought promptly before a judge or other officer authorized by law to exercise judicial power and shall be entitled to trial within a reasonable time or to release. It shall not be the general rule that persons awaiting trial shall be detained in custody, but release may be subject to guarantees to appear for trial, at any other stage of the judicial proceedings, and, should occasion arise, for execution of the judgement.

4. Anyone who is deprived of his liberty by arrest or detention shall be entitled to take proceedings before a court, in order that that court may decide without delay on the lawfulness of his detention and order his release if the detention is not lawful.

5. Anyone who has been the victim of unlawful arrest or detention shall have an enforceable right to compensation.

Article 10

1. All persons deprived of their liberty shall be treated with humanity and with respect for the inherent dignity of the human person.

2. (a) Accused persons shall, save in exceptional circumstances, be segregated from convicted persons and shall be subject to separate treatment appropriate to their status as unconvicted persons;

(b) Accused juvenile persons shall be separated from adults and brought as speedily as possible for adjudication.

3. The penitentiary system shall comprise treatment of prisoners the essential aim of which shall be their reformation and social rehabilitation. Juvenile offenders shall be segregated from adults and be accorded treatment appropriate to their age and legal status.

Article 11

No one shall be imprisoned merely on the ground of inability to fulfil a contractual obligation.

Article 12

1. Everyone lawfully within the territory of a State shall, within that territory, have the right to liberty of movement and freedom to choose his residence.

2. Everyone shall be free to leave any country, including his own.

3. The above-mentioned rights shall not be subject to any restrictions except those which are provided by law, are necessary to protect national security, public order (ordre public), public health or morals or the rights and freedoms of others, and are consistent with the other rights recognized in the present Covenant.

4. No one shall be arbitrarily deprived of the right to enter his own country.

Article 13

An alien lawfully in the territory of a State Party to the present Covenant may be expelled therefrom only in pursuance of a decision reached in accordance with law and shall, except where compelling reasons of national security otherwise require, be allowed to submit the reasons against his expulsion and to have his case reviewed by, and be represented for the purpose before, the competent authority or a person or persons especially designated by the competent authority.

Article 14

1. All persons shall be equal before the courts and tribunals. In the determination of any criminal charge against him, or of his rights and obligations in a suit at law, everyone shall be entitled to a fair and public hearing by a competent, independent and impartial tribunal established by law. The Press and the public may be excluded from all or part of a trial for reasons of morals, public order (ordre public) or national security in a democratic society, or when the interest of the private lives of the parties so requires, or to the extent strictly necessary in the opinion of the court in special circumstances where publicity would prejudice the interests of justice; but any judgement rendered in a criminal case or in a suit at law shall be made public except where the interest of juvenile persons otherwise requires or the proceedings concern matrimonial disputes or the guardianship of children.

2. Everyone charged with a criminal offence shall have the right to be presumed innocent until proved guilty according to law.

3. In the determination of any criminal charge against him, everyone shall be entitled to the following minimum guarantees, in full equality:

(a) To be informed promptly and in detail in a language which he understands of the nature and cause of the charge against him;

(b) To have adequate time and facilities for the preparation of his defence and to communicate with counsel of his own choosing;

(c) To be tried without undue delay;

(d) To be tried in his presence, and to defend himself in person or through legal assistance of his own choosing; to be informed, if he does not have legal assistance, of this right; and to have legal assistance assigned to him, in any case where the interests of justice so require, and without payment by him in any such case if he does not have sufficient means to pay for it;

(e) To examine, or have examined, the witnesses against him and to obtain the attendance and examination of witnesses on his behalf under the same conditions as witnesses against him;

(f) To have the free assistance of an interpreter if he cannot understand or speak the language used in court;

(g) Not to be compelled to testify against himself or to confess guilt.

4. In the case of juvenile persons, the procedure shall be such as will take account of their age and the desirability of promoting their rehabilitation.

5. Everyone convicted of a crime shall have the right to his conviction and sentence being reviewed by a higher tribunal according to law.

6. When a person has by a final decision been convicted of a criminal offence and when subsequently his conviction has been reversed or he has been pardoned on the ground that a new or newly discovered fact shows conclusively that there

...as been a miscarriage of justice, the person who has suffered punishment as a result of such conviction shall be compensated according to law, unless it is proved that the non-disclosure of the unknown fact in time is wholly or partly attributable to him.

7. No one shall be liable to be tried or punished again for an offence for which he has already been finally convicted or acquitted in accordance with the law and penal procedure of each country.

Article 15

1. No one shall be held guilty of any criminal offence on account of any act or omission which did not constitute a criminal offence, under national or international law, at the time when it was committed. Nor shall a heavier penalty be imposed than the one that was applicable at the time when the criminal offence was committed. If, subsequent to the commission of the offence, provision is made by law for the imposition of a lighter penalty, the offender shall benefit thereby.

2. Nothing in this article shall prejudice the trial and punishment of any person for any act or omission which, at the time when it was committed, was criminal according to the general principles of law recognized by the community of nations.

Article 16

Everyone shall have the right to recognition everywhere as a person before the law.

Article 17

1. No one shall be subjected to arbitrary or unlawful interference with his privacy, family, home or correspondence, nor to unlawful attacks on his honour and reputation.

2. Everyone has the right to the protection of the law against such interference or attacks.

Article 18

1. Everyone shall have the right to freedom of thought, conscience and religion. This right shall include freedom to have or to adopt a religion or belief of his choice, and freedom, either individually or in community with others and in public or private, to manifest his religion or belief in worship, observance, practice and teaching.

2. No one shall be subject to coercion which would impair his freedom to have or to adopt a religion or belief of his choice.

3. Freedom to manifest one's religion or beliefs may be subject only to such limitations as are prescribed by law and are necessary to protect public safety, order, health, or morals or the fundamental rights and freedoms of others.

4. The States Parties to the present Covenant undertake to have respect for the liberty of parents and, when applicable, legal guardians to ensure the religious and moral education of their children in conformity with their own convictions.

Article 19

1. Everyone shall have the right to hold opinions without interference.

2. Everyone shall have the right to freedom of expression; this right shall include freedom to seek, receive and impart information and ideas of all kinds, regardless of frontiers, either orally, in writing or in print, in the form of art, or through any other media of his choice.

3. The exercise of the rights provided for in paragraph 2 of this article carries with it special duties and responsibilities. It may therefore be subject to certain restrictions, but these shall only be such as are provided by law and are necessary:

(a) For respect of the rights or reputations of others;

(b) For the protection of national security or of public order (*ordre public*), or of public health or morals.

Article 20

1. Any propaganda for war shall be prohibited by law.

2. Any advocacy of national, racial or religious hatred that constitutes incitement to discrimination, hostility or violence shall be prohibited by law.

Article 21

The right of peaceful assembly shall be recognized. No restrictions may be placed on the exercise of this right other than those imposed in conformity with. the law and which are necessary in a democratic society in the interests of national security or public safety, public order (*ordre public*), the protection of public health or morals or the protection of the rights and freedoms of others.

Article 22

1. Everyone shall have the right to freedom of association with others, including the right to form and join trade unions for the protection of his interests.

2. No restrictions may be placed on the exercise of this right other than those which are prescribed by law and which are necessary in a democratic society in the interests of national security or public safety, public order (*ordre public*), the protection of public health or morals or the protection of the rights and freedoms of others. This article shall not prevent the imposition of lawful restrictions on members of the armed forces and of the police in their exercise of this right.

3. Nothing in this article shall authorize States Parties to the International Labour Organisation Convention of 1948 concerning Freedom of Association and Protection of the Right to Organize to take legislative measures which would prejudice, or to apply the law in such a manner as to prejudice, the guarantees provided for in that Convention.

Article 23

1. The family is the natural and fundamental group unit of society and is entitled to protection by society and the State.

2. The right of men and women of marriageable age to marry and to found a family shall be recognized.

3. No marriage shall be entered into without the free and full consent of the intending spouses.

4. States Parties to the present Covenant shall take appropriate steps to ensure equality of rights and responsibilities of spouses as to marriage, during marriage and at its dissolution. In the case of dissolution, provision shall be made for the necessary protection of any children.

Article 24

1. Every child shall have, without any discrimination as to race, colour, sex, language, religion, national or social origin, property or birth, the right to such measures of protection as are required by his status as a minor, on the part of his family, society and the State.

2. Every child shall be registered immediately after birth and shall have a name.

3. Every child has the right to acquire a nationality.

Article 25

Every citizen shall have the right and the opportunity, without any of the distinctions mentioned in article 2 and without unreasonable restrictions:

(a) To take part in the conduct of public affairs, directly or through freely chosen representatives;

(b) To vote and to be elected at genuine periodic elections which shall be by universal and equal suffrage and shall be held by secret ballot, guaranteeing the free expression of the will of the electors;

(c) To have access, on general terms of equality, to public service in his country.

Article 26

All persons are equal before the law and are entitled without any discrimination to the equal protection of the law. In this respect, the law shall prohibit any discrimination and guarantee to all persons equal and effective protection against discrimination on any ground such as race, colour, sex, language, religion, political or other opinion, national or social origin, property, birth or other status.

Article 27

In those States in which ethnic, religious or linguistic minorities exist, persons belonging to such minorities shall not be denied the right, in community with the other members of their group, to enjoy their own culture, to profess and practice their own religion, or to use their own language.

PART IV

Article 28

1. There shall be established a Human Rights Committee (hereafter referred to in the present Covenant as the Committee). It shall consist of eighteen members and shall carry out the functions hereinafter provided.

2. The Committee shall be composed of nationals of the States Parties to the present Covenant who shall be persons of high moral character and recognized competence in the field of human rights, consideration being given to the usefulness of the participation of some persons having legal experience.

3. The members of the Committee shall be elected and shall serve in their personal capacity.

Article 29

1. The members of the Committee shall be elected by secret ballot from a list of persons possessing the qualifications prescribed in article 28 and nominated for the purpose by the State Parties to the present Covenant.

2. Each State Party to the present Covenant may nominate not more than two persons. These persons shall be nationals of the nominating State.

3. A person shall be eligible for renomination.

Article 30

1. The initial election shall be held no later than six months after the date of the entry into force of the present Covenant.

2. At least four months before the date of each election to the Committee, other than an election to fill a vacancy declared in accordance with article 34, the Secretary-General of the United Nations shall address a written invitation to the States Parties to the present Covenant to submit their nominations for membership of the Committee within three months.

3. The Secretary-General of the United Nations shall prepare a list in alphabetical order of all the persons thus nominated, with an indication of the States Parties which have nominated them, and shall submit it to the States Parties to the present Covenant no later than one month before the date of each election.

4. Elections of the members of the Committee shall be held at a meeting of the States Parties to the present Covenant convened by the Secretary-General of the United Nations at the Headquarters of the United Nations. At that meeting, for which two thirds of the States Parties to the present Covenant shall constitute a quorum, the persons elected to the Committee shall be those nominees who obtain the largest number of votes and an absolute majority of the votes of the representatives of States Parties present and voting.

Article 31

1. The Committee may not include more than one national of the same State.

2. In the election of the Committee, consideration shall be given to equitable geographical distribution of membership and to the representation of the different forms of civilization and of the principal legal systems.

Article 32

1. The members of the Committee shall be elected for a term of four years. They shall be eligible for re-election if renominated. However, the terms of nine of the members elected at the first election shall expire at the end of two years; immediately after the first election, the names of these nine members shall be chosen by lot by the Chairman of the meeting referred to in article 30, paragraph 4.

2. Elections at the expiry of office shall be held in accordance with the preceding articles of this part of the present Covenant.

Article 33

1. If, in the unanimous opinion of the other members, a member of the Committee has ceased to carry out his functions for any cause other than absence of a temporary character, the Chairman of the Committee shall notify the Secretary-General of the United Nations, who shall then declare the seat of that member to be vacant.

2. In the event of the death or the resignation of a member of the Committee, the Chairman shall immediately notify the Secretary-General of the United Nations, who shall declare the seat vacant from the date of death or the date on which the resignation takes effect.

Article 34

1. When a vacancy is declared in accordance with article 33 and if the term of office of the member to be replaced does not expire within six months of the declaration of the vacancy, the Secretary-General of the United Nations shall notify each of the States Parties to the present Covenant, which may within two months submit nominations in accordance with article 29 for the purpose of filling the vacancy.

2. The Secretary-General of the United Nations shall prepare a list in alphabetical order of the persons thus nominated and shall submit it to the States Parties to the present Covenant. The election to fill the vacancy shall then take place in accordance with the relevant provisions of this part of the present Covenant.

3. A member of the Committee elected to fill a vacancy declared in accordance with article 33 shall hold office for the remainder of the term of the member who vacated the seat on the Committee under the provisions of that article.

Article 35

The members of the Committee shall, with the approval of the General Assembly of the United Nations, receive emoluments from United Nations resources on such terms and conditions as the General Assembly may decide, having regard to the importance of the Committee's responsibilities.

Article 36

The Secretary-General of the United Nations shall provide the necessary staff and facilities for the effective performance of the functions of the Committee under the present Covenant.

Article 37

1. The Secretary-General of the United Nations shall convene the initial meeting of the Committee at the Headquarters of the United Nations.

2. After its initial meeting, the Committee shall meet at such times as shall be provided in its rules of procedure.

3. The Committee shall normally meet at the Headquarters of the United Nations or at the United Nations Office at Geneva.

Article 38

Every member of the Committee shall, before taking up his duties, make a solemn declaration in open committee that he will perform his functions impartially and conscientiously.

Article 39

1. The Committee shall elect its officers for a term of two years. They may be re-elected.

2. The Committee shall establish its own rules of procedure, but these rules shall provide, *inter alia*, that :

(*a*) Twelve members shall constitute a quorum;

(*b*) Decisions of the Committee shall be made by a majority ote of the members present.

Article 40

1. The States Parties to the present Covenant undertake to ubmit reports on the measures they have adopted which give ffect to the rights recognized herein and on the progress aade in the enjoyment of those rights:

(*a*) Within one year of the entry into force of the present Covenant for the States Parties concerned;

(*b*) Thereafter whenever the Committee so requests.

2. All reports shall be submitted to the Secretary-General f the United Nations, who shall transmit them to the Committee for consideration. Reports shall indicate the factors and ifficulties, if any, affecting the implementation of the present Covenant.

3. The Secretary-General of the United Nations may, after onsultation with the Committee, transmit to the specialized gencies concerned copies of such parts of the reports as may all within their field of competence.

4. The Committee shall study the reports submitted by he States Parties to the present Covenant. It shall transmit ts reports, and such general comments as it may consider ppropriate, to the States Parties. The Committee may also ransmit to the Economic and Social Council these comments long with the copies of the reports it has received from States Parties to the present Covenant.

5. The States Parties to the present Covenant may submit to he Committee observations on any comments that may be made n accordance with paragraph 4 of this article.

Article 41

1. A State Party to the present Covenant may at any time declare under this article that it recognizes the competence of the Committee to receive and consider communications to the effect that a State Party claims that another State Party is not fulfilling its obligations under the present Covenant. Communications under this article may be received and considered only if submitted by a State Party which has made a declaration recognizing in regard to itself the competence of the Committee. No communication shall be received by the Committee if it concerns a State Party which has not made such a declaration. Communications received under this article shall be dealt with in accordance with the following procedure:

(*a*) If a State Party to the present Covenant considers that another State Party is not giving effect to the provisions of the present Covenant, it may, by written communication, bring the matter to the attention of that State Party. Within three months after the receipt of the communication, the receiving State shall afford the State which sent the communication an explanation or any other statement in writing clarifying the matter, which should include, to the extent possible and pertinent, reference to domestic procedures and remedies taken, pending, or available in the matter.

(*b*) If the matter is not adjusted to the satisfaction of both States Parties concerned within six months after the receipt by the receiving State of the initial communication, either State shall have the right to refer the matter to the Committee, by notice given to the Committee and to the other State.

(*c*) The Committee shall deal with a matter referred to it only after it has ascertained that all available domestic remedies have been invoked and exhausted in the matter, in conformity with the generally recognized principles of international law. This shall not be the rule where the application of the remedies is unreasonably prolonged.

(*d*) The Committee shall hold closed meetings when examining communications under this article.

(*e*) Subject to the provisions of sub-paragraph (*c*), the Committee shall make available its good offices to the States Parties concerned with a view to a friendly solution of the matter on the basis of respect for human rights and fundamental freedoms as recognized in the present Covenant.

(*f*) In any matter referred to it, the Committee may call upon the States Parties concerned, referred to in sub-paragraph (*b*), to supply any relevant information.

(*g*) The States Parties concerned, referred to in sub-paragraph (*b*), shall have the right to be represented when the matter is being considered in the Committee and to make submissions orally and/or in writing.

(*h*) The Committee shall, within twelve months after the date of receipt of notice under sub-paragraph (*b*), submit a report:

(i) If a solution within the terms of sub-paragraph (*e*) is reached, the Committee shall confine its report to a brief statement of the facts and of the solution reached;

(ii) If a solution within the terms of sub-paragraph (*e*) is not reached, the Committee shall confine its report to a brief statement of the facts; the written submissions and record of the oral submissions made by the States Parties concerned shall be attached to the report.

In every matter, the report shall be communicated to the States Parties concerned.

2. The provisions of this article shall come into force when ten States Parties to the present Covenant have made declarations under paragraph 1 of this article. Such declarations shall be deposited by the States Parties with the Secretary-General of the United Nations, who shall transmit copies thereof to the other States Parties. A declaration may be withdrawn at any time by notification to the Secretary-General. Such a withdrawal shall not prejudice the consideration of any matter which is the subject of a communication already transmitted under this article; no further communication by any State Party shall be received after the notification of withdrawal of the declaration has been received by the Secretary-General, unless the State Party concerned has made a new declaration.

Article 42

1. (*a*) If a matter referred to the Committee in accordance with article 41 is not resolved to the satisfaction of the States Partes concerned, the Committee may, with the prior consent of the States Parties concerned, appoint an *ad hoc* Conciliation Commission (hereinafter referred to as the Commission). The good offices of the Commission shall be made available to the States Parties concerned with a view to an amicable solution of the matter on the basis of respect for the present Covenant;

(*b*) The Commission shall consist of five persons acceptable to the States Parties concerned. If the States Parties concerned fail to reach agreement within three months on all or part of the composition of the Commission, the members of the Commission concerning whom no agreement has been reached shall be elected by secret ballot by a two-thirds majority vote of the Committee from among its members.

2. The members of the Commission shall serve in their personal capacity. They shall not be nationals of the States Parties concerned, or of a State not party to the present Covenant, or of a State Party which has not made a declaration under article 41.

3. The Commission shall elect its own Chairman and adopt its own rules of procedure.

4. The meetings of the Commission shall normally be held at the Headquarters of the United Nations or at the United Nations Office at Geneva. However, they may be held at such other convenient places as the Commission may determine in consultation with the Secretary-General of the United Nations and the States Parties concerned.

5. The secretariat provided in accordance with article 36 shall also service the commissions appointed under this article.

6. The information received and collated by the Committee shall be made available to the Commission and the Commission may call upon the States Parties concerned to supply any other relevant information.

7. When the Commission has fully considered the matter, but in any event not later than twelve months after having been seized of the matter, it shall submit to the Chairman of the Committee a report for communication to the States Parties concerned:

(a) If the Commission is unable to complete its consideration of the matter within twelve months, it shall confine its report to a brief statement of the status of its consideration of the matter;

(b) If an amicable solution to the matter on the basis of respect for human rights as recognized in the present Covenant is reached, the Commission shall confine its report to a brief statement of the facts and of the solution reached;

(c) If a solution within the terms of sub-paragraph (b) is not reached, the Commission's report shall embody its findings on all questions of fact relevant to the issues between the States Parties concerned, and its views on the possibilities of an amicable solution of the matter. This report shall also contain the written submissions and a record of the oral submissions made by the States Parties concerned;

(d) If the Commission's report is submitted under subparagraph (c), the States Parties concerned shall, within three months of the receipt of the report, notify the Chairman of the Committee whether or not they accept the contents of the report of the Commission.

8. The provisions of this article are without prejudice to the responsibilities of the Committee under article 41.

9. The States Parties concerned shall share equally all the expenses of the members of the Commission in accordance with estimates to be provided by the Secretary-General of the United Nations.

10. The Secretary-General of the United Nations shall be empowered to pay the expenses of the members of the Commission, if necessary, before reimbursement by the States Parties concerned, in accordance with paragraph 9 of this article.

Article 43

The members of the Committee, and of the *ad hoc* conciliation commissions which may be appointed under article 42, shall be entitled to the facilities, privileges and immunities of experts on mission for the United Nations as laid down in the relevant sections of the Convention on the Privileges and Immunities of the United Nations.

Article 44

The provisions for the implementation of the present Covenant shall apply without prejudice to the procedures prescribed in the field of human rights by or under the constituent instruments and the conventions of the United Nations and of the specialized agencies and shall not prevent the States Parties to the present Covenant from having recourse to other procedures for settling a dispute in accordance with general or special international agreements in force between them.

Article 45

The Committee shall submit to the General Assembly of the United Nations, through the Economic and Social Council, an annual report on its activities.

PART V

Article 46

Nothing in the present Covenant shall be interpreted as impairing the provisions of the Charter of the United Nations and of the constitutions of the specialized agencies which define the respective responsibilities of the various organs of the United Nations and of the specialized agencies in regard to the matters dealt within the present Covenant.

Article 47

Nothing in the present Covenant shall be interpreted as impairing the inherent right of all peoples to enjoy and utilize fully and freely their natural wealth and resources.

PART VI

Article 48

1. The present Covenant is open for signature by any State Member of the United Nations or member of any of its specialized agencies, by any State Party to the Statute of the International Court of Justice, and by any other State which has been invited by the General Assembly of the United Nations to become a party to the present Covenant.

2. The present Covenant is subject to ratification. Instruments of ratification shall be deposited with the Secretary-General of the United Nations.

3. The present Covenant shall be open to accession by any State referred to in paragraph 1 of this article.

4. Accession shall be effected by the deposit of an instrument of accession with the Secretary-General of the United Nations.

5. The Secretary-General of the United Nations shall inform all States which have signed this Covenant or acceded to it of the deposit of each instrument of ratification or accession.

Article 49

1. The present Covenant shall enter into force three months after the date of the deposit with the Secretary-General of the United Nations of the thirty-fifth instrument of ratification or instrument of accession.

2. For each State ratifying the present Covenant or acceding to it after the deposit of the thirty-fifth instrument of ratification or instrument of accession, the present Covenant shall enter into force three months after the date of the deposit of its own instrument of ratification or instrument of accession.

Article 50

The provisions of the present Covenant shall extend to all parts of federal States without any limitations or exceptions.

Article 51

1. Any State Party to the present Covenant may propose an amendment and file it with the Secretary-General of the United Nations. The Secretary-General of the United Nations shall thereupon communicate any proposed amendments to the States Parties to the present Covenant with a request that they notify him whether they favour a conference of States Parties for the purpose of considering and voting upon the proposals. In the event that at least one third of the States Parties favours such a conference, the Secretary-General shall convene the conference under the auspices of the United Nations. Any amendment adopted by a majority of the States Parties present and voting at the conference shall be submitted to the General Assembly of the United Nations for approval.

2. Amendments shall come into force when they have been approved by the General Assembly of the United Nations and accepted by a two-thirds majority of the States Parties to the present Covenant in accordance with their respective constitutional processes.

3. When amendments come into force, they shall be binding on those States Parties which have accepted them, other States Parties still being bound by the provisions of the present Covenant and any earlier amendment which they have accepted.

Article 52

Irrespective of the notifications made under article 48, paragraph 5, the Secretary-General of the United Nations shall inform all States referred to in paragraph 1 of the same article of the following particulars:

(a) Signatures, ratifications and accessions under article 48;

(b) The date of the entry into force of the present Covenant under article 49 and the date of the entry into force of any amendments under article 51.

Article 53

1. The present Covenant, of which the Chinese, English, French, Russian and Spanish texts are equally authentic, shall be deposited in the archives of the United Nations.

2. The Secretary-General of the United Nations shall transmit certified copies of the present Covenant to all States referred to in article 48.

Optical Protocol to the International Covenant on Civil and Political Rights

The States Parties to the present Protocol,

Considering that in order further to achieve the purposes of the Covenant on Civil and Political Rights (hereinafter referred to as the Covenant) and the implementation of its provisions it would be appropriate to enable the Human Rights Committee set up in part IV of the Covenant (hereinafter referred to as the Committee) to receive and consider, as provided in the present Protocol, communications from individuals claiming to be victims of violations of any of the rights set forth in the Covenant,

Have agreed as follows:

Article 1

A State Party to the Covenant that becomes a party to the present Protocol recognizes the competence of the Committee to receive and consider communications from individuals subject to its jurisdiction who claim to be victims of a violation by that State Party of any of the rights set forth in the Covenant. No communication shall be received by the Committee if it concerns a State Party to the Covenant which is not a party to the present Protocol.

Article 2

Subject to the provisions of article 1, individuals who claim that any of their rights enumerated in the Covenant have been violated and who have exhausted all available domestic remedies may submit a written communication to the Committee for consideration.

Article 3

The Committee shall consider inadmissible any communication under the present Protocol which is anonymous, or which it considers to be an abuse of the right of submission of such communications or to be incompatible with the provisions of the Covenant.

Article 4

1. Subject to the provisions of article 3, the Committee shall bring any communications submitted to it under the present Protocol to the attention of the State Party to the present Protocol alleged to be violating any provision of the Covenant.

2. Within six months, the receiving State shall submit to the Committee written explanations or statements clarifying the matter and the remedy, if any, that may have been taken by that State.

Article 5

1. The Committee shall consider communications received under the present Protocol in the light of all written information made available to it by the individual and by the State Party concerned.

2. The Committee shall not consider any communication from an individual unless it has ascertained that:

(a) The same matter is not being examined under another procedure of international investigation or settlement;

(b) The individual has exhausted all available domestic remedies.

This shall not be the rule where the application of the remedies is unreasonably prolonged.

3. The Committee shall hold closed meetings when examining communications under the present Protocol.

4. The Committee shall forward its views to the State Party concerned and to the individual.

Article 6

The Committee shall include in its annual report under article 45 of the Covenant a summary of its activities under the present Protocol.

Article 7

Pending the achievement of the objectives of resolution 1514 (XV) adopted by the General Assembly of the United Nations on 14 December 1960 concerning the Declaration on the Granting of Independence to Colonial Countries and Peoples, the provisions of the present Protocol shall in no way limit the right of petition granted to these peoples by the Charter of the United Nations and other international conventions and instruments under the United Nations and its specialized agencies.

Article 8

1. The present Protocol is open for signature by any State which has signed the Covenant.

2. The present Protocol is subject to ratification by any State which has ratified or acceded to the Covenant. Instruments of ratification shall be deposited with the Secretary-General of the United Nations.

3. The present Protocol shall be open to accession by any State which has ratified or acceded to the Covenant.

4. Accession shall be effected by the deposit of an instrument of accession with the Secretary-General of the United Nations.

5. The Secretary-General of the United Nations shall inform all States which have signed the present Protocol or acceded to it of the deposit of each instrument of ratification or accession.

Article 9

1. Subject to the entry into force of the Covenant, the present Protocol shall enter into force three months after the date of the deposit with the Secretary-General of the United Nations of the tenth instrument of ratification or instrument of accession.

2. For each State ratifying the present Protocol or acceding to it after the deposit of the tenth instrument of ratification or instrument of accession, the present Protocol shall enter into force three months after the date of the deposit of its own instrument of ratification or instrument of accession.

Article 10

The provisions of the present Protocol shall extend to all parts of federal States without any limitations or exceptions.

Article 11

1. Any State Party to the present Protocol may propose an amendment and file it with the Secretary-General of the United Nations. The Secretary-General shall thereupon communicate any proposed amendments to the States Parties to the present Protocol with a request that they notify him whether they favour a conference of States Parties for the purpose of considering and voting upon the proposal. In the event that at least one third of the States Parties favours such a conference, the Secretary-General shall convene the conference under the auspices of the United Nations. Any amendment adopted by a majority of the States Parties present and voting at the conference shall be submitted to the General Assembly of the United Nations for approval.

2. Amendments shall come into force when they have been approved by the General Assembly of the United Nations and accepted by a two-thirds majority of the States Parties to the present Protocol in accordance with their respective constitutional processes.

3. When amendments come into force, they shall be binding on those States Parties which have accepted them, other States Parties still being bound by the provisions of the present Protocol and any earlier amendment which they have accepted.

Article 12

1. Any State Party may denounce the present Protocol at any time by written notification addressed to the Secretary-General of the United Nations. Denunciation shall take effect three months after the date of receipt of the notification by the Secretary-General.

2. Denunciation shall be without prejudice to the continued application of the provisions of the present Protocol to any communication submitted under article 2 before the effective date of denunciation.

Article 13

Irrespective of the notifications made under article 8, paragraph 5, of the present Protocol, the Secretary-General of the United Nations shall inform all States referred to in article 48, paragraph 1, of the Covenant of the following particulars:

(*a*) Signatures, ratifications and accessions under article 8;

(*b*) The date of the entry into force of the present Protocol under article 9 and the date of the entry into force of any amendments under article 11;

(*c*) Denunciations under article 12.

Article 14

1. The present Protocol, of which the Chinese, English, French, Russian and Spanish texts are equally authentic, shall be deposited in the archives of the United Nations.

2. The Secretary-General of the United Nations shall transmit certified copies of the present Protocol to all States referred to in article 48 of the Covenant.

1386 (XIV). Declaration of the Rights of the Child

PREAMBLE

Whereas the peoples of the United Nations have, in the Charter, reaffirmed their faith in fundamental human rights and in the dignity and worth of the human person, and have determined to promote social progress and better standards of life in larger freedom,

Whereas the United Nations has, in the Universal Declaration of Human Rights, proclaimed that everyone is entitled to all the rights and freedoms set forth therein, without distinction of any kind, such as race, colour, sex, language, religion, political or other opinion, national or social origin, property, birth or other status,

Whereas the child, by reason of his physical and mental immaturity, needs special safeguards and care, including appropriate legal protection, before as well as after birth,

Whereas the need for such special safeguards has been stated in the Geneva Declaration of the Rights of the Child of 1924, and recognized in the Universal Declaration of Human Rights and in the statutes of specialized agencies and international organizations concerned with the welfare of children,

Whereas mankind owes to the child the best it has to give,

Now therefore,

The General Assembly

Proclaims this Declaration of the Rights of the Child to the end that he may have a happy childhood and enjoy for his own good and for the good of society the rights and freedoms herein set forth, and calls upon parents, upon men and women as individuals, and upon voluntary organizations, local authorities and national Governments to recognize these rights and strive for their observance by legislative and other measures progressively taken in accordance with the following principles:

PRINCIPLE 1

The child shall enjoy all the rights set forth in this Declaration. Every child, without any exception whatsoever, shall be entitled to these rights, without distinction or discrimination on account of race, colour, sex, language, religion, political or other opinion, national or social origin, property, birth or other status, whether of himself or of his family.

PRINCIPLE 2

The child shall enjoy special protection, and shall be given opportunities and facilities, by law and by other means, to enable him to develop physically, mentally, morally, spiritually and socially in a healthy and normal manner and in conditions of freedom and dignity. In the enactment of laws for this purpose, the best interests of the child shall be the paramount consideration.

PRINCIPLE 3

The child shall be entitled from his birth to a name and a nationality.

PRINCIPLE 4

The child shall enjoy the benefits of social security. He shall be entitled to grow and develop in health; to this end, special care and protection shall be provided both to him and to his mother, including adequate pre-natal and post-natal care. The child shall have the right to adequate nutrition, housing, recreation and medical services.

PRINCIPLE 5

The child who is physically, mentally or socially handicapped shall be given the special treatment, education and care required by his particular condition.

PRINCIPLE 6

The child, for the full and harmonious development of his personality, needs love and understanding. He shall, wherever possible, grow up in the care and under the responsibility of his parents, and, in any case, in an atmosphere of affection and of moral and material security; a child of tender years shall not, save in exceptional circumstances, be separated from his mother. Society and the public authorities shall have the duty to extend particular care to children without a family and to those without adequate means of support. Payment of State and other assistance towards the maintenance of children of large families is desirable.

PRINCIPLE 7

The child is entitled to receive education, which shall be free and compulsory, at least in the elementary stages. He shall be given an education which will promote his general culture, and enable him, on a basis of equal opportunity, to develop his abilities, his individual judgement, and his sense of moral and social responsibility, and to become a useful member of society.

The best interests of the child shall be the guiding principle of those responsible for his education and guidance; that responsibility lies in the first place with his parents.

The child shall have full opportunity for play and recreation, which should be directed to the same purposes as education; society and the public authorities shall endeavour to promote the enjoyment of this right.

PRINCIPLE 8

The child shall in all circumstances be among the first to receive protection and relief.

PRINCIPLE 9

The child shall be protected against all forms of neglect, cruelty and exploitation. He shall not be the subject of traffic, in any form.

The child shall not be admitted to employment before an appropriate minimum age; he shall in no case be caused or permitted to engage in any occupation or employment which would prejudice his health or education, or interfere with his physical, mental or moral development.

PRINCIPLE 10

The child shall be protected from practices which may foster racial, religious and any other form of discrimination. He shall be brought up in a spirit of understanding, tolerance, friendship among peoples, peace and universal brotherhood, and in full consciousness that his energy and talents should be devoted to the service of his fellow men.

*841st plenary meeting,
20 November 1959.*

1514 (XV). Declaration on the granting of independence to colonial countries and peoples

The General Assembly,

Mindful of the determination proclaimed by the peoples of the world in the Charter of the United Nations to reaffirm faith in fundamental human rights, in the dignity and worth of the human person, in the equal rights of men and women and of nations large and small and to promote social progress and better standards of life in larger freedom,

Conscious of the need for the creation of conditions of stability and well-being and peaceful and friendly relations based on respect for the principles of equal rights and self-determination of all peoples, and of universal respect for, and observance of, human rights and fundamental freedoms for all without distinction as to race, sex, language or religion,

Recognizing the passionate yearning for freedom in all dependent peoples and the decisive role of such peoples in the attainment of their independence,

Aware of the increasing conflicts resulting from the denial of or impediments in the way of the freedom of such peoples, which constitute a serious threat to world peace,

Considering the important role of the United Nations in assisting the movement for independence in Trust and Non-Self-Governing Territories,

Recognizing that the peoples of the world ardently desire the end of colonialism in all its manifestations,

Convinced that the continued existence of colonialism prevents the development of international economic co-operation, impedes the social, cultural and economic development of dependent peoples and militates against the United Nations ideal of universal peace,

Affirming that peoples may, for their own ends, freely dispose of their natural wealth and resources without prejudice to any obligations arising out of international economic co-operation, based upon the principle of mutual benefit, and international law,

Believing that the process of liberation is irresistible and irreversible and that, in order to avoid serious crises, an end must be put to colonialism and all practices of segregation and discrimination associated therewith,

Welcoming the emergence in recent years of a large number of dependent territories into freedom and independence, and recognizing the increasingly powerful trends towards freedom in such territories which have not yet attained independence,

Convinced that all peoples have an inalienable right to complete freedom, the exercise of their sovereignty and the integrity of their national territory,

Solemnly proclaims the necessity of bringing to a speedy and unconditional end colonialism in all its forms and manifestations;

And to this end

Declares that:

1. The subjection of peoples to alien subjugation, domination and exploitation constitutes a denial of fundamental human rights, is contrary to the Charter of the United Nations and is an impediment to the promotion of world peace and co-operation.

2. All peoples have the right to self-determination; by virtue of that right they freely determine their political status and freely pursue their economic, social and cultural development.

3. Inadequacy of political, economic, social or educational preparedness should never serve as a pretext for delaying independence.

4. All armed action or repressive measures of all kinds directed against dependent peoples shall cease in order to enable them to exercise peacefully and freely their right to complete independence, and the integrity of their national territory shall be respected.

5. Immediate steps shall be taken, in Trust and Non-Self-Governing Territories or all other territories which have not yet attained independence, to transfer all powers to the peoples of those territories, without any conditions or reservations, in accordance with their freely expressed will and desire, without any distinction as to race, creed or colour, in order to enable them to enjoy complete independence and freedom.

6. Any attempt aimed at the partial or total disruption of the national unity and the territorial integrity of a country is incompatible with the purposes and principles of the Charter of the United Nations.

7. All States shall observe faithfully and strictly the provisions of the Charter of the United Nations, the Universal Declaration of Human Rights and the present Declaration on the basis of equality, non-interference in the internal affairs of all States, and respect for the sovereign rights of all peoples and their territorial integrity.

947th plenary meeting,
14 December 1960.

2263 (XXII). Declaration on the Elimination of Discrimination against Women

The General Assembly,

Considering that the peoples of the United Nations have, in the Charter, reaffirmed their faith in fundamental human¹ rights, in the dignity and worth of the human person and in the equal rights of men and women,

Considering that the Universal Declaration on Human Rights asserts the principle of non-discrimination and proclaims that all human beings are born free and equal in dignity and rights and that everyone is entitled to all the rights and freedoms set forth therein, without distinction of any kind, including any distinction as to sex,

Taking into account the resolutions, declarations, conventions and recommendations of the United Nations and the specialized agencies designed to eliminate all forms of discrimination and to promote equal rights for men and women,

Concerned that, despite the Charter of the United Nations, the Universal Declaration of Human Rights, the International Covenants on Human Rights and other instruments of the United Nations and the specialized agencies and despite the progress made in the matter of equality of rights, there continues to exist considerable discrimination against women,

Considering that discrimination against women is incompatible with human dignity and with the welfare of the family and of society, prevents their participation, on equal terms with men, in the political, social, economic and cultural life of their countries and is an obstacle to the full development of the potentialities of women in the service of their countries and of humanity,

Bearing in mind the great contribution made by women to social, political, economic and cultural life and the part they play in the family and particularly in the rearing of children,

Convinced that the full and complete development of a country, the welfare of the world and the cause of peace require the maximum participation of women as well as men in all fields,

Considering that it is necessary to ensure the universal recognition in law and in fact of the principle of equality of men and women,

Solemnly proclaims this Declaration:

Article 1

Discrimination against women, denying or limiting as it does their equality of rights with men, is fundamentally unjust and constitutes an offence against human dignity.

Article 2

All appropriate measures shall be taken to abolish existing laws, customs, regulations and practices which are discriminatory against women, and to establish adequate legal protection for equal rights of men and women, in particular:

(*a*) The principle of equality of rights shall be embodied in the constitution or otherwise guaranteed by law;

(*b*) The international instruments of the United Nations and the specialized agencies relating to the elimination of discrimination against women shall be ratified or acceded to and fully implemented as soon as practicable.

Article 3

All appropriate measures shall be taken to educate public opinion and to direct national aspirations towards the eradication of prejudice and the abolition of customary and all other practices which are based on the idea of the inferiority of women.

Article 4

All appropriate measures shall be taken to ensure to women on equal terms with men, without any discrimination:

(*a*) The right to vote in all elections and be eligible for election to all publicly elected bodies;

(*b*) The right to vote in all public referenda;

(*c*) The right to hold public office and to exercise all public functions.
Such rights shall be guaranteed by legislation.

Article 5

Women shall have the same rights as men to acquire, change or retain their nationality. Marriage to an alien shall not automatically affect the nationality of the wife either by rendering her stateless or by forcing upon her the nationality of her husband.

Article 6

1. Without prejudice to the safeguarding of the unity and the harmony of the family, which remains the basic unit of any society, all appropriate measures, particularly legislative measures, shall be taken to ensure to women, married or unmarried, equal rights with men in the field of civil law, and in particular:

(*a*) The right to acquire, administer, enjoy, dispose of and inherit property, including property acquired during marriage;

(*b*) The right to equality in legal capacity and the exercise thereof;

(*c*) The same rights as men with regard to the law on the movement of persons.

2. All appropriate measures shall be taken to ensure the principle of equality of status of the husband and wife, and in particular:

(*a*) Women shall have the same right as men to free choice of a spouse and to enter into marriage only with their free and full consent;

(*b*) Women shall have equal rights with men during marriage and at its dissolution. In all cases the interest of the children shall be paramount;

(*c*) Parents shall have equal rights and duties in matters relating to their children. In all cases the interest of the children shall be paramount.

3. Child marriage and the betrothal of young girls before puberty shall be prohibited, and effective action, including legislation, shall be taken to specify a minimum age for marriage and to make the registration of marriages in an official registry compulsory.

Article 7

All provisions of penal codes which constitute discrimination against women shall be repealed.

Article 8

All appropriate measures, including legislation, shall be taken to combat all forms of traffic in women and exploitation of prostitution of women.

Article 9

All appropriate measures shall be taken to ensure to girls and women, married or unmarried, equal rights with men in education at all levels, and in particular:

(*a*) Equal conditions of access to, and study in, educational institutions of all types, including universities and vocational, technical and professional schools;

(*b*) The same choice of curricula, the same examinations, teaching staff with qualifications of the same standard, and school premises and equipment of the same quality, whether the institutions are co-educational or not;

(*c*) Equal opportunities to benefit from scholarships and other study grants;

(*d*) Equal opportunities for access to programmes of continuing education, including adult literacy programmes;

(*e*) Access to educational information to help in ensuring the health and well-being of families.

Article 10

1. All appropriate measures shall be taken to ensure to women, married or unmarried, equal rights with men in the field of economic and social life, and in particular:

(*a*) The right, without discrimination on grounds of marital status or any other grounds, to receive vocational training, to work, to free choice of profession and employment, and to professional and vocational advancement;

(*b*) The right to equal remuneration with men and to equality of treatment in respect of work of equal value;

(*c*) The right to leave with pay, retirement privileges and provision for security in respect of unemployment, sickness, old age or other incapacity to work;

(*d*) The right to receive family allowances on equal terms with men.

2. In order to prevent discrimination against women on account of marriage or maternity and to ensure their effective right to work, measures shall be taken to prevent their dismissal in the event of marriage or maternity and to provide paid maternity leave, with the guarantee of returning to former employment, and to provide the necessary social services, including child-care facilities.

3. Measures taken to protect women in certain types of work, for reasons inherent in their physical nature, shall not be regarded as discriminatory.

Article 11

1. The principle of equality of rights of men and women demands implementation in all States in accordance with the principles of the Charter of the United Nations and of the Universal Declaration of Human Rights.

2. Governments, non-governmental organizations and individuals are urged, therefore, to do all in their power to promote the implementation of the principles contained in this Declaration.

1597th plenary meeting,
7 November 1967.

201 (S-VI). Declaration on the Establishment of a New International Economic Order

The General Assembly

Adopts the following Declaration:

DECLARATION ON THE ESTABLISHMENT OF A NEW INTERNATIONAL ECONOMIC ORDER

We, the Members of the United Nations,

Having convened a special session of the General Assembly to study for the first time the problems of raw materials and development, devoted to the consideration of the most important economic problems facing the world community,

Bearing in mind the spirit, purposes and principles of the Charter of the United Nations to promote the economic advancement and social progress of all peoples,

Solemnly proclaim our united determination to work urgently for THE ESTABLISHMENT OF A NEW INTERNATIONAL ECONOMIC ORDER based on equity, sovereign equality, interdependence, common interest and co-operation among all States, irrespective of their economic and social systems which shall correct inequalities and redress existing injustices, make it possible to eliminate the widening gap between the developed and the developing countries and ensure steadily accelerating economic and social development and peace and justice for present and future generations, and, to that end, declare:

1. The greatest and most significant achievement during the last decades has been the independence from colonial and alien domination of a large number of peoples and nations which has enabled them to become members of the community of free peoples. Technological progress has also been made in all spheres of economic activities in the last three decades, thus providing a solid potential for improving the well-being of all peoples. However, the remaining vestiges of alien and colonial domination, foreign occupation, racial discrimination, *apartheid* and neo-colonialism in all its forms continue to be among the greatest obstacles to the full emancipation and progress of the developing countries and all the peoples involved. The benefits of technological progress are not shared equitably by all members of the international community. The developing countries, which constitute 70 per cent of the world's population, account for only 30 per cent of the world's income. It has proved impossible to achieve an even and balanced development of the international community under the existing international economic order. The gap between the developed and the developing countries continues to widen in a system which was established at a time when most of the developing countries did not even exist as independent States and which perpetuates inequality.

2. The present international economic order is in direct conflict with current developments in international political and economic relations. Since 1970, the world economy has experienced a series of grave crises which have had severe repercussions, especially on the developing countries because of their generally greater vulnerability to external economic impulses. The developing world has become a powerful factor that makes its influence felt in all fields of international activity. These irreversible changes in the relationship of forces in the world necessitate the active, full and equal participation of the developing countries in the formulation and application of all decisions that concern the international community.

3. All these changes have thrust into prominence the reality of interdependence of all the members of the world community. Current events have brought into sharp focus the realization that the interests of the developed countries and those of the developing countries can no longer be isolated from each other, that there is a close interrelationship between the prosperity of the developed countries and the growth and development of the developing countries, and that the prosperity of the international community as a whole depends upon the prosperity of its constituent parts. International co-operation for development is the shared goal and common duty of all countries. Thus the political, economic and social well-being of present and future generations depends more than ever on co-operation between all the

members of the international community on the basis of sovereign equality and the removal of the disequilibrium that exists between them.

4. The new international economic order should be founded on full respect for the following principles:

(a) Sovereign equality of States, self-determination of all peoples, inadmissibility of the acquisition of territories by force, territorial integrity and non-interference in the internal affairs of other States;

(b) The broadest co-operation of all the States members of the international community, based on equity, whereby the prevailing disparities in the world may be banished and prosperity secured for all;

(c) Full and effective participation on the basis of equality of all countries in the solving of world economic problems in the common interest of all countries, bearing in mind the necessity to ensure the accelerated development of all the developing countries, while devoting particular attention to the adoption of special measures in favour of the least developed, land-locked and island developing countries as well as those developing countries most seriously affected by economic crises and natural calamities, without losing sight of the interests of other developing countries;

(d) The right of every country to adopt the economic and social system that it deems the most appropriate for its own development and not to be subjected to discrimination of any kind as a result;

(e) Full permanent sovereignty of every State over its natural resources and all economic activities. In order to safeguard these resources, each State is entitled to exercise effective control over them and their exploitation with means suitable to its own situation, including the right to nationalization or transfer of ownership to its nationals, this right being an expression of the full permanent sovereignty of the State. No State may be subjected to economic, political or any other type of coercion to prevent the free and full exercise of this inalienable right;

(f) The right of all States, territories and peoples under foreign occupation, alien and colonial domination or *apartheid* to restitution and full compensation for the exploitation and depletion of, and damages to, the natural resources and all other resources of those States, territories and peoples;

(g) Regulation and supervision of the activities of transnational corporations by taking measures in the interest of the national economies of the countries where such transnational corporations operate on the basis of the full sovereignty of those countries;

(h) The right of the developing countries and the peoples of territories under colonial and racial domination and foreign occupation to achieve their liberation and to regain effective control over their natural resources and economic activities;

(i) The extending of assistance to developing countries, peoples and territories which are under colonial and alien domination, foreign occupation, racial discrimination or *apartheid* or are subjected to economic, political or any other type of coercive measures to obtain from them the subordination of the exercise of their sovereign rights and to secure from them advantages of any kind, and to neo-colonialism in all its forms, and which have estab-

lished or are endeavouring to establish effective control over their natural resources and economic activities that have been or are still under foreign control;

(j) Just and equitable relationship between the prices of raw materials, primary commodities, manufactured and semi-manufactured goods exported by developing countries and the prices of raw materials, primary commodities, manufactures, capital goods and equipment imported by them with the aim of bringing about sustained improvement in their unsatisfactory terms of trade and the expansion of the world economy;

(k) Extension of active assistance to developing countries by the whole international community, free of any political or military conditions;

(l) Ensuring that one of the main aims of the reformed international monetary system shall be the promotion of the development of the developing countries and the adequate flow of real resources to them;

(m) Improving the competitiveness of natural materials facing competition from synthetic substitutes;

(n) Preferential and non-reciprocal treatment for developing countries, wherever feasible, in all fields of international economic co-operation whenever possible;

(o) Securing favourable conditions for the transfer of financial resources to developing countries;

(p) Giving to the developing countries access to the achievements of modern science and technology, and promoting the transfer of technology and the creation of indigenous technology for the benefit of the developing countries in forms and in accordance with procedures which are suited to their economies;

(q) The need for all States to put an end to the waste of natural resources, including food products;

(r) The need for developing countries to concentrate all their resources for the cause of development;

(s) The strengthening, through individual and collective actions, of mutual economic, trade, financial and technical co-operation among the developing countries, mainly on a preferential basis;

(t) Facilitating the role which producers' associations may play within the framework of international co-operation and, in pursuance of their aims, *inter alia* assisting in the promotion of sustained growth of the world economy and accelerating the development of developing countries.

5. The unanimous adoption of the International Development Strategy for the Second United Nations Development Decade[5] was an important step in the promotion of international economic co-operation on a just and equitable basis. The accelerated implementation of obligations and commitments assumed by the international community within the framework of the Strategy, particularly those concerning imperative development needs of developing countries, would contribute significantly to the fulfilment of the aims and objectives of the present Declaration.

6. The United Nations as a universal organization should be capable of dealing with problems of international economic co-operation in a compre-

---

[5] Resolution 2626 (XXV).

hensive manner and ensuring equally the interests of all countries. It must have an even greater role in the establishment of a new international economic order. The Charter of Economic Rights and Duties of States, for the preparation of which the present Declaration will provide an additional source of inspiration, will constitute a significant contribution in this respect. All the States Members of the United Nations are therefore called upon to exert maximum efforts with a view to securing the implementation of the present Declaration, which is one of the principal guarantees for the creation of better conditions for all peoples to reach a life worthy of human dignity.

7. The present Declaration on the Establishment of a New International Economic Order shall be one of the most important bases of economic relations between all peoples and all nations.

2229th plenary meeting
1 May 1974

3202 (S-VI). Programme of Action on the Establishment of a New International Economic Order

The General Assembly

Adopts the following Programme of Action:

PROGRAMME OF ACTION ON THE ESTABLISHMENT OF A NEW INTERNATIONAL ECONOMIC ORDER

CONTENTS

INTRODUCTION

1. In view of the continuing severe economic imbalance in the relations between developed and developing countries, and in the context of the constant and continuing aggravation of the imbalance of the economies of the developing countries and the consequent need for the mitigation of their current economic difficulties, urgent and effective measures need to be taken by the international community to assist the developing countries, while devoting particular attention to the least developed, land-locked and island developing countries and those developing countries most seriously

affected by economic crises and natural calamities leading to serious retardation of development processes.

2. With a view to ensuring the application of the Declaration on the Establishment of a New International Economic Order,[6] it will be necessary to adopt and implement within a specified period a programme of action of unprecedented scope and to bring about maximum economic co-operation and understanding among all States, particularly between developed and developing countries, based on the principles of dignity and sovereign equality.

I. FUNDAMENTAL PROBLEMS OF RAW MATERIALS AND PRIMARY COMMODITIES AS RELATED TO TRADE AND DEVELOPMENT

1. *Raw materials*

All efforts should be made:

(*a*) To put an end to all forms of foreign occupation, racial discrimination, *apartheid*, colonial, neocolonial and alien domination and exploitation through the exercise of permanent sovereignty over natural resources;

(*b*) To take measures for the recovery, exploitation, development, marketing and distribution of natural resources, particularly of developing countries, to serve their national interests, to promote collective self-reliance among them and to strengthen mutually beneficial international economic co-operation with a view to bringing about the accelerated development of developing countries;

(*c*) To facilitate the functioning and to further the aims of producers' associations, including their joint marketing arrangements, orderly commodity trading, improvement in the export income of producing developing countries and in their terms of trade, and sustained growth of the world economy for the benefit of all;

(*d*) To evolve a just and equitable relationship between the prices of raw materials, primary commodities, manufactured and semi-manufactured goods exported by developing countries and the prices of raw materials, primary commodities, food, manufactured and semi-manufactured goods and capital equipment imported by them, and to work for a link between the prices of exports of developing countries and the prices of their imports from developed countries;

(*e*) To take measures to reverse the continued trend of stagnation or decline in the real price of several commodities exported by developing countries, despite a general rise in commodity prices, resulting in a decline in the export earnings of these developing countries;

(*f*) To take measures to expand the markets for natural products in relation to synthetics, taking into account the interests of the developing countries, and to utilize fully the ecological advantages of these products;

(*g*) To take measures to promote the processing of raw materials in the producer developing countries.

2. *Food*

All efforts should be made:

(*a*) To take full account of specific problems of developing countries, particularly in times of food

---

[6] Resolution 3201 (S-VI).

shortages, in tne international efforts connected with the food problem;

(*b*) To take into account that, owing to lack of means, some developing countries have vast potentialities of unexploited or underexploited land which, if reclaimed and put into practical use, would contribute considerably to the solution of the food crisis;

(*c*) By the international community to undertake concrete and speedy measures with a view to arresting desertification, salination and damage by locusts or any other similar phenomenon involving several developing countries, particularly in Africa, and gravely affecting the agricultural production capacity of these countries, and also to assist the developing countries affected by any such phenomenon to develop the affected zones with a view to contributing to the solution of their food problems;

(*d*) To refrain from damaging or deteriorating natural resources and food resources, especially those derived from the sea, by preventing pollution and taking appropriate steps to protect and reconstitute those resources;

(*e*) By developed countries, in evolving their policies relating to production, stocks, imports and exports of food, to take full account of the interests of:

(i) Developing importing countries which cannot afford high prices for their imports;

(ii) Developing exporting countries which need increased market opportunities for their exports;

(*f*) To ensure that developing countries can import the necessary quantity of food without undue strain on their foreign exchange resources and without unpredictable deterioration in their balance of payments, and, in this context, that special measures are taken in respect of the least developed, land-locked and island developing countries as well as those developing countries most seriously affected by economic crises and natural calamities;

(*g*) To ensure that concrete measures to increase food production and storage facilities in developing countries are introduced, *inter alia*, by ensuring an increase in all available essential inputs, including fertilizers, from developed countries on favourable terms;

(*h*) To promote exports of food products of developing countries through just and equitable arrangements, *inter alia*, by the progressive elimination of such protective and other measures as constitute unfair competition.

3. *General trade*

All efforts should be made:

(*a*) To take the following measures for the amelioration of terms of trade of developing countries and concrete steps to eliminate chronic trade deficits of developing countries:

(i) Fulfilment of relevant commitments already undertaken in the United Nations Conference on Trade and Development and in the International Development Strategy for the Second United Nations Development Decade;[7]

(ii) Improved access to markets in developed countries through the progressive removal of tariff and non-tariff barriers and of restrictive business practices;

---

[7] Resolution 2626 (XXV).

(iii) Expeditious formulation of commodity agreements where appropriate, in order to regulat as necessary and to stabilize the world mar kets for raw materials and primary com modities;

(iv) Preparation of an over-all integrated pro gramme, setting out guidelines and takin into account the current work in this field for a comprehensive range of commoditie of export interest to developing countries;

(v) Where products of developing countries com pete with the domestic production in devel oped countries, each developed countr should facilitate the expansion of import from developing countries and provide a fai and reasonable opportunity to the develop ing countries to share in the growth of th market;

(vi) When the importing developed countries de rive receipts from customs duties, taxes an other protective measures applied to import of these products, consideration should b given to the claim of the developing countrie that these receipts should be reimbursed i full to the exporting developing countries o devoted to providing additional resources t meet their development needs;

(vii) Developed countries should make appropri ate adjustments in their economies so as t facilitate the expansion and diversification o imports from developing countries and there by permit a rational, just and equitable inter national division of labour;

(viii) Setting up general principles for pricing policy for exports of commodities of developing countries, with a view to rectifying and achieving satisfactory terms of trade for them

(ix) Until satisfactory terms of trade are achieved for all developing countries, consideratior should be given to alternative means, including improved compensatory financing schemes for meeting the development needs of the developing countries concerned;

(x) Implementation, improvement and enlargement of the generalized system of preferences for exports of agricultural primary commodities, manufactures and semi-manufactures from developing to developed countries and consideration of its extension to commodities, including those which are processed or semiprocessed; developing countries which are or will be sharing their existing tariff advantages in some developed countries as the result of the introduction and eventual enlargement of the generalized system of preferences should, as a matter of urgency, be granted new openings in the markets of other developed countries which should offer them export opportunities that at least compensate for the sharing of those advantages;

(xi) The setting up of buffer stocks within the framework of commodity arrangements and their financing by international financial institutions, wherever necessary, by the developed countries and, when they are able to do so, by the developing countries, with the aim of favouring the producer developing and consumer developing countries and of contributing to the expansion of world trade as a whole;

(xii) In cases where natural materials can satisfy the requirements of the market, new investment for the expansion of the capacity to produce synthetic materials and substitutes should not be made;

(b) To be guided by the principles of non-reciprocity and preferential treatment of developing countries in multilateral trade negotiations between developed and developing countries, and to seek sustained and additional benefits for the international trade of developing countries, so as to achieve a substantial increase in their foreign exchange earnings, diversification of their exports and acceleration of the rate of their economic growth.

4. *Transportation and insurance*

All efforts should be made:

(a) To promote an increasing and equitable participation of developing countries in the world shipping tonnage;

(b) To arrest and reduce the ever-increasing freight rates in order to reduce the costs of imports to, and exports from, the developing countries;

(c) To minimize the cost of insurance and re-insurance for developing countries and to assist the growth of domestic insurance and reinsurance markets in developing countries and the establishment to this end, where appropriate, of institutions in these countries or at the regional level;

(d) To ensure the early implementation of the code of conduct for liner conferences;

(e) To take urgent measures to increase the import and export capability of the least developed countries and to offset the disadvantages of the adverse geographic situation of land-locked countries, particularly with regard to their transportation and transit costs, as well as developing island countries in order to increase their trading ability;

(f) By the developed countries to refrain from imposing measures or implementing policies designed to prevent the importation, at equitable prices, of commodities from the developing countries or from frustrating the implementation of legitimate measures and policies adopted by the developing countries in order to improve prices and encourage the export of such commodities.

II. INTERNATIONAL MONETARY SYSTEM AND FINANCING OF THE DEVELOPMENT OF DEVELOPING COUNTRIES

1. *Objectives*

All efforts should be made to reform the international monetary system with, *inter alia*, the following objectives:

(a) Measures to check the inflation already experienced by the developed countries, to prevent it from being transferred to developing countries and to study and devise possible arrangements within the International Monetary Fund to mitigate the effects of inflation in developed countries on the economies of developing countries;

(b) Measures to eliminate the instability of the international monetary system, in particular the uncertainty of the exchange rates, especially as it affects adversely the trade in commodities;

(c) Maintenance of the real value of the currency reserves of the developing countries by preventing their erosion from inflation and exchange rate depreciation of reserve currencies;

(d) Full and effective participation of developing countries in all phases of decision-making for the formulation of an equitable and durable monetary system and adequate participation of developing countries in all bodies entrusted with this reform and, particularly, in the proposed Council of Governors of the International Monetary Fund;

(e) Adequate and orderly creation of additional liquidity with particular regard to the needs of the developing countries through the additional allocation of special drawing rights based on the concept of world liquidity needs to be appropriately revised in the light of the new international environment; any creation of international liquidity should be made through international multilateral mechanisms;

(f) Early establishment of a link between special drawing rights and additional development financing in the interest of developing countries, consistent with the monetary characteristics of special drawing rights;

(g) Review by the International Monetary Fund of the relevant provisions in order to ensure effective participation by developing countries in the decision-making process;

(h) Arrangements to promote an increasing net transfer of real resources from the developed to the developing countries;

(i) Review of the methods of operation of the International Monetary Fund, in particular the terms for both credit repayments and "stand-by" arrangements, the system of compensatory financing, and the terms of the financing of commodity buffer stocks, so as to enable the developing countries to make more effective use of them.

2. *Measures*

All efforts should be made to take the following urgent measures to finance the development of developing countries and to meet the balance-of-payment crises in the developing world:

(a) Implementation at an accelerated pace by the developed countries of the time-bound programme, as already laid down in the International Development Strategy for the Second United Nations Development Decade, for the net amount of financial resource transfers to developing countries; increase in the official component of the net amount of financial resource transfers to developing countries so as to meet and even to exceed the target of the Strategy;

(b) International financing institutions should effectively play their role as development financing banks without discrimination on account of the political or economic system of any member country, assistance being untied;

(c) More effective participation by developing countries, whether recipients or contributors, in the decision-making process in the competent organs of the International Bank for Reconstruction and Development and the International Development Association, through the establishment of a more equitable pattern of voting rights;

(d) Exemption, wherever possible, of the developing countries from all import and capital outflow controls imposed by the developed countries;

(e) Promotion of foreign investment, both public and private, from developed to developing countries in accordance with the needs and requirements in sectors of their economies as determined by the recipient countries;

(f) Appropriate urgent measures, including international action, should be taken to mitigate adverse consequences for the current and future development of developing countries arising from the burden of external debt contracted on hard terms;

(g) Debt renegotiation on a case-by-case basis with a view to concluding agreements on debt cancellation, moratorium, rescheduling or interest subsidization;

(h) International financial institutions should take into account the special situation of each developing country in reorienting their lending policies to suit these urgent needs; there is also need for improvement in practices of international financial institutions in regard to, *inter alia*, development financing and international monetary problems;

(i) Appropriate steps should be taken to give priority to the least developed, land-locked and island developing countries and to the countries most seriously affected by economic crises and natural calamities, in the availability of loans for development purposes which should include more favourable terms and conditions.

III. INDUSTRIALIZATION

All efforts should be made by the international community to take measures to encourage the industrialization of the developing countries, and to this end:

(a) The developed countries should respond favourably, within the framework of their official aid as well as international financial institutions, to the requests of developing countries for the financing of industrial projects;

(b) The developed countries should encourage investors to finance industrial production projects, particularly export-oriented production, in developing countries, in agreement with the latter and within the context of their laws and regulations;

(c) With a view to bringing about a new international economic structure which should increase the share of the developing countries in world industrial production, the developed countries and the agencies of the United Nations system, in co-operation with the developing countries, should contribute to setting up new industrial capacities including raw materials and commodity-transforming facilities as a matter of priority in the developing countries that produce those raw materials and commodities;

(d) The international community should continue and expand, with the aid of the developed countries and the international institutions, the operational and instruction-oriented technical assistance programmes, including vocational training and management development of national personnel of the developing countries, in the light of their special development requirements.

IV. TRANSFER OF TECHNOLOGY

All efforts should be made:

(a) To formulate an international code of condu for the transfer of technology corresponding to nee and conditions prevalent in developing countries;

(b) To give access on improved terms to mode technology and to adapt that technology, as appropr ate, to specific economic, social and ecological cond tions and varying stages of development in developir countries;

(c) To expand significantly the assistance fro developed to developing countries in research and de velopment programmes and in the creation of suitab indigenous technology;

(d) To adapt commercial practices governing tran fer of technology to the requirements of the develop ing countries and to prevent abuse of the rights c sellers;

(e) To promote international co-operation in re search and development in exploration and exploita tion, conservation and the legitimate utilization c natural resources and all sources of energy.

In taking the above measures, the special needs of th least developed and land-locked countries should b borne in mind.

V. REGULATION AND CONTROL OVER THE ACTIVITIE OF TRANSNATIONAL CORPORATIONS

All efforts should be made to formulate, adopt an implement an international code of conduct for trans national corporations:

(a) To prevent interference in the internal affair of the countries where they operate and their collab oration with racist régimes and colonial administrations

(b) To regulate their activities in host countries, tc eliminate restrictive business practices and to conform to the national development plans and objectives ol developing countries, and in this context facilitate, as necessary, the review and revision of previously concluded arrangements;

(c) To bring about assistance, transfer of technology and management skills to developing countries on equitable and favourable terms;

(d) To regulate the repatriation of the profits accruing from their operations, taking into account the legitimate interests of all parties concerned;

(e) To promote reinvestment of their profits in developing countries.

VI. CHARTER OF ECONOMIC RIGHTS AND DUTIES OF STATES

The Charter of Economic Rights and Duties of States, the draft of which is being prepared by a working group of the United Nations and which the General Assembly has already expressed the intention of adopting at its twenty-ninth regular session, shall constitute an effective instrument towards the establishment of a new system of international economic relations based on equity, sovereign equality, and interdependence of the interests of developed and developing countries. It is therefore of vital importance that the forementioned Charter be adopted by the General Assembly at its twenty-ninth session.

VII. PROMOTION OF CO-OPERATION AMONG DEVELOPING COUNTRIES

1. Collective self-reliance and growing co-operation among developing countries will further strengthen their role in the new international economic order. Developing countries, with a view to expanding co-operation at the regional, subregional and interregional levels, should take further steps, *inter alia*:

(*a*) To support the establishment and/or improvement of an appropriate mechanism to defend the prices of their exportable commodities and to improve access to and stabilize markets for them. In this context the increasingly effective mobilization by the whole group of oil-exporting countries of their natural resources for the benefit of their economic development is to be welcomed. At the same time there is the paramount need for co-operation among the developing countries in evolving urgently and in a spirit of solidarity all possible means to assist developing countries to cope with the immediate problems resulting from this legitimate and perfectly justified action. The measures already taken in this regard are a positive indication of the evolving co-operation between developing countries;

(*b*) To protect their inalienable right to permanent sovereignty over their natural resources;

(*c*) To promote, establish or strengthen economic integration at the regional and subregional levels;

(*d*) To increase considerably their imports from other developing countries;

(*e*) To ensure that no developing country accords to imports from developed countries more favourable treatment than that accorded to imports from developing countries. Taking into account the existing international agreements, current limitations and possibilities and also their future evolution, preferential treatment should be given to the procurement of import requirements from other developing countries. Wherever possible, preferential treatment should be given to imports from developing countries and the exports of those countries;

(*f*) To promote close co-operation in the fields of finance, credit relations and monetary issues, including the development of credit relations on a preferential basis and on favourable terms;

(*g*) To strengthen efforts which are already being made by developing countries to utilize available financial resources for financing development in the developing countries through investment, financing of export-oriented and emergency projects and other long-term assistance;

(*h*) To promote and establish effective instruments of co-operation in the fields of industry, science and technology, transport, shipping and mass communication media.

2. Developed countries should support initiatives in the regional, subregional and interregional co-operation of developing countries through the extension of financial and technical assistance by more effective and concrete actions, particularly in the field of commercial policy.

VIII. ASSISTANCE IN THE EXERCISE OF PERMANENT SOVEREIGNTY OF STATES OVER NATURAL RESOURCES

All efforts should be made:

(*a*) To defeat attempts to prevent the free and effective exercise of the rights of every State to full and permanent sovereignty over its natural resources;

(*b*) To ensure that competent agencies of the United Nations system meet requests for assistance from developing countries in connexion with the operation of nationalized means of production.

IX. STRENGTHENING THE ROLE OF THE UNITED NATIONS SYSTEM IN THE FIELD OF INTERNATIONAL ECONOMIC CO-OPERATION

1. In furtherance of the objectives of the International Development Strategy for the Second United Nations Development Decade and in accordance with the aims and objectives of the Declaration on the Establishment of a New International Economic Order, all Member States pledge to make full use of the United Nations system in the implementation of the present Programme of Action, jointly adopted by them, in working for the establishment of a new international economic order and thereby strengthening the role of the United Nations in the field of world-wide co-operation for economic and social development.

2. The General Assembly of the United Nations shall conduct an over-all review of the implementation of the Programme of Action as a priority item. All the activities of the United Nations system to be undertaken under the Programme of Action as well as those already planned, such as the World Population Conference, 1974, the World Food Conference, the Second General Conference of the United Nations Industrial Development Organization and the mid-term review and appraisal of the International Development Strategy for the Second United Nations Development Decade should be so directed as to enable the special session of the General Assembly on development, called for under Assembly resolution 3172 (XXVIII) of 17 December 1973, to make its full contribution to the establishment of the new international economic order. All Member States are urged, jointly and individually, to direct their efforts and policies towards the success of that special session.

3. The Economic and Social Council shall define the policy framework and co-ordinate the activities of all organizations, institutions and subsidiary bodies within the United Nations system which shall be entrusted with the task of implementing the present Programme of Action. In order to enable the Economic and Social Council to carry out its tasks effectively:

(*a*) All organizations, institutions and subsidiary bodies concerned within the United Nations system shall submit to the Economic and Social Council progress reports on the implementation of the Programme of Action within their respective fields of competence as often as necessary, but not less than once a year;

(*b*) The Economic and Social Council shall examine the progress reports as a matter of urgency, to which end it may be convened, as necessary, in special session or, if need be, may function continuously. It shall draw the attention of the General Assembly to the problems and difficulties arising in connexion with the implementation of the Programme of Action.

4. All organizations, institutions, subsidiary bodies and conferences of the United Nations system are entrusted with the implementation of the Programme of Action. The activities of the United Nations Conference on Trade and Development, as set forth in General Assembly resolution 1995 (XIX) of 30 December 1964, should be strengthened for the purpose of following in collaboration with other competent organizations the development of international trade in raw materials throughout the world.

5. Urgent and effective measures should be taken to review the lending policies of international financial institutions, taking into account the special situation of each developing country, to suit urgent needs, to improve the practices of these institutions in regard to, *inter alia*, development financing and international monetary problems, and to ensure more effective participation by developing countries—whether recipients or contributors—in the decision-making process through appropriate revision of the pattern of voting rights.

6. The developed countries and others in a position to do so should contribute substantially to the various organizations, programmes and funds established within the United Nations system for the purpose of accelerating economic and social development in developing countries.

7. The present Programme of Action complements and strengthens the goals and objectives embodied in the International Development Strategy for the Second United Nations Development Decade as well as the new measures formulated by the General Assembly at its twenty-eighth session to offset the shortfalls in achieving those goals and objectives.

8. The implementation of the Programme of Action should be taken into account at the time of the mid-term review and appraisal of the International Development Strategy for the Second United Nations Development Decade. New commitments, changes, additions and adaptations in the Strategy should be made, as appropriate, taking into account the Declaration on the Establishment of a New International Economic Order and the present Programme of Action.

X. Special Programme

The General Assembly adopts the following Special Programme, including particularly emergency measures to mitigate the difficulties of the developing countries most seriously affected by economic crisis, bearing in mind the particular problem of the least developed and land-locked countries:

The General Assembly,

Taking into account the following considerations:

(a) The sharp increase in the prices of their essential imports such as food, fertilizers, energy products, capital goods, equipment and services, including transportation and transit costs, has gravely exacerbated the increasingly adverse terms of trade of a number of developing countries, added to the burden of their foreign debt and, cumulatively, created a situation which, if left untended, will make it impossible for them to finance their essential imports and development and result in a further deterioration in the levels and conditions of life in these countries. The present crisis is the outcome of all the problems that have accumulated over the years: in the field of trade, in monetary reform, the world-wide inflationary situation, inadequacy and delay in provision of financial assistance and many other similar problems in the economic and developmental fields. In facing the crisis, this complex situation must be borne in mind so as to ensure that the Special Programme adopted by the international community provides emergency relief and timely assistance to the most seriously affected countries. Simultaneously, steps are being taken to resolve these outstanding problems through fundamental restructuring of the world economic system, in order to allow these countries while solving the present difficulties to reach an acceptable level of development.

(b) The special measures adopted to assist the most seriously affected countries must encompass not only the relief which they require on an emergency basis to maintain their import requirements but also, beyond that, steps to consciously promote the capacity of these countries to produce and earn more. Unless such a comprehensive approach is adopted, there is every likelihood that the difficulties of the most seriously affected countries may be perpetuated. Nevertheless, the first and most pressing task of the international community is to enable these countries to meet the shortfall in their balance-of-payments positions. But this must be simultaneously supplemented by additional development assistance to maintain and thereafter accelerate their rate of economic development.

(c) The countries which have been most seriously affected are precisely those which are at the greatest disadvantage in the world economy: the least developed, the land-locked and other low income developing countries as well as other developing countries whose economies have been seriously dislocated as a result of the present economic crisis, natural calamities, and foreign aggression and occupation. An indication of the countries thus affected, the level of the impact on their economies and the kind of relief and assistance they require can be assessed on the basis, *inter alia*, of the following criteria:

(i) Low *per capita* income as a reflection of relative poverty, low productivity, low level of technology and development;

(ii) Sharp increase in their import cost of essentials relative to export earnings;

(iii) High ratio of debt servicing to export earnings;

(iv) Insufficiency in export earnings, comparative inelasticity of export incomes and unavailability of exportable surplus;

(v) Low level of foreign exchange reserves or their inadequacy for requirements;

(vi) Adverse impact of higher transportation and transit costs;

(vii) Relative importance of foreign trade in the development process.

(d) The assessment of the extent and nature of the impact on the economies of the most seriously affected countries must be made flexible, keeping in mind the present uncertainty in the world economy, the adjustment policies that may be adopted by the developed countries and the flow of capital and investment. Estimates of the payments situation and needs of these countries can be assessed and projected reliably only on the basis of their average performance over a number of years. Long-term projections, at this time, cannot but be uncertain.

(e) It is important that, in the special measures to mitigate the difficulties of the most seriously affected countries, all the developed countries as well as the developing countries should contribute according to their level of development and the capacity and strength of their economies. It is notable that some developing countries, despite their own difficulties and development needs, have shown a willingness to play a concrete and helpful role in ameliorating the difficulties faced by the poorer developing countries. The various initiatives and measures taken recently by certain developing countries with adequate resources on a bilateral and multilateral basis to contribute to alleviating the difficulties of other developing countries are a reflection of their commitment to the principle of effective economic co-operation among developing countries.

(f) The response of the developed countries which have by far the greater capacity to assist the affected countries in overcoming their present difficulties must be commensurate with their responsibilities. Their assistance should be in addition to the presently available levels of aid. They should fulfil and if possible exceed the targets of the International Development Strategy for the Second United Nations Development Decade on financial assistance to the developing countries, especially that relating to official development assistance. They should also give serious consideration to the cancellation of the external debts of the most seriously affected countries. This would provide the simplest and quickest relief to the affected countries. Favourable consideration should also be given to debt moratorium and rescheduling. The current situation should not lead the industrialized countries to adopt what will ultimately prove to be a self-defeating policy aggravating the present crisis.

Recalling the constructive proposals made by His Imperial Majesty the Shahanshah of Iran[8] and His Excellency Mr. Houari Boumediène, President of the People's Democratic Republic of Algeria,[9]

1. *Decides* to launch a Special Programme to provide emergency relief and development assistance to the developing countries most seriously affected, as a matter of urgency, and for the period of time necessary, at least until the end of the Second United Nations Development Decade, to help them overcome their present difficulties and to achieve self-sustaining economic development;

2. *Decides* as a first step in the Special Programme to request the Secretary-General to launch an emergency operation to provide timely relief to the most seriously affected developing countries, as defined in subparagraph (c) above, with the aim of maintaining unimpaired essential imports for the duration of the coming twelve months and to invite the indus-

trialized countries and other potential contributors to announce their contributions for emergency assistance, or intimate their intention to do so, by 15 June 1974 to be provided through bilateral or multilateral channels, taking into account the commitments and measures of assistance announced or already taken by some countries, and further requests the Secretary-General to report the progress of the emergency operation to the General Assembly at its twenty-ninth session, through the Economic and Social Council at its fifty-seventh session;

3. *Calls upon* the industrialized countries and other potential contributors to extend to the most seriously affected countries immediate relief and assistance which must be of an order of magnitude that is commensurate with the needs of these countries. Such assistance should be in addition to the existing level of aid and provided at a very early date to the maximum possible extent on a grant basis and, where not possible, on soft terms. The disbursement and relevant operational procedures and terms must reflect this exceptional situation. The assistance could be provided either through bilateral or multilateral channels, including such new institutions and facilities that have been or are to be set up. The special measures may include the following:

(a) Special arrangements on particularly favourable terms and conditions including possible subsidies for and assured supplies of essential commodities and goods;

(b) Deferred payments for all or part of imports of essential commodities and goods;

(c) Commodity assistance, including food aid, on a grant basis or deferred payments in local currencies, bearing in mind that this should not adversely affect the exports of developing countries;

(d) Long-term suppliers' credits on easy terms;

(e) Long-term financial assistance on concessionary terms;

(f) Drawings from special International Monetary Fund facilities on concessional terms;

(g) Establishment of a link between the creation of special drawing rights and development assistance, taking into account the additional financial requirements of the most seriously affected countries;

(h) Subsidies, provided bilaterally or multilaterally, for interest on funds available on commercial terms borrowed by the most seriously affected countries;

(i) Debt renegotiation on a case-by-case basis with a view to concluding agreements on debt cancellation, moratorium or rescheduling;

(j) Provision on more favourable terms of capital goods and technical assistance to accelerate the industrialization of the affected countries;

(k) Investment in industrial and development projects on favourable terms;

(l) Subsidizing the additional transit and transport costs, especially of the land-locked countries;

4. *Appeals* to the developed countries to consider favourably the cancellation, moratorium or rescheduling of the debts of the most seriously affected developing countries, on their request, as an important contribution to mitigating the grave and urgent difficulties of these countries;

---

[8] A/9548, annex.
[9] *Official Records of the General Assembly, Sixth Special Session, Plenary Meetings*, 2208th meeting, paras. 3-152.

5. *Decides* to establish a Special Fund under the auspices of the United Nations, through voluntary contributions from industrialized countries and other potential contributors, as a part of the Special Programme, to provide emergency relief and development assistance, which will commence its operations at the latest by 1 January 1975;

6. *Establishes* an *Ad Hoc* Committee on the Special Programme, composed of thirty-six Member States appointed by the President of the General Assembly, after appropriate consultations, bearing in mind the purposes of the Special Fund and its terms of reference:

(*a*) To make recommendations, *inter alia,* on the scope, machinery and modes of operation of the Special Fund, taking into account the need for:

(i) Equitable representation on its governing body;

(ii) Equitable distribution of its resources;

(iii) Full utilization of the services and facilities of existing international organizations;

(iv) The possibility of merging the United Nations Capital Development Fund with the operations of the Special Fund;

(v) A central monitoring body to oversee the various measures being taken both bilaterally and multilaterally;

and, to this end, bearing in mind the different ideas and proposals submitted at the sixth special session, including those put forward by Iran[10] and those made at the 2208th plenary meeting, and the comments thereon, and the possibility of utilizing the Special Fund to provide an alternative channel for normal development assistance after the emergency period;

(*b*) To monitor, pending commencement of the operations of the Special Fund, the various measures being taken both bilaterally and multilaterally to assist the most seriously affected countries;

(*c*) To prepare, on the basis of information provided by the countries concerned and by appropriate agencies of the United Nations system, a broad assessment of:

(i) The magnitude of the difficulties facing the most seriously affected countries;

(ii) The kind and quantities of the commodities and goods essentially required by them;

(iii) Their need for financial assistance;

(iv) Their technical assistance requirements, including especially access to technology;

7. *Requests* the Secretary-General of the United Nations, the Secretary-General of the United Nations Conference on Trade and Development, the President of the International Bank for Reconstruction and Development, the Managing Director of the International Monetary Fund, the Administrator of the United Nations Development Programme and the heads of the other competent international organizations to assist the *Ad Hoc* Committee on the Special Programme in performing the functions assigned to it under paragraph 6 above, and to help, as appropriate, in the operations of the Special Fund;

8. *Requests* the International Monetary Fund to expedite decisions on:

(*a*) The establishment of an extended special facility with a view to enabling the most seriously affected developing countries to participate in it on favourable terms;

(*b*) The creation of special drawing rights and the early establishment of the link between their allocation and development financing;

(*c*) The establishment and operation of the proposed new special facility to extend credits and subsidize interest charges on commercial funds borrowed by Member States, bearing in mind the interests of the developing countries and especially the additional financial requirements of the most seriously affected countries;

9. *Requests* the World Bank Group and the International Monetary Fund to place their managerial, financial and technical services at the disposal of Governments contributing to emergency financial relief so as to enable them to assist without delay in channelling funds to the recipients, making such institutional and procedural changes as may be required;

10. *Invites* the United Nations Development Programme to take the necessary steps, particularly at the country level, to respond on an emergency basis to requests for additional assistance which it may be called upon to render within the framework of the Special Programme;

11. *Requests* the *Ad Hoc* Committee on the Special Programme to submit its report and recommendations to the Economic and Social Council at its fifty-seventh session and invites the Council, on the basis of its consideration of that report, to submit suitable recommendations to the General Assembly at its twenty-ninth session;

12. *Decides* to consider as a matter of high priority at its twenty-ninth session, within the framework of a new international economic order, the question of special measures for the most seriously affected countries.

2229th plenary meeting
1 May 1974

*
*   *

The President of the General Assembly subsequently informed the Secretary-General[11] that, in pursuance of section X, paragraph 6, of the above resolution, he had appointed the members of the Ad Hoc Committee on the Special Programme.

As a result, the Ad Hoc Committee will be composed of the following Member States: ALGERIA, ARGENTINA, AUSTRALIA, BRAZIL, CHAD, COSTA RICA, CZECHOSLOVAKIA, FRANCE, GERMANY (FEDERAL REPUBLIC OF), GUYANA, INDIA, IRAN, JAPAN, KUWAIT, MADAGASCAR, NEPAL, NETHERLANDS, NIGERIA, NORWAY, PAKISTAN, PARAGUAY, PHILIPPINES, SOMALIA, SRI LANKA, SUDAN, SWAZILAND, SYRIAN ARAB REPUBLIC, TURKEY, UNION OF SOVIET SOCIALIST REPUBLICS, UNITED KINGDOM OF GREAT BRITAIN AND NORTHERN IRELAND, UNITED STATES OF AMERICA, UPPER VOLTA, URUGUAY, VENEZUELA, YUGOSLAVIA and ZAIRE.

---

[10] A/AC.166/L.15; see also A/9548, annex.

[11] A/9558 and Add.1.

*
*   *

3281 (XXIX) Charter of Economic Rights and Duties of States

The General Assembly,

Recalling that the United Nations Conference on Trade and Development, in its resolution 45 (III) of 18 May 1972,[34] stressed the urgency to establish generally accepted norms to govern international economic relations systematically and recognized that it is not feasible to establish a just order and a stable world as long as a charter to protect the rights of all countries, and in particular the developing States, is not formulated,

Recalling further that in the same resolution it was decided to establish a Working Group of governmental representatives to draw up a draft Charter of Economic Rights and Duties of States, which the General Assembly, in its resolution 3037 (XXVII) of 19 December 1972, decided should be composed of forty Member States,

Noting that, in its resolution 3082 (XXVIII) of 6 December 1973, it reaffirmed its conviction of the urgent need to establish or improve norms of universal application for the development of international economic relations on a just and equitable basis and urged the Working Group on the Charter of Economic Rights and Duties of States to complete, as the first step in the codification and development of the matter, the elaboration of a final draft Charter of Economic Rights and Duties of States, to be considered and approved by the General Assembly at its twenty-ninth session,

Bearing in mind the spirit and terms of its resolutions 3201 (S-VI) and 3202 (S-VI) of 1 May 1974, containing, respectively, the Declaration and the Programme of Action on the Establishment of a New International Economic Order, which underlined the vital importance of the Charter to be adopted by the General Assembly at its twenty-ninth session and stressed the fact that the Charter shall constitute an effective instrument towards the establishment of a new system of international economic relations based on equity, sovereign equality and interdependence of the interests of developed and developing countries,

Having examined the report of the Working Group on the Charter of Economic Rights and Duties of States on its fourth session,[35] transmitted to the General Assembly by the Trade and Development Board at its fourteenth session,

Expressing its appreciation to the Working Group on the Charter of Economic Rights and Duties of States which, as a result of the task performed in its four sessions held between February 1973 and June 1974, assembled the elements required for the completion and adoption of the Charter of Economic Rights and Duties of States at the twenty-ninth session of the General Assembly, as previously recommended,

Adopts and solemnly proclaims the following Charter:

---

[34] See *Proceedings of the United Nations Conference on Trade and Development, Third Session,* vol. I, *Report and Annexes* (United Nations publication, Sales No.: E.73.II.D.4), annex I.A.

[35] TD/B/AC.12/4 and Corr.1.

CHARTER OF ECONOMIC RIGHTS AND DUTIES OF STATES

PREAMBLE

The General Assembly,

Reaffirming the fundamental purposes of the United Nations, in particular the maintenance of international peace and security, the development of friendly relations among nations and the achievement of international co-operation in solving international problems in the economic and social fields,

Affirming the need for strengthening international co-operation in these fields,

Reaffirming further the need for strengthening international co-operation for development,

Declaring that it is a fundamental purpose of the present Charter to promote the establishment of the new international economic order, based on equity, sovereign equality, interdependence, common interest and co-operation among all States, irrespective of their economic and social systems,

Desirous of contributing to the creation of conditions for:

(*a*) The attainment of wider prosperity among all countries and of higher standards of living for all peoples,

(*b*) The promotion by the entire international community of the economic and social progress of all countries, especially developing countries,

(*c*) The encouragement of co-operation, on the basis of mutual advantage and equitable benefits for all peace-loving States which are willing to carry out the provisions of the present Charter, in the economic, trade, scientific and technical fields, regardless of political, economic or social systems,

(*d*) The overcoming of main obstacles in the way of the economic development of the developing countries,

(*e*) The acceleration of the economic growth of developing countries with a view to bridging the economic gap between developing and developed countries,

(*f*) The protection, preservation and enhancement of the environment,

Mindful of the need to establish and maintain a just and equitable economic and social order through:

(*a*) The achievement of more rational and equitable international economic relations and the encouragement of structural changes in the world economy,

(*b*) The creation of conditions which permit the further expansion of trade and intensification of economic co-operation among all nations,

(*c*) The strengthening of the economic independence of developing countries,

(*d*) The establishment and promotion of international economic relations, taking into account the agreed differences in development of the developing countries and their specific needs,

Determined to promote collective economic security for development, in particular of the developing countries, with strict respect for the sovereign equality of each State and through the co-operation of the entire international community,

Considering that genuine co-operation among States, based on joint consideration of and concerted action regarding international economic problems, is essential for fulfilling the international community's common desire to achieve a just and rational development of all parts of the world,

Stressing the importance of ensuring appropriate conditions for the conduct of normal economic relations among all States, irrespective of differences in social and economic systems, and for the full respect of the rights of all peoples, as well as strengthening instruments of international economic co-operation as a means for the consolidation of peace for the benefit of all,

Convinced of the need to develop a system of international economic relations on the basis of sovereign equality, mutual and equitable benefit and the close interrelationship of the interests of all States,

Reiterating that the responsibility for the development of every country rests primarily upon itself but that concomitant and effective international co-operation is an essential factor for the full achievement of its own development goals,

Firmly convinced of the urgent need to evolve a substantially improved system of international economic relations,

Solemnly adopts the present Charter of Economic Rights and Duties of States.

CHAPTER I

FUNDAMENTALS OF INTERNATIONAL ECONOMIC RELATIONS

Economic as well as political and other relations among States shall be governed, *inter alia*, by the following principles:

(*a*) Sovereignty, territorial integrity and political independence of States;

(*b*) Sovereign equality of all States;

(*c*) Non-aggression;

(*d*) Non-intervention;

(*e*) Mutual and equitable benefit;

(*f*) Peaceful coexistence;

(*g*) Equal rights and self-determination of peoples;

(*h*) Peaceful settlement of disputes;

(*i*) Remedying of injustices which have been brought about by force and which deprive a nation of the natural means necessary for its normal development;

(*j*) Fulfilment in good faith of international obligations;

(*k*) Respect for human rights and fundamental freedoms;

(*l*) No attempt to seek hegemony and spheres of influence;

(*m*) Promotion of international social justice;

(*n*) International co-operation for development;

(*o*) Free access to and from the sea by land-locked countries within the framework of the above principles.

CHAPTER II

ECONOMIC RIGHTS AND DUTIES OF STATES

Article 1

Every State has the sovereign and inalienable right to choose its economic system as well as its political, social and cultural systems in accordance with the will of its people, without outside interference, coercion or threat in any form whatsoever.

Article 2

1. Every State has and shall freely exercise full permanent sovereignty, including possession, use and disposal, over all its wealth, natural resources and economic activities.

2. Each State has the right:

(*a*) To regulate and exercise authority over foreign investment within its national jurisdiction in accordance with its laws and regulations and in conformity with its national objectives and priorities. No State shall be compelled to grant preferential treatment to foreign investment;

(*b*) To regulate and supervise the activities of transnational corporations within its national jurisdiction and take measures to ensure that such activities comply with its laws, rules and regulations and conform with its economic and social policies. Transnational corporations shall not intervene in the internal affairs of a host State. Every State should, with full regard for its sovereign rights, co-operate with other States in the exercise of the right set forth in this subparagraph;

(*c*) To nationalize, expropriate or transfer ownership of foreign property, in which case appropriate compensation should be paid by the State adopting such measures, taking into account its relevant laws and regulations and all circumstances that the State considers pertinent. In any case where the question of compensation gives rise to a controversy, it shall be settled under the domestic law of the nationalizing State and by its tribunals, unless it is freely and mutually agreed by all States concerned that other peaceful means be sought on the basis of the sovereign equality of States and in accordance with the principle of free choice of means.

Article 3

In the exploitation of natural resources shared by two or more countries, each State must co-operate on the basis of a system of information and prior consultations in order to achieve optimum use of such resources without causing damage to the legitimate interest of others.

Article 4

Every State has the right to engage in international trade and other forms of economic co-operation irrespective of any differences in political, economic and social systems. No State shall be subjected to discrimination of any kind based solely on such differences. In the pursuit of international trade and other forms of economic co-operation, every State is free to choose the forms of organization of its foreign economic relations and to enter into bilateral and multilateral arrangements consistent with its international obligations and with the needs of international economic co-operation.

Article 5

All States have the right to associate in organizations of primary commodity producers in order to develop their national economies, to achieve stable financing for their development and, in pursuance of their aims, to assist in the promotion of sustained growth of the world economy, in particular accelerating the development of developing countries. Correspondingly, all States have the duty to respect that right by refraining from applying economic and political measures that would limit it.

Article 6

It is the duty of States to contribute to the development of international trade of goods, particularly by means of arrangements and by the conclusion of long-term multilateral commodity agreements, where appropriate, and taking into account the interests of producers and consumers. All States share the responsibility to promote the regular flow and access of all commercial goods traded at stable, remunerative and equitable prices, thus contributing to the equitable development of the world economy, taking into account, in particular, the interests of developing countries.

Article 7

Every State has the primary responsibility to promote the economic, social and cultural development of its people. To this end, each State has the right and the responsibility to choose its means and goals of development, fully to mobilize and use its resources, to implement progressive economic and social reforms and to ensure the full participation of its people in the process and benefits of development. All States have the duty, individually and collectively, to co-operate in eliminating obstacles that hinder such mobilization and use.

Article 8

States should co-operate in facilitating more rational and equitable international economic relations and in encouraging structural changes in the context of a balanced world economy in harmony with the needs and interests of all countries, especially developing countries, and should take appropriate measures to this end.

Article 9

All States have the responsibility to co-operate in the economic, social, cultural, scientific and technological fields for the promotion of economic and social progress throughout the world, especially that of the developing countries.

Article 10

All States are juridically equal and, as equal members of the international community, have the right to participate fully and effectively in the international decision-making process in the solution of world economic, financial and monetary problems, *inter alia*, through the appropriate international organizations in accordance with their existing and evolving rules, and to share equitably in the benefits resulting therefrom.

Article 11

All States should co-operate to strengthen and continuously improve the efficiency of international organizations in implementing measures to stimulate the general economic progress of all countries, particularly of developing countries, and therefore should co-operate to adapt them, when appropriate, to the changing needs of international economic co-operation.

Article 12

1. States have the right, in agreement with the parties concerned, to participate in subregional, regional and interregional co-operation in the pursuit of their economic and social development. All States engaged in such co-operation have the duty to ensure that the policies of those groupings to which they belong correspond to the provisions of the present Charter and are outward-looking, consistent with their international obligations and with the needs of international economic co-operation, and have full regard for the legitimate interests of third countries, especially developing countries.

2. In the case of groupings to which the States concerned have transferred or may transfer certain competences as regards matters that come within the scope of the present Charter, its provisions shall also apply to those groupings in regard to such matters, consistent with the responsibilities of such States as members of such groupings. Those States shall co-operate in the observance by the groupings of the provisions of this Charter.

Article 13

1. Every State has the right to benefit from the advances and developments in science and technology for the acceleration of its economic and social development.

2. All States should promote international scientific and technological co-operation and the transfer of technology, with proper regard for all legitimate interests including, *inter alia*, the rights and duties of holders, suppliers and recipients of technology. In particular, all States should facilitate the access of developing countries to the achievements of modern science and technology, the transfer of technology and the creation of indigenous technology for the benefit of the developing countries in forms and in accordance with procedures which are suited to their economies and their needs.

3. Accordingly, developed countries should co-operate with the developing countries in the establishment, strengthening and development of their scientific and technological infrastructures and their scientific research and technological activities so as to help to expand and transform the economies of developing countries.

4. All States should co-operate in research with a view to evolving further internationally accepted guidelines or regulations for the transfer of technology, taking fully into account the interests of developing countries.

Article 14

Every State has the duty to co-operate in promoting a steady and increasing expansion and liberalization of world trade and an improvement in the welfare and living standards of all peoples, in particular those of developing countries. Accordingly, all States should co-operate, *inter alia*, towards the progressive dismantling of obstacles to trade and the improvement of the international framework for the conduct of world trade and, to these ends, co-ordinated efforts shall be made to solve in an equitable way the trade problems of all countries, taking into account the specific trade problems of the developing countries. In this connexion, States shall take measures aimed at securing additional benefits for the international trade of developing countries so as to achieve a substantial increase in their foreign exchange earnings, the diversification of their exports, the acceleration of the rate of growth of their trade, taking into account their development needs, an improvement in the possibilities for these countries to participate in the expansion of world trade and a balance more favourable to developing countries in the sharing of the advantages resulting from this expansion, through, in the largest possible measure, a substantial improvement in the conditions of access for the products of interest to the developing countries and, wherever appropriate, measures designed to attain stable, equitable and remunerative prices for primary products.

Article 15

All States have the duty to promote the achievement of general and complete disarmament under effective international control and to utilize the resources released by effective disarmament measures for the economic and social development of countries, allocating a substantial portion of such resources as additional means for the development needs of developing countries.

Article 16

1. It is the right and duty of all States, individually and collectively, to eliminate colonialism, *apartheid*, racial discrimination, neo-colonialism and all forms of foreign aggression, occupation and domination, and the economic and social consequences thereof, as a prerequisite for development. States which practise such coercive policies are economically responsible to the countries, territories and peoples affected for the restitution and full compensation for the exploitation and depletion of, and damages to, the natural and all other resources of those countries, territories and peoples. It is the duty of all States to extend assistance to them.

2. No State has the right to promote or encourage investments that may constitute an obstacle to the liberation of a territory occupied by force.

Article 17

International co-operation for development is the shared goal and common duty of all States. Every State should co-operate with the efforts of developing countries to accelerate their economic and social development by providing favourable external conditions and by extending active assistance to them, consistent with their development needs and objectives, with strict respect for the sovereign equality of States and free of any conditions derogating from their sovereignty.

Article 18

Developed countries should extend, improve and enlarge the system of generalized non-reciprocal and non-discriminatory tariff preferences to the developing countries consistent with the relevant agreed conclusions and relevant decisions as adopted on this subject, in the framework of the competent international organizations. Developed countries should also give serious consideration to the adoption of other differential measures, in areas where this is feasible and appropriate and in ways which will provide special and more favourable treatment, in order to meet the trade and development needs of the developing countries. In the conduct of international economic relations the developed countries should endeavour to avoid measures having a negative effect on the development of the national economies of the developing countries, as promoted by generalized tariff preferences and other generally agreed differential measures in their favour.

Article 19

With a view to accelerating the economic growth of developing countries and bridging the economic gap between developed and developing countries, developed countries should grant generalized preferential, non-reciprocal and non-discriminatory treatment to developing countries in those fields of international economic co-operation where it may be feasible.

Article 20

Developing countries should, in their efforts to increase their over-all trade, give due attention to the possibility of expanding their trade with socialist countries, by granting to these countries conditions for trade not inferior to those granted normally to the developed market economy countries.

Article 21

Developing countries should endeavour to promote the expansion of their mutual trade and to this end may, in accordance with the existing and evolving provisions and procedures of international agreements where applicable, grant trade preferences to other developing countries without being obliged to extend such preferences to developed countries, provided these arrangements do not constitute an impediment to general trade liberalization and expansion.

Article 22

1. All States should respond to the generally recognized or mutually agreed development needs and objectives of developing countries by promoting increased net flows of real resources to the developing countries from all sources, taking into account any obligations and commitments undertaken by the States concerned, in order to reinforce the efforts of developing countries to accelerate their economic and social development.

2. In this context, consistent with the aims and objectives mentioned above and taking into account any obligations and commitments undertaken in this regard, it should be their endeavour to increase the net amount of financial flows from official sources to developing countries and to improve the terms and conditions thereof.

3. The flow of development assistance resources should include economic and technical assistance.

Article 23

To enhance the effective mobilization of their own resources, the developing countries should strengthen their economic co-operation and expand their mutual trade so as to accelerate their economic and social development. All countries, especially developed countries, individually as well as through the competent international organizations of which they are members, should provide appropriate and effective support and co-operation.

Article 24

All States have the duty to conduct their mutual economic relations in a manner which takes into account the interests of other countries. In particular, all States should avoid prejudicing the interests of developing countries.

Article 25

In furtherance of world economic development, the international community, especially its developed members, shall pay special attention to the particular needs and problems of the least developed among the developing countries, of land-locked developing countries and also island developing countries, with a view to helping them to overcome their particular difficulties and thus contribute to their economic and social development.

Article 26

All States have the duty to coexist in tolerance and live together in peace, irrespective of differences in political, economic, social and cultural systems, and to facilitate trade between States having different economic and social systems. International trade should be conducted without prejudice to generalized non-discriminatory and non-reciprocal preferences in favour of developing countries, on the basis of mutual advantage, equitable benefits and the exchange of most-favoured-nation treatment.

Article 27

1. Every State has the right to enjoy fully the benefits of world invisible trade and to engage in the expansion of such trade.

2. World invisible trade, based on efficiency and mutual and equitable benefit, furthering the expansion of the world economy, is the common goal of all States. The role of developing countries in world invisible trade should be enhanced and strengthened consistent with the above objectives, particular attention being paid to the special needs of developing countries.

3. All States should co-operate with developing countries in their endeavours to increase their capacity to earn foreign exchange from invisible transactions, in accordance with the potential and needs of each developing country and consistent with the objectives mentioned above.

Article 28

All States have the duty to co-operate in achieving adjustments in the prices of exports of developing countries in relation to prices of their imports so as to promote just and equitable terms of trade for them, in a manner which is remunerative for producers and equitable for producers and consumers.

CHAPTER III

COMMON RESPONSIBILITIES TOWARDS THE INTERNATIONAL COMMUNITY

Article 29

The sea-bed and ocean floor and the subsoil thereof, beyond the limits of national jurisdiction, as well as the resources of the area, are the common heritage of mankind. On the basis of the principles adopted by the General Assembly in resolution 2749 (XXV) of 17 December 1970, all States shall ensure that the exploration of the area and exploitation of its resources are carried out exclusively for peaceful purposes and that the benefits derived therefrom are shared equitably by all States, taking into account the particular interests and needs of developing countries; an international régime applying to the area and its resources and including appropriate international machinery to give effect to its provisions shall be established by an international treaty of a universal character, generally agreed upon.

Article 30

The protection, preservation and enhancement of the environment for the present and future generations is the responsibility of all States. All States shall endeavour to establish their own environmental and developmental policies in conformity with such responsibility. The environmental policies of all States should enhance and not adversely affect the present and future development potential of developing countries. All States have the responsibility to ensure that activities within their jurisdiction or control do not cause damage to the environment of other States or of areas beyond the limits of national jurisdiction. All States should co-operate in evolving international norms and regulations in the field of the environment.

CHAPTER IV

FINAL PROVISIONS

Article 31

All States have the duty to contribute to the balanced expansion of the world economy, taking duly into account the close interrelationship between the well-being of the developed countries and the growth and development of the developing countries, and the fact that the prosperity of the international community as a whole depends upon the prosperity of its constituent parts.

Article 32

No State may use or encourage the use of economic, political or any other type of measures to coerce another State in order to obtain from it the subordination of the exercise of its sovereign rights.

Article 33

1. Nothing in the present Charter shall be construed as impairing or derogating from the provisions of the Charter of the United Nations or actions taken in pursuance thereof.

2. In their interpretation and application, the provisions of the present Charter are interrelated and each provision should be construed in the context of the other provisions.

Article 34

An item on the Charter of Economic Rights and Duties of States shall be included in the agenda of the General Assembly at its thirtieth session, and thereafter on the agenda of every fifth session. In this way a systematic and comprehensive consideration of the implementation of the Charter, covering both progress achieved and any improvements and additions which might become necessary, would be carried out and appropriate measures recommended. Such consideration should take into account the evolution of all the economic, social, legal and other factors related to the principles upon which the present Charter is based and on its purpose.

2315th plenary meeting
12 December 1974

3362 (S-VII). Development and international economic co-operation

The General Assembly,

Determined to eliminate injustice and inequality which afflict vast sections of humanity and to accelerate the development of developing countries,

Recalling the Declaration and the Programme of Action on the Establishment of a New International Economic Order,[10] as well as the Charter of Economic Rights and Duties of States,[11] which lay down the foundations of the new international economic order.

Reaffirming the fundamental purposes of the above-mentioned documents and the rights and duties of all States to seek and participate in the solutions of the problems afflicting the world, in particular the imperative need of redressing the economic imbalance between developed and developing countries,

Recalling further the International Development Strategy for the Second United Nations Development Decade,[12] which should be reviewed in the light of the Programme of Action on the Establishment of a New International Economic Order, and determined to implement the targets and policy measures contained in the International Development Strategy,

Conscious that the accelerated development of developing countries would be a decisive element for the promotion of world peace and security,

Recognizing that greater co-operation among States in the fields of trade, industry, science and technology as well as in other fields of economic activities, based on the principles of the Declaration and the Programme of Action on the Establishment of a New International Economic Order and of the Charter of Economic Rights and Duties of States, would also contribute to strengthening peace and security in the world,

Believing that the over-all objective of the new international economic order is to increase the capacity of developing countries, individually and collectively, to pursue their development,

Decides, to this end and in the context of the foregoing, to set in motion the following measures as the basis and framework for the work of the competent bodies and organizations of the United Nations system:

I. INTERNATIONAL TRADE

1. Concerted efforts should be made in favour of the developing countries towards expanding and diversifying their trade, improving and diversifying their productive capacity, improving their productivity and increasing their export earnings, with a view

[10] Resolutions 3201 (S-VI) and 3202 (S-VI).
[11] Resolution 3281 (XXIX).
[12] Resolution 2626 (XXV).

to counteracting the adverse effects of inflation—thereby sustaining real incomes—and with a view to improving the terms of trade of the developing countries and in order to eliminate the economic imbalance between developed and developing countries.

2. Concerted action should be taken to accelerate the growth and diversification of the export trade of developing countries in manufactures and semi-manufactures and in processed and semi-processed products in order to increase their share in world industrial output and world trade within the framework of an expanding world economy.

3. An important aim of the fourth session of the United Nations Conference on Trade and Development, in addition to work in progress elsewhere, should be to reach decisions on the improvement of market structures in the field of raw materials and commodities of export interest to the developing countries, including decisions with respect to an integrated programme and the applicability of elements thereof. In this connexion, taking into account the distinctive features of individual raw materials and commodities, the decisions should bear on the following:

(*a*) Appropriate international stocking and other forms of market arrangements for securing stable, remunerative and equitable prices for commodities of export interest to developing countries and promoting equilibrium between supply and demand, including, where possible, long-term multilateral commitments;

(*b*) Adequate international financing facilities for such stocking and market arrangements;

(*c*) Where possible, promotion of long-term and medium-term contracts;

(*d*) Substantial improvement of facilities for compensatory financing of export revenue fluctuations through the widening and enlarging of the existing facilities. Note has been taken of the various proposals regarding a comprehensive scheme for the stabilization of export earnings of developing countries and for a development security facility as well as specific measures for the benefit of the developing countries most in need;

(*e*) Promotion of processing of raw materials in producing developing countries and expansion and diversification of their exports, particularly to developed countries;

(*f*) Effective opportunities to improve the share of developing countries in transport, marketing and distribution of their primary commodities and to encourage measures of world significance for the evolution of the infrastructure and secondary capacity of developing countries from the production of primary commodities to processing, transport and marketing, and to the production of finished manufactured goods, their transport, distribution and exchange, including advanced financial and exchange institutions for the remunerative management of trade transactions.

4. The Secretary-General of the United Nations Conference on Trade and Development should present a report to the Conference at its fourth session on the impact of an integrated programme on the imports of developing countries which are net importers of raw materials and commodities, including those lacking in natural resources, and recommend any remedial measures that may be necessary.

5. A number of options are open to the international community to preserve the purchasing power of developing countries. These need to be further studied on a priority basis. The Secretary-General of the United Nations Conference on Trade and Development should continue to study direct and indirect indexation schemes and other options with a view to making concrete proposals before the Conference at its fourth session.

6. The Secretary-General of the United Nations Conference on Trade and Development should prepare a preliminary study on the proportion between prices of raw materials and commodities exported by developing countries and the final consumer price, particularly in developed countries, and submit it, if possible, to the Conference at its fourth session.

7. Developed countries should fully implement agreed provisions on the principle of standstill as regards imports from developing countries, and any departure should be subjected to such measures as consultations and multilateral surveillance and compensation, in accordance with internationally agreed criteria and procedures.

8. Developed countries should take effective steps within the framework of multilateral trade negotiations for the reduction or removal, where feasible and appropriate, of non-tariff barriers affecting the products of export interest to developing countries on a differential and more favourable basis for developing countries. The generalized scheme of preferences should not terminate at the end of the period of ten years originally envisaged and should be continuously improved through wider coverage, deeper cuts and other measures, bearing in mind the interests of those developing countries which enjoy special advantages and the need for finding ways and means for protecting their interests.

9. Countervailing duties should be applied only in conformity with internationally agreed obligations. Developed countries should exercise maximum restraint within the framework of international obligations in the imposition of countervailing duties on the imports of products from developing countries. The multilateral trade negotiations under way should take fully into account the particular interests of developing countries with a view to providing them differential and more favourable treatment in appropriate cases.

10. Restrictive business practices adversely affecting international trade, particularly that of developing countries, should be eliminated and efforts should be made at the national and international levels with the objective of negotiating a set of equitable principles and rules.

11. Special measures should be undertaken by developed countries and by developing countries in a position to do so to assist in the structural transformation of the economy of the least developed, land-locked and island developing countries.

12. Emergency measures as spelled out in section X of General Assembly resolution 3202 (S-VI) should be undertaken on a temporary basis to meet the specific problems of the most seriously affected countries as defined in Assembly resolutions 3201 (S-VI) and 3202 (S-VI) of 1 May 1974, without any detriment to the interests of the developing countries as a whole.

13. Further expansion of trade between the socialist countries of Eastern Europe and the developing countries should be intensified as is provided for in resolutions 15 (II) of 25 March 1968[13] and 53 (III) of 19 May 1972[14] of the United Nations Conference on Trade and Development. Additional measures and appropriate orientation to achieve this end are necessary.

II. TRANSFER OF REAL RESOURCES FOR FINANCING THE DEVELOPMENT OF DEVELOPING COUNTRIES AND INTERNATIONAL MONETARY REFORMS

1. Concessional financial resources to developing countries need to be increased substantially, their terms and conditions ameliorated and their flow made predictable, continuous and increasingly assured so as to facilitate the implementation by developing countries of long-term programmes for economic and social development. Financial assistance should, as a general rule, be untied.

2. Developed countries confirm their continued commitment in respect of the targets relating to the transfer of resources, in particular the official development assistance target of 0.7 per cent of gross national product, as agreed in the International Development Strategy for the Second United Nations Development Decade, and adopt as their common aim an effective increase in official development assistance with a view to achieving these targets by the end of the decade. Developed countries which have not yet made a commitment in respect of these targets undertake to make their best efforts to reach these targets in the remaining part of this decade.

3. The establishment of a link between the special drawing rights and development assistance should form part of the consideration by the International Monetary Fund of the creation of new special drawing rights as and when they are created according to the needs of international liquidity. Agreement should be reached at an early date on the establishment of a trust fund, to be financed partly through the International Monetary Fund gold sales and partly through voluntary contributions and to be governed by an appropriate body, for the benefit of developing countries. Consideration of other means of transfer of real resources which are predictable, assured and continuous should be expedited in appropriate bodies.

---

[13] *Proceedings of the United Nations Conference on Trade and Development, Second Session,* vol. I and Corr.1 and 3 and Add.1 and 2, *Report and Annexes* (United Nations publication, Sales No. E.68.II.D.14), p. 32.

[14] See *Proceedings of the United Nations Conference on Trade and Development, Third Session,* vol. I, *Report and Annexes* (United Nations publication, Sales No. E.73.II.D.4), annex I.A.

4. Developed countries and international organizations should enhance the real value and volume of assistance to developing countries and ensure that the developing countries obtain the largest possible share in the procurement of equipment, consultants and consultancy services. Such assistance should be on softer terms and, as a general rule, untied.

5. In order to enlarge the pool of resources available for financing development, there is an urgent need to increase substantially the capital of the World Bank Group, in particular the resources of the International Development Association, to enable it to make additional capital available to the poorest countries on highly concessional terms.

6. The resources of the development institutions of the United Nations system, in particular the United Nations Development Programme, should also be increased. The funds at the disposal of the regional development banks should be augmented. These increases should be without prejudice to bilateral development assistance flows.

7. To the extent desirable, the World Bank Group is invited to consider new ways of supplementing its financing with private management, skills, technology and capital and also new approaches to increase financing of development in developing countries, in accordance with their national plans and priorities.

8. The burden of debt on developing countries is increasing to a point where the import capacity as well as reserves have come under serious strain. At its fourth session the United Nations Conference on Trade and Development shall consider the need for, and the possibility of, convening as soon as possible a conference of major donor, creditor and debtor countries to devise ways and means to mitigate this burden, taking into account the development needs of developing countries, with special attention to the plight of the most seriously affected countries as defined in General Assembly resolutions 3201 (S-VI) and 3202 (S-VI).

9. Developing countries should be granted increased access on favourable terms to the capital markets of developed countries. To this end, the joint Development Committee of the International Monetary Fund and the International Bank for Reconstruction and Development should progress as rapidly as possible in its work. Appropriate United Nations bodies and other related intergovernmental agencies should be invited to examine ways and means of increasing the flow of public and private resources to developing countries, including proposals made at the current session to provide investment in private and public enterprises in the developing countries. Consideration should be given to the examination of an international investment trust and to the expansion of the International Finance Corporation capital without prejudice to the increase in resources of other intergovernmental financial and development institutions and bilateral assistance flows.

10. Developed and developing countries should further co-operate through investment of financial resources and supply of technology and equipment to developing countries by developed countries and by developing countries in a position to do so.

11. Developed countries, and developing countries in a position to do so, are urged to make adequate contributions to the United Nations Special Fund with a view to an early implementation of a programme of lending, preferably in 1976.

12. Developed countries should improve terms and conditions of their assistance so as to include a preponderant grant element for the least developed, land-locked and island developing countries.

13. In providing additional resources for assisting the most seriously affected countries in helping them to meet their serious balance-of-payments deficits, all developed countries, and developing countries in a position to do so, and international organizations such as the International Bank for Reconstruction and Development and the International Monetary Fund, should undertake specific measures in their favour, including those provided in General Assembly resolutions 3201 (S-VI) and 3202 (S-VI).

14. Special attention should be given by the international community to the phenomena of natural disasters which frequently afflict many parts of the world, with far-reaching devastating economic, social and structural consequences, particularly in the least developed countries. To this end, the General Assembly at its thirtieth session, in considering this problem, should examine and adopt appropriate measures.

15. The role of national reserve currencies should be reduced and the special drawing rights should become the central reserve asset of the international monetary system in order to provide for greater international control over the creation and equitable distribution of liquidity and in order to limit potential losses as a consequence of exchange rate fluctuations. Arrangements for gold should be consistent with the agreed objective of reducing the role of gold in the system and with equitable distribution of new international liquidity and should in particular take into consideration the needs of developing countries for increased liquidity.

16. The process of decision-making should be fair and responsive to change and should be most specially responsive to the emergence of a new economic influence on the part of developing countries. The participation of developing countries in the decision-making process in the competent organs of international finance and development institutions should be adequately increased and made more effective without adversely affecting the broad geographic representation of developing countries and in accordance with the existing and evolving rules.

17. The compensatory financing facility now available through the International Monetary Fund should be expanded and liberalized. In this connexion, early consideration should be given by the Fund and other appropriate United Nations bodies to various proposals made at the current session—including the examination of a new development security facility—which would mitigate export earnings shortfalls of developing countries, with special regard to the poorest countries, and thus provide greater assistance to their continued economic development. Early consideration should also be given by the International Monetary Fund to proposals to expand and liberalize its coverage of current transactions to include manufactures and services, to ensure that, whenever possible, compensation for export shortfalls takes place at the same time they

occur, to take into account, in determining the quantum of compensation, movements in import prices and to lengthen the repayment period.

18. Drawing under the buffer stock financing facility of the International Monetary Fund should be accorded treatment with respect to floating alongside the gold tranche, similar to that under the compensatory financing facility, and the Fund should expedite its study of the possibility of an amendment of the Articles of Agreement, to be presented to the Interim Committee, if possible at its next meeting, that would permit the Fund to provide assistance directly to international buffer stocks of primary products.

III. SCIENCE AND TECHNOLOGY

1. Developed and developing countries should co-operate in the establishment, strengthening and development of the scientific and technological infrastructure of developing countries. Developed countries should also take appropriate measures, such as contribution to the establishment of an industrial technological information bank and consideration of the possibility of regional and sectoral banks, in order to make available a greater flow to developing countries of information permitting the selection of technologies, in particular advanced technologies. Consideration should also be given to the establishment of an international centre for the exchange of technological information for the sharing of research findings relevant to developing countries. For the above purposes institutional arrangements within the United Nations system should be examined by the General Assembly at its thirtieth session.

2. Developed countries should significantly expand their assistance to developing countries for direct support to their science and technology programmes, as well as increase substantially the proportion of their research and development devoted to specific problems of primary interest to developing countries, and in the creation of suitable indigenous technology, in accordance with feasible targets to be agreed upon. The General Assembly invites the Secretary-General to carry out a preliminary study and to report to the Assembly at its thirty-first session on the possibility of establishing, within the framework of the United Nations system, an international energy institute to assist all developing countries in energy resources research and development.

3. All States should co-operate in evolving an international code of conduct for the transfer of technology, corresponding, in particular, to the special needs of the developing countries. Work on such a code should therefore be continued within the United Nations Conference on Trade and Development and concluded in time for decisions to be reached at the fourth session of the Conference, including a decision on the legal character of such a code with the objective of the adoption of a code of conduct prior to the end of 1977. International conventions on patents and trade marks should be reviewed and revised to meet, in particular, the special needs of the developing countries, in order that these conventions may become more satisfactory instruments for aiding developing countries in the transfer and development of technology. National patents systems should, without delay, be brought into line with the international patent system in its revised form.

4. Developed countries should facilitate the access of developing countries on favourable terms and conditions, and on an urgent basis, to *informatique*, to relevant information on advanced and other technologies suited to their specific needs as well as on new uses of existing technology, new developments and possibilities of adapting them to local needs. Inasmuch as in market economies advanced technologies with respect to industrial production are most frequently developed by private institutions, developed countries should facilitate and encourage these institutions in providing effective technologies in support of the priorities of developing countries.

5. Developed countries should give developing countries the freest and fullest possible access to technologies whose transfer is not subject to private decision.

6. Developed countries should improve the transparency of the industrial property market in order to facilitate the technological choices of developing countries. In this respect, relevant organizations of the United Nations system, with the collaboration of developed countries, should undertake projects in the fields of information, consultancy and training for the benefit of developing countries.

7. A United Nations Conference on Science and Technology for Development should be held in 1978 or 1979 with the main objectives of strengthening the technological capacity of developing countries to enable them to apply science and technology to their own development; adopting effective means for the utilization of scientific and technological potentials in the solution of development problems of regional and global significance, especially for the benefit of developing countries; and providing instruments of co-operation to developing countries in the utilization of science and technology for solving socio-economic problems that cannot be solved by individual action, in accordance with national priorities, taking into account the recommendations made by the Intergovernmental Working Group of the Committee on Science and Technology for Development.

8. The United Nations system should play a major role, with appropriate financing, in achieving the above-stated objectives and in developing scientific and technological co-operation between all States in order to ensure the application of science and technology to development. The work of the relevant United Nations bodies, in particular that of the United Nations Conference on Trade and Development, the United Nations Industrial Development Organization, the International Labour Organisation, the United Nations Educational, Scientific and Cultural Organization, the Food and Agriculture Organization of the United Nations, the World Intellectual Property Organization and the United Nations Development Programme, to facilitate the transfer and diffusion of technology should be given urgent priority. The Secretary-General of the United Nations should take steps to ensure that the technology and experience available within the United Nations system is widely disseminated and readily available to the developing countries in need of it.

9. The World Health Organization and the competent organs of the United Nations system, in particular the United Nations Children's Fund, should intensify the international effort aimed at improving health conditions in developing countries by giving

priority to prevention of disease and malnutrition and by providing primary health services to the communities, including maternal and child health and family welfare.

10. Since the outflow of qualified personnel from developing to developed countries seriously hampers the development of the former, there is an urgent need to formulate national and international policies to avoid the "brain drain" and to obviate its adverse effects.

IV. INDUSTRIALIZATION

1. The General Assembly endorses the Lima Declaration and Plan of Action on Industrial Development Co-operation[15] and requests all Governments to take individually and/or collectively the necessary measures and decisions required to implement effectively their undertakings in terms of the Lima Declaration and Plan of Action.

2. Developed countries should facilitate the development of new policies and strengthen existing policies, including labour market policies, which would encourage the redeployment of their industries which are less competitive internationally to developing countries, thus leading to structural adjustments in the former and a higher degree of utilization of natural and human resources in the latter. Such policies may take into account the economic structure and the economic, social and security objectives of the developed countries concerned and the need for such industries to move into more viable lines of production or into other sectors of the economy.

3. A system of consultations as provided for by the Lima Plan of Action should be established at the global, regional, interregional and sectoral levels within the United Nations Industrial Development Organization and within other appropriate international bodies, between developed and developing countries and among developing countries themselves, in order to facilitate the achievement of the goals set forth in the field of industrialization, including the redeployment of certain productive capacities existing in developed countries and the creation of new industrial facilities in developing countries. In this context, the United Nations Industrial Development Organization should serve as a forum for negotiation of agreements in the field of industry between developed and developing countries and among developing countries themselves, at the request of the countries concerned.

4. The Executive Director of the United Nations Industrial Development Organization should take immediate action to ensure the readiness of that organization to serve as a forum for consultations and negotiation of agreements in the field of industry. In reporting to the next session of the Industrial Development Board on actions taken in this respect, the Executive Director should also include proposals for the establishment of a system of consultations. The Industrial Development Board is invited to draw up, at an early date, the rules of procedure according to which this system would operate.

5. To promote co-operation between developed and developing countries, both should endeavour to disseminate appropriate information about their priority areas for industrial co-operation and the form

they would like such co-operation to take. The efforts undertaken by the United Nations Conference on Trade and Development on tripartite co-operation between countries having different economic and social systems could lead to constructive proposals for the industrialization of developing countries.

6. Developed countries should, whenever possible, encourage their enterprises to participate in investment projects within the framework of the development plans and programmes of the developing countries which so desire; such participation should be carried out in accordance with the laws and regulations of the developing countries concerned.

7. A joint study should be undertaken by all Governments under the auspices of the United Nations Industrial Development Organization, in consultation with the Secretary-General of the United Nations Conference on Trade and Development, making full use of the knowledge, experience and capacity existing in the United Nations system of methods and mechanisms for diversified financial and technical co-operation which are geared to the special and changing requirements of international industrial co-operation, as well as of a general set of guidelines for bilateral industrial co-operation. A progress report on this study should be submitted to the General Assembly at its thirty-first session.

8. Special attention should be given to the particular problems in the industrialization of the least developed, land-locked and island developing countries—in order to put at their disposal those technical and financial resources as well as critical goods which need to be provided to them to enable them to overcome their specific problems and to play their due role in the world economy, warranted by their human and material resources.

9. The General Assembly endorses the recommendation of the Second General Conference of the United Nations Industrial Development Organization to convert that organization into a specialized agency and decides to establish a Committee on the Drafting of a Constitution for the United Nations Industrial Development Organization, which shall be an intergovernmental committee of the whole, including States which participated in the Second General Conference, to meet in Vienna to draw up a constitution for the United Nations Industrial Development Organization as a specialized agency, to be submitted to a conference of plenipotentiaries to be convened by the Secretary-General in the last quarter of 1976.

10. In view of the importance of the forthcoming Tripartite World Conference on Employment, Income Distribution, Social Progress and the International Division of Labour, Governments should undertake adequate preparations and consultations.

V. FOOD AND AGRICULTURE

1. The solution to world food problems lies primarily in rapidly increasing food production in the developing countries. To this end, urgent and necessary changes in the pattern of world food production should be introduced and trade policy measures should be implemented, in order to obtain a notable increase in agricultural production and the export earnings of developing countries.

2. To achieve these objectives, it is essential that developed countries, and developing countries in a

---

[15] See A/10112, chap. IV.

position to do so, should substantially increase the volume of assistance to developing countries for agriculture and food production, and that developed countries should effectively facilitate access to their markets for food and agricultural products of export interest to developing countries, both in raw and processed form, and adopt adjustment measures, where necessary.

3. Developing countries should accord high priority to agricultural and fisheries development, increase investment accordingly and adopt policies which give adequate incentives to agricultural producers. It is a responsibility of each State concerned, in accordance with its sovereign judgement and development plans and policies, to promote interaction between expansion of food production and socio-economic reforms, with a view to achieving an integrated rural development. The further reduction of post-harvest food losses in developing countries should be undertaken as a matter of priority, with a view to reaching at least a 50 per cent reduction by 1985. All countries and competent international organizations should co-operate financially and technically in the effort to achieve this objective. Particular attention should be given to improvement in the systems of distribution of food-stuffs.

4. The Consultative Group on Food Production and Investment in Developing Countries should quickly identify developing countries having the potential for most rapid and efficient increase of food production, as well as the potential for rapid agricultural expansion in other developing countries, especially the countries with food deficits. Such an assessment would assist developed countries and the competent international organizations to concentrate resources for the rapid increase of agricultural production in the developing countries.

5. Developed countries should adopt policies aimed at ensuring a stable supply and sufficient quantity of fertilizers and other production inputs to developing countries at reasonable prices. They should also provide assistance to, and promote investments in, developing countries to improve the efficiency of their fertilizer and other agricultural input industries. Advantage should be taken of the mechanism provided by the International Fertilizer Supply Scheme.

6. In order to make additional resources available on concessional terms for agricultural development in developing countries, developed countries and developing countries in a position to do so should pledge, on a voluntary basis, substantial contributions to the proposed International Fund for Agricultural Development so as to make it to come into being by the end of 1975, with initial resources of SDR 1,000 million. Thereafter, additional resources should be provided to the Fund on a continuing basis.

7. In view of the significant impact of basic and applied agricultural research on increasing the quantity and quality of food production, developed countries should support the expansion of the work of the existing international agricultural research centres. Through their bilateral programmes they should strengthen their links with these international research centres and with the national agricultural research centres in developing countries. With respect to the improvement of the productivity and

competitiveness with synthetics of non-food agricultural and forestry products, research and technological assistance should be co-ordinated and financed through an appropriate mechanism.

8. In view of the importance of food aid as a transitional measure, all countries should accept both the principle of a minimum food aid target and the concept of forward planning of food aid. The target for the 1975-1976 season should be 10 million tons of food grains. They should also accept the principle that food aid should be channelled on the basis of objective assessment of requirements in the recipient countries. In this respect all countries are urged to participate in the Global Information and Early Warning System on Food and Agriculture.

9. Developed countries should increase the grant component of food aid, where food is not at present provided as grants, and should accept multilateral channelling of these resources at an expanding rate. In providing food grains and financing on soft terms to developing countries in need of such assistance, developed countries and the World Food Programme should take due account of the interests of the food-exporting developing countries and should ensure that such assistance includes, wherever possible, purchases of food from the food-exporting developing countries.

10. Developed countries, and developing countries in a position to do so, should provide food grains and financial assistance on most favourable terms to the most seriously affected countries, to enable them to meet their food and agricultural development requirements within the constraints of their balance-of-payments position. Donor countries should also provide aid on soft terms, in cash and in kind, through bilateral and multilateral channels, to enable the most seriously affected countries to obtain their estimated requirements of about 1 million tons of plant nutrients during 1975-1976.

11. Developed countries should carry out both their bilateral and multilateral food aid channelling in accordance with the procedures of the Principles of Surplus Disposal of the Food and Agriculture Organization of the United Nations so as to avoid causing undue fluctuations in market prices or the disruption of commercial markets for exports of interest to exporting developing countries.

12. All countries should subscribe to the International Undertaking on World Food Security. They should build up and maintain world food-grain reserves, to be held nationally or regionally and strategically located in developed and developing, importing and exporting countries, large enough to cover foreseeable major production shortfalls. Intensive work should be continued on a priority basis in the World Food Council and other appropriate forums in order to determine, *inter alia*, the size of the required reserve, taking into account among other things the proposal made at the current session that the components of wheat and rice in the total reserve should be 30 million tons. The World Food Council should report to the General Assembly on this matter at its thirty-first session. Developed countries should assist developing countries in their efforts to build up and maintain their agreed shares of such reserves. Pending the establishment of the world food-grain reserve, developed countries and developing countries in a position to do so

should earmark stocks and/or funds to be placed at the disposal of the World Food Programme as an emergency reserve to strengthen the capacity of the Programme to deal with crisis situations in developing countries. The aim should be a target of not less than 500,000 tons.

13. Members of the General Assembly reaffirm their full support for the resolutions of the World Food Conference and call upon the World Food Council to monitor the implementation of the provisions under section V of the present resolution and to report to the General Assembly at its thirty-first session.

VI. CO-OPERATION AMONG DEVELOPING COUNTRIES

1. Developed countries and the United Nations system are urged to provide, as and when requested, support and assistance to developing countries in strengthening and enlarging their mutual co-operation at subregional, regional and interregional levels. In this regard, suitable institutional arrangements within the United Nations development system should be made and, when appropriate, strengthened, such as those within the United Nations Conference on Trade and Development, the United Nations Industrial Development Organization and the United Nations Development Programme.

2. The Secretary-General, together with the relevant organizations of the United Nations system, is requested to continue to provide support to ongoing projects and activities, and to commission further studies through institutions in developing countries, which would take into account the material already available within the United Nations system, including in particular the regional commissions and the United Nations Conference on Trade and Development, and in accordance with existing subregional and regional arrangements. These further studies, which should be submitted to the General Assembly at its thirty-first session, should, as a first step, cover:

(*a*) Utilization of know-how, skills, natural resources, technology and funds available within developing countries for promotion of investments in industry, agriculture, transport and communications;

(*b*) Trade liberalization measures including payments and clearing arrangements, covering primary commodities, manufactured goods and services, such as banking, shipping, insurance and reinsurance;

(*c*) Transfer of technology.

3. These studies on co-operation among developing countries, together with other initiatives, would contribute to the evolution towards a system for the economic development of developing countries.

VII. RESTRUCTURING OF THE ECONOMIC AND SOCIAL SECTORS OF THE UNITED NATIONS SYSTEM

1. With a view to initiating the process of restructuring the United Nations system so as to make it more fully capable of dealing with problems of inter-

national economic co-operation and development in a comprehensive and effective manner, in pursuance of General Assembly resolutions 3172 (XXVIII) of 17 December 1973 and 3343 (XXIX) of 17 December 1974, and to make it more responsive to the requirements of the provisions of the Declaration and the Programme of Action on the Establishment of a New International Economic Order as well as those of the Charter of Economic Rights and Duties of States, an *Ad Hoc* Committee on the Restructuring of the Economic and Social Sectors of the United Nations System, which shall be a committee of the whole of the General Assembly open to the participation of all States,[16] is hereby established to prepare detailed action proposals. The *Ad Hoc* Committee should start its work immediately and inform the General Assembly at its thirtieth session on the progress made, and submit its report to the Assembly at its thirty-first session, through the Economic and Social Council at its resumed session. The *Ad Hoc* Committee should take into account in its work, *inter alia*, the relevant proposals and documentation submitted in preparation for the seventh special session of the General Assembly pursuant to Assembly resolution 3343 (XXIX) and other relevant decisions, including the report of the Group of Experts on the Structure of the United Nations System entitled *A New United Nations Structure for Global Economic Co-operation*,[17] the records of the relevant deliberations of the Economic and Social Council, the Trade and Development Board, the Governing Council of the United Nations Development Programme and the seventh special session of the General Assembly, as well as the results of the forthcoming deliberations on institutional arrangements of the United Nations Conference on Trade and Development at its fourth session and of the Governing Council of the United Nations Environment Programme at its fourth session. All United Nations organs, including the regional commissions, as well as the specialized agencies and the International Atomic Energy Agency, are invited to participate at the executive level in the work of the *Ad Hoc* Committee and to respond to requests that the Committee may make to them for information, data or views.

2. The Economic and Social Council should meanwhile continue the process of rationalization and reform which it has undertaken in accordance with Council resolution 1768 (LIV) of 18 May 1973 and General Assembly resolution 3341 (XXIX) of 17 December 1974, and should take into full consideration those recommendations of the *Ad Hoc* Committee that fall within the scope of these resolutions, at the latest at its resumed sixty-first session.

*2349th plenary meeting
16 September 1975*

---

[16] It is the understanding of the General Assembly that the "all States" formula will be applied in accordance with the established practice of the General Assembly.

[17] E/AC.62/9 (United Nations publication, Sales No. E.75. II.A.7).

*
*   *

APPENDIX
INTERGOVERNMENTAL ORGANIZATIONS
RELATED TO THE UNITED NATIONS

INTERGOVERNMENTAL ORGANIZATIONS RELATED
TO THE UNITED NATIONS

Each of the following organizations would require
a separate book for adequate treatment; it was felt,
however, that some basic information about them might be
helpful to users of this reference work.*

―――――――* See also Chapter 6 (The United Nations System
of Organizations) and Part IV (General
Bibliography).

SPECIALIZED AGENCIES

(A) FOOD AND AGRICULTURE ORGANIZATION OF THE UNITED
NATIONS (FAO)

<u>Headquarters</u>: Via delle Terme di Caracalla
00100 Rome, Italy

<u>Establishment</u>: the United Nations Conference on Food and
Agriculture met at Hot Springs, Virginia, U.S.A. in May
1943. The Conference established an interim commission
which drafted a Constitution. Upon the acceptance of the
Constitution by over twenty states, FAO was established
on 16 October 1945. FAO's relationship with the United
Nations was approved by the UN General Assembly on
14 December 1946.

<u>Main purposes</u>: to raise levels of nutrition and standards
of living; to improve the production and distribution of
food and agricultural products; to improve the conditions
of rural populations.

<u>Structure</u>: General Conference (chief policy-making body,
meets every other year); Council (functions continuously);

Secretariat (chief officer: Edouard Saouma (Lebanon),
Director-General).

Gross budget (for 1976): U.S. $87,174,000.

Members (136): Afghanistan, Albania, Algeria, Argentina,
Australia, Austria, Bahamas, Bahrain, Bangladesh, Barbados
Belgium, Benin, Bolivia, Botswana, Brazil, Bulgaria, Burma
Burundi, Canada, Cape Verde, Central African Empire, Chad,
Chile, China, Colombia, Congo, Costa Rica, Cuba, Cyprus,
Czechoslovakia, Democratic Kampuchea, Democratic Yemen,
Denmark, Dominican Republic, Ecuador, Egypt, El Salvador,
Ethiopia, Fiji, Finland, France, Gabon, Gambia, Germany
(Federal Republic of), Ghana, Greece, Grenada, Guatemala,
Guinea, Guinea-Bissau, Guyana, Haiti, Honduras, Hungary,
Iceland, India, Indonesia, Iran, Iraq, Ireland, Israel,
Italy, Ivory Coast, Jamaica, Japan, Jordan, Kenya, Kuwait,
Lao People's Democratic Republic, Lebanon, Lesotho,
Liberia, Libyan Arab Republic, Luxembourg, Madagascar,
Malawi, Malaysia, Maldives, Mali, Malta, Mauritania,
Mauritius, Mexico, Mongolia, Morocco, Nepal, Netherlands,
New Zealand, Nicaragua, Niger, Nigeria, Norway, Oman,
Pakistan, Panama, Papua New Guinea, Paraguay, Peru,
Philippines, Poland, Portugal, Qatar, Republic of Korea,
Romania, Rwanda, Saudi Arabia, Senegal, Sierra Leone,
Socialist Republic of Viet Nam, Somalia, Spain, Sri Lanka,
Sudan, Surinam, Swaziland, Sweden, Switzerland, Syrian
Arab Republic, Thailand, Togo, Trinidad and Tobago,
Tunisia, Turkey, Uganda, United Arab Emirates, United
Kingdom of Great Britain and Northern Ireland, United
Republic of Cameroon, United Republic of Tanzania,
United States of America, Upper Volta, Uruguay, Venezuela,
Yemen Arab Republic, Yugoslavia, Zaire, Zambia.

Select list of FAO publications:

Agricultural development papers
Agricultural studies
Animal health yearbook
Annual fertilizer review
Atomic energy series
Basic texts (Constitution, General Rules of the
  Organization, etc.)
Ceres; FAO review on development
FAO commodity reports
FAO documentation; current bibliography

FAO plant protection bulletin
Food and agricultural legislation
Food and nutrition
Freedom from Hunger Campaign; basic studies
Monthly bulletin of agricultural economics and statistics
National grain policies
Production yearbook
Report of the Conference of FAO
So bold an aim
The state of food and agriculture
Trade yearbook
Unasylva; an international journal of forestry and forest
    products
World animal review
World Food Programme studies
World grain trade statistics
Yearbook of fishery statistics
Yearbook of forest products statistics

(B) INTERGOVERNMENTAL MARITIME CONSULTATIVE ORGANIZATION (IMCO)

Headquarters: 101-104 Piccadilly
              London, WlV OAE, England

Establishment: the United Nations Maritime Conference,
held in Geneva in 1948, prepared IMCO's Convention. The
Convention came into force on 17 March 1958. IMCO was
formally established on 13 January 1959. Its relationship
with the United Nations had been approved by the UN
General Assembly on 18 November 1948.

Main purposes: to facilitate co-operation and information
exchange among governments on technical matters affecting
shipping; to assure high standards of maritime safety and
efficient navigation; to promote safety of life at sea;
to encourage removal of discriminatory and restrictive
practices.

Structure: Assembly (policy-making body, meets every two
years); Council (meets twice a year); Maritime Safety
Committee; Secretariat (chief officer: Chandrika Prasad
Srivastava (India), Secretary-General).

<u>Gross budget</u> (for 1976): U.S. $5,259,800.

<u>Members</u> (101): Algeria, Argentina, Australia, Austria,
Bahamas, Bahrain, Bangladesh, Barbados, Belgium, Brazil,
Bulgaria, Burma, Canada, Cape Verde, Chile, China, Colomb
Congo, Cuba, Cyprus, Czechoslovakia, Democratic Kampuchea
Denmark, Dominican Republic, Ecuador, Egypt, Equatorial
Guinea, Ethiopia, Finland, France, Gabon, German Democrat
Republic, Germany (Federal Republic of), Ghana, Greece,
Guinea, Haiti, Honduras, Hungary, Iceland, India,
Indonesia, Iran, Iraq, Ireland, Israel, Italy, Ivory
Coast, Jamaica, Japan, Jordan, Kenya, Kuwait, Lebanon,
Liberia, Libyan Arab Republic, Madagascar, Malaysia,
Maldives, Malta, Mauritania, Mexico, Morocco, Netherlands,
New Zealand, Nigeria, Norway, Oman, Pakistan, Panama,
Papua New Guinea, Peru, Philippines, Poland, Portugal,
Republic of Korea, Romania, Saudi Arabia, Senegal, Sierra
Leone, Singapore, Spain, Sri Lanka, Sudan, Surinam,
Sweden, Switzerland, Syrian Arab Republic, Thailand,
Trinidad and Tobago, Tunisia, Turkey, Union of Soviet
Socialist Republics, United Kingdom, United Republic of
Cameroon, United Republic of Tanzania, United States of
America, Uruguay, Venezuela, Yugoslavia, Zaire.

<u>Associate member</u> (1977): Hong Kong.

<u>Select list of IMCO publications</u>:

Basic documents (Convention, rules of procedure, etc.)
Glossary of maritime technical terms
IMCO bulletin
IMCO index
IMCO publications (catalogue)
International maritime dangerous goods code
Report of the Council
Resolutions and other decisions of the Assembly

(C) INTERNATIONAL CIVIL AVIATION ORGANIZATION (ICAO)

<u>Headquarters</u>: Place de l'Aviation Internationale
             1000 Sherbrooke Street West
             Montréal, Québec, Canada H3A 2R2

<u>Establishment</u>: The International Civil Aviation
Conference, held in Chicago from 1 November to 7 December
1944, drafted the ICAO Convention. Upon ratification by

6 states, the Convention came into force and ICAO came
into being on 4 April 1947. (A provisional civil aviation
organization operated from 6 June 1945 until the formal
establishment of ICAO.) ICAO's relationship with the
United Nations had been approved by the UN General
Assembly on 14 December 1946.

Main purposes: to develop the principles and techniques
of air navigation; to foster the planning and development
of international air transport; to establish international
standards and regulations for civil aviation; to promote
efficient, safe and economical civil air transport.

Structure: Assembly (chief policy-making body, meets at
least once every three years); Council (executive body);
Secretariat (chief officer: Yves Lambert, Secretary-
General).

Gross budget (for 1976): U.S. $18,101,000.

Members (140): Afghanistan, Algeria, Angola, Argentina,
Australia, Austria, Bahamas, Bahrain, Bangladesh,
Barbados, Belgium, Benin, Bolivia, Brazil, Bulgaria,
Burma, Burundi, Canada, Cape Verde, Central African
Empire, Chad, Chile, China, Colombia, Congo, Costa Rica,
Cuba, Cyprus, Czechoslovakia, Democratic Kampuchea,
Democratic Yemen, Denmark, Dominican Republic, Ecuador,
Egypt, El Salvador, Equatorial Guinea, Ethiopia, Fiji,
Finland, France, Gabon, Gambia, Germany (Federal Republic
of), Ghana, Greece, Guatemala, Guinea, Guyana, Haiti,
Honduras, Hungary, Iceland, India, Indonesia, Iran, Iraq,
Ireland, Israel, Italy, Ivory Coast, Jamaica, Japan,
Jordan, Kenya, Kuwait, Lao People's Democratic Republic,
Lebanon, Lesotho, Liberia, Libyan Arab Republic,
Luxembourg, Madagascar, Malawi, Malaysia, Maldives, Mali,
Malta, Mauritania, Mauritius, Mexico, Morocco, Mozambique,
Nauru, Nepal, Netherlands, New Zealand, Nicaragua, Niger,
Nigeria, Norway, Oman, Pakistan, Panama, Papua New Guinea,
Paraguay, Peru, Philippines, Poland, Portugal, Qatar,
Republic of Korea, Romania, Rwanda, São Tomé and Príncipe,
Saudi Arabia, Senegal, Seychelles, Sierra Leone, Singapore,
Socialist Republic of Viet Nam, Somalia, South Africa,
Spain, Sri Lanka, Sudan, Surinam, Swaziland, Sweden,
Switzerland, Syrian Arab Republic, Thailand, Togo,
Trinidad and Tobago, Tunisia, Turkey, Uganda, USSR,*
United Arab Emirates, United Kingdom, United Republic of

Cameroon, United Republic of Tanzania, United States of America, Upper Volta, Uruguay, Venezuela, Yemen Arab Republic, Yugoslavia, Zaire, Zambia.

* USSR membership in ICAO covers the Byelorussian SSR and the Ukrainian SSR.

Select list of ICAO publications:

Action of the Council
Aircraft accident digest
Annual report of the Council to the Assembly
Basic documents (Convention, rules of procedure, etc.)
Catalogue of ICAO publications
ICAO bulletin
ICAO digest of statistics
ICAO training manual
Index of ICAO publications
Manual of airport and air navigation facility tariffs
Reports and minutes of the Assembly

(D) INTERNATIONAL LABOUR ORGANISATION (ILO)

Headquarters: 4, route des Morillons
CH-1211 Geneva 22, Switzerland

Establishment: ILO's Constitution formed part of the 1919 Treaty of Versailles. The Constitution came into force on 11 April 1919. On the same day, ILO came into being as an autonomous institution associated with the League of Nations. The Declaration of Philadelphia, adopted by the International Labour Conference in 1944, was later annexed to the Constitution. The revised Constitution came into force on 20 April 1948. ILO became the first specialized agency to be associated with the United Nations: this relationship was approved by the UN General Assembly on 14 December 1946.

Main purposes: to advance social justice; to improve living and working conditions; to promote full employment; to ensure the fundamental rights of workers; to protect the life and health of workers; to promote co-operation between workers and employers.

Structure: ILO's unique feature is its tripartite structure: employers' and workers' organizations as well as governments take part in its work. The International

abour Conference is the supreme deliberative body,
eeting annually; the Governing Body is the executive
rgan; the International Labour Office is the secretariat
chief officer: Francis Blanchard (France), Director-
eneral).

ross budget (for 1976): U.S. $90,603,000.

embers (136): Afghanistan, Algeria, Angola, Argentina,
ustralia, Austria, Bahamas, Bahrain, Bangladesh, Barbados,
elgium, Benin, Bolivia, Brazil, Bulgaria, Burma, Burundi,
yelorussian SSR, Canada, Central African Empire, Chad,
hile, China, Colombia, Congo, Costa Rica, Cuba, Cyprus,
zechoslovakia, Democratic Kampuchea, Democratic Yemen,
enmark, Dominican Republic, Ecuador, Egypt, El Salvador,
thiopia, Fiji, Finland, France, Gabon, German Democratic
Republic, Germany (Federal Republic of), Ghana, Greece,
Guatemala, Guinea, Guinea-Bissau, Guyana, Haiti, Honduras,
Hungary, Iceland, India, Indonesia, Iran, Iraq, Ireland,
Israel, Italy, Ivory Coast, Jamaica, Japan, Jordan, Kenya,
Kuwait, Lao People's Democratic Republic, Lebanon, Liberia,
Libyan Arab Republic, Luxembourg, Madagascar, Malawi,
Malaysia, Mali, Malta, Mauritania, Mauritius, Mexico,
Mongolia, Morocco, Mozambique, Nepal, Netherlands, New
Zealand, Nicaragua, Niger, Nigeria, Norway, Pakistan,
Panama, Papua New Guinea, Paraguay, Peru, Philippines,
Poland, Portugal, Qatar, Romania, Rwanda, Saudi Arabia,
Senegal, Seychelles, Sierra Leone, Singapore, Socialist
Republic of Viet Nam, Somalia, Spain, Sri Lanka, Sudan,
Surinam, Swaziland, Sweden, Switzerland, Syrian Arab
Republic, Thailand, Togo, Trinidad and Tobago, Tunisia,
Turkey, Uganda, Ukrainian SSR, Union of Soviet Socialist
Republics, United Arab Emirates, United Kingdom, United
Republic of Cameroon, United Republic of Tanzania, United
States of America, Upper Volta, Uruguay, Venezuela, Yemen
Arab Republic, Yugoslavia, Zaire, Zambia.

Select list of ILO publications:

Activities of the ILO; report of the Director-General
    to the International Labour Conference
Bulletin of labour statistics
Conventions and recommendations, 1919-1966
Cooperative information
The cost of social security
Documents of the International Labour Conference

Encyclopaedia of occupational health and safety
The ILO and the world of work
ILO catalogue of publications in print
Industry and labour
International directory of co-operative organisation
International labour documentation
International labour review
Labour-management information series
Legislative series
Members of the Governing Body
Occupational safety and health series
Official bulletin
Record of proceedings of the International Labour
   Conference
Social and labour bulletin
The story of fifty years
Studies and reports
Subject guide to publications of the ILO, 1919-1964
Year book of labour statistics

(E) INTERNATIONAL MONETARY FUND (IMF)

Headquarters: 700, 19th Street N.W.
                Washington, D.C. 20431, U.S.A.

Establishment: the United Nations Monetary and Financial
Conference, held at Bretton Woods, New Hampshire, U.S.A.,
in July 1944, drafted the Articles of Agreement of the
IMF. The Articles of Agreement came into force on 27
December 1945. The Fund began operation on 1 March 1947.
IMF's relationship with the United Nations was approved
by the UN General Assembly on 15 November 1947.

Main purposes: to promote international monetary co-
operation; to facilitate the expansion and balanced growth
of international trade; to promote exchange stability; to
make its resources available to member states in order to
assist these states in correcting balance-of-payments
difficulties.

Structure: Board of Governors (in which all powers of the
Fund are vested); Board of Executive Directors (responsible
for the operations of the Fund); the Managing Director and
Chairman of the Board of Executive Directors (H. Johannes

Vitteveen, Netherlands) and his staff.

Administrative budget (for fiscal 1975/76): 60,976,755
(in Special Drawing Rights). (SDR 1=U.S. $1.15 in 1976
average).

Members (130): Afghanistan, Algeria, Argentina, Australia,
Austria, Bahamas, Bahrain, Bangladesh, Barbados, Belgium,
Benin, Bolivia, Botswana, Brazil, Burma, Burundi, Canada,
Central African Empire, Chad, Chile, China*, Colombia,
Comoros, Congo, Costa Rica, Cyprus, Democratic Kampuchea,
Democratic Yemen, Denmark, Dominican Republic, Ecuador,
Egypt, El Salvador, Equatorial Guinea, Ethiopia, Fiji,
Finland, France, Gabon, Gambia, Germany (Federal Republic
of), Ghana, Greece, Grenada, Guatemala, Guinea, Guyana,
Haiti, Honduras, Iceland, India, Indonesia, Iran, Iraq,
Ireland, Israel, Italy, Ivory Coast, Jamaica, Japan,
Jordan, Kenya, Kuwait, Lao People's Democratic Republic,
Lebanon, Lesotho, Liberia, Libyan Arab Republic,
Luxembourg, Madagascar, Malawi, Malaysia, Mali, Malta,
Mauritania, Mauritius, Mexico, Morocco, Nepal, Netherlands,
New Zealand, Nicaragua, Niger, Nigeria, Norway, Oman,
Pakistan, Panama, Papua New Guinea, Paraguay, Peru,
Philippines, Portugal, Qatar, Republic of Korea, Romania,
Rwanda, Samoa, Saudi Arabia, Senegal, Sierra Leone,
Singapore, Socialist Republic of Viet Nam, Somalia, South
Africa, Spain, Sri Lanka, Sudan, Swaziland, Sweden, Syrian
Arab Republic, Thailand, Togo, Trinidad and Tobago,
Tunisia, Turkey, Uganda, United Arab Emirates, United
Kingdom, United Republic of Cameroon, United Republic of
Tanzania, United States of America, Upper Volta, Uruguay,
Venezuela, Yemen Arab Republic, Yugoslavia, Zaire, Zambia.

* With respect to China's representation, the Fund has not
  implemented General Assembly resolution 2758 (XXVI) of
  25 October 1971.

Select list of IMF publications:

Annual report of the Board of Executive Directors
Annual report on exchange restrictions
Balance of payments yearbook
Catalog of publications
Central banking legislation
Direction of trade
Finance and development

Financial statement
International financial news survey
International financial statistics
Special Drawing Rights: character and use
Staff papers
The stand-by arrangements of the International Monetary
   Fund
Summary proceedings of the annual meeting of the Board
   of Governors

(F) INTERNATIONAL REFUGEE ORGANIZATION (IRO)

Headquarters: were in Geneva, Switzerland.

History: The Constitution of the IRO was approved by the
United Nations General Assembly on 15 December 1946.   On
1 July 1947, the IRO Preparatory Commission took over the
functions previously exercised by the United Nations
Relief and Rehabilitation Administration (UNRRA).   IRO
itself succeeded the Preparatory Commission on 20 August
1948.   On 18 November 1948, the United Nations General
Assembly approved a relationship agreement.   IRO ceased
its operation in February 1952, whereupon its functions
were transferred to the Office of the United Nations High
Commissioner for Regufees (UNHCR).

Main purposes: to assist and resettle or repatriate
refugees and displaced persons.

Structure: General Council (policy-making body);
Executive Committee; Secretariat (the last chief officer
was J. Donald Kingsley (United States), Director General).

Gross budget (for nineteen months ended 31 Januarv 1952)
was U.S. $102,827,440.

Members (18 as of 31 December 1951):

Australia, Belgium, Canada, China, Denmark, Dominican
Republic, France, Guatemala, Iceland, Italy, Luxembourg,
Netherlands, New Zealand, Norway, Switzerland, United
Kingdom, United States, Venezuela.

Official history (including basic documents):

Louise W. Holborn, The International Refugee Organization, a specialized agency of the United Nations; its history and work, 1946-1952 (London: Oxford University Press, 1956).

(G) INTERNATIONAL TELECOMMUNICATION UNION (ITU)

Headquarters: Place des Nations
1211 Geneva 10, Switzerland

Establishment: ITU's forerunner, the International Telegraph Union, was established by a convention signed in Paris on 17 May 1865. The International Radiotelegraph Convention was signed in Berlin on 3 November 1906. The International Telegraph Convention and the International Radiotelegraph Convention were merged to form the International Telecommunication Convention, which was signed in 1932 and came into force on 1 January 1934. Under the new 1932 Convention, the International Telecommunication Union became the successor to the International Telegraph Union. ITU became a specialized agency of the United Nations on 15 November 1947, upon approval of that relationship by the UN General Assembly. Subsequently, a number of new conventions governing ITU were adopted, each in turn succeeding or modifying the previous one. The most recent convention, signed at Malaga-Torremolinos in 1973, came into force on 1 January 1975.

Main purposes: to maintain and extend international cooperation for the improvement and rational use of all types of telecommunications; to promote the development and efficient operation of technical facilities, and to make these facilities generally available to the public; to harmonize national telecommunication activities.

Structure: Plenipotentiary Conference (supreme organ, normally meets every five years); Administrative Conferences (on telegraph and telephone regulations, on radio regulations, on regional needs, etc.); Administrative Council (meets annually and supervises ITU's administrative functions); General Secretariat (chief officer: Mohamed Mili (Tunisia), Secretary-General); other permanent organs (International Frequency Registration Board,

International Radio Consultative Committee, International Telegraph and Telephone Consultative Committee).

<u>Gross budget</u> (for 1976): U.S. $23,695,000 (actual budget is in Swiss francs, here converted at the 1976 rate of Sw.fr.2.68 = U.S. $1).

<u>Members</u> (152): Afghanistan, Albania, Algeria, Angola, Argentina, Australia, Austria, Bahamas, Bahrain, Bangladesh, Barbados, Belgium, Benin, Bolivia, Botswana, Brazil, Bulgaria, Burma, Burundi, Byelorussian SSR, Canada, Cape Verde, Central African Empire, Chad, Chile, China, Colombia, Comoros, Congo, Costa Rica, Cuba, Cyprus, Czechoslovakia, Democratic Kampuchea, Democratic People's Republic of Korea, Democratic Yemen, Denmark, Dominican Republic, Ecuador, Egypt, El Salvador, Equatorial Guinea, Ethiopia, Fiji, Finland, France, Gabon, Gambia, German Democratic Republic, Germany (Federal Republic of), Ghana, Greece, Guatemala, Guinea, Guinea-Bissau, Guyana, Haiti, Holy See, Honduras, Hungary, Iceland, India, Indonesia, Iran, Iraq, Ireland, Israel, Italy, Ivory Coast, Jamaica, Japan, Jordan, Kenya, Kuwait, Lao People's Democratic Republic, Lebanon, Lesotho, Liberia, Libyan Arab Republic, Liechtenstein, Luxembourg, Madagascar, Malawi, Malaysia, Maldives, Mali, Malta, Mauritania, Mauritius, Mexico, Monaco, Mongolia, Morocco, Mozambique, Nauru, Nepal, Netherlands, New Zealand, Nicaragua, Niger, Nigeria, Norway, Oman, Pakistan, Panama, Papua New Guinea, Paraguay, Peru, Philippines, Poland, Portugal, Qatar, Republic of Korea, Romania, Rwanda, São Tomé and Príncipe, Saudi Arabia, Senegal, Sierra Leone, Singapore, Socialist Republic of Viet Nam, Somalia, South Africa, Spain, Sri Lanka, Sudan, Surinam, Swaziland, Sweden, Switzerland, Syrian Arab Republic, Thailand, Togo, Tonga, Trinidad and Tobago, Tunisia, Turkey, Uganda, Ukrainian SSR, Union of Soviet Socialist Republics, United Arab Emirates, United Kingdom, United Republic of Cameroon, United Republic of Tanzania, United States of America, Upper Volta, Uruguay, Venezuela, Yemen Arab Republic, Yugoslavia, Zaire, Zambia.

<u>Select list of ITU publications</u>:

From semaphore to satellite
International Telecommunication Convention
List of stations in the space service and in the radio

astronomy service
Minutes of the Plenipotentiary Conference
1865-1965; a hundred years of international co-operation
Radio regulations
Report on telecommunication and the peaceful uses of
   outer space
Report on the activities of the International
   Telecommunication Union
Resolutions and decisions of the Administrative Council
Telecommunication journal
Telecommunication statistics
Telegraph regulations
Telephone regulations

(H) UNITED NATIONS EDUCATIONAL, SCIENTIFIC AND CULTURAL
      ORGANIZATION (UNESCO)

<u>Headquarters</u>: 7, Place de Fontenoy
                75015 Paris, France

<u>Establishment</u>: a conference held in London from 1 to 16
November 1945 drafted UNESCO's Constitution and established
a Preparatory Educational, Scientific and Cultural
Commission. This Preparatory Commission functioned until
4 November 1946 when UNESCO's Constitution came into force
and UNESCO came into being. UNESCO's relationship with
the United Nations was approved by the UN General
Assembly on 14 December 1946.

<u>Main purposes</u>: to contribute to peace and security by
promoting collaboration among nations through education,
science and culture; to further universal respect for
justice, for the rule of law, and for human rights and
fundamental freedoms for all.

<u>Structure</u>: General Conference (policy-making body, meets
every two years); Executive Board (meets at least twice
a year); Secretariat (chief officer: Amadou-Mahtar
M'Bow (Senegal), Director-General).

<u>Gross budget</u> (for 1976): U.S. $104,144,000.

<u>Members</u> (141): Afghanistan, Albania, Algeria, Angola,
Argentina, Australia, Austria, Bahrain, Bangladesh,
Barbados, Belgium, Benin, Bolivia, Brazil, Bulgaria,
Burma, Burundi, Byelorussian SSR, Canada, Central African

Empire, Chad, Chile, China, Colombia, Congo, Costa Rica, Cuba, Cyprus, Czechoslovakia, Democratic Kampuchea, Democratic People's Republic of Korea, Democratic Yemen, Denmark, Dominican Republic, Ecuador, Egypt, El Salvador, Ethiopia, Finland, France, Gabon, Gambia, German Democrati Republic, Germany (Federal Republic of), Ghana, Greece, Grenada, Guatemala, Guinea, Guinea-Bissau, Guyana, Haiti, Honduras, Hungary, Iceland, India, Indonesia, Iran, Iraq, Ireland, Israel, Italy, Ivory Coast, Jamaica, Japan, Jordan, Kenya, Kuwait, Lao People's Democratic Republic, Lebanon, Lesotho, Liberia, Libyan Arab Republic, Luxembourg, Madagascar, Malawi, Malaysia, Mali, Malta, Mauritania, Mauritius, Mexico, Monaco, Mongolia, Morocco, Mozambique, Nepal, Netherlands, New Zealand, Nicaragua, Niger, Nigeria, Norway, Oman, Pakistan, Panama, Papua New Guinea, Paraguay, Peru, Philippines, Poland, Portugal, Qatar, Republic of Korea, Romania, Rwanda, San Marino, Saudi Arabia, Senegal, Seychelles, Sierra Leone, Singapore, Socialist Republic of Viet Nam, Somalia, Spain, Sri Lanka, Sudan, Surinam, Sweden, Switzerland, Syrian Arab Republic, Thailand, Togo, Trinidad and Tobago, Tunisia, Turkey, Uganda, Ukrainian SSR, Union of Soviet Socialist Republics, United Arab Emirates, United Kingdom, United Republic of Cameroon, United Republic of Tanzania, United States of America, Upper Volta, Uruguay, Venezuela, Yemen Arab Republic, Yugoslavia, Zaire, Zambia.

<u>Associate members</u> (2): British Eastern Caribbean Group, Namibia.

<u>Select list of UNESCO publications</u>:

Annual summary of information on natural disasters
Bibliography, documentation, terminology
Bibliography of publications issued by Unesco or under
   its auspices
Book promotion news
Cultures
Educational documentation and information
Financing educational systems (country case studies)
In the minds of men; UNESCO, 1946 to 1971
Index translationum
International social science journal
Nature and resources

Official records of the General Conference
Prospects; quarterly review of education
Report of the Director-General on the activities of
the Organization
Reports and papers on mass communication
Statistical yearbook
Studies and documents on cultural policies
Study abroad
UNESCO bibliographical handbooks
UNESCO bulletin for libraries
UNESCO chronicle
UNESCO courier
UNESCO list of documents and publications

(I) UNIVERSAL POSTAL UNION (UPU)

Headquarters: Weltpoststrasse 4
Berne, Switzerland

Establishment: the first International Postal Congress
met in Berne, Switzerland and adopted the Berne Treaty,
which was signed on 9 October 1874. The Berne Treaty
came into force on 1 July 1875, formally establishing
the General Postal Union. The second International
Postal Congress, held in Paris in 1878, changed the name
of the organization to Universal Postal Union. By an
agreement between the United Nations and UPU, signed in
Paris on 4 July 1947, UPU was recognized as a specialized
agency of the UN. The UN General Assembly approved the
relationship on 15 November 1947. A revised UPU
Constitution came into force on 1 January 1966 and an
Additional Protocol on 1 January 1976.

Main purposes: to secure the organization and improvement
of postal services; to promote international postal co-
operation; to give technical assistance to member states;
to promote the reciprocal exchange of letter-post items.

Structure: Universal Postal Congress (supreme organ,
generally meets every five years); Executive Council
(meets yearly); Consultative Committee for Postal Studies;
International Bureau (UPU's secretariat; chief officer:
Mohamed Ibrahim Sobhi (Egypt), Director-General).

Gross budget (for 1976): U.S. $5,287,000 (actual budget is in Swiss francs, here converted at the 1976 rate of Sw. fr. 2.68 = U.S. $1).

Members (156): Afghanistan, Albania, Algeria, Argentina, Australia, Austria, Bahamas, Bahrain, Bangladesh, Barbados, Belgium, Benin, Bhutan, Bolivia, Botswana, Brazil, Bulgaria, Burma, Burundi, Byelorussian SSR, Canada, Cape Verde, Central African Empire, Chad, Chile, China, Colombia, Comoros, Congo, Costa Rica, Cuba, Cyprus, Czechoslovakia, Democratic Kampuchea, Democratic People's Republic of Korea, Democratic Yemen, Denmark, Dominican Republic, Ecuador, Egypt, El Salvador, Equatorial Guinea, Ethiopia, Fiji, Finland, France, French Overseas Territories, Gabon, Gambia, German Democratic Republic, Germany (Federal Republic of), Ghana, Greece, Guatemala, Guinea, Guinea-Bissau, Guyana, Haiti, Holy See, Honduras, Hungary, Iceland, India, Indonesia, Iran, Iraq, Ireland, Israel, Italy, Ivory Coast, Jamaica, Japan, Jordan, Kenya, Kuwait, Lao People's Democratic Republic, Lebanon, Lesotho, Liberia, Libyan Arab Republic, Liechtenstein, Luxembourg, Madagascar, Malawi, Malaysia, Maldives, Mali, Malta, Mauritania, Mauritius, Mexico, Monaco, Mongolia, Morocco, Nauru, Nepal, Netherlands, Netherlands Antilles, New Zealand, Nicaragua, Niger, Nigeria, Norway, Oman, Pakistan, Panama, Papua New Guinea, Paraguay, Peru, Philippines, Poland, Portugal, Portuguese Provinces in Asia and Oceania, Qatar, Republic of Korea, Romania, Rwanda, San Marino, Saudi Arabia, Senegal, Sierra Leone, Singapore, Socialist Republic of Viet Nam, Somalia, South Africa, Spain, Sri Lanka, Sudan, Surinam, Swaziland, Sweden, Switzerland, Syrian Arab Republic, Thailand, Togo, Tonga, Trinidad and Tobago, Tunisia, Turkey, Uganda, Ukrainian SSR, Union of Soviet Socialist Republics, United Arab Emirates, United Kingdom, United Kingdom Overseas Territories, United Republic of Cameroon, United Republic of Tanzania, United States of America, United States Territories (including the Trust Territory of the Pacific Islands), Upper Volta, Uruguay, Venezuela, Yemen Arab Republic, Yugoslavia, Zaire, Zambia.

Select list of UPU publications:

Genèse des Actes de l'UPU
Liste des publications du Bureau international
Report on the work of the Union

Resolutions and decisions of the Executive Council
Statistique des services postaux
Union postale

(J) WORLD BANK GROUP:

INTERNATIONAL BANK FOR RECONSTRUCTION AND
DEVELOPMENT (IBRD)
INTERNATIONAL DEVELOPMENT ASSOCIATION (IDA)
INTERNATIONAL FINANCE CORPORATION (IFC)

IBRD

Headquarters: 1818 H Street, N.W.
Washington, D.C. 20433, U.S.A.

Establishment: IBRD's Articles of Agreement were drawn up
at the Monetary and Financial Conference held at Bretton
Woods, New Hampshire, U.S.A. in July 1944. The Articles
of Agreement came into force on 27 December 1945 and IBRD
began operation on 25 June 1946. Its relationship with
the United Nations was approved by the UN General Assembly
on 15 November 1947.

Main purposes: to promote the international flow of
capital for productive purposes; to assist in the economic
development of its member states; to promote private
foreign investment. The main original aim of IBRD was
financial assistance for post-World-War-II reconstruction.

Structure: Board of Governors (in which all powers of the
Bank are vested); Executive Directors (they functions as
a Board, to which the Board of Governors has delegated
most powers); the President who is also ex officio
Chairman of the Executive Directors (Robert S. McNamara,
United States) and his staff.

Administrative budget for fiscal 1974/75: U.S. $157,539,000
(including IDA's administrative budget).

IBRD members (128): Afghanistan, Algeria, Argentina,
Australia, Austria, Bahamas, Bahrain, Bangladesh, Barbados,
Belgium, Benin, Bolivia, Botswana, Brazil, Burma, Burundi,
Canada, Central African Empire, Chad, Chile, China*,

Colombia, Comoros, Congo, Costa Rica, Cyprus, Democratic
Kampuchea, Democratic Yemen, Denmark, Dominican Republic,
Ecuador, Egypt, El Salvador, Equatorial Guinea, Ethiopia,
Fiji, Finland, France, Gabon, Gambia, Germany (Federal
Republic of), Ghana, Greece, Grenada, Guatemala, Guinea,
Guyana, Haiti, Honduras, Iceland, India, Indonesia, Iran,
Iraq, Ireland, Israel, Italy, Ivory Coast, Jamaica, Japan,
Jordan, Kenya, Kuwait, Lao People's Democratic Republic,
Lebanon, Lesotho, Liberia, Libyan Arab Republic,
Luxembourg, Madagascar, Malawi, Malaysia, Mali, Mauritania,
Mauritius, Mexico, Morocco, Nepal, Netherlands, New
Zealand, Nicaragua, Niger, Nigeria, Norway, Oman, Pakistan,
Panama, Papua New Guinea, Paraguay, Peru, Philippines,
Portugal, Qatar, Republic of Korea, Romania, Rwanda,
Samoa, Saudi Arabia, Senegal, Sierra Leone, Singapore,
Socialist Republic of Viet Nam, Somalia, South Africa,
Spain, Sri Lanka, Sudan, Swaziland, Sweden, Syrian Arab
Republic, Thailand, Togo, Trinidad and Tobago, Tunisia,
Turkey, Uganda, United Arab Emirates, United Kingdom,
United Republic of Cameroon, United Republic of Tanzania,
United States of America, Upper Volta, Uruguay, Venezuela,
Yemen Arab Republic, Yugoslavia, Zaire, Zambia.

* With respect to China's representation, IBRD has not
implemented General Assembly resolution 2758 (XXVI)
of 25 October 1971.

Select list of IBRD publications: see Select list of
publications of the World Bank Group.

IDA

Headquarters: see IBRD

Establishment: IDA's Articles of Agreement came into force
on 24 September 1960, establishing IDA as an affiliate of
IBRD. IDA began operation on 8 November 1960. Its relationship with the United Nations was approved by the UN
General Assembly on 27 March 1961.

Main purposes: to promote economic development in its
less developed member states, by providing financing on
easier terms than conventional loans.

Structure: the Board of Governors, the Executive Directors, and the President and his staff are those of the IBRD.

Administrative budget: see IBRD.

IDA members (116, comprising 'Part I' [high income] and 'Part II'[developing] states):

Afghanistan, Algeria, Argentina, Australia, Austria, Bangladesh, Belgium, Benin, Bolivia, Botswana, Brazil, Burma, Burundi, Canada, Central African Empire, Chad, Chile, China*, Colombia, Congo, Costa Rica, Cyprus, Democratic Kampuchea, Democratic Yemen, Denmark, Dominican Republic, Ecuador, Egypt, El Salvador, Equatorial Guinea, Ethiopia, Fiji, Finland, France, Gabon, Gambia, Germany (Federal Republic of), Ghana, Greece, Grenada, Guatemala, Guinea, Guyana, Haiti, Honduras, Iceland, India, Indonesia, Iran, Iraq, Ireland, Israel, Italy, Ivory Coast, Japan, Jordan, Kenya, Kuwait, Lao People's Democratic Republic, Lebanon, Lesotho, Liberia, Libyan Arab Republic, Luxembourg, Madagascar, Malawi, Malaysia, Mali, Mauritania, Mauritius, Mexico, Morocco, Nepal, Netherlands, New Zealand,Nicaragua, Niger, Nigeria, Norway, Oman, Pakistan, Panama, Papua New Guinea, Paraguay, Peru, Philippines, Republic of Korea, Rwanda, Samoa, Saudi Arabia, Senegal, Sierra Leone, Socialist Republic of Viet Nam, Somalia, South Africa, Spain, Sri Lanka, Sudan, Swaziland, Sweden, Syrian Arab Republic, Thailand, Togo, Trinidad and Tobago, Tunisia, Turkey, Uganda, United Kingdom, United Republic of Cameroon, United Republic of Tanzania, United States of America, Upper Volta, Yemen Arab Republic, Yugoslavia, Zaire, Zambia.

* With respect to China's representation, IDA has not implemented General Assembly resolution 2758 (XXVI) of 25 October 1971.

Select list of IDA publications: see Select list of publications of the World Bank Group.

IFC

Headquarters: see IBRD

Establishment: IFC's Charter came into force on 20 July

1956, establishing IFC as an affiliate of IBRD, although a separate legal entity with its own funds and staff. IFC's relationship with the United Nations was approved by the UN General Assembly on 20 February 1957.

Main purposes: to invest, without government guarantees of repayment, in productive private enterprises in member states (particularly in less developed ones), thus supplementing IBRD's activities.

Structure: Board of Governors (supreme organ, meets annually in conjunction with the IBRD/IDA); Board of Directors (supervises IFC's operations); President and Chairman of the Board of Directors who is also President of IBRD (Robert S. McNamara, United States) and his staff.

Administrative expenses (for fiscal year 1974/75): U.S. $10,446,809.

IFC members (105): Afghanistan, Argentina, Australia, Austria, Bangladesh, Belgium, Bolivia, Brazil, Burma, Canada, Chile, China*, Colombia, Costa Rica, Cyprus, Denmark, Dominican Republic, Ecuador, Egypt, El Salvador, Ethiopia, Finland, France, Gabon, Germany (Federal Republic of), Ghana, Greece, Grenada, Guatemala, Guyana, Haiti, Honduras, Iceland, India, Indonesia, Iran, Iraq, Ireland, Israel, Italy, Ivory Coast, Jamaica, Japan, Jordan, Kenya, Kuwait, Lebanon, Lesotho, Liberia, Libyan Arab Republic, Luxembourg, Madagascar, Malawi, Malaysia, Mauritania, Mauritius, Mexico, Morocco, Nepal, Netherlands, New Zealand, Nicaragua, Nigeria, Norway, Oman, Pakistan, Panama, Papua New Guinea, Paraguay, Peru, Philippines, Portugal, Republic of Korea, Rwanda, Samoa, Saudi Arabia, Senegal, Sierra Leone, Singapore, Socialist Republic of Viet Nam, Somalia, South Africa, Spain, Sri Lanka, Sudan, Swaziland, Sweden, Syrian Arab Republic, Thailand, Togo, Trinidad and Tobago, Tunisia, Turkey, Uganda, United Kingdom, United Republic of Cameroon, United Republic of Tanzania, United States of America, Upper Volta, Uruguay, Venezuela, Yemen Arab Republic, Yugoslavia, Zaire, Zambia.

* With respect to China's representation, IFC has not implemented General Assembly resolution 2758 (XXVI) of 25 October 1971.

Select list of IFC publications: see Select list of

publications of the World Bank Group.

Select list of publications of the World Bank Group:

Annual report of the IBRD and the IDA
Annual report of the IFC
Basic instruments (IBRD and IDA Articles of Agreement,
    IFC Charter, etc.)
Credit number . . . (statement of development credits;
    IDA)
Facts about the World Bank
Finance and development
Loan number . . . (statement of loans; IBRD)
Sector policy papers (IBRD)
Summary proceedings of the annual meetings of the
    Boards of Governors
Trends in developing countries
World Bank staff occasional papers

(K) WORLD HEALTH ORGANIZATION (WHO)

Headquarters: 20, avenue Appia
              1211 Geneva 27, Switzerland

Establishment: an international health conference held in
New York in June and July 1946 drafted WHO's Constitution
and established an Interim Commission. The WHO Constitution came into force on 7 April 1948 and WHO succeeded
the Interim Commission on 1 September 1948. WHO's relationship with the United Nations had been approved by
the UN General Assembly on 15 November 1947.

Main purpose: the attainment by all peoples of the
highest possible level of health, 'health' being defined
in the WHO Constitution as "a state of complete physical,
mental and social well-being."

Structure: World Health Assembly (policy-making body,
meets every year); Executive Board (meets at least twice
a year); Secretariat (chief officer: Dr. Halfdan Mahler
(Denmark), Director-General).

Gross budget (for 1976): U.S. $153,436,000.

Members (149): Afghanistan, Albania, Algeria, Angola,
Argentina, Australia, Austria, Bahamas, Bahrain,

Bangladesh, Barbados, Belgium, Benin, Bolivia, Brazil, Bulgaria, Burma, Burundi, Byelorussian SSR, Canada, Cape Verde, Central African Empire, Chad, Chile, China, Colombia, Comoros, Congo, Costa Rica, Cuba, Cyprus, Czechoslovakia, Democratic Kampuchea, Democratic People's Republic of Korea, Democratic Yemen, Denmark, Dominican Republic, Ecuador, Egypt, El Salvador, Ethiopia, Fiji, Finland, France, Gabon, Gambia, German Democratic Republic, Germany (Federal Republic of), Ghana, Greece, Grenada, Guatemala, Guinea, Guinea-Bissau, Guyana, Haiti, Honduras, Hungary, Iceland, India, Indonesia, Iran, Iraq, Ireland, Israel, Italy, Ivory Coast, Jamaica, Japan, Jordan, Kenya, Kuwait, Lao People's Democratic Republic, Lebanon, Lesotho, Liberia, Libyan Arab Republic, Luxembourg, Madagascar, Malawi, Malaysia, Maldives, Mali, Malta, Mauritania, Mauritius, Mexico, Monaco, Mongolia, Morocco, Mozambique, Nepal, Netherlands, New Zealand, Nicaragua, Niger, Nigeria, Norway, Oman, Pakistan, Panama, Papua New Guinea, Paraguay, Peru, Philippines, Poland, Portugal, Qatar, Republic of Korea, Romania, Rwanda, Samoa, São Tomé and Príncipe, Saudi Arabia, Senegal, Sierra Leone, Singapore, Socialist Republic of Viet Nam, Somalia, South Africa, Spain, Sri Lanka, Sudan, Surinam, Swaziland, Sweden, Switzerland, Syrian Arab Republic, Thailand, Togo, Tonga, Trinidad and Tobago, Tunisia, Turkey, Uganda, Ukrainian SSR, Union of Soviet Socialist Republics, United Arab Emirates, United Kingdom, United Republic of Cameroon, United Republic of Tanzania, United States of America, Upper Volta, Uruguay, Venezuela, Yemen Arab Republic, Yugoslavia, Zaire, Zambia.

Associate members (2): Namibia, Southern Rhodesia (the associate membership of the latter is regarded as being suspended).

Select list of WHO publications:

Basic documents (Constitution, regulations, etc.)
International digest of health legislation
Manual of the international statistical classification
   of diseases, injuries, and causes of death
The medical research programme of the World Health
   Organization
Public health papers

Publications of the WHO; a bibliography
Report on the world health situation
Resolutions and decisions of the World Health Assembly
WHO chronicle
Weekly epidemiological record
The work of WHO; annual report of the Director-General
World health
World health statistics annual
World health statistics report

(L) WORLD INTELLECTUAL PROPERTY ORGANIZATION (WIPO)

<u>Headquarters</u>: 32, chemin des Colombettes
                Geneva, Switzerland

<u>Establishment</u>: the Paris Union (International Union for
the Protection of Industrial Property) and the Berne
Union (International Union for the Protection of Literary
and Artistic Works) exist under separate conventions
originally concluded, respectively, in 1883 and 1886.
The two international bureaux serving as secretariats of
these two unions were united in 1893, and subsequently
named United International Bureaux for the Protection of
Intellectual Property (BIRPI). WIPO is the successor of
BIRPI, although BIRPI continues its legal existence for
those members of the Paris and Berne unions which are not
member states of WIPO. WIPO's Convention was drawn up at
a conference held in Stockholm on 14 July 1967. The
Convention came into force on 26 April 1970. WIPO's relationship with the United Nations was approved by the UN
General Assembly on 17 December 1974.

<u>Main purposes</u>: to promote the protection of intellectual
property through international co-operation; to ensure
administrative co-operation among the Paris and Berne
unions in the observance of agreements on trademarks,
patents, protection of artistic and literary works, etc.

<u>Structure</u>: General Assembly (policy-making body, meets
every three years); Conference (meets simultaneously with
the General Assembly); Co-ordination Committee (joint
executive committees of the Paris and Berne unions);
International Bureau (WIPO's secretariat; chief officer:
Arpad Bogsch (United States), Director-General).

Gross budget (for 1976): U.S. $7,591,000 (actual budget is in Swiss francs, here converted at the 1976 rate of Sw. fr. 2.68 = U.S. $1).

Members (73): Algeria, Australia, Austria, Bahamas, Belgium, Benin, Brazil, Bulgaria, Byelorussian SSR, Canada, Chad, Chile, Congo, Cuba, Czechoslovakia, Democratic People's Republic of Korea, Denmark, Egypt, Fiji, Finland, France, Gabon, German Democratic Republic, Germany (Federal Republic of), Ghana, Greece, Holy See, Hungary, India, Iraq, Ireland, Israel, Ivory Coast, Japan, Jordan, Kenya, Libyan Arab Republic, Liechtenstein, Luxembourg, Malawi, Mauritania, Mauritius, Mexico, Monaco, Morocco, Netherlands, Niger, Norway, Poland, Portugal, Qatar, Romania, Senegal, Socialist Republic of Viet Nam*, South Africa, Spain, Sudan, Surinam, Sweden, Switzerland, Togo, Tunisia, Turkey, Uganda, Ukrainian SSR, Union of Soviet Socialist Republics, United Arab Emirates, United Kingdom, United Republic of Cameroon, United States of America, Upper Volta, Yugoslavia, Zaire.

* The situation of the Socialist Republic of Viet Nam in respect of the WIPO Convention is under examination.

Select list of WIPO publications:

Basic texts (Berne Convention, Paris Convention, etc.)
Copyright; monthly review
Industrial property; monthly review
Industrial property statistics
Publications of the WIPO (catalogue)

(M) WORLD METEOROLOGICAL ORGANIZATION (WMO)

Headquarters: 41, avenue Giuseppe-Motta
1211 Geneva 20, Switzerland

Establishment: the International Meteorological Organization, a non-governmental organization, was established at a conference held in 1878 at Utrecht, Netherlands. A Conference of Directors of national meteorological services, held in Washington, D.C. in 1947, adopted the World Meteorological Convention, thus establishing WMO, an intergovernmental organization. The Convention came into force on 23 March 1950. WMO began operation on 4 April 1951, replacing the International

Meteorological Organization. WMO's relationship with the United Nations was approved by the UN General Assembly on 20 December 1951.

<u>Main purposes</u>: to facilitate international co-operation in establishing networks of meteorological observation stations; to promote the rapid exchange of weather information; to promote standardization of meteorological observations; to further the application of meteorology to aviation, shipping, agriculture and other activities; to encourage research and training in meteorology.

<u>Structure</u>: World Meteorological Congress (policy-making body, meets at least every four years); Executive Committee (meets at least once a year); six regional meteorological associations (Africa, Asia, South America, North and Central America, Europe, Southwest Pacific); eight technical commissions (for instruments and methods of observation, for marine meteorology, for hydrology, etc.); Secretariat (chief officer: David A. Davies (United Kingdom), Secretary-General).

<u>Gross budget</u> (for 1976): U.S. $11,304,000.

<u>Members</u> (145): Afghanistan, Albania, Algeria, Angola, Argentina, Australia, Austria, Bahamas, Bangladesh, Barbados, Belgium, Benin, Bolivia, Botswana, Brazil, British Caribbean Territories, Bulgaria, Burma, Burundi, Byelorussian SSR, Canada, Cape Verde, Central African Empire, Chad, Chile, China, Colombia, Comoros, Congo, Costa Rica, Cuba, Cyprus, Czechoslovakia, Democratic Kampuchea, Democratic People's Republic of Korea, Democratic Yemen, Denmark, Dominican Republic, Ecuador, Egypt, El Salvador, Ethiopia, Finland, France, French Polynesia, French Territory of the Afars and Issas, Gabon, German Democratic Republic, Germany (Federal Republic of), Ghana, Greece, Guatemala, Guinea, Guyana, Haiti, Honduras, Hong Kong, Hungary, Iceland, India, Indonesia, Iran, Iraq, Ireland, Israel, Italy, Ivory Coast, Jamaica, Japan, Jordan, Kenya, Kuwait, Lao People's Democratic Republic, Lebanon, Liberia, Libyan Arab Republic, Luxembourg, Madagascar, Malawi, Malaysia, Mali, Mauritania, Mauritius, Mexico, Mongolia, Morocco, Mozambique, Nepal, Netherlands, Netherlands Antilles, New Caledonia, New Zealand, Nicaragua, Niger, Nigeria, Norway, Oman, Pakistan, Panama, Papua New Guinea, Paraguay, Peru, Philippines, Poland,

Portugal, Qatar, Republic of Korea, Romania, Rwanda, St. Pierre and Miquelon, São Tomé and Príncipe, Saudi Arabia, Senegal, Sierra Leone, Singapore, Socialist Republic of Viet Nam, Somalia, South Africa, Southern Rhodesia, Spain, Sri Lanka, Sudan, Surinam, Sweden, Switzerland, Syrian Arab Republic, Thailand, Togo, Trinidad and Tobago, Tunisia, Turkey, Uganda, Ukrainian SSR, Union of Soviet Socialist Republics, United Kingdom, United Republic of Cameroon, United Republic of Tanzania, United States of America, Upper Volta, Uruguay, Venezuela, Yemen Arab Republic, Yugoslavia, Zaire, Zambia.

Select list of WMO publications:

Abridged final report of the World Meteorological
  Congress, with resolutions
Annual report of the WMO
Basic documents (Convention, regulations, etc.)
Catalogue of publications
International meteorological tables
Operational hydrology reports
Reports on marine science affairs
Special environmental reports
Technical note[s]
WMO bulletin
WMO/IHD project reports
  (IHD - International Hydrological Decade)
World Weather Watch planning reports

OTHER INSTITUTIONS IN THE UNITED NATIONS SYSTEM OF
ORGANIZATIONS

(N)   GENERAL AGREEMENT ON TARIFFS AND TRADE (GATT)

Headquarters: Villa Le Bocage
              Palais des Nations
              1211 Geneva 10, Switzerland

Establishment: the United Nations Economic and Social Council decided, in 1946, to convene an international conference on trade and employment and to establish a Preparatory Committee to draft a convention for an international trade organization. As a result of meetings of the Preparatory Committee and various tariff negotiations, the following two instruments were framed: the General Agreement on Tariffs and Trade (GATT), signed on

30 October 1947, and a draft charter for an International Trade Organization (ITO). Both GATT and the draft ITO Charter were considered at the United Nations Conference on Trade and Employment, held at Havana from November 1947 to March 1948. GATT, which came into force on 1 January 1948, was at first considered a stopgap measure until the establishment of ITO; but because of the unwillingness of some states to ratify the ITO Charter (known as the Havana Charter), ITO never came into existence. Thus, GATT has stood as the only international instrument which lays down rules of conduct for international trade: it now governs about eighty per cent of international trade. Comprehensive reviews of GATT were undertaken by its contracting parties in 1955 and in 1967. GATT co-operates with the United Nations at the Secretariat and intergovernmental levels.

<u>Main purposes</u>: GATT is an multilateral trade agreement embodying the following general principles: trade should be conducted on a non-discriminatory basis (the 'most-favoured-nation' clause); domestic industries should be protected through customs tariffs, rather than through quantitative and other restrictions; tariffs should be reduced through multilateral negotiations, in order to avoid damage to the trading interests of GATT's contracting parties; and GATT should provide the framework for negotiations for the reduction of tariff and non-tariff barriers to trade. (Two major steps in this process: the 'Kennedy Round' of trade negotiations of 1964-1967 and the 'Tokyo Round' which began in 1973.)

<u>Structure</u>: Contracting Parties (supreme organ); Council of Representatives (meets every four to six weeks); Committee on Trade and Development; International Trade Centre (administered jointly with the United Nations Conference on Trade and Development); Secretariat (originally established to serve the Interim Commission for the International Trade Organization; chief officer: Olivier Long (Switzerland), Director-General).

<u>Gross budget</u>: (for 1976): U.S. $12,480,072 (actual budget is in Swiss francs, here converted at the 1976 rate of Sw. fr. 2.74=U.S. $1).

<u>Contracting parties</u> (83): Argentina, Australia, Austria, Bangladesh, Barbados, Belgium, Benin, Brazil, Burma,

Burundi, Canada, Central African Empire, Chad, Chile, Congo, Cuba, Cyprus, Czechoslovakia, Denmark, Dominican Republic, Egypt, Finland, France, Gabon, Gambia, Germany (Federal Republic of), Ghana, Greece, Guyana, Haiti, Hungary, Iceland, India, Indonesia, Ireland, Israel, Italy, Ivory Coast, Jamaica, Japan, Kenya, Kuwait, Luxembourg, Madagascar, Malawi, Malaysia, Malta, Mauritania, Mauritius, Netherlands, New Zealand, Nicaragua, Niger, Nigeria, Norway, Pakistan, Peru, Poland, Portugal, Republic of Korea, Romania, Rwanda, Senegal, Sierra Leone, Singapore, South Africa, Southern Rhodesia, Spain, Sri Lanka, Sweden, Switzerland, Togo, Trinidad and Tobago, Turkey, Uganda, United Kingdom, United Republic of Cameroon, United Republic of Tanzania, United States of America, Upper Volta, Uruguay, Yugoslavia, Zaire.

In addition to the 83 contracting parties, the following 3 states have provisionally acceded to GATT: Colombia, Philippines, Tunisia.

The following 24 states, to whose territories GATT had been applied before they attained independence and which now, as independent states, maintain a de facto application of GATT pending final decisions as to their future commercial policy: Algeria, Angola, Bahamas, Bahrain, Botswana, Cape Verde, Democratic Kampuchea, Democratic Yemen, Equatorial Guinea, Fiji, Grenada, Guinea-Bissau, Lesotho, Maldives, Mali, Mozambique, Papua New Guinea, Qatar, São Tomé and Príncipe, Surinam, Swaziland, Tonga, United Arab Emirates, Zambia.

<u>Select list of GATT publications</u>:

Basic instruments and selected documents
GATT activities
GATT; status of legal instruments
International trade
International trade forum
World directory of industry and trade associations

(0)   INTERNATIONAL ATOMIC ENERGY AGENCY (IAEA)

<u>Headquarters</u>: Kärntnerring 11
                    A-1010 Vienna I, Austria

<u>Establishment</u>: the President of the United States

(Eisenhower) made a proposal to the United Nations General Assembly on 8 December 1953 for the establishment of an international organization devoted to the peaceful uses of atomic energy. IAEA's Statute was approved on 26 October 1956 at a conference held at UN Headquarters. The Statute came into force and the Agency thus came into being on 29 July 1957. IAEA's relationship with the United Nations was approved by the UN General Assembly on 14 November 1957.

Main purposes: to increase the contribution of atomic energy to peace, health and prosperity throughout the world; to ensure that the assistance and services IAEA provides are not used to further any military purposes.

Structure: General Conference (supreme organ, meets annually); Board of Governors (executive body, meets every three months); Director-General: (Sigvard Eklund, Sweden) and his staff.

Gross budget (for 1976): U.S. $37,002,000.

Members (109): Afghanistan, Albania, Algeria, Argentina, Australia, Austria, Bangladesh, Belgium, Bolivia, Brazil, Bulgaria, Burma, Byelorussian SSR, Canada, Chile, Colombia, Costa Rica, Cuba, Cyprus, Czechoslovakia, Democratic Kampuchea, Democratic People's Republic of Korea, Denmark, Dominican Republic, Ecuador, Egypt, El Salvador, Ethiopia, Finland, France, Gabon, German Democratic Republic, Germany (Federal Republic of), Ghana, Greece, Guatemala, Haiti, Holy See, Hungary, Iceland, India, Indonesia, Iran, Iraq, Ireland, Israel, Italy, Ivory Coast, Jamaica, Japan, Jordan, Kenya, Kuwait, Lebanon, Liberia, Libyan Arab Republic, Liechtenstein, Luxembourg, Madagascar, Malaysia, Mali, Mauritius, Mexico, Monaco, Mongolia, Morocco, Netherlands, New Zealand, Niger, Nigeria, Norway, Pakistan, Panama, Paraguay, Peru, Philippines, Poland, Portugal, Qatar, Republic of Korea, Romania, Saudi Arabia, Senegal, Sierra Leone, Singapore, Socialist Republic of Viet Nam, South Africa, Spain, Sri Lanka, Sudan, Sweden, Switzerland, Syrian Arab Republic, Thailand, Tunisia, Turkey, Uganda, Ukrainian SSR, Union of Soviet Socialist Republics, United Arab Emirates, United Kingdom, United Republic of Cameroon, United Republic of Tanzania, United States of America, Uruguay, Venezuela, Yugoslavia, Zaire, Zambia.

<u>Select list of IAEA publications</u>:

The Agency's accounts
The Agency's budget
The Agency's programme
Annual report
Directory of nuclear reactors
IAEA bulletin
IAEA publications catalogue
INIS atomindex
Journal of the General Conference
Legal series
Progress in peaceful applications of nuclear energy
Resolutions and other decisions of the General Conference
Statute
Waste management research abstracts

GENERAL INDEX

This Index should be used in conjunction with the Table of Contents and with the Index to the Bibliography (pp. 307-326).